U0504891

世界文明对话研究报告

（2002—2012年）

总顾问：［中国］许嘉璐　［德国］孔汉思　［美国］杜维明　［加拿大］沈青松

尼山世界文明论坛组委会　编著

人民出版社

责任编辑：王　萍　刘　恋

封面设计：石笑梦

图书在版编目（CIP）数据

世界文明对话研究报告：2002~2012年：中文、英文／尼山世界文明论坛组委会 编著 .
　　－北京：人民出版社，2013.12

ISBN 978－7－01－012815－3

I. ①世…　 II. ①尼…　 III. ①文化交流－研究报告－世界－汉、英　 IV. ① G115

中国版本图书馆 CIP 数据核字（2013）第 266478 号

世界文明对话研究报告

SHIJIE WENMING DUIHUA YANJIU BAOGAO

（2002—2012 年）

尼山世界文明论坛组委会　编著

人民出版社 出版发行

（100706　北京市东城区隆福寺街 99 号）

北京新华印刷有限公司印刷　新华书店经销

2013 年 12 月第 1 版　2013 年 12 月北京第 1 次印刷

开本：787 毫米 ×1092 毫米 1/16　印张：26.5

字数：558 千字

ISBN 978－7－01－012815－3　定价：66.00 元

邮购地址 100706　北京市东城区隆福寺街 99 号

人民东方图书销售中心　电话（010）65250042　65289539

目　录

序 .... 许嘉璐　1

回顾与展望：世界文明对话的动力和原则 .... 谢文郁　1

　一、普世价值说法的起源 2
　二、权利和责任 4
　三、寻找文明交流——对话模式 6
　四、文明对话的基本原则 9

文明对话：联合国教科文组织的努力 .... 刘铁娃　13

　一、UNESCO 从倡导普世价值到倡导文化多样性的转变 14
　二、联合国教科文组织支持文明对话的努力 19
　小　　结 26

联合国文明联盟与文明对话 .... 张贵洪　杨濡嘉　28

　一、从文明对话到文明联盟 28
　二、文明对话：联合国文明联盟在行动 32
　三、文明对话：联合国的使命和中国的作用 37

罗德岛世界公众论坛 .... 倪培民　41

　一、文明对话本身作为一个历史现象 41
　二、"世界公众论坛：文明对话"的活动 44
　三、一些反思 47

1

中华文明对欧美文明的挑战 ················· 谭明冉 51

　　一、经济上的挑战 ································ 52

　　二、政治上的挑战 ································ 54

　　三、文化上的挑战 ································ 56

　　四、中国挑战的潜力 ······························ 58

　　五、西方的回应 ································ 59

　　六、和平对话的可能性 ·························· 61

东方的努力：尼山世界文明论坛 ··········· 高述群 65

　　一、尼山论坛的组织建制与前期工作 ·············· 66

　　二、尼山论坛开创文明对话新局面 ················ 68

　　三、尼山论坛走进联合国总部大厦 ················ 75

　　四、儒家文明重返世界文明中心舞台 ·············· 82

文明对话的动态与趋势 ··················· 高述群 85

跋 ································· 徐向红 90

附　录

　　附录一：世界文化多样性宣言 ···················· 93

　　附录二：保护和促进文化表现形式多样性公约 ·········· 97

　　附录三："文明联盟"高级名人小组报告 ············ 111

　　附录四：人类和谐宣言 ························ 128

　　附录五：青年人积极参与世界文明对话倡议书 ········ 130

　　附录六：世界古文明国家文化遗产保护与促进文明对话尼山共识 ····· 131

　　附录七：十年文明对话大事记 ·················· 133

　　附录八：十年文明对话名人录 ·················· 154

序

许嘉璐

在世界范围内，开展不同文明对话、强调人类文化的多样性，已经形成一股不大不小的潮流。说它不大，是因为这一潮流基本上还停留在学者、神学家和一些国家前政要这一狭小的圈子里；说它不小，是因为经联合国教科文组织和各国民间团体的努力，不同文明对话、提倡文化多样性的声音所产生的效应是巨大的，它不但催生了"公共外交"概念的提出，而且开始让一个多世纪以来只认定某种价值观就该"普世"——不论使用什么手段——的帝国，现在也不得不承认不同文明应该对话，文化多样性应该得到保护。虽然有可能出现言与行极为明显相悖的情况，但是，随着世界各国人民理性认识的提高，最终"公共外交"会越来越按照其原旨成为国际关系的主流。

在倡导文化多样性的浪潮中，联合国教科文组织起了很大的不可代替的作用。而前殖民地国家的独立和兴起则是其背后主要的支撑力量。前殖民地国家在政治上获得独立后，对文化上独立的诉求，即要求自己的文化和传统得到承认、尊重和保护，自然会在要求经济上独立的同时向世界呐喊。在这样的背景下，教科文组织近十多年来开展了许多有效的工作，包括主办和组织相关国家举办文明对话活动。

但是，在众多对话活动中，中国缺席了。一个拥有 13 亿多人口，具有世界最古老文明，正在迅速复兴的中国，理应和众多前殖民地一样，在世界舞台上发出自己的声音，让全球人民了解中国的过去、现在和对未来的憧憬。中国人民也将在与本土文明对话过程中全面接触并学习和吸收别的民族和国家的文化与经验。从另外一个角度看，在世界不同文明对话场景中看不到中国人的身影，文化多样性的舞台就很难称得上是"世界"的或"全球"的。

中国在世界文化舞台上的话语权，在很大程度上决定于中国人民自己：对不同文明对话重要性的认识是否到位？在当今世界强势文化与弱势文化的既博弈又对话的大局中，中国文化与谁"同命"？在不同文明的相较中，对自己的文化特质是否已经了然于胸？是否渴望并且学会了对不同文化背景的人们讲述自己的故事？——显然，任何一种文化在参与不同文明对话时，本应该对自身和他者有着清醒的认识。就这点而言，我们并没有做好准备。

当然，在强势文化笼罩全球的今天，大多数国家和民族的话语权，也受着经济和科技水平以及三百年来文化偏见的制约；但是"谋事在人"，高尚、美好、真诚而正义的声音即使不能成为跨国媒体上的主流，却也是阻挡不住的强音。中国人之所谓"成事在天"者，其实说的是经努力而水到渠成。强势文化虽然其势仍强，但君不见已如《红楼梦》上所说，其内囊已尽上来了么？

对于中国而言，即使仓促，也需上阵。走在前面的通常是"社会精英"，按旧话说，即先觉者。这是古今中外的规律。这是因为，在知识、语言、人脉等方面，知识精英有着显著的优势；他们是社会的良心，而民族文化之力主要在民间。一般来讲，学者和神学家在与异国同行相遇相论时会直插心底，而且可以下学而上达。中国的人文社会学者，任重道远矣！

新千年将要到来之际，中国的学术界、宗教界开始在世界范围里"发话"了，走出去，请进来，参与多国举行的国际性论坛，多机构、多省市举行各种形式的论坛、研讨会。这一动向，在一定程度上激活了许多国家过去相对沉寂的"中国学"，引发了更多学者和宗教家对了解和研究中国的兴趣，这一势头方兴未艾，无人能遏之。

中国话语和中国真实故事要走向世界，还需要长期的努力。我们不能永远仓促从事，永远准备不足。准备工作之一，是了解世界不同文明对话及其相关理念的起始、历程、背景和现状，了解国际和国内就文明对话在理论研究领域的成果和分歧；换言之，中国应该有人与机构对不同文明对话和文化多样性进行深入研究，跨文化交际问题自然也包括在内。研究的成果将为所有关心和参与文明对话乃至所有置身于国际文化交流活动的人们参考。

尼山世界文明论坛就是为了中国参与不同文明对话而设。国际性、学术性、民间性是其主要特征，加上今年举行的"北京尼山论坛"，四年间在国内外一共举办了五次。上面我所说的一番话，就是我们在筹备和举办尼山论坛过程中的感受之一。现在奉献在读者面前的这本《世界文明对话研究报告》则是举办尼山论坛的副产品，是组委会工作的有意延伸。

这本书的篇幅不大，几位作者都是多年来关注并研究国际问题，尤其是不同文明对话的学者。读者从八篇言简意赅的文章中可以感到，作者们有着广阔的视野和强烈的历史感，是怀着对"中华文化走出去"的殷切期望，对投入到这一人类从未有过的世界文化"运动"的热情而执笔的。文后的八篇附录，是为读者们思考和研究世界文明对话而提供的资料。需要说明的是，《十年文明对话大事记》的编写，由于国内外对话活动甚多，我们搜集有关资料未能穷尽，必然有所遗漏，这并不意味着编者不以其为"大事"。

对文明对话的研究，是全新的课题。这本小书的编纂带有探索性。在这里，说句俗套话吧：希望此书成为引玉之砖。我们不但期待读者有以教之，更希望文化学、宗教学、哲学、国际关系学等领域的专家们关注这块范围虽小却很有意义且可伸缩自如的处女地，为我国以更加自信而包容、昂扬而谦逊的姿态，在世界文化交流的大潮中尽到应有的责任提供智力的支撑。

2013 年 7 月 28 日

于日读一卷书屋

回顾与展望：世界文明对话的动力和原则

谢文郁

不同文明之间一旦发生接触，就开始交往。交往的模式很多。有外部冲突式的不打不相识；有相互渗透式的相辅相成；有教化式的大鱼吃小鱼；甚至还有灭绝式的你死我活等等。在宽泛的意义上，这些交往活动也可以称为文明对话。我这里并不打算对这些交往—对话方式进行逐一分析讨论。我们注意，近代西方文明产生后，以其强盛的科学技术力量把世界各文明的地理距离大大拉近，从而使世界各文明之间的交往—对话具有直接的迫切性。

冷战结束之后，在世界各文明交往—对话中开始流行一种所谓的"普世价值—文明转型"对话模式。这是一种教化式的对话模式。在西方文明优势这个大语境中，人们有意识或无意识地接受了一种预设，即：世界文明发展应该有一个共同的方向，而调整文明发展方向的指示性标志便是普世价值。因此，各文明应该按照这个普世价值进行自我改造，并以此为目标实现自我转型，或通过外力强迫转型。这种文明交往—对话模式是否是一种我们应该推行的文明对话模式？我们希望通过追踪这一对话模式的来龙去脉，揭示当代文明对话在这一模式的主导下所陷入的困境，进而提出并论证一种新的文明对话模式：核心价值—文明自觉模式。其基本思路是，各文明的自身生长乃是由自身的原始责任意识所推动和维持的，因而不同文明必然形成自身所独有的核心价值。因此，文明对话的目的不是促成普世价值的实现，而是引导各文明（包括弱势的和强势的）在对话中深入认识自己的核心价值，不断消除自身的视觉盲点而自我更新。进一步，我们还将探讨文明对话的"核心价值—文明自觉"模式在实践上的指导性原则。

一、普世价值说法的起源

20 世纪 90 年代，苏联解体。这个事件宣告了以美国为首的资本主义阵营和以苏联为首的共产主义阵营之间的冷战结束。冷战是二次世界大战之后的产物。冷战结束之后，在世界政治版图上，美国成为唯一的超级大国。同时，西方文明似乎也因此牢固地主导着世界文明方向。

关于这个事件，人们可以从不同角度进行分析和解释。有意思的是，在过去的 20 余年中，有一点可以肯定的是，解释者都来自作为胜利者的西方世界。苏联解体后留下的俄国（原苏联的主要构成）面临生存危机，因而全力关注自身的生存问题。对于俄国人来说，他们不希望担当苏联解体的责任。因此，他们对于冷战的形成和结束这件事显得漠不关心。这就是说，他们希望对冷战问题冷却处理。这种做法等于放弃发言权。同时，作为这场冷战的胜利者，西方学者对于自己的胜利激动不已，喋喋不休。在他们看来，这场胜利来自普世价值的胜利，并很快就形成了一个共识：在全世界推广普世价值。

我们需要追踪"普世价值"这一提法的历史演变。一般来说，普世价值是二次大战后慢慢流行起来的说法。冷战结束之后，这一说法开始主导以西方政治为中心的国际关系。而且，在当前的国际政治关系中，这一说法仍然扮演着重要角色。虽然其中包括积极的作用（如推动弱势文明反省自身的核心价值及其视角盲点），但是，更多地，它所倡导的文明转型引发弱势国家的内乱，危害世界和平。在很大程度上，它妨碍未来国际政治的健康发展。因此，对这个说法的起源、演变及其困境进行一些分析和讨论，从而呈现普世价值观在冷战问题以及当前国际关系处理上的解释误区，就显得十分重要了。

普世价值这一提法的前身来自《世界人权宣言》（*Universal Declaration of Human Rights*；另一种解读和译法为：人权普世宣言）。1948 年 12 月 10 日，联合国在巴黎发表了这个宣言，认为二次世界大战给我们留下的最深刻教训是我们对人权的不尊重，因而联合国必须公开地对基本人权进行全面认可并进行保护。就文字而言，《世界人权宣言》没有直接提到普世价值一词，但在解释上被认为这些人权具有普世价值。这个宣言共有 30 条，涉及了和人的生存有直接或间接关系的各种权利。为了进一步分析和讨论的方便，我们这里自行翻译并列出《世界人权宣言》的一些与当前国际关系有密切关系的所谓普世价值条款：

第 1 条：所有的人生而自由，在尊严和权利上彼此平等。他们拥有理性和良心，相待以兄弟之情。

第2条：所有的人都拥有生活、自由和人身安全的权利。

第13条：所有的人都有在国内出行和迁居的自由。所有的人都有离开和返回自己国家的自由。

第17条：所有的人都有独占财产和共享财产的权利。任何人的财产都不能被强行剥夺。

第18条：所有的人都拥有思想自由、良心自由和宗教自由的权利。这个权利包括改变宗教或信念的自由，以及独自地或集体地和公开地或私下地，仅仅通过自愿而非强迫的教导、实践、敬拜、约束等方式，表达其宗教或信念的自由。

第19条：所有的人都拥有意见表达自由。这个权利包括不受干涉地坚持自己的意见和追寻、接受以及通过媒体分享信息和观念的自由，且不受国界限制。

第20条：所有的人都拥有和平集会和结社的自由。任何人都不能被迫隶属一个社团。

我们看到，这些条文使用了"所有的人"这样的字样。这就是说，这些条文是适用于所有的人的，因而是普世的。在这种导向中，人们在阅读这个宣言时不小心就会把它读成《普世人权宣言》（有些中文翻译就是这样做的）。1966年，联合国还采纳了另外两个有关人权的文件：《经济、社会、文化权利公约》（*International Covenant on Economic, Social and Cultural Rights*）和《公民权利与政治权利公约》（*International Covenant on Civil and Political Rights*）。1976年，上述三个文件合并为《国际人权法》（*International Bill of Human Rights*），作为联合国在人权问题上的官方文件和处理人权问题的依据，要求各成员国认可并保护这些权利。

中国政府没有参与这些文件的制定。1971年，中华人民共和国取得了联合国常务理事国的席位。1980年，中国政府决定认可并签署了《国际人权法》。不过，这个文件在中国境内并无法律效力。严格来说，这个文件不是法律文件，而是政治文件。我们可以从这个角度分析。从法律的角度看，这个《国际人权法》不是联合国的宪法或法律。无论执行什么法律，执法者首先需要明确对相关法律的理解和解释；并且，一旦出现对法律理解的不同意见，在执法程序上就必须确立最高解释权威。缺乏最高解释权威，任何法律都无法落实。我们也注意到，有些国家采纳《国际人权法》作为法律。然而，他们在实际操作中都是依据本国法律权威的解释，并不求助于联合国。这就是说，《国际人权法》只有在符合本国法律（或至少不与之矛盾）的基础上才具有法律效力。从这个意义上看，认可和采纳其实并无实质上的区别。更准确地说，这些文件对于联合国成员国来说仅仅具有意识导向作用，联合国对此并无执法功能。

然而，苏联解体之后，西方在意识形态上展现了某种强势，在《国际人权法》解释上占据高位。比如，在当代国际关系中，西方政治家强调民主选举、宗教自由、言论自由、结社自由等，认为它们是人权的核心内容，具有普世价值，各国应该建立相应社会制度加以保障。① 对于那些未能按照西方政治家的解释进行政治治理的国家来说，西方国家便利用强大的经济、舆论和军事力量强迫他们实行社会制度转型。显然，受这种强势意识形态的影响，世界各文明之间的对话和交流就变得很简单：宣传并推动世界各文明采纳普世价值，促使文明转型而趋向一个拥有普世价值的大同世界。美国哥伦比亚大学的萨缪尔·莫恩教授在他的新著《最后的乌托邦：在历史中的人权》一书的序言中谈道："这个词（人权）意味着一个改善世界的方案，催化一个新世界的到来，让每一个体的尊严都得到国际性的保护。"② 我们称这种倾向为"普世价值—文明转型"世界文明对话模式。

二、权利和责任

人权是人类生存的出发点。没有权利的人不可能进行任何判断选择，从而无法生存。但是，对于人类生存来说，个体并不是孤立的瞬间存在，而是在群体中走向未来的持续存在。因此，人的存在还涉及责任，包括每个人在进行生存选择时对自己未来的责任和对他人存在的责任。人是在一定的责任意识中进行判断选择的。权利意识不过是一种责任意识的表达形式而已。我们可以这样分析。有些"权利"和人的实际生存可以毫不相关，即使"拥有"也不会去使用它们。比如，对于一个不愿迁居的人来说，迁居自由和他的生存毫无关系。如果把这些不在人的意识中的权利奉为普世权利，那么，我们就要进行大力宣传，使那些缺乏权利

---

① 西方世界在和发展中国家的政治文化交往时一般都是围绕着自己的意识形态来谈论人权。篇幅所限，这里就不展开分析讨论了。这里仅仅举出一个简单例子。《世界人权宣言》第 13 条为出入国境自由权。我们知道，中国传统社会持以天下概念，因而迁居自由在过去几千年来一直是天经地义的事。但是，近代西方社会引入现代政治学的国家概念，从而大大地限制了中国的天下概念。目前，中国人口众多十分拥挤；相对而言，美国、加拿大以及欧洲的一些国家可居住面积广大。西方政治家在谈论中国的人权问题时，往往不涉及迁居自由权。

② 译自 Samuel Moyn, *The Last Utopia: Human Rights in History*（《最后的乌托邦：在历史中的人权》），Harvard University Press, 2010, p.1.

意识的人对此有所意识。宣传是一种责任意识培养。对于那些接受权利意识教育的人来说，他们接受教育在先，享用权利在后。在这种情况下，权利是某种责任意识的形式化表达。于是，我们看到，对于人的生存来说，一方面，人必须拥有某种权利进行判断选择，因而权利在先；另一方面，人是在某种责任意识中拥有权利的，因而是在一定的责任意识中行使权利（责任在先）。权利和责任的这种生存关系值得我们十分重视。①

西方意识形态中对某些人权的偏好其实也是由某种责任意识来引导的。我们来分析《世界人权宣言》的第1条。我们读到："所有的人生而自由，在尊严和权利上彼此平等。他们拥有理性和良心，相待以兄弟之情。"这里，开头在谈论平等权利，接着却谈论理性、良心和兄弟之情。显然，理性、良心和兄弟之情不是一种权利，而是一种责任意识。我们在哪个意义上能够说一个人是有理性和良心的呢？对于一个以杀人为乐趣的人来说，他可以有条不紊地设计并执行杀人计划。这个人是否有理性？一个人的兄弟之情是天生的吗？抑或需要后天培养？在哪个层次上他才算具有了兄弟之情？不难指出，我们只能在责任范畴中使用理性、良心和兄弟之情这些语词。不同的责任意识，具有不同的关于理性、良心和兄弟之情的理解。

就历史发展而言，文明的差异性来自于不同的责任意识。一种文明的原始责任意识之培养是一个十分复杂的问题，涉及生存环境、语言文化、自身努力等等。在许多情况下，一个微不足道的偶然因素就可以培养出一种责任意识。比如，对于一对双胞胎，母亲随意指定其中之一为长，另一为幼，将导致他们形成不同的责任意识以及不同的成长之路。一个文明的原始责任意识的出现也是这样的。我们更加关心的是，一种责任意识形成之后，人们就开始自觉或不自觉地受之引导，从此出发关心周围事物、判断并处理人际关系、设计未来生活等等。因此，对于个人来说，不同的责任意识引导不同的生存方式。对于一个文明来说，不同的原始责任意识会造就不同文明性格。任何一种文明都具有某种独特的原始责任意识，并在它的驱动和引导下生存发展。文明的这种原始责任意识需要我们特别重视。

我们进一步分析。责任意识是流动性的。它必须形式化而成为某种固定的价值，才能作为人的判断选择之根据。因此，就其表现形式而言，一种文明是通过

---

①　关于权利和责任之间的关系，更详细的分析讨论可参阅谢文郁"自由与责任：一种政治哲学的分析"，《浙江大学学报》（人文社会科学版）2010年第1期，第182—195页。

一系列权利、美德、规范、榜样、愿望等确定的价值来表达自己的。其中，那些表达原始责任意识的价值，我们称为文明的核心价值。不同文明之间的冲突主要表现为不同价值间的冲突。这种冲突一开始是一些次要价值之间的冲突，如见面时应该如何打招呼？看见他人的奇怪动作应该如何回应？等等。这些次要价值间的冲突在进一步交往中形成习惯而一一化解。但是，当冲突触及核心利益时，冲突的双方便呈现为势不两立。

就现象而言，人在一种文明中生活，其判断选择都受到他所接受的核心价值的左右。但是，核心价值是在一定原始责任意识中培养出来的。原始责任意识是基础性的。因此，我们必须反省并进入自身文明的原始责任意识中。在价值判断中，人们把任何符合这种原始责任意识的命题和事件评价为天经地义、理所当然。

值得注意的是，人们不可能追问作为文明基础的原始责任意识之合法性问题。归根到底，它是一切合法性的基础，因而在它后面没有任何其他原则。由此，我们可以有两个推论。首先，在没有外来文明的影响下，一种文明的发展始终受其原始责任意识驱动而自我发展、自生自灭。而且，人们不可能对自身的原始责任意识进行反思和分析——很显然，他们没有反思的基础。任何文明都有自己的观察角度；而人们是在一定的原始责任意识和价值观中观察世界的。因此，考虑到一种文明的有限性，我们可以说，一种封闭的文明无法消除自己的视角盲点（略后我们还要对视角盲点一词的用法进行分析）。其次，我们也注意到，限制或破坏一种文明的原始责任意识等于阉割或摧毁这个文明的存在。原始责任意识是一种文明借以生存的基础；丧失自己的原始责任意识，等于丧失自己的存在基础。因此，任何一种文明的生存，都必须清楚自身的原始责任意识。

我们认为，在文明对话这一话题上，充分认识文明的原始责任意识和核心价值，是我们寻找文明交流——对话模式的关键所在。

三、寻找文明交流——对话模式

在全球经济的推动下，无论是自愿还是被迫，世界诸文明被结合为一个经济共同体，彼此受益。同时，诸文明在这个共同体中发生直接联系。在当今世界，文明的孤立发展已属罕见。随着诸文明之间的交往加深，不可避免地会触及各自的核心价值，发生冲突。因此，如何使世界各文明之间的交往交流成为祝福，而非演变为外在冲突而危害各文明的生存，对于当今国际关系来说，乃是当务之急，需要我们认真对待。

西方思想界比较早认识到这个问题，并希望建立各种文明对话模式作为解决方案。然而，西方思想家在思路上无法摆脱普世价值—文明转型的谈论方式。尽管有些学者小心翼翼地企图摆脱西方中心论，强调诸文明之间的平等，但是，他们所提供的各种对话模式仍然无法指出世界文明对话的出路。我们这里试图追踪约翰·希克（John Hick，1922—2012）多元主义视角下的宗教对话，第二轴心时代的跨文化对话，以及亨廷顿的文明冲突理论，展示普世价值—文明转型这一模式在理论上和实践上的困境。

希克在 20 世纪 70 年代提出了宗教多元主义的说法。在这种说法中，各宗教（可引申为诸文明或文化）就其终极诉求而言都自认为把握住了终极实在。但是，究竟谁才真正地把握了终极实在，各方充其量不过是自说自话。结果是，强势文化自认为自己把握了终极实在，因而往往会对弱势文化进行外在压制。然而，我们没有完全的证据来证明，强势文化把握了终极实在。希克认为，没有任何宗教能够完全把握这个终极实在。各宗教充其量不过是把握住了它的某个方面。如果对这一点有确切认识，那么，不同宗教就可以放下自己的自以为是，相互尊重，相互学习，进行对话交流。在希克看来，只要诸宗教放下身段，承认其他宗教和自己一样也拥有关于终极实在的认识，那样，诸宗教之间的交流和对话就不成问题。① 我们看到，希克是努力在多元主义名义下为诸宗教对话寻找途径。这一努力并不成功。从文明对话的角度看，每一文明都有自己的核心诉求，并且在情感和责任意识中坚持自己的核心诉求。且不说多元主义的说法在逻辑上无法自圆其说，在实践上，它加给弱势文明的压力要远远大于对强势文明的压力。遵循希克的对话模式等于要求弱势文明不再坚持自己的核心诉求。

"第二轴心时代"在理论上是对多元主义的某种修补。希克的"终极实在"隐含着某种"轴心时代"的痕迹，在肯定诸宗教的平等地位的同时要求诸宗教改变自己的核心诉求而转向追求终极实在。当代一些西方学者企图修补这一缺陷。他们（包括尤尔特·卡曾斯 [Ewert Cousins]，雷蒙·潘尼卡 [Raimon Panikkar]，保罗·尼特 [Paul F. Knitter] 等人）提出并企图打造"第二轴心时代"。他们分享

① 参阅希克的《上帝和信仰之宇宙》(*God and the Universe of Faiths*. Oxford: OneWorld Publications Ltd., 1973）；以及《宗教哲学对话》(*Dialogues in the Philosophy of Religion*, Palgrave Macmillan, 2001）。

了多元主义的忧患情结：多元宗教如何能够平等相处、进入对话？"第二轴心时代"强调全球意识，认为人类共处一个地球，有共同利益；不同宗教（文化、文明）之间应该一起来爱护而不是损害这个地球。① 仅仅凭这一点，不同宗教（文化、文明）之间就应该避免冲突和战争，通过和平对话来增进彼此的理解，解决彼此之间的争端。为达此目的，他们当中的有些人愿意进入多种宗教身份，比如，潘尼卡就身兼天主教神父、印度教古鲁、佛教和尚以及世俗主义者。身份转换在他们看来可以使他们对不同宗教（文化、文明）拥有切身理解。不过，我们注意到，这种不断转换身份的生存大概只有几位学者能够做到，对于普通百姓来说是不可能的。普通百姓只能生活在自己的宗教（文化、文明）中。因此，"第二轴心时代"乃是一座空中楼阁，与现实生活无关。

1993 年，哈佛大学教授萨缪尔·亨廷顿（Samuel P. Huntington，1927—2008）在美国的《外交》季刊夏季号上发表了《文明的冲突》一文，并在 1996 年出版他的完整论述《文明的冲突与世界秩序的重建》② 一书。亨廷顿注意到了普世价值—文明转型模式在国际关系上的危险导向。他在第一章阐述本书第四部分主题时，谈道："西方国家的普世主义日益把它引向同其他文明的冲突，最严重的是同伊斯兰和中国的冲突。"而第五部分主题，用他的话来说："西方的生存依赖于……西方人把自己的文明看作独特的而不是普遍的，并且团结起来更新和保护自己的文化，使它免受来自非西方社会的挑战。避免全球的文明战争要靠世界领导人愿意维持全球政治的多文明特征，并为此进行合作。"亨廷顿是在西方文明强势而其他文明的自觉意识已经兴起这种语境中发表这种议论的。我们可以称之为普世价值思路中的焦虑意识。尽管他批评西方的普世主义在国际关系中的负面作用，但是，在他看来，原因在于西方文明对非西方文明的过于强烈的冲击，导致了非西方文明的强烈反弹。因此，西方人在全球范围内推广普世价值必须有所收敛。他在第十二章中有这样的话："西方的普世主义对于世界来说是危险的，因为它可能导致核心国家之间的重大文明间战争；它对于西方来说也是危险的，因为它可能导致西方的失败。"在亨廷顿心中，西方文化必须有所收敛并强调自己的独特性，只有这样才能生存下去并保持强势。这是亨廷顿式的韬晦之计。

---

① 相关讨论参阅保罗·尼特《一个地球，多种宗教：多信仰对话与全球责任》，王志成等译，宗教文化出版社 2003 年版。英文见 Paul F. Knitter, *One Earth-Many Religions: Multifaith Dialogue and Global Responsibilities*，Orbis Books，1995。

② *The Clash of Civilizations and the Remaking of World Order*，New York: Simon & Schuster，1996. 中文版见《文明的冲突与世界秩序的重建》，周琪等译，新华出版社 1998 年版。

在世界文明史上，有些文明消失了，有些文明延续下来。前面谈到，任何文明都是在某种原始责任意识中发展起来的。在原始责任意识中，维持自身的生存是首要原则。当诸文明进行直接接触和交流时，每一个文明都只能从自身的角度对对方进行理性评判，并在评判中赞美并吸收对方的优点，忽略并排斥对方的丑陋。理性评判是带着普遍主义和自我中心倾向的。没有人会赞美并吸收对方的丑陋，忽略并排斥对方的优点。因此，无视文明的普遍主义和自我中心倾向就无法讨论文明间的冲突和对话。换句话说，这种无视，如果不是别有用心（如亨廷顿的韬晦之计），那么，等于要求自阉，即：放弃自己的原始责任意识，放弃自身文明的生存。

我们指出，任何一个微不足道的因素都可以引导一种责任意识。在前面的双胞胎例子上，或长或幼只凭母亲一句话，而此后这对双胞胎的责任意识培养却可以在完全不同方向上。一个文明的原始责任意识也可以是这样产生的，即：它可能产生于某种偶然因素。任何文明都建立在一定的原始责任意识之上。不同的责任意识给出不同的价值观，形成一定的视角，并在此基础上进行各种评判。受着自己的原始责任意识的制约，任何文明都有自己的视角盲点。比如，如果一件事在某种责任意识中被判断为毫无意义，那么，无论这件事在其他责任意识中被认为多么重要，在这个视角中，这件事就是可以忽略不计的。我们称此为视角盲点。

而且，任何文明都不可能通过自己的努力（包括反省、反思）来呈现自己的视角盲点，就好像自己的眼睛不可能看自己的眼睛一样。消除视角盲点需要其他文明在场作为对照物。就好像人的眼睛面对镜子一样，视角盲点只能在和其他文明的交流中对照出来。可以这样看，对于一个文明认为毫无意义的事，却在其他文明中被认为极为重要，那么，这一文明的价值观就难免受到冲击，即视角盲点被暴露。面对这一冲击，如果两种文明之间处于敌对状态，彼此没有信任，那么，这一冲击就导向外部冲突和战争。如果两种文明之间处于和好信任状态，那么，视角盲点的暴露就会被当作善意的礼物而接受下来。在信任中，两种文明将相互呈现对方视角盲点，共同扩展视野。这里，和好信任乃是关键点。

四、文明对话的基本原则

我们对文明进行了分析，发现其中有两个关键因素，即：原始责任意识和视角盲点。进一步，我们分析了文明间的交流和对话，发现，一种健康的世界诸文明关系必须建立在彼此信任的基础上。任何文明都带着普世主义倾向。实际上，这种普世主义倾向是不同文明之间对话的动力。在彼此信任的基础上，文明对话可以帮助指出对方盲点，推动对方发展自己的原始责任意识，共同扩展视野，自我更新。对于弱势文明来说，它需要对自己的原始责任意识有深刻的反省和清楚的认识，需要在其他强势文明的对照下认识并消除自己的视角盲点。对于强势文明来说，它同样需要其他文明来对照自己的视角盲点，深化自己的原始责任意识。任何文明，只有在信任和好的气氛中和其他文明进行直接接触和交流，才能继续生存下去。我们称这样的文明对话为"核心价值—文明自觉"模式。在这种模式中，我们要从诸文明的自觉意识出发来面对文明冲突问题，即：建立文明对话平台，突出各文明的平等尊严，彼此帮助消除对方的视角盲点，推动并深化各文明对自身核心价值的认识，导向一种和而不同的诸文明共存的和谐世界。

我们从历史、理论和当代实践的角度对"普世价值—文明转型"和"核心价值—文明自觉"这两种模式进行了分析和论证。就思维性格而言，"核心价值—文明自觉"模式具有相当浓重的中国传统思维特性，即和而不同的情感取向。《中庸》有这样的句子："万物并育而不相害。道并行而不相悖。小德川流；大德敦化。此天地之所以为大也。"① 每一文明都是一"物"，在自己的原始责任意识中生存发展，但可以"并育而不相害"。每一文明在自己的原始责任意识中都走自己的道路，但可以"并行而不相悖"。只有这样，这个世界才能和谐共存。

从中国立场出发，我们认为，文明对话的"核心价值—文明自觉"模式具有优越性。也许，对于那些坚持"普世价值—文明转型"模式的人来说，"核心价值—文明自觉"模式过于保守。然而，只有这种模式才能切实地在实践上推进世界文明对话。在此基础上，我们提出如下5条文明对话原则。

首先，我们必须尊重诸文明的平等话语权。在当代世界文明的交往和对话中，我们不得不面对其他文明的存在。从一种文明的角度看，其他文明的问题关注、思维方式、待人接事、行为规范等等都是陌生的。一般来说，这种陌生性会引发某种恶感，即排斥对方的倾向。但是，这种恶感并不一定是消极的破坏性的。不难指出，交往各方都希望向对方推荐或推行各自认定的良善因素，同时也情不自禁地会批评乃至教导对方以改变对方的丑恶因素。也就是说，交往中的恶感可以作为交往—对话的动力。然而，这里的推荐—推行和批评—教化，即使充满善意，我们也必须在尊重对方意愿的前提下进行。否则，不同文明间的交往—

---

① 《中庸》第30章。

对话不可避免地将引起情绪上的对抗，并导致冲突。这就要求我们在尊重诸文明的平等话语权的前提下进行对话。

其次，推动诸文明在对话中深入认识自己的核心价值。任何文明都有其历史和传统，因而拥有自身的核心价值。坚持自身价值，并使之发扬光大，乃是各文明的本分。文明发展有历史长短和发展方向的差异。抹杀这种差异，等于摧毁弱势文明。但是，我们也注意到，受到自身的视角限制，任何文明，无论是强势还是弱势，历史或长或短，都有自己的视角盲点。人们无法在盲点中发现自己的盲点。文明对话提供了一个暴露自身视角盲点的平台。盲点暴露对一个文明自身存在和发展来说当然会形成巨大的冲击，甚至导致旧体系的解体。但是，它不会破坏文明的核心价值。相反，解体的同时也在推动重构，形成新体系。这是一个自身核心价值发扬光大的过程。我们认为，文明对话的目的正是要推动各文明对自身核心价值的自我意识，使之发扬光大。

第三，在平等对话和文明自觉这两条原则的基础上，各文明在政治上应该采纳互不干涉对方内政，并鼓励各国实行符合本国民众心理结构的政治制度。政治是一种强制性的社会管理，涉及社会内部各种力量。我们指出，文明发展史是由一定的责任意识所驱动的。这种责任意识只有当事人才能拥有恰当的把握。当然，当事人（即文明内部的诸个体）关于这种责任意识—核心价值的认识和把握是多样的，甚至彼此相互冲突。但是，究竟谁的认识和把握才是正确的？究竟怎样的表达才是准确的？——对于这样的问题，只有当事人才最清楚。因此，站在文明的外部，尽管可以在平等对话中给当事人提供一种观察角度，但决策者必须是当事人，而不能来自外部。实际上，我们注意到，强势文明在普世价值—文明转型模式中追求从外部对弱势文明的政治介入，这种做法在过去的经验中证明无助于文明对话，反而在相当大程度上破坏弱势文明的生存。因此，我们认为，当代世界文明对话不允许简单地从外部强力推行某种政治制度这样的做法。相反，各文明在政治上要奉行不干涉内政原则，鼓励各国从本文明的责任意识出发建立适合的政治制度。这一政治要求应该成为文明对话的基本原则。

第四，走向全球融合的经济关系。文明之间可以通过不同纽带建立关系，如地缘毗邻、贸易需要、艺术爱好、思想魅力等等。在这些纽带中，在贸易需要基础上发展起来的经济关系特别需要注意。长期以来，地理距离阻碍着文明间的交往。然而，在过去几十年来，由于交通工具的发展，地球各个角落的地理距离大大缩短，各文明之间的经济关系日益密切。贸易需要已经进入日常生活，达到了相互依赖的程度。实际上，如果没有这种密切的经济纽带关系，各文明对话充其量是局部的和表面的。当人的衣食住行依赖于其他文明时，切割和其他文明的关系等于直接损害自己的生存。这种相互依赖的经济关系是文明对话的推手。因此，经济上的全球融合趋势要求文明之间在深层次上进行相互了解。同时，文明对话加深了彼此了解，也反过来进一步促进经济上的融合，使各方都能得到实实在在的益处。因此，我们认为，全球经济一体化和文明对话是相辅相成的。

第五，推动搭建宗教对话平台。人在生存上不可能没有终极诉求。宗教是这种终极诉求的一种表达。终极诉求指向完善存在。也就是说，这种诉求就其目标而言不是现实的。但是，不同的诉求引导不同的生存方向。因此，宗教在表达人的终极诉求的同时，对人的现实生活发挥直接作用。各文明在终极诉求上有不同的宗教表达形式。考虑到宗教的超越性和现实性，我们必须十分谨慎地处理不同文明在宗教问题上的交往关系，在充分尊重各宗教人士的情感的前提下，搭建宗教对话平台。

以上5条原则仅仅具有指导性作用。在实践上采用"核心价值—文明自觉"模式，推进文明对话，我们还需要就事论事，具体问题具体分析和处理。然而，我们指出，"普世价值—文明转型"模式无法满足世界文明对话的内在要求。在未来文明对话中，我们相信，由"核心价值—文明自觉"模式来主导将是对世界文明生存和发展的祝福！

作者简介：

谢文郁：北京大学硕士，美国克莱门特研究生大学博士；现为山东大学哲学与社会发展学院教授、博士生导师、山东大学希腊思想研究中心主任。著有：*The Concept of Freedom*（2002）；《自由与生存》（2007）；《道路与真理》（2012）等，以及80余篇学术论文。目前致力于宗教哲学、基督教思想、比较哲学研究。

文明对话：联合国教科文组织的努力

刘铁娃

作为联合国的重要专门机构之一，联合国教科文组织（UNESCO）所关注的领域包括教育、科学、文化、交流。通过"致力于在尊重共同价值观的基础上为不同文明、文化和民族之间开展对话创造条件。正是通过这种对话，世界才能实现可持续发展的全球愿景，包括尊重人权、相互尊重和减轻贫困，所有这一切都是教科文组织的核心使命和活动"①。联合国教科文组织对于文化多样性的提倡，在冷战结束、大国之间的紧张和冲突减少、但是民族矛盾、宗教矛盾等涉及文化、文明的冲突却越来越上升的背景下具有了特别重要的意义。一些学者将此称之为"文明的冲突"②。对于文化多样性的肯定，实际上涉及肯定"普世价值"与肯定不同文明"相对价值"两种观点之间的争论。全球化背景下的伦理精神就逻辑的存在两种基本的价值观。一是普世价值观，所谓"普世伦理"或"普遍伦理"；一是相对价值观，所谓"特殊伦理"或"民族伦理"。前者与"文化全球一体化"立场相一致，主张普世主义；后者与"文化全球多元化"的立场相适合，主张特殊主义。③"一方面，文化多元意识的增强，促使人们更多地偏执于'特殊主义'或'地域主义'的文化价值立场，对人类普遍价值理想和道德规范的信心大大减弱。""另一方面，现代人和现代世界愈是强烈地意识到文化多元分庭竞争的现实，其寻求某种形式的跨文化差异的普遍共识之愿望愈发强烈。"④

---

① http://unesdoc.unesco.org/images/0014/001473/147330c.pdf.

② [美]塞缪尔·亨廷顿：《文明的冲突与世界秩序的重建》，周琪等译，新华出版社1998年版，第18页。

③ 樊浩：《伦理精神的生态对话与生态发展——中国伦理应对"全球化"的价值理念》，《中国社会科学院研究生院学报》2001年第6期，第16页。

④ 万俊人：《寻求普世伦理》，商务印书馆2001年版，第303页。

本文的关注点并不是就普世价值和相对价值两种观点孰优孰劣进行评述，而是试图就联合国教科文组织在倡导文化多样性、推动文明对话这一方面所发挥的作用进行探讨，同时展示该组织如何从建立之初致力于传播普世价值到致力于倡导文化多样性的转变。在联合国教科文组织如何倡导文化多样性的努力方面，本文将梳理自 2000 年以来该机构在推动文明对话方面的主要决议和行动进行说明。

一、UNESCO 从倡导普世价值到倡导文化多样性的转变

联合国教科文组织是教育、科学和文化领域最为重要的政府间国际组织。可以说，教科文组织在有关文化、文明关系的领域具有相当大的发言权。但是，联合国教科文组织并不是从一开始就积极倡导文化多样性的，这里经历了一个明显的转变过程，即战后初期美国主导下的教科文组织被用来作为传播西方意识形态的一个重要工具，但到了 20 世纪 60 年代中期以后 UNESCO 越来越转向倡导文化多样性、反对文化领域的"殖民主义"与帝国主义。

与战后其他许多政府间国际组织不同，联合国教科文组织的起源主要在欧洲。①1941 年，英国政府倡议建立"国际教育组织"，并且召开了同盟国教育部长会议（Conference of Allied Ministers of Education）。② 美国代表团为会议提供了一份宪章草案并被大会所接受，草案的标题是《将同盟国教育部长会议发展为联合国教育和文化重建组织的建议》。经过这些协商和妥协，这个新组织的宗旨被确定为"通过教育、科学和文化，促进国际合作，以推动对正义、法治、人权和基本自由的普遍尊重。根据联合国的宪章，这些权利应该是不分种族、性别、语言或者宗教为世界上各民族都享有的。"③ 因此，联合国教科文组织是按照西方自由主义政治意识形态和价值观所建立的。

---

① Roger A. Coate, "Changing Patterns of Conflict: the United States and UNESCO", in Magaret P. Karns and Karen A. Mingst（ed.），*The United States and Multilateral Institutions: Patterns of Changing Instrumentality and Influence*, London: Routledge, p. 232.

② 这一机构是在英国文化委员会（British Council）主席的邀请下建立的。除了英国的代表以外，它最开始包括 8 个联合国成员政府的代表。这一机构的主要目标是战后的教育重建。1943 年的同盟国教育部长会议成员也是伦敦国际大会（London International Assembly）的成员。这次会议表明了创建一个永久性的国际教育组织的呼声。

③ See UNESCO，*Constitution*, Article 1, paragraph 1, http://portal.unesco.org/en/ev.php-URL_ID=15244&URL_DO=DO_TOPIC&URL_SECTION=201.html.

如果在美苏冲突和意识形态斗争的背景下考察该组织，我们可以看到，联合国教科文组织的最初原则渗透了强调个体权利、新闻自由的美国价值观和世界秩序观念。具体来说，联合国教科文组织的宪章中是这样规定其推动"普世价值"的使命的："文化的广泛差异，以及有关人类正义、自由和和平的教育，对于人的尊严是不可缺少的。所有的国家必须相互支持、关心来完成这一神圣的任务。"[1] 因此，建立之初，联合国教科文组织的首要任务是推动人权、民主、自由等普世性的价值理念；人的权利的概念从此进入了国际组织中专门的项目规划。联合国教科文组织有关国际人权的项目在 UNESCO 建立后的很多年里都主要由美国所推动。它甚至还包括揭露苏联违反人权的工作计划——这实际上反映了普世价值的理念本质上是美国主导下的一种价值观。按照联合国教科文组织社会和人文科学部门简报的说法，"促进人权是成立联合国教科文组织的核心目标。在 UNESCO 出现以前，人权被粗暴地践踏，因此全球范围内对人权的尊重是宪章中第一条所设定的根本目标。这一宪章于 1945 年 11 月 16 日在伦敦得到通过。"[2]

为了传播自由主义的意识形态和美国的价值观、政治制度，美国坚持认为联合国教科文组织的任务应该扩大到加强国际通讯方面。因此，宪章的第一条第二款规定，UNESCO 应该"通过一切可能的大众通讯手段来增进各民族的相互了解。为了达到这一目标，建立这些方面的国际协定可能是促进思想的自由流动所必需的。"[3] 实际上，自从联合国教科文组织建立之日起，通讯传播就是美国政治领导人首要关注的问题之一。美国人在 1946 年的 UNESCO 第一次大会上就提出，建立联合国教科文组织的广播网络，"使用强度信号覆盖地球上的每一片土地"[4]。联合国教科文组织在朝鲜战争中所扮演的角色，是该组织深刻地卷入政治事态的又一典型例子。[5] 在朝鲜战争中，联合国教科文组织实际上成为了美国政府的一

---

① Roger A. Coate, *Unilateralism, Ideology, & U. S. Foreign Policy: The United States In and Out of UNESCO*, Boulder, Lynne Rienner Publishers, 1988, p. 38.

② See the Official Website of UNESCO, http://portal.unesco.org/shs/en/ev.php-URL_ID=8736&URL_DO=DO_TOPIC&URL_SECTION=201.html.

③ See *UNESCO, Constitution*, Article 1, Section 2, http://portal.unesco.org/en/ev.php-URL_ID=15244&URL_DO=DO_TOPIC&URL_SECTION=201.html.

④ Robert W. Cox and Harold K. Jacobson, *The Anatomy of Influence: Decision Making in International Organization*, New Haven: Yale University Press, 1973, p. 162.

⑤ See Agenda item 4 of the 23rd session of the Executive Board in September 1950. 参见 Executive Board document 23 EX/Decisions, p. 2, http://unesdoc.unesco.org/images/0011/001139/113905E.pdf.

个宣传工具。在提到联合国教科文组织对朝鲜提供援助的原因时，UNESCO 的决议是这样表达的，"这是考虑到联合国教科文组织的主要目的之一，正像在宪章第一款中规定的那样，'通过教育、科学和文化，促进国际合作，以推动对正义、法治、人权和基本自由的普遍尊重。根据联合国的宪章，这些权利应该是不分种族、性别、语言或者宗教为世界上各民族都享有的。'"执行局也表示，"他们对韩国受到的武装攻击感到十分震动"[1]。

到了 1954 年，苏联改变了原来的政策，决定不再远离联合国教科文组织。这一做法也使得它的追随者们积极地寻求加入到 UNESCO 中来，其中包括已经加入而又退出的捷克斯洛伐克、波兰和匈牙利。保加利亚、罗马尼亚和阿尔巴尼亚在苏联重新进入组织后不久就加入了该组织。在联合国教科文组织中，第三世界国家的实力和影响力也有大幅度增长，在意识形态的对抗斗争中优势也不断增加，[2] 美国政府的利益和影响力已经开始下降。美国代表团强烈反对罗马尼亚和保加利亚加入联合国教科文组织，因为美国认为这两个国家严重违反了人权，而人权观念是该组织宪章中的核心组成部分。但是在对这两个国家进行谴责时，美国在联合国教科文组织中"有选择的道德观"也受到了质疑。正如我们所知，南非共和国虽然也不断违反人权，但是并没有被拒绝加入联合国教科文组织。1954 年 UNESCO 大会的第八次会议中，苏联和捷克斯洛伐克的代表团对罗马尼亚在教育、科学和文化方面所做出的努力和取得的成就表示了高度的赞赏。苏联代表团还指出，美国对罗马尼亚侵犯人权的指控并没有提供任何的证据，因此是不能被接受的。最终，大会"决定这个问题不是一个值得进一步考虑的问题，因为应该赋予人民的权利以及罗马尼亚的文化和科学发展证明了所有的这些指控都是错误的。"[3]

自 20 世纪 60 年代早期开始，UNESCO 内部的非西方国家就试图重新定义联合国教科文组织的目标和原则，而它们所提出的目标和原则与西方的自由主义意识形态是不同的。这使得 UNESCO 内部的思维方式、工作哲学和政策偏好都逐步发生了明显变化。例如，第三世界国家努力在该组织中倡导非殖民主义的思

---

① See Executive Board document 23EX/Decisions, p.2, http://unesdoc.unesco.org/images/0011/001139/113905E.pdf.

② UNESCO 的成员从最初的 27 国上升到 1960 年的 100 国。1962 年，34 国加入了 UNESCO，其中大多数是非洲国家。仅仅在 1960 年，18 国加入了 UNESCO。它们中绝大多数是非洲国家。

③ See "Proceedings of the General Conference," 8th Session, 3rd Plenary Meeting, Montevideo, 1954, p.48, also at http://unesdoc.unesco.org/images/0011/001145/114586E.pdf.

想。实际上最终的 UNESCO 决议采纳了第三世界的很多观点。1960 年大会通过的决议被称为《联合国教科文组织为了殖民地国家和人民获得独立做出贡献》。"无论是何种形式，何种表现的殖民主义都应该迅速被废除；获得自由和独立的进程不能再拖延下去了。认为某些特定的领域还没有在经济、社会、教育和文化事务等方面达到足够高的标准是错误的想法。""联合国教科文组织最紧迫的任务是帮助新独立的国家、准备独立的国家克服任何有害的殖民主义遗留的影响，例如经济、社会和文化发展的低水平；文盲以及受过训练的人员的紧缺。"①

自 20 世纪 60 年代末开始，反对文化帝国主义、坚持文化主权的问题成为了国际政治斗争的焦点之一。这场斗争的主要目标是消除来自霸权国的压倒性的文化和交流渗透。1972 年，苏联准备了一份《大众传媒使用的宣言草案》，以默许的形式支持国家对媒体的控制。1974 年，苏联的宣言草案变成了一个确定的议题。当时一些西方代表们走出会场，抗议反以色列的语言，并且认为这是试图破坏新闻自由的表现。1974 年 UNESCO 大会的结论认为，"正因为世界的信息状况缺少平衡，倾向一方面并忽视其他，不结盟国家和其他发展中国家有义务改变这种形势，以在信息领域实现非殖民化，并且表达在信息领域建立新的国际秩序的坚定决心。"②1976 年，联合国教科文组织主持召开了一次讨论拉丁美洲通讯政策的会议。这次会议一致接受了以下原则：国家间信息交换的更公正的标准；允许按照主权自决的需要以及与国际信息流动有关的优先选择来决定国际政策倾向；承认真正的信息自由流动只有在所有国家都能够平等对话，平等控制所有信息资源并使用国际发射渠道的条件下才能够实现。③ 这一切都表明，联合国教科文组织的工作目标已经从建立之初美国主导下、旨在传播某种普世价值观转向了逐步被第三世界主导、肯定和倡导文化多样性的方面。

那么，这一转变的根本原因是什么呢？主要的原因还在于联合国教科文组织在决策方面的民主原则，即一国一票。按照它的宪章规定，联合国教科文组织可以被定义为一个非常开放的组织，"所有的国家在大会上拥有平等的投票权；根

① See the records of 11th Session of General Conference in 1960, at http://unesdoc.unesco.org/images/0011/001145/114583E.pdf, p.74; also see the records of Executive Board meeting, http://unesdoc.unesco.org/images/0011/001132/113245E.pdf.

② See "Final Report," Tunis, March26-30, Symposium of the Non-Aligned on Information, 1976.

③ Herbert I. Schiller, "Decolonization of Information: Efforts toward a New International Order", *Latin American Perspectives*, Vol.5, No.1, *Culture in the Age of Mass Media*（Winter, 1978）, pp.35-48.

据宪章的最初规定，大会每年召开一次。但是，从 1948 年以来，大会两年才仅仅召开一次。执行局的成员们由大会代表中选出。"①"执行局的成员都只有一票。执行局的决定应该是出席会议的简单多数决定，除了某些特别场合。"② 而且，"联合国组织的成员应该同时拥有成为联合国教科文组织成员的权利。"③ 这意味着如果一个国家已经是联合国的成员国，如果它愿意的话，它将自动成为联合国教科文组织的成员国。1954 年之前，联合国教科文组织的开放性在某种程度上被削弱了，因为当时很多社会主义国家被排除在外、许多的第三世界国家还没有实现民族独立。④ 从 1945 年到 1954 年，西方国家成员构成了该组织的绝大部分；只有三个社会主义国家加入了该组织，分别是波兰、捷克斯洛伐克和匈牙利。这三个国家经常反对大会或者执行局做出的反共产主义的政治化决定，但是几乎没有什么积极的结果。最终，它们退出了联合国教科文组织。当时，第三世界的大多数国家还刚刚独立，在参与多边外交方面既没有什么经验也缺少相应的能力。值得注意的是，当时第三世界的许多成员国是拉丁美洲国家，因此它们深受发达的北方国家的影响。它们还未能进行一定的协调和合作，就像后来所做的那样。所以 UNESCO 的大多数成员毫无疑问地接受了西方国家特别是美国的领导。⑤

但是，随着大批成员的加入，UNESCO 构成了国际组织体系中开放程度最高的几个之一。用学者理查德·比斯尔（Richard Bissell）的话来说，"联合国成员范围扩大，特别是新成员性质的变化，所导致的一个重要后果是组织的主要关注的变化。例如，在像联合国教科文组织这样的组织中，各成员国享有同等的投票权，最初只关注大国政治利益的态度逐渐转为对发展中国家的同等关注，包括它们对经济繁荣的关心，或者是世界信息新秩序。通常来说，国际社会的主要关

---

① Sources come from the official website of UNESCO, http://unesdoc.unesco.org/images/0013/001337/133729cb.pdf#page=7 〈br/〉.

② 下列情况需要出席和投票的国家的三分之二多数批准：提案的再考虑（规则 45）；通信协商（consultation by correspondence）（规则 60）；程序规则的修正（规则 66）；程序规则的中止（规则 67）；确认哪些非 UNESCO 成员国可以派观察员参加大会的会议。See http://unesdoc.unesco.org/images/0013/001390/139080e.pdf.

③ 参见 Constitution of the United Nations Educational, Scientific and Cultural Organization, Article II, at http://portal.unesco.org/en/ev.php-URL_ID=15244&URL_DO=DO_TOPIC&URL_SECTION=201.html.

④ 值得注意的是，宪章的第二条声明如下："经由执行局推荐，以及大会三分之二多数票支持，不是联合国成员的国家也可以成为 UNESCO 的成员。"

⑤ Sagarika Dutt, *The Politicization of the United Nations Specialized Agencies, A Case Study of UNESCO*, Mellen University Press, 1995, p.44.

注点已经转为人口、食品、能源、居住和环境问题，同时也强调国家之间的相互依存而不是单方依附。"① 这主要是基于其"一国一票"的平等决策方式。由于联合国教科文组织的开放程度很高，以及大批第三世界国家的加入，美国发现自己越来越不能够操纵或者完全主导联合国教科文组织来推行所谓的"普世价值"。从 20 世纪 60 年代中期开始，教科文组织内部反对文化殖民主义、坚持文化主权的呼声越来越强烈，文化多样性成为了教科文组织的一个新目标。到了 1984 年，美国退出了联合国教科文组织，因为它发现苏联和第三世界国家几乎主导了该组织的议程设置，做出的许多决议也往往是对它不利的。美国国务院认为联合国教科文组织"在每个议题上都表现得极端政治化；对自由社会、自由市场和自由出版的基本制度表现得很有敌意。"②

二、联合国教科文组织支持文明对话的努力

如果说冷战结束之前联合国教科文组织内部存在着推动普世价值和反对殖民主义两种带有对抗性的思潮的话，那么，冷战结束之后联合国教科文组织的目标还是有适度的变化。这一适度的变化并不是说 UNESCO 改变了倡导文化多样性的基本原则，而是说更多在肯定文化多样性的基础上推动文明对话、促进不同文明之间的和谐与共同繁荣。1998 年联合国大会通过 53/22 号决议，确定 2001 年为"各种文明间对话年"（International Year of Dialogue among Civilizations）。教科文组织在 1998 年世界文化报告中申述了坚持文化多样性的七大根据。这七项根据是："第一，文化多样性作为人类精神创造性的一种表达，它本身就具有价值。第二，它为平等、人权和自决权原则所要求。第三，类似于生物的多样性，文化多样性可以帮助人类适应世界有限的环境资源。在这一背景下多元性与可持续性相连。第四，文化多样性是反对政治与经济的依赖和压迫的需要。第五，从美学上讲，文化多样性呈现一种不同文化的系列，令人愉悦。第六，文化多样性启迪人们的思想。第七，文化多样性可以储存好的和有用的做事方法，储存这方

---

① Richard E. Bissell, "The United States in the UN: Past and Present", *The US, the UN and the Management of Global Change*, edited by Toby Trister Gati, New York University Press, 1983, pp.90-91.

② "US Statement on UNESCO", *New York Times*, Dec.30, 1983, p.A4.

面的知识和经验。① 这里我将集中关注 2000 年以来联合国教科文组织所通过的主要决议和所做的主要工作，来说明其推动文明对话的努力。

1. 全球层面的宣言、公约和活动

UNESCO 组织从 1999 年开始不定期举行国际文化部长圆桌会议，来自世界各国的文化部长和代表围绕不同的主题开展讨论。2000 年 12 月 11 日至 12 日，UNESCO 组织召开了第二届国际文化部长圆桌会议，其主题为"2000 至 2010 年的文化多样性：市场的挑战"。此次圆桌会议的主要议题为：文化怎样适应市场化的需求；市场化所附带的追逐经济利益最大化对文化多样性所造成的冲击以及应对措施。会议得出的结论是：各国文化产业的发展既要适应市场经济的发展，利用全球广阔的市场空间，又要着重保护文化多样性避免对经济利益的追逐侵蚀文化的多样性。② 从 2000 年开始，联合国教科文组织开始举办"国际母语日"活动。2000 年的主题是："首次国际母语日庆典"（Inaugural Celebration of International Mother Language Day）。国际母语日活动旨在促进语言和文化的多样性以及多语种化。

2001 年 4 月 23—26 日，联合国教科文组织在立陶宛的维尔纽斯召开了"文明间对话的国际会议"，以辩论为主要形式，共同探讨了当今世界中文明和文化的重要复杂问题，此次会议的成果为《文明对话》。会议以人类团结和共同的价值观为出发点，承认世界文化多样性和各文明、文化和个人间的平等与尊严。强调需要防止出现新的偏见与成见。这一对话会议为 2001 年 11 月联合国教科文组织大会第 31 届会议的《世界文化多样性宣言》打下了基础。《宣言》认为："文化在各不相同的时空中会有各不相同的表现形式。这种多样性的具体表现形式，便是构成各人类群体所具有的独特性和多样性。文化的多样性是交流、革新和创作的源泉，对人类来说，保护它就像与保护生物多样性进而维持生物平衡一样必不可少。从这个意义上讲，文化多样性是人类的共同遗产，应从当代人和子孙后代的利益考虑予以承认和肯定。"③ 依据联合国教科文组织 2001 大会决议发起的"全球文化多样性联盟"是一个建立在伙伴关系基础上的倡议，2002 年进入实施

---

① 联合国教科文组织《世界文化报告（1998）》，阿里斯佩：《前言》，北京大学出版社 2000 年版，第 3 页。

② http://www.unesco.org.cn/ViewInfoText.jsp？INFO_ID=94&KEYWORD=.

③ 资料来自中国政务信息网：http://www.fsa.gov.cn/web_db/sdzg2006/adv/BLDPX/DYMB/zhc/jcjy020.htm。

阶段。在联盟的支持下，至少有 20 多个试点项目正在秘鲁、阿尔及利亚、牙买加、中国和津巴布韦开展活动。这些项目涉及许多领域，如音乐、出版、博物馆的衍生产品、卡通电影生产和小手工艺品厂等。项目的开发是建立在团结、互利的原则之上。①UNESCO 于 2002 年 12 月 20 日宣布，从 2003 年开始把 5 月 21 日定为世界文化多样性促进对话和发展日，确认文化多样性的保护与不同文明之间对话的大框架之间存在密切联系。

2002 年 9 月 12 日，美国布什总统在联合国大会上宣布："作为对人类尊严做出承诺的象征，美国决定返回联合国教科文组织。这个组织经过了改革，美国将全面地参加到它的活动中去，以推进人权、宽容和学习。"② 联合国基金和创造更好世界基金会（United Nations Foundation and Better World Fund）主席蒂莫西·沃思（Timothy E. Wirth）认为"联合国教科文组织在全世界推动美国价值观方面扮演着关键的角色，无论是在教育、民主还是人权方面。"③ 然而，不可否认的是，使美国的利益与联合国教科文组织的运作相一致并不是件简单的事情。倡导文化多样性、推动文明对话依然是联合国教科文组织在全球层面最主要的工作目标之一。2002 年 9 月 16 日至 17 日，UNESCO 组织召开了第三次国际文化部长圆桌会议，在土耳其伊斯坦布尔举行。这次会议的主题是："非物质文化遗产——文化多样性的体现。"各成员国经过充分协商，通过了保护非物质文化遗产的《伊斯坦布尔宣言》。④ 2003 年 10 月 9 日至 10 日，UNESCO 召开了第四次国际文化部长圆桌会议，此次会议以"迈向知识社会"为主题。会议通过讨论认为，"知识社会确定、生产、加工、转化、传播和使用信息以便为人类的发展建立并应用知识的能力。知识社会需要具有多样性、包容性、团结性与参与性特点的强烈的社会愿景。"⑤ UNESCO 从 2004 年开始举办"世界文化论坛"，截至 2011 年共举行了 3 次，分别是 2004 年巴塞罗那世界文化论坛、2007 年蒙特雷世界文化论坛、2010 年瓦尔帕莱索世界文化论坛。2004 年 5 月 9 日—9 月 26 日在西班牙的巴塞罗那举办的"世界文化论坛"，突出主题为"文化的多样性"。来自世界各国的众多文化项目参加了论坛活动，共有展览 50 个、音乐会 56 场、戏剧 31 台、电影

---

① http://www.ncac.gov.cn/cms/html/205/2094/200401/671932.html.

② "President's Remarks at the United Nations General Assembly," at the website of Whitehouse: http://www.whitehouse.gov/news/releases/2002/09/20020912-1.html.

③ http://betterworldfund.org/multimedia/pdf/2004/Congress_Funds_UNESC_030904.pdf.

④ 《伊斯坦布尔宣言》详见联合国官网：http://www.un.org/zh/。

⑤ http://www.unesco.org/dialogue/en/publications.html.

300 场，另有杂技和舞蹈表演等。作为论坛的主要活动，四场大型主题展览帮助观众理解文化的多样性、可持续发展以及和平的环境等多个问题，这四场展览分别是"声音"、"城市—角落"、"栖身于世界"和"西安兵马俑"。①

《文化多样性公约》的通过是分析美国、联合国教科文组织与倡导文化多样化之间关系的很好例子。2005 年 10 月 20 日 UNESCO 大会通过了《保护和促进文化表现形式多样性公约》，主要内容包括：要求缔约方采取具体措施保护文化多样性，并以适当方式促进向世界其他国家开放文化，为各国在文化多样性保护方面开展合作提供了必要的法律框架。② 主要内容包括：要求缔约方采取具体措施保护文化多样性，并以适当方式促进向世界其他国家开放文化，为各国在文化多样性保护方面开展合作提供了必要的法律框架。其中，"文化表现形式"，指个人、群体和社会创造的具有文化内容的表现形式。"文化多样性"，指各群体和社会借以表现其文化的多种不同形式。这些表现形式在他们内部及其间传承，不仅体现在人类文化遗产通过丰富多彩的文化表现形式来表达、弘扬和传承的多种方式，也体现在借助各种方式和技术进行的艺术创造、生产、传播、销售和消费的多种方式。该公约于 2007 年 3 月 18 日正式生效。

美国对文化多样性的公约草案非常不满，但是，它发现自己仍然不能够控制谈判进程。正像美国代表在最后陈词中所抱怨的那样，"UNESCO 会议的习惯并不是为了激励协商和进一步的思考。程序原则——以及联合国教科文组织总的实践——都不是一贯执行的，有的时候甚至完全被忽视。在'暗示'下的投票并不是为了促进共识而是鼓励分歧。"③ 因此，美国投票反对《文化表达多样性的保护和促进公约》（*Convention on the Protection and Promotion of the Diversity of Cultural Expressions*）。④ 在这次投票过程中，以色列是美国唯一的跟随者。因此，在像联合国教科文组织这样非常开放的组织中，每个国家都拥有平等的投票权。虽然有些成员国对美国的态度表示尊重，并且会有一些美国偏好的价值观被加入到公约中去，美国不得不承认它还是不能够独自决定联合国教科文组织的结果。

2007 年 12 月，大会通过了《联合国土著人民权利宣言》。《宣言》为世界土

---

① http://static.chinavisual.com/storage/contents/2006/10/15/8555T20061015132854_1.shtml.

② http://www.fmprc.gov.cn/chn/pds/ziliao/tytj/tyfg/t311879.htm.

③ See "Final Statement of the United States Delegation," http://www.amb—usa.fr/usunesco/texts/Cultural_Diversity_Final.pdf.

④ About the Convention, please refer to http://unesdoc.unesco.org/images/0014/001429/142919e.pdf.

著人民的生存、尊严、福祉和权利确立了全球最低标准全球框架。《宣言》规定歧视土著人民为非法，促进土著人民全面有效地参与与其相关的一切事项。《宣言》还确保他们有权保持其独特性，在经济、社会和文化发展中制定自己的优先重点。①2009 年 9 月 UNESCO 第 35 届大会第 34C/4 号文件继续明确了推动文明对话和文化多样性的行动纲领。"在不同文明文化之间对话方面，教科文组织将继续采取具体和切实可行的行动，其中包括重点关注土著人民和不同宗教间对话、地区和分地区一级的各种举措、形成一套共同的价值观和原则、以其五个主管领域为基础的核心主题以及将对话作为增进妇女人权的一种手段。""教科文组织还将挖掘以音乐和艺术为手段开展对话的潜力，将其作为加强相互了解和相互作用，建设和平文化，促进对文化多样性的尊重的手段。""加强宗教间对话，确保：(i) 尊重宗教信仰和宽容的共同价值观在学校课程和教科书中得到体现，(ii) 在一个有助于对话目标的世俗框架内探讨信仰问题。"②

　　不同宗教文明之间的对话是联合国教科文组织倡导文化多样性、推进文明对话的重点领域之一。2006 年 1 月 20 日，在 UNESCO 的推动下，联合国大会第 61 届会议通过第 60/150 号决议"遏制对宗教的诽谤"，承认所有宗教对现代文明做出宝贵贡献和表明整个国际社会都渴望保持不同文化间的对话及合作来促进和平。③2006 年 3 月 30 日，教科文组织执行局举行第 174 届会议，通过了"尊重言论自由与尊重宗教信仰和价值观以及宗教和文化象征"④ 的决定，体现了国际社会对和平、宽容和各种文明、文化、民族和宗教情况的关注，为了使其有所保障，吁请寻找教科文组织可以采取的行动方法和方式。2006 年 12 月，UNESCO 决定在 2007 年举行宗教间和文化间合作高级别对话，以期促进相互容忍、理解、对宗教或信仰自由和文化多样性的普遍尊重，并同该领域其他行动相互协调⑤。2007 年 12 月，UNESCO 大会申明相互了解和宗教间对话是不同文明间的对话与和平文化的重要方面，鼓励会员国酌情审议那些确定在社会所有阶层和级别采取实际行动以促进宗教间和文化间对话、宽容、了解与合作的举措。大会还鼓励各种文化和文明的媒体相互开展对话。⑥

① http://www.un.org/esa/socdev/unpfii/documents/DRIPS_zh.pdf.

② http://unesdoc.unesco.org/images/0018/001836/183612c.pdf.

③ 详见联合国官网：http://www.un.org/zh/。

④ 详见 UNESCO 执行局举行第 174 届会议记录。

⑤ 详见联合国官网：http://www.un.org/zh/。

⑥ 详见 UNESCO2007 年大会记录。

世界范围内的以宗教为核心的推进文明间对话的行动主要包括：2007 年 10 月 26—28 日在马其顿文化名城奥赫里德市，马其顿共和国文化部与联合国教科文组织联合举办"世界宗教与文明对话会议"。此次会议主题为"宗教与文化对和平的贡献，互敬与共存"。来自马其顿、阿尔巴尼亚、波黑美国、俄罗斯、德国、瑞士、奥地利、爱尔兰、梵蒂冈、约旦、印度、日本、韩国、中国等 20 多个国家的 200 多名宗教界人士和学者出席了会议。此次"宗教与文明对话会议"为首届会议，以后将每三年召开一次。大会选举 70 名各国代表作为下届会议的组委会委员，并通过了大会宣言，呼吁各宗教与文明加强对话，放弃偏见，尊重宗教与文明的多样性，谴责宗教暴力，加强宗教教育，尊重女权。①2009 年 5 月 26 日至 28 日在马尼拉举行的关于不同信仰间开展对话与合作以促进和平与发展的不结盟运动部长级特别会议。2009 年 12 月 3 日至 9 日在澳大利亚墨尔本举行的世界宗教议会。②2009 年 7 月 1 日和 2 日在阿斯塔纳举行的第三次世界宗教和传统宗教领袖大会。③

2. 推动不同国家、地区之间的文明对话

联合国教科文组织不仅在全球层面通过了许多的《宣言》、制定行动计划和开展文明对话活动，它也致力于推动不同国家、地区之间的文明对话活动。这些文明对话活动都围绕着文化多样化的主题，致力于促进不同文明之间的和谐共处、互相学习。

2002 年 9 月 16 日至 17 日 UNESCO 组织召开了第三次国际文化部长圆桌会议，在土耳其伊斯坦布尔举行。这次会议的主题是"非物质文化遗产——文化多样性的体现"。会议期间，代表们围绕非物质文化遗产的范围及面临的威胁、文化多样性与可持续性发展的关系、建立保护非物质文化遗产的国内制度、加强国际间合作等问题展开了热烈的讨论。各成员国经过充分协商，通过了保护非物质文化遗产的《伊斯坦布尔宣言》。宣言陈述了非物质文化遗产的重要性及加强非物质文化遗产保护的紧迫性，呼吁各国尽快制定保护非物质文化遗产的政策和法规，加强国际间的交流和协作。此次会议之后，《保护非物质文化遗产公约》进入起草阶段。④2003 年 8 月 29 日至 30 日，在前南斯拉夫的马其顿共和国奥赫里德，

---

① http://www.unesco.org/dialogue/en/events.htm.

② http://www.chinatibetnews.com/zongjiao/2009-12/21/content_370405.htm.

③ http://www.qikan.com.cn/Article/zgdj/zgdj200806/zgdj20080627.html.

④ http://www.bjww.gov.cn/2004/7-12/1633.html.

东南欧地区的八个国家元首——前南斯拉夫马其顿共和国（东道国）、阿尔巴尼亚、波斯尼亚—黑塞哥维那、保加利亚、克罗地亚、匈牙利、塞尔维亚和黑山及斯洛文尼亚以及教科文组织大会主席、联合国秘书长的个人代表等都出席了在此举行的文明对话论坛。会议通过了《奥赫里德公报》，包含针对东南欧地区在价值观教育、文化遗产与科学合作等领域开展进一步合作所采取的具体措施。① 此次会议成为了以解决区域间或区域内问题为目标而开展对话的先例。

2004年2月10日至11日联合国教科文组织在也门萨那举办"文化与文明间对话"专题讨论会。来自阿拉伯世界和其他地区的约50名代表参与此会。讨论会主要从下列5个角度探讨文化与文明间对话：全球化与对话；教育对对话的贡献；阿拉伯文化对其他文化的贡献；对话在遏制恐怖主义的过程中发挥的作用；东西方的对话，突出主题为"遏制恐怖主义"。主要成果：萨那关于文化和文明间对话的呼吁，它提出了一些要在未来实施的具体建议，强调应追求共同价值观、教育对培育和维持对话具有不可缺少的作用、应争取文化多样性。② 接下来2004年12月20日至21日，UNESCO组织在越南河内举办了亚太地区"和平与持续发展"文化与文明对话大会。由亚太地区的30多个国家的部长级官员参会。会议成果为《河内宣言》，呼吁采取一系列具体措施，以增强人类安全，加强人与人之间，特别是年轻人之间的文化和科学交流与合作；通过国民教育改革，如对课程、课本及其他教育材料的审核与更新，来调整教育计划，以便推进素质教育。主要内容：为致力于不同文化和文明间对话的机构和个人提供展开直接、公开对话的平台，以便探讨在不同层面和交叉部门开展的政治行动的方向、战略和措施。③

2005年5月20日—21日，在保加利亚瓦尔纳举办了第三届东南欧国家首脑会议，此次主题为"东南欧文化走廊"。主办方为保加利亚政府、联合国教科文组织、欧洲委员会。参与方为阿尔巴尼亚、波黑、保加利亚、希腊、马其顿、土耳其、克罗地亚7国总统以及代表罗马尼亚和塞黑两国总统的两国文化部长出席。会议主要探讨推广该地区的文化遗产和文化走廊，采取紧急措施推动区域内濒危文化遗产的保护，包括继续采取行动打击非法贩运文化财产。会议成果包括"东南欧文化走廊——共同的历史，共同的遗产，未来伙伴关系的钥匙"声明：

---

① http://unesdoc.unesco.org/images/0013/001319/131973c.pdf.

② http://www.unesco.org/dialogue/en/conferences.html.

③ http://www.unesco.org/dialogue/en/conferences.html.

东南欧9国共同承诺，努力挖掘、保护和传扬本地区的文化历史遗产，共同采取措施，联合打击破坏和走私文物及历史遗产的行为，使"文化走廊"成为联系本地区各国和各国人民的"纽带"。①

联合国教科文组织也致力于推动不同国家、地区之间的宗教文明对话。2000年9月，在乌兹别克斯坦的塔什干地区举办了宗教间对话的国际会议。此次会议的主题为"精神融合与文化间对话"以及"关注于中亚的东西方文明间对话"。伊斯兰教是中亚地区颇具影响的主要宗教。② 所以，此次对话着重于伊斯兰文明与西方基督教文明之间的相互理解。2004年12月，在阿尔巴尼亚地拉那举行的东南欧国家"宗教和民族事务首脑会议"，会议通过了《地拉那首脑会议宣言》，强调所有宗教领袖与其他公民社会和社区的领袖一样，拥有对人们在社会中相互理解与互动的方式施加积极的道德影响的潜力和责任。③2009年在澳大利亚举行了第五次亚太区域宗教间对话。2010年5月在巴西召开的文化联盟第三届论坛，此次论坛是关于文化间友谊的研讨会，主题为"拉丁美洲宗教间青年对话：历史与展望"；等等。

小　结

通过以上研究，本文主要解答两个方面的问题，即联合国教科文组织如何从传播普世价值到倡导文化多样性的转变，以及冷战结束以来、尤其是2000年以来，联合国教科文组织如何在倡导文化多样性的原则下积极推动文明对话，在全球层面和地区层面展开了一系列重要活动。论文指出，联合国教科文组织具有十分开放的决策原则，这导致美国和西方国家并不能主导这一国际组织的议程设置和决策结果，坚持和促进文化多样性而不是传播西方的意识形态和价值观成为了联合国教科文组织在推动文明对话方面的主要目标。我们看到，联合国教科文组织的工作是十分全面而积极的，不仅涵盖了语言、电影等，还涉及宗教文明、土著人的权利等方面。作为教育、科学、文化领域最重要的政府间国际组织，UNESCO的工作对于在全球范围内促进文化的多样性起到了不可替代的巨

---

① http://news.xinhuanet.com/world/2005-05/21/content_2985210.htm.
② http://www.unesco.org/dialogue/en/events.htm.
③ http://gb.cri.cn/3821/2004/07/28/561@246635.htm.

大作用。

作者简介：

刘铁娃：日本早稻田大学国际关系学博士，北京大学法学博士，北京外国语大学国际关系学院讲师，北外联合国与国际组织研究中心副主任。专业研究方向为联合国与东北亚研究。教授课程包括高年级本科生《经济外交》(双语)，硕士研究生《联合国与国际组织研究》(双语)，《国际关系经典文献选读》(英文)。主要学术兼职为澳大利亚亚太保护责任研究中心学术顾问、中国项目协调人，韩国首尔亚洲和平与安全研究中心顾问。

联合国文明联盟与文明对话

张贵洪　杨濡嘉

冷战结束后，国际关系发生深刻的变革。东西方对抗结束了，世界政治会往什么方向发展？当时有人提出了文明冲突论，认为文明冲突将取代国家间的冲突成为国际政治的新范式。20 世纪 90 年代初，国际社会团结一致采取行动恢复科威特的主权和领土完整，联合国通过加强维和行动，在维护国际和平与安全中的作用有所上升。但西方国家提出"人权高于主权"和人道主义干预等主张，特别是北约绕过联合国安理会对科索沃采取军事行动，联合国的威信受到削弱，国际社会也出现新的分裂。同时，因种族、民族、宗教和文化等因素而造成的冲突越来越多，而且往往是由国内冲突而引发地区动荡。国际社会迫切需要通过加强不同文化之间的对话和理解，推广容忍、平等、多元等价值来缓和紧张、消除冲突。

作为最具普遍性、代表性和权威性的政府间国际组织，联合国不仅是实践多边主义的最佳场所，是集体应对各种威胁和挑战的有效平台，同时也是世界文明多样性的典型代表，是不同文明汇聚的论坛，在推动不同文明间对话方面有着不可替代的作用。联合国文明联盟就是文明对话的倡导者、组织者、参与者和推动者。

一、从文明对话到文明联盟

联合国文明联盟（United Nations Alliance of Civilizations，UNAOC）作为世界最高层次的不同文明对话组织，由联合国秘书长科菲·安南（Kofi Annan）发起创立，旨在促进不同文化和宗教的国家和人们之间的相互理解与合作，帮助反对那些引发分裂和极端主义的力量。文明联盟通过与政府、国际性和地区性组织、民间社会团体、基金会以及私营机构的通力合作，支持一系列旨在为不同文化和共同体之间搭建桥梁的项目和活动。

联合国文明联盟的发展要追溯至联合国文明对话的产生。1998 年 11 月 4 日，第53 届联大一致通过决议（A/RES/53/22），决定宣布 2001 年为"联合国不同文明之间对话年"，以增进各种文明间的了解和沟通，减少不同文明间的冲突。决议认为，"不同文明所取得的成果是人类共同的文化遗产，为全人类提供了进步的源泉"。决议承认文化多元化和人类创造活动的多样性，强调应当把对话作为实现理解、消除对和平的威胁、加强相互联系以及在不同文明间加强交流的一种手段。此后，不同文明之间的对话，包括不同信仰、不同宗教之间的平等对话，在全球广泛展开。

1999 年第 54 届联大和 2000 年第 55 届联大都将题为"联合国不同文明之间对话年"的项目列入大会的临时议程（A/RES/54/113, A/RES/55/23）。2001 年 11月，第 56 届联大就促进不同文明之间的对话问题举行全体会议，以增进各种文明间的了解和沟通，减少不同文明间的冲突。会议在美国"9·11"恐怖袭击事件后举行，因此如何通过不同文明间对话推动各国预防和打击国际恐怖主义的斗争成为会议的重要议题之一。联合国秘书长安南就"联合国不同文明间对话年"发表报告，指出"文化和宗教多样化是力量的源泉，而不是分裂和对抗的起因"。2002 年，联合国大会一致通过决议（A/RES/57/249），宣布每年的 5 月 21 日为"世界文化多样性促进对话和发展日"。

文明联盟的倡议最初由西班牙前首相萨帕特罗（José Luis Rodríguez Zapatero）在 2004 年第 59 届联大上提出，并与土耳其前总理埃尔多安（Recep Tayyip Erdoan）共同发起。2005 年 7 月，时任联合国秘书长安南发言（SG/SM/10004）宣布正式成立文明联盟，并任命一个由 20 位国际知名人士组成的名人小组（High Level Group）指导文明联盟的活动。2006 年 11 月，该小组向安南提交了一份报告。报告指出，造成西方与伊斯兰世界隔阂的核心因素不是宗教信仰，而是冲突、恐怖主义以及过去几年里发生的各种激化矛盾的事件。报告为重建拥有不同文化和信仰的人民之间的互信提出了具体建议，如通过教育、媒体、移民等手段推动文明间的交流和理解，强调国际社会必须同时致力于解决一系列悬而未决的政治问题。2007 年 4 月，刚刚接任联合国秘书长的潘基文任命葡萄牙前总统若热·桑帕约（Jorge Sampaio）为负责文明联盟工作的高级代表。①

联合国文明联盟由高级代表领导，设有一个由 16 人组成的秘书处，在秘书处主

---

① 从 2013 年 1 月 1 日起，联合国文明联盟高级代表由曾经担任第 66 届联大主席和卡塔尔常驻联合国代表的纳赛尔（Nassir Abdulaziz）担任。

任的管理下支持高级代表的各项工作。此外，筹备联合国文明联盟成立期间成立的名人小组成员被任命为文明联盟大使，该小组成员仍为联合国文明联盟活动的开展提供建议。联合国秘书长根据名人小组报告的建议，还建立了一个志愿性质的信托基金①，用以支持联合国文明联盟的项目开展。联合国文明联盟拥有 134 名伙伴成员 (members of group of friends)，包括世界主要国家和联合国其他机构和国际组织，如教科文组织（UNESCO）和国际移民组织（IOM）等，这些伙伴共同推进文明联盟在教育、青年、媒体和移民四大问题上的项目在全球的开展。文明联盟还设有一个全球化的智囊网络（UNAOC Research Network），从阿根廷的 ESEADE 大学到土耳其的伊斯兰文化研究中心，这一网络包括了全球诸多的从事于文明联盟事务相关领域研究的研究机构，它们为文明联盟的项目开展提供智力支持。下图展示了联合国文明联盟的组织架构：

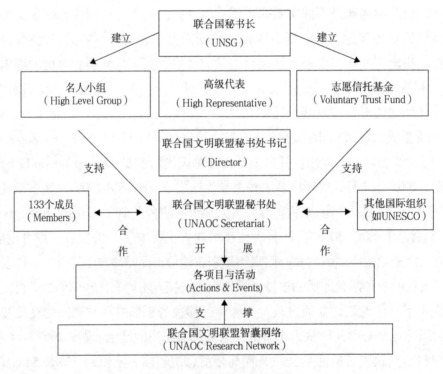

联合国文明联盟组织架构图

---

① 该信托基金设在联合国大会下管理，资金来源主要来自于各国政府的自愿捐助。该基金遵循联合国财务管理规则，基金的项目管理将由联合国项目管理办公室（UNOPS）负责。

联合国文明联盟主要致力于处理交叉领域问题。联盟在选取工作领域时主要基于下列认识：在 21 世纪诸多影响人们生活的跨文明冲突问题中，教育起到帮助人们认识到文明是人类冲突根源的基础性作用。培养公民理解文明多样性的能力和技能是促进文明对话的关键。青年是联盟要争取的主要支持者和活动受众。粗略计算，世界人口的五分之一就是 15 岁至 24 岁的青年人口。具有创新力和想法的年轻人是社会变革、经济发展、技术革新的关键力量。与此同时，传统媒体与社交媒体和新信息技术一起，塑造人们的观点和态度。它们具备沟通不同文明和宗教的桥梁性作用和营造公众对文明多样性的积极态度的潜力。增强媒体的建设性作用是文明联盟的一项核心工作。移民和人口流动使得当前社会的文明多样性更加明显，它们为创新和发展带来可能性，但同时也对建立一个包容性社会提出挑战，这一领域同样需要文明联盟的参与。基于上述考虑，联合国文明联盟主要在教育、青年、媒体、移民四大方面开展活动。

联盟在开展各项活动时的宗旨是：1. 尊重和维护《世界人权宣言》；2. 为保护和推动世界各国的公民、政治、经济、社会和文化权利而奋斗；3. 加强各国实现民主和尊重人权（包括少数人的权利和发展权）的能力；4. 确保在所有社会中实现尊重和保护移民人权，消除种族主义和排外行为，实现更大限度的社会和谐与包容；5. 反对任何形式的针对妇女的暴力；6. 积极欢迎各方的参与；7. 确保媒体自由和公众掌握信息的渠道通畅。

自 2007 年至 2012 年的 5 年期间，联合国文明联盟逐渐在全球层面发展起来，在世界各地建立起合作伙伴、成员和项目网络。其覆盖网络由起初的以欧洲和南美为主、不足全球范围三分之一的区域迅速发展至新增北美、澳洲、亚洲、非洲大部分地区后全球范围的五分之四的区域。在其网络不断扩大的情况下，联合国文明联盟在过去 5 年里还实现了：第一，为跨文明的对话与合作提供一个组织完善信誉良好的联合国平台。尽管文明联盟的性质特殊，它并非联合国的一个分支机构，但却与联合国的分支机构及其他政府间组织实现良好互补。第二，逐步将自己塑造成一个以消除不同文明间敌视情绪加强文明对话的软实力工具。第三，作为搭建桥梁者、催化剂和会议召集人角色的文明联盟，不仅与自己传统意义上的利益相关者（成员国）保持密切联系，同时得以与各国国内社会和草根阶层密切接触，并通过多方合作开发一系列创新性的项目推进文明的交流和理解。第四，在文明联盟内多样性日益增加的同时，建立清晰的组织架构和工作机制。

二、文明对话：联合国文明联盟在行动

在联合国文明联盟宗旨的指导下，文明联盟的核心项目及其主要成就如下：

1. 年度论坛

迄今为止，联盟举行了四次全球论坛。2008年1月，联合国文明联盟首届论坛在西班牙的马德里举行，来自各国政府、基金会、国际组织、民间社会、媒体和工商界的人士齐聚一堂，共同探讨如何弥合不同国家和文化之间的分歧，并为推动跨文化交流建立伙伴关系。会议主要探讨了"在全球化时代管理多样性"、"建立不同文明间认同的政治挑战"和"从全球对话到具体行动"等议题。2009年4月，第二届论坛在土耳其的伊斯坦布尔举行，就"良好治理文明多样性的重要性"、"创新政策与创新举措的结合"、"教育与文明对话"等议题展开讨论。2010年5月，第三届论坛在巴西的里约热内卢举行，主题为"沟通不同文化，构建世界和平"。2011年12月，第四届论坛在卡塔尔的多哈举行，探讨"文明多样性与发展"、"增进互信，维护和平"、"文明对话的新战略"等内容。另外，论坛还将焦点对准了"9·11"十周年后的穆斯林与西方关系。第五届论坛计划于2013年3月在奥地利的维也纳举行。年度论坛不仅为解决全球问题提供了一个跨文化对话的平台，更在会后提供一系列联盟项目的开展机会，同时也促进联盟的合作伙伴间开展跨文化交流项目的机会。

2. 国家计划与区域战略

国家计划是文明联盟通过影响会员国在跨文明问题上的政策制定来营造一个更好的文明多样性环境的手段。联盟帮助会员国制定计划来处理多领域交叉问题：从教育到青年，从媒体到移民等。在此基础上，区域性战略从更广泛的层面影响会员国的包容性社会的建立。区域战略是一套实现跨文明对话与合作的框架，它整合国家计划和相关项目，把政府、地方当局、媒体、社会公众和私人部门的力量集合起来，实现一定国际区域的联合行动。目前，两大区域战略已被采纳并正在实施：一是东南欧战略（2009年由波斯尼亚和黑塞哥维那采用），二是地中海战略（2010年由马耳他采用）。这两大战略涉及了欧洲40多个国家，包括巴尔干半岛、北非和中东地区。

区域战略通过联盟与其官方和私人合作伙伴的合作转化为三种项目：1. 作为

文明联盟的旗舰项目在一定区域实施；2.合作组织或联盟自己开发的新项目；3.由各国国内社会组织提交申请得以通过的项目。上述项目的实践帮助联盟实现消除跨文明冲突、增进文明多样性了解、反对仇外心理和种族主义等目标。

3.媒体项目

文明联盟媒体项目的核心是环球专家计划。环球专家是一个专家网络，同时提供网上资源，为全球的记者提供世界意见领袖在政治、社会、宗教事务上的看法与观点。这一计划帮助全球的记者在报道时取得多样化的评论和分析，实现在敏感事务报道中观点多样性的平衡。环球专家计划在过去三年间取得了如下的成就：其一，建立了一个约有350位专家的数据库，包括专家的简历和联系方式，读者可以通过专业领域、地域和关键字来搜索各位专家的观点和信息。其二，向世界各地的编辑分发文章和评论以提高信息库中分析的质量和多样性。其三，在重大国际事件发生时通报全球的记者和其他利益相关方。其四，开发移动应用，使得记者和媒体从业者们可以通过移动设备随时在网上找到相关专家。

记者培训是媒体项目的第二重要组成部分。这些培训由高级记者和专家们组织，用以提高记者们报道跨文明事务。培训组织的工作坊已经在巴基斯坦、印度尼西亚、阿拉伯世界、欧洲和北美举办多次。培训帮助记者们提高在电子信息时代报道冲突，如"穆斯林—西方"关系时的能力。很多电视节目、文章、广播采访和博客等都是记者培训的成果。

与之相类似的，媒体培训是针对社会团体的领导者，特别是在文明领域固守成见的社会团体的领导者的培训，鼓励他们突破成见，通过传媒了解不同的文化。

媒体领导者论坛将具有影响力的媒体领导者——编辑、媒体业主和投资人等聚集在一起，讨论在报道跨文化冲突时的新的报道策略。最近的一次大型媒体领导者论坛是于2011年举行的死海论坛。

最后，媒体项目还包括视频和多媒体项目。该项目由联盟的合作伙伴，如顶尖的传媒院校等共同举办，用以提供对复杂的文明多样性事务的纪实报道和评论。目前共举办了两次以身份认知和伊斯兰为主题的项目。

4.青年团结基金

青年团结基金（YSF）为青年组织开展理解地区层面、国家层面和国际层面的文明多样性活动提供最高30000美元的资金。各项目由青年组织向联盟申报，项目必须利于青年（18 至 30 岁），并具备持续的多重影响力。例如，在索马里举办的工作坊以"武力冲突下的人权教育"为主题向当地青年进行教育。很多受训者现在已成为培训人员并鼓励其他武装战士参与培训。YSF 项目目前进行了两期，取得如下成就：其一，24 个项目（申请项目数的 4%）在 22 个国家中成功举办，耗资 570000 美元。其二，超过 15 万的青年受众从项目获益。其三，绝大部分的项目包括文明意识提升、培训、与决策者对话、建立支持网络等。其四，增加社会边缘青年的参与，建立代际、不同文明和宗教间的沟通桥梁。

5. 奖学金项目

文明联盟的奖学金项目由德国政府、爱马仕和平基金会支持，在与阿拉伯国家联盟、ISESCO（伊斯兰教育科学与文化组织）、卡塔尔政府、约旦政府、伊斯兰合作组织（OIC）、英国文化协会和国际教育学院合作下开展。该项目主要致力于增加伊斯兰世界（以阿拉伯国家为主）和西方世界（以欧洲为主）的人民的相互理解。该项目邀请来自西欧和阿拉伯地区的领导者齐聚一堂，增进彼此的理解和互信。目前，在 2010 年和 2011 年，两期实验性项目已经完成，招收了来自阿拉伯世界和西欧、北美地区的 15 位参与者。他们中有知名记者、外交官和一些阿拉伯国家地区的领导人。参与者们与成功企业的首席执行官、基金会和各组织的领导人会谈，并在项目结束返回本国后将自己学到的内容应用于本国社会的改革中。

6. 教育项目

文明联盟坚信青年是影响社会转变的主力。文明联盟暑期学校基本是以一周时长为限的夏季课程，以参与者来自不同文明背景为出发点，通过培训使得年轻的领导者们更好地理解文明多样性的社会，并让他们回到本国后投身推动包容性社会的建设中去。暑期学校的执教队伍由专业人员构成，包括顶级高校的教授、行业的专家、政治家等等。每期暑期学校在确保区域、性别、文化背景均衡的条件下，召集 100 位左右的年龄从 18 岁至 35 岁的年轻领导者参与。暑期学校的举办地在文明联盟的合作高校中选择，在 2010 年和 2011 年，暑期学校在葡萄牙举行，分别在阿威罗和里斯本两座城市。2012 年，两期暑期学校在葡萄牙的科安布拉和约旦的安曼举行。另有两期冬季学校计划举办，分别在拉丁美洲和亚洲。2013 年有三期暑期学校在筹划中，两期在地中海地区，一期在非洲。此外，还有三期冬季学校在筹划中，分别计划在亚洲、拉丁美洲和中东开展。

其他教育项目还包括网上宗教和信仰教育，文明联盟研究网络，减少文盲率的媒体和教育的信息交流中心等。此外，UNITWIN 项目，由联合国文明联盟与联合国教科文组织合作举办的全球传媒与信息交流和文明对话项目也是教育项目中的重要一环。全球八所大学参与该项目，研究减少跨文化交流中的偏见和阻碍。

7. 公民跨文化交往能力建设项目

在这一方面，文明联盟主要有三大主题活动。

第一，跨文化创新奖和无线局域网。2011 年，文明联盟与宝马集团合作，启动了跨文化创新宝马奖。这一奖项的设立是为了奖励全球文明对话与合作中的创新项目。2011 年获奖的前 10 个创新项目被邀请在多哈论坛上展出。每一年都有 10 个新的组织加入这一创新奖的无线网络。该网络连接草根阶层与媒体、捐赠人和政府，将公民对文明对话和跨文化交流的创新思想在更广的领域予以宣传。

第二，"为多样性和包容性做一件事"运动。2011 年 5 月，一个创新性的活动在公共和私人组织中展开。该活动鼓励人们在日常生活中选择一件小事去理解不同文明。2012 年活动还提出"10 件你可以做的小事来庆祝世界文明对话日"的倡议，如"去参观一个你原本不了解的文明的博物馆"等。

第三，PLURAL+ 项目，青年拍摄以移民、多样性与包容性主题的电影节。联合国文明联盟与国际联盟组织合作创办的 PLURAL+ 项目鼓励全球各地的青年针对移民、多样性和社会包容力等主题拍摄反映自身经历或观点的视频。自2009 至 2011 年，该活动征集了来自 72 个国家的 450 个视频，该活动还选取优秀视频在多媒体平台上播放。PLURAL+ 项目为青年人参与文明对话、表达思想提供了新的机会和平台。

8. 移民项目

移民与融合——建立包容性社会（IBIS）项目于 2010 年由联合国文明联盟和国际移民组织合作建立。该项目提供成功的移民融入当地社会信息和案例，推动利益有关方的参与解决移民问题。该项目同时通过媒体传播解决移民问题的积极态度，其中一项计划为将移民融入当地生活的成功经验拍摄成视频传播。第一个计划已经在意大利政府的支持下于意大利拍摄完成，目前还有其他计划在拍摄过程中。该项目还计划对地方当局的移民机构给予培训，争取取得当局政策制定时针对移民等少数团体的均衡考虑。

9. 文明对话咖啡

文明对话咖啡是一个通过运用前沿的视频会议技术实现不同文化群体的人们进行面对面交流的非盈利的计划。该项目帮助不同文明背景的人们分享经历、消除误解并互相学习。文明对话咖啡已经在第一批城市巴黎、里斯本、阿姆斯特丹、里约热内卢、克利夫兰、拉马拉中展开。2012 年夏季，该项目在伦敦、贝鲁特、弗罗茨瓦夫和圣保罗也得到开展。新的文明对话咖啡活动正在突尼斯、贝尔格莱德、拉各斯和布里斯班作为试点展开，并将于 2013 年年中正式开展。通过该项活动，组织和个人都得以与不同文明背景的人进行交流，以消除对其他文明的误解。根据活动反馈，该项目成果颇丰：来自贝鲁特、拉马拉和巴塞罗那的年轻人通过文明对话咖啡交流他们不同的传统；来自开罗、多哈、阿姆斯特丹和里约热内卢的女性讨论在赋予妇女权力中教育和工作的重要性；以气候变化、创新和人口老龄化等为题的城市会议将北京、旧金山、东京和墨尔本联系起来。在塞内加尔举办的音乐会能够在开普敦、伦敦和里斯本直播。

10. 新项目

值得注意的是，联盟的行动计划随时间的发展不断革新。2011 年 12 月的多哈论坛又为联盟新活动提供灵感，包括：（1）防止不同文明间的紧张和危机：建立博物馆和中心网络，提升公众对文化多样性的包容力；开展一项网上青年运动，邀请政治领导人、决策者和市民公开发言反对恐慌、不包容和仇外心理。（2）提高对文明多样性的价值的认识——这不只是一项自由，更是一种财富：在联盟 2012 至 2013 计划中关注创新型工业支持女性发展；由人类生存发展国际基金会、俄罗斯外交部、联合国教科文组织、联合国儿童基金会和非政府组织与联合国文明联盟合作开展的"2030 代"项目将深入开展。（3）鼓励不同文明背景的人们沟通，建立包容性社会：开展题为"统一多样性与凝聚力"的系列研讨会，通过邀请政府、地方当局、社会活动家和媒体，共同推动社会政策的改善；在 2012 至 2013 年间开展青年文化节，使来自不同文明背景的青年齐聚一堂、相互了解学习，并建立全球青年合作关系。（4）推动关于多领域交叉问题（青年、教育、移民、媒体等）的政策制定和行动，研发新工具：建立一个网上信息平台来汇集知识和交换专家意见，帮助联盟的参与者深化了解会员国的情况，并为联盟开展的文明对话、活动等提供信息支持。

三、文明对话：联合国的使命和中国的作用

进入新世纪，国际社会继续发生重大的变革和调整：第一，国际关系发展变化的不确定性和复杂性更加突出。国际关系特别是大国之间的关系不断处于调整之中，新的国际格局一直没有成型。非国家行为体的作用在不断上升，跨国和跨地区的活动有加速的趋势，全球性问题越来越突出。这些变化大大增加了国际关系中的不确定性和复杂性。第二，世界和人类发展的依赖性和脆弱性越来越明显。技术的进步使人类对自然界的依赖程度有所下降，但国家之间、人们相互之间的依赖性却大大增强。技术的进步还使人、物和信息的流动加速，但人类自身的脆弱性反而更加突出。第三，国际体系的转型进入一个关键时期。经过20多年的调整，大国关系正从变革走向稳定，新兴大国的利益日益向海外扩张，其经济力量正向政治力量转化，新时期国际关系的主题逐渐明朗，从国际货币基金组织到联合国安理会，从货币体系到安理会席位，国际规则和秩序正面临重大的修改和变革。第四，国际社会的组织化和法制化趋势继续得到加强。通过组织化和法制化的方法和途径，规范国家的对外行为和国家间的利益关系，越来越成为国际社会的共识并得到大多数国家的支持。对大国和发达国家来说，可以利用其资金、技术、制度和外交的优势，在国际组织和法律中占据主导和有利地位；对发展中国家而言，则可以利用国际组织和法律保证其基本的权力和利益，并通过集体的力量影响国际关系的发展。第五，新兴国家和力量的崛起正孕育着国际秩序的某种变革。亚、非、拉一些新兴国家已在所在地区发挥主导作用，成为地区力量中心和地区新秩序的倡导者和推动者。这些新兴国家的力量和利益还不断向周边和更远的地区扩展，并提出在国际社会拥有更多发言权、参与权和决定权的要求。

面对这些调整和变革，一方面联合国具有的普遍性、代表性和权威性可能在未来不会有大的变化，联合国在某种程度上仍然具有稀缺性和不可替代性。但另一方面，联合国内外受到很多挑战，内部如联合国大会的有效性、安理会的代表性以及联合国一些机构（如托管理事会）的作用，受到质疑；外部如二十国集团的兴起，以及北约继续存在，甚至在利比亚问题上发挥主导性的作用，使得联合国在某种程度、某些方面、某些时候有被边缘化的危险。如何在新的全球治理结构中进行定位并发挥更重要的作用，是联合国面临的新课题。文明对话，可以成为联合国维护和平、实现发展、促进人权的重要抓手。

通过对话达成相互理解。文明对话的首要功能是达成相互理解。历史经验表明，在人类文明交流的过程中，不仅需要克服自然的屏障和隔阂，还需要超越思想的障碍和束缚，更需要克服形形色色的偏见和误解。通过对话，相互了解对方的利益和需要、各自的观念和思想，才有可能进行沟通、交流、协商和谈判，求同存异，达成相互理解和信任。文明对话能够在三方面发挥重要的桥梁作用。首先，通过文明对话能够推动政府、国际组织、民间社会和非政府组织之间的合作，推动社区不同文化间的对话和交流。其次，通过文明对话能够推动各国政府间就正确对待文化差异、弥合分歧而采取共同的行动。第三，通过文明对话还有助于加强联合国体系作为一个整体在防止战争、推动和平方面的工作。

通过理解推动彼此合作。理解和信任是合作的关键。意识形态、社会制度、发展模式的差异不应成为合作的障碍，更不能成为相互对抗的理由。世界的多样性、文明和文化的差异不应是世界冲突的根源，而应是世界交流和合作的动力与起点。文化交流是达成相互理解的基本手段和途径，但文化之间的理解和信任却需要一个长期的过程，需要宽容、容忍、谦让和尊重的精神。有了相互之间的理解，才有可能就促进共同利益、消除各种分歧开展合作。在国际关系中，利益是合作的基础，但也是冲突的来源。有了深入理解基础上的信任，这种合作才有可能持久和有效。

通过合作实现和平发展。和平和发展只有通过合作才能实现。正如前联合国秘书长安南就"联合国不同文明间对话年"发表的报告中所说："联合国的一个主要使命是预防冲突。我们要完成这一使命就必须开展不同文明间的对话。通过实现理解和相互尊重，我们可以减少误解和不信任，奠定采用非暴力方式解决冲突的基础。"现任联合国秘书长潘基文也表示，联合国文明联盟的努力是对执行联大2006年通过的反恐战略的有益补充，也是对联合国开展预防外交及推动可持续和平的有力支持。在世界经济全球化、文化多元化的当下，不同文明间的对话，是化解各国家、民族、种族、宗教、文明间种种冲突的有效方式和最佳选择。联合国的另一使命是促进发展，对话对于这一使命也非常重要。通过交流经验和共同寻找解决办法，我们可以解决我们目前和今后面临的经济和社会问题。

在联合国文明对话活动中，中国有独特的条件和优势，完全能大有可为：

第一，中国一贯支持联合国在国际事务和多边外交中的核心地位，也积极参与联合国主导的文明对话活动。2001年9月，为响应联合国"不同文明对话年"，全国政协外事委员会在北京举办"21世纪论坛——不同文明对话"研讨会，邀请国内外知名人士和专家学者，就不同文明对话问题进行多方面的交流与探讨。

全国政协副主席宋健应科菲·安南秘书长邀请，成为"不同文明间对话名人小组"的 19 名成员之一。中国积极倡导在亚欧会议框架下开展文化与文明对话交流，并于 2003 年主办了亚欧会议进程中的第一届文化与文明会议。2007 年，亚欧会议不同信仰间对话会议又在南京举行。

第二，文明对话与中国未来的发展战略相契合。党的十七届六中全会通过的《中共中央关于深化文化体制改革　推动社会主义文化大发展大繁荣若干重大问题的决定》提出：当前，增强国家软实力和中华文化国际影响力的要求更加紧迫，必须提高文化开放水平，推动中华文化走向世界。为此，要开展多渠道多形式多层次的对外文化交流，广泛参与世界文明对话，促进文化相互借鉴，增强中华文化在世界上的感召力和影响力。

第三，以儒家思想为重要代表的中华文化是参与世界文明对话的重要力量。源于儒家思想的和谐观作为中华民族独特的文化精神和生存智慧，其合理的思想内核为当代世界的和平、发展、合作提供了可供借鉴的精神资源，具有重要的时代价值。它不仅为追求人与人之间、不同社会阶层之间以及人与自然之间的相互和谐提供智慧，还为追求民族与民族、国与国之间的相互和谐提供智慧。

第四，尼山论坛是中国为主体的文明对话平台。尼山世界文明论坛以开展世界不同文明对话为主题，以弘扬中华文化、促进中外文化交流、推动建设和谐世界为目的，开展以学术性与民间性、国际性与开放性相结合为特色的国际文化学术交流活动。首届尼山世界文明论坛于 2010 年 9 月在孔子出生地曲阜尼山举办，主题是"和而不同与和谐世界"。2011 年 4 月，尼山论坛还走出中国和亚洲，在联合国教科文组织总部举办以"儒家思想与全球化世界中的新人文主义"为主题的巴黎尼山论坛。2012 年 11 月 10—11 日，在联合国总部举办纽约尼山世界文明论坛，主题为"超越国度、不同信仰，共同价值：儒家与基督文明对话"，就哲学价值、宗教文化、世界和谐等话题展开对话和探讨。

第五，联合国文明联盟正把文明对话的重心转向东方。联盟的初期活动集中在推动穆斯林和西方社会之间的对话与和解。目前，联盟致力于扩大在亚太地区的活动，推动各种文化（包括儒教文化）之间的理解与合作，并希望中国在其中发挥关键的作用。作为联合国倡导的一项活动，联盟在亚太地区开展活动主要有以下几点考虑：第一，组成亚太地区的大多数社会在文化、语言、宗教、政治上具有多样性，联盟可以提供一个相对低调、非干预性但又实用的政策工具，以帮助本地区的各个社会更好地发挥其多样性的优势。第二，国内的多样性很多时候又反映在地区层面，在亚太，儒教、穆斯林教、基督教、佛教、道教、印度教和世俗社会不得不就一系列问题上的差异进行协商。第三，宗教和文化能为亚太地区国家在发展高层次的地区合作和更有效的地区机构的持续努力方面提供重大的帮助。第四，东方文明目前的发言权还很有限，但是在文明联盟看来，东方文明可以在文化理解的全球对话方面有更重要的贡献。2012 年 11 月 29—30 日，联盟与中国联合国协会共同在上海主办亚洲和南太平洋地区磋商会议，主题是"通过对话和多样性促进和谐"(Harmony through Dialogue and Diversity)。会议就"文化传统与现代生活的结合"、"世俗主义和宗教的复兴"、"文化和文明对话作为国际关系的新兴范式"、"联合国体系与亚洲文化"、"中国传统文化的精髓如何为'多元文化、一个人类'作贡献"、"民族主义与地区文化"、"青年如何为跨文化对话与和谐作贡献"、"教育如何适应跨文化对话与和谐"等议题开展广泛研讨，来自中国、印度、澳大利亚、新西兰、马来西亚、泰国、菲律宾、印度尼西亚、日本、韩国、中国台湾等数十个国家和地区的代表、国际和地区组织的代表、私人机构和非政府组织领袖、媒体代表等 150 人左右应邀与会。

可以预见，以儒家文化为主体的东方文明将在联合国文明对话中占据重要一席，中国必将为文明对话作出新的贡献。

作者介绍：

张贵洪：复旦大学国际问题研究院联合国研究中心执行主任，教授、博士生导师。兼任中国联合国协会常务理事、中国南亚学会常务理事、上海国际关系学会常务理事、中印友好协会理事，亚洲学者联合会副会长兼中国同学会召集人。出版专著《超越均势：冷战后的美国南亚安全战略》，合著《中美印三边关系研究》，主编《联合国秘书长》、《联合国与文明对话》、《联合国发展报告 2012》、《联合国研究》等。主要研究领域包括联合国问题、中美印关系、亚太地区安全等。目前担任教育部重大课题攻关项目首席专家，主持多项科研项目。

罗德岛世界公众论坛

倪培民

一、文明对话本身作为一个历史现象

10 年前（2002），联合国宣布将每年的 5 月 21 日定为世界文明对话年。回顾这 10 年的文明对话历程，我们有必要首先简单梳理一下文明对话这个概念及文明对话的主要方式，以便将这 10 年的文明对话放到宏观的人类历史背景当中来予以审视。

提到对话，我们通常想到的就是柏拉图式的、通过对话各方之间的理性交谈、辩论，以澄清概念、达成共识的那种对话。的确，"对话"一词在希腊语里的原意来自 δια（diá，通）和 λόγos（logos，话语、词句、事理）。它意味着"对话"这个词与语言和理性的运用有着原初的联系。但这个原意也可以被理解为"意义的流通"。基于后者这个宽泛的理解，"文明对话"可以包括各种形式的文化传播、碰撞、竞争、互补和交融。由此不仅中国历史上春秋战国的百家争鸣和古希腊各派哲学的论辩可以看作文明对话，文成公主的西嫁吐蕃、郑和的南下西洋、十字军的东征、哥伦布的"发现"美洲大陆都可以看作是文明对话活动。

这种广义上的文明对话，从其形式来看，可大致概括为"文、武、商、政"四种："文"是指文明的交流形式，包括和平的传教活动、翻译介绍、学术讨论、体育艺术活动等。"武"是指运用武力的征服、强权的制约等手段来传播一种文明或意识形态的方式。"商"包括贸易、投资和以物质生存条件为目的而移民导致的文明交流和传播。"政"是政治外交的形式，如国际谈判、政府代表的访问等。这几种方式当中还可以细分，比如"文"的方式还可以进一步区分为语言的（学术探讨、翻译等）和非语言的（音乐舞蹈体育等）交流、无对话目的的和有组织、有目的的文化交流、单向的传播或者双向或多向的平等交流、不同文明之间的交流和同一文明内部的交流等。

联合国文明对话日所标志的对话，显然不是广义的文明对话。它指的主要是"文"的形式当中使用语言的、有组织的、多向的、文明间的对话。这种特殊意义上的文明对话不仅不同于以"武"为形式的文明交流，而且是与武力征服和强制截然相反的文明交流形式。它与"商"、"政"的文明交流形式也不同，虽然它们可以有部分的重合，如人们在从事商业或政治活动的时候，可以采取对话的方式。它甚至不是泛指所有"文"的形式的文明交流。非语言的体育艺术活动、单向的文化传播、无对话目的的意义流通和同一文明内部的讨论等，都不是这个特殊意义上的文明对话。换句话说，我们今天所探讨和推广的文明对话指的是人类自觉地把不同文明的代表组织起来，用语言的方式进行平等的交流，以促进相互的了解和共识的对话。

从历史上看，这种特殊意义上的文明对话直到 19 世纪末才出现。[①] 其最著名的标志性事件是 1893 年在芝加哥召开的"世界宗教议会"（World's Parliament of Religions）。那次大会被公认为是现代文明对话正式开端的标志。虽然在整整 17 天的会议上，英语世界的基督教占据了绝对优势[②]，难能可贵的是，所有的发言者在这个大会上的地位是平等的。可惜的是，那个会议在以后的很多年里中断了。在这以后的两次世界大战、共产主义革命以及民族独立运动当中，各文明的主要交往的方式是武力和强权的方式。但这些武力冲突和强权的横行也促使人们更深刻地认识到文明对话的必要，所以第二次世界大战的后期和战后，文明对话的活动开始逐渐多了起来。1939 年，夏威夷大学就开始举办"东西方哲学家大会"，力图在哲学的根子上，促进东西方的相互了解和交流。[③] 二战结束不久，联合国于 1948 年通过了著名的《人权宣言》。它既是对两次世界大战中西方文明中滋生出来的那种残酷现实的反省，同时也是文明对话的产物。[④] 这以后，文明对

---

① 近代以前即便有过类似的对话，也只是很个别的现象，如宋代儒家学者与佛教高僧之间的个人的交流，近代耶稣教的利玛窦与徐光启等儒者的交流，等等。

② 大会总共 194 个发言里，基督教占了 152 篇。其他的发言所占的比例是：佛教 12，犹太教 11，印度教 8，伊斯兰教 2，帕西教（Parsi）2，神道教 2，儒教 2，道教 1，耆那教 1。（R. H. Seager,"The World's Parliament of Religions，Chicago, Illinois, 1893: America's Religious Coming of Age." Ph.D.Diss., Harvard University, 1986, p.87）。

③ 这个大会后来先是 10 年一次，继而又变成 5 年一次，至今已经举办了 10 届。

④ 宣言的起草委员会里，就有中国的代表张彭春与吴德耀。张和吴两位都是杰出的儒家人物。宣言中的"所有的人应当像兄弟一样相互对待"的口号，就是儒家的"四海之内皆兄弟也"（论语 12.5）的思想，而它就是在张彭春的建议下加进去的。

话活动越来越频繁和广泛。1958 年张君劢、唐君毅、牟宗三、徐复观共同发表了《为中国文化敬告世界人士宣言》。1967 年，"国际亚洲哲学与比较哲学学会"（Society for Asian and Comparative Philosophy）在美国成立。1978 年，美国天普大学（Temple）成立"跨宗教跨文化研究院"。[①]1988 年，"世界宗教议会理事会"（Council for a Parliament of the World's Religions）成立，并于 1993 年，即世界宗教议会百年之际，在芝加哥集结了来自全世界各国家和地区的 8000 多位代表，召开了一次规模空前的盛会，并通过了一个非常著名的文件——《走向全球伦理宣言》（*Towards a Global Ethic: An Initial Declaration*），表达了世界各宗教和精神传统所达成的对伦理道德的基本共识。牛津大学也在同年成立了"国际跨宗教研究中心"（The International Interfaith Centre，Oxford，1993）。此后，世界宗教议会于 1999 年在南非的开普敦、2004 年在西班牙的巴塞罗那、2009 年在澳大利亚的墨尔本又连续召开了三届世界宗教议会大会，每 5 年一次。参会人数由 1999 年的 7000 多人增加到 2009 年的 10000 多人。1998 年 11 月联合国大会响应伊朗总统哈塔米（Mohammad Khatami）的提议通过决议，将 2001 年作为文明对话年。1999 年，"跨宗教和跨文化研究和对话基金会"（The Foundation for Interreligious and Intercultural Research and Dialogue [FIIRD]）在瑞士日内瓦成立。2000 年 8 月，2000 名宗教界领袖聚集在联合国，举行"世纪之交宗教与精神领袖世界和平峰会"。

2001 年，也就是联合国的文明对话年，发生了震惊世界的"911 事件"。这个巧合正是我们这个时代的象征。一方面是武力冲突的升级及其破坏性的凸显，一方面是文明对话的兴起及其迫切性的凸显。2001 年 11 月 9 日，联合国教科文组织大会通过了《世界文化多样性宣言》，将人类历史上文明之间的对话推向了一个新的高潮。各种以促进文明对话为主旨的研究机构、教育机构、团体组织、基金会、刊物和书籍等纷纷出现，数不胜数。[②]

---

① Institute for interreligious, Intercultural Dialogue，简称 IIID，后来在 2008 年演变为"全球对话研究院"（Global Dialogue Institute）。

② 如 2001 年成立的"世界公众论坛：文明对话"、2002 年在泰国成立的"世界宗教领袖议会"（World Council of Religious Leaders）、2005 年成立的"联合国文明联盟"（United Nations Alliance of Civilizations）、2006 年在澳大利亚墨尔本成立的"对话中心"（The Centre for Dialogue）和伊朗前总统卡塔米领导成立的"国际文明对话中心"（the International Center for Dialogue among Civilizations）、2008 年在孟加拉国达卡 Dhaka 大学成立的"跨宗教与跨文化对话中心"（Centre for Inter-religious and Intercultural Dialogue, CIID）等等。

中国比较明确地参与和推动文明对话，是在联合国文明对话年以后开始的。①

这段历史非常丰富，它的来龙去脉，其中各个国家、宗教、文明在这个过程中的态度，都很值得研究，足可由此形成一组非常丰富的专题。从总体来说，可以看出，过去的"世界文明对话日"10年不是随机的事件。它是人们对人类乃至整个地球生态在当代所面临的深刻危机的理性反应，是20世纪后半期那许许多多有关文明对话的呼声和实践在世纪之交时达到高潮的标志。如果说一个人的成熟不能以他的肌肉有多发达、体魄有多健壮来衡量，而应当以心智的发达和道德水准来衡量，那么这10年的文明对话，可以说是人类在危机和磨难中走向成熟的表现。

二、"世界公众论坛：文明对话"的活动

过去的10年中，全世界最重要的文明对话机制之一是"世界公众论坛：文明对话"（World Public Forum"Dialogue of Civilizations"）。它成立于2002年（也就是联合国确立世界文明对话日的那一年），在莫斯科和日内瓦设有常设机构，并且与联合国教科文组织（UNESCO）、阿拉伯联盟教科文组织（ALECSO）、欧亚基金会（ASEF）、国际跨文化教育协会（IAIE）等许多国际组织有着密切的合作关系。这个组织的基本宗旨是集结国际上各方面致力于团结与合作的力量，保护人类的精神和文化价值，为世界各主要文明创造积极对话的平台，促进各文明的相互合作与理解，共同面对和应付人类所面临的种种危机与挑战。从2003年

---

① 中国在"文革"以后，就开始了关于文化和文明的讨论。著名的电视片《河殇》，就是关于文明的思考和比较。但那个时候不仅文明对话这个概念在中国还没有流行，而且当时中国面临的主要是如何摆脱"文革"的阴影，对外开放和学习西方的现代化经验，还没有作为一个古老文明与其他文明有组织地展开对话。但进入21世纪以后，情况就不同了。2003年中国主办了亚欧会议进程中的第一届文化与文明会议。自2005年起，中国每两年举办一届"中阿（阿拉伯）关系暨中阿文明对话研讨会"。《北京论坛》也是世纪之交以后出现的一个重要的文明对话的机制。从2004年开始每年举办一次，迄今已经有70多个国家，2700多位名流政要和知名学者参加了会议，文明对话是其重要内容。同样是2004年开始的上海《世界中国学论坛》，是由国务院新闻办公室和上海市政府合作举办的，每两年一次，至今已经成功举办了四届。它也是文明对话的一个重要平台。2007年，"亚欧会议不同信仰间对话会议"在中国南京举行。2011年6月，首届"回儒文明对话论坛"国际学术研讨会在云南举行，由云南大学和伊朗穆斯塔法国际大学联合主办。2011年，在许嘉璐的倡导下，《中国尼山论坛》召开首届文明对话会议。这是又一个重要的标志性的事件。

起，"论坛"每年都在西方文明起源地希腊的罗德岛举办一次年会，每次出席人数有五六百，其中有来自世界各国和地区的学者、宗教界领袖、国际组织的代表、政府官员（包括个别的国家元首）和媒体。[①] 除了罗德岛年会之外，"论坛"还不定期地就各种专题在全世界各地召集文明对话会议[②]，包括 2010 年在北京与中国国际问题研究基金会合作召开的题为"文明对话与和谐世界"的会议，以及与上海国际问题研究院合作在上海召开的"世界经济体系转化中的中俄经济合作"会议。从 2010 年开始，"世界公众论坛"还在罗德岛论坛之外开辟了"罗德岛青年论坛"。首届罗德岛青年论坛有来自 34 个国家的 150 位青年代表出席，共同讨论他们所面临的未来，以及他们自己在当今世界中的身份和使命。至今，青年论坛已经召开了三届年会和一届在新德里召开的特别会议，发起了一个叫做"青年时代"（Youth Time）的国际运动，举办了暑期班，开辟了网页，创办了刊物。此外，"世界公众论坛"还举办了一些休闲式的文化活动，促进文化的交流。[③]

　　"世界公众论坛"是一个公民层面的机制。其参与者都是独立的个人，代表各个文明，而不是代表政府或政治团体。论坛的联合主席、美国学者达奥梅尔（Fred Dallmayr）曾用五个"不是"一个"是"来概括它的性质：1."世界公众论坛"和许多政府有良好的关系，但它不是一个政府机构或跨国政府机构（诸如联合国、联合国教科文组织、世界卫生组织之类）。2.它欢迎任何政党或其他团体的

----

　　① 其大致比例是：各领域的专家学者 73%，宗教领袖 4%，政府官员和国际组织 14%，媒体 9%。在学者中，比例分别为经济学 17%、政治学 11%、法律 11%、社会学 10%。出席论坛的政府官员比例分别为俄国 21%、印度 9%、奥地利 9%（根据"世界公众论坛"网页上所列的国际协作委员会名单和专家名单统计）。

　　② 如在印度新德里的尼赫鲁大学召开的"全球化背景下的对话"会议（2004）和"发展模式与全球的一体化"会议（2007）；在古巴哈瓦那召开的"21 世纪的拉丁美洲：普遍主义与独创性"会议（2005）；在捷克的布拉格召开的"21 世纪的欧洲：文明的十字路口"会议（2004），"东方与西方—整合与发展"会议（2006）和"21 世纪的欧洲：布拉格对话"会议（2009）；在约旦召开的"基督教与穆斯林教对话"圆桌会议（2006）；2007 年 3 月在法国巴黎联合国教科文组织总部召开的"文化与文明对话：人权与道德价值的桥梁"会议（2007 年 3 月）和"古代文明与新的起点：关于变化的对话"的小型会议（2007 年 12 月）；在芬兰的坦佩雷（Tampere）召开的"欧洲文明的空间：波罗的海对话"会议（2007 年 6 月）；在巴林召开的"巴林文明对话会议"（2008）；在渥太华召开的"教育作为社会发展的对话模式"会议（2008 年 6 月）；在卡萨克斯坦举办的"历史与文化遗产在文明对话中的地位"会议（2009）；以及在维也纳召开的讨论世界面临的最为迫切的社会与文化问题的峰会（2008）。

　　③ 比如 2011 年 5 月 19 日，2500 多人应"世界公众论坛"的邀请参加了维也纳弗洛伊德公园的"文化约请桌"活动，一起欣赏丰富的音乐、舞蹈和各民族的美食。

人士参加，但它不是一个追求自己特殊利益的政党或企业。3.它涉及各个学术领域，但它不是一个旨在发展理论或学说的学术组织。4.它的参与者中有很多宗教界的人士，但它不是一个宗教团体。5.它希望其参与者能够在彼此交流中得到快乐，但它不是一个俱乐部。"世界公众论坛"就是它的名字所标示的，是一个文明对话的全球的、公众的论坛。它确实有自己的立场——一个伦理道德的立场，那就是要实现这样一个世界，在这个世界里公众的问题不是通过文明的冲突，而是通过文明的对话来解决。[①]

"世界公众论坛"的主要发起者和主席是弗拉基米尔·亚库宁（Vladimir Yakunin）。他是俄国铁道部长、铁路公司总裁，并曾经是2006年继任俄罗斯总统的人选之一。作为一个身兼国家重要官员和企业界巨头双重身份的人物，亚库宁的主要精力却是在促进世界文明对话上。"世界公众论坛"的大量而又频繁的活动，几乎都是他亲自主持、从头到尾出席的。由于亚库宁的关系，"世界公众论坛"的文明对话有较强的俄罗斯背景。每次年会，俄罗斯的与会代表总是最多的。在参与其文明对话的主要代表当中，俄国占23%，印度占7%，中国占2.5%[②]，俄国的人数几乎是中国的10倍。这当然是因为那是他们搭建的平台，但同时也说明了冷战以后的俄罗斯对文明对话的重视，说明了他们努力在世界文明当中给自己定位，找到自己的坐标，并意欲在文明对话上成为世界的主导力量。另外，印度文明的代表在"世界公众论坛"中的地位也很突出。这当然也和论坛的发起者之一和联合主席、印度知名公共知识分子和企业家卡普尔（Jagdish Chandra Kapur）有关。但同样，这背后有更加深刻的内涵。卡普尔曾经亲口对笔者说："如果俄国、印度和中国在一起主导世界的文明对话，这力量足以抗衡西方强权！"

确实，"世界公众论坛"的参与者当中虽然来自美国和西欧的比例不低，但这些人士几乎都代表了反对国际政治舞台上的西方强权和对西方近代启蒙理性持批判态度的声音。这也凸显了这样一个事实，即论坛和其他许多文明对话机制一样，实际上并非纯粹中立的平台。它们的基本宗旨和倾向性都是反对文明冲突，提倡文明对话。在前面所说的文、武、商、政这四种广义的文明对话方式中，美国和西方世界的政府在武、商、政三个方面都处于强势地位。尤其是美国，其军

---

① Dallmayr, Fred. 2011, *Who are We? What is WPF–Dialogue of Civilizations?* http://www.wpfdc.org/en/328-who-are-we-what-is-wpf-dialogue-of-civilizations.

② 其他的参与者比例是北美12%，欧洲41%，中东8.5%，南美3%，非洲2%，澳大利亚0.5%。（根据"世界公众论坛"网页上所列的国际协作委员会名单和专家名单统计）。

费的开支相当于全世界其他国家军费开支的总和。唯独在"文"的方面，它不但没有站在创导者的地位上，而且常常被看作是文明冲突的制造者，是文明对话所要制约、批评、甚至抗衡的势力。

三、一些反思

怎么来看待文明对话才比较准确和具有建设性？按照亨廷顿的理论，世界各文明之间一旦发生际遇，就必然导致冲突。这种文明冲突论可以称作为"丛林模式"。为了生存，各文明之间只能是或者你取代我，或者我取代你，别无他路。基于这样的假设来看广义的文明对话，显然首选是"武"和"政"的形式，其次是"商"，即通过贸易金融的扩张来使某种文明占据绝对优势，最终取代别的文明。这些方式要比试图说服其他文明归顺自己更加直截了当。① 美国和西方世界的政府对联合国文明对话日所倡导的那种文明对话缺乏兴趣，和这种思路有密切关系。

当然，把美国和西方国家纯粹理解为丛林猛兽，也有失公允。这些国家在保护少数民族和文化多元化方面，取得了相当的成就。但稍加观察就能发现，他们从未使其他文化有机会影响其主流文化。他们的文化多元化，可以称作为"动物园模式"——其中虽然各种动物都有，但在各自的笼子里展出，相互之间没有真正的交流和互动。其主流文化则像是动物园的管理员。他也关心那些动物的生存，也为那些动物提供必要的条件，还会今天举办"猴子周"，明天举办"熊猫月"，来增进公众的动物保护意识。我们所提倡的文明对话，如果纳入了这个模式，虽然有胜于无，但其意义最多也就是使其他文明得到有限的宽容，为主流文化增添一些吸引人的"多元"色彩，以掩盖社会依然为单一文明所主宰的现实。

文明对话的另外一个模式是"舞台模式"。我们常常把文明对话的论坛比作

---

① 虽然亨廷顿有关文明冲突的咒语不断地被作为文明对话的对立面受到抨击，文明冲突在文明对话当中也同样可能发生。把文明对话看作是论战，是通过辩驳来压倒论敌、赢得支持的手段，就是丛林模式在狭义的文明对话当中的表现。它与健康的对话之间并没有一个很明显的分界线。公平地说，那些把文明对话看作论战的人甚至可能出于善意，想帮助别人摆脱错误的观念和价值。真正的对话和简单的论战之间的区别不在于我们是否回避分歧，也不在于我们能否开展论辩，而在于论辩的方式和目的。真正的对话是通过理性的讨论，以达到互相的理解和反思，而不是运用论辩技巧去压倒对方，以缄其口。

平台，在这些平台上，代表不同文明的人们可以演示他们各自的观点和价值。这个模式显然优于前面两个模式，只要这些平台是公众的，也就是说是真正对每个人都开放的。它更好地体现了文明对话的"文"的性质，说明文明对话既不是丛林式的竞争，也不是动物园式的展览。它不仅让不同的"演员"在同一个舞台上演示，而且允许他们互相之间发生真正的际遇和互动。把各个对话机制看作不同的舞台，也有利于突出在文明对话中争取话语权的必要和拥有自己的平台的必要。① 但是用舞台模式来描述文明对话仍然有其局限。即便我们让舞台对各种声音都开放，站到舞台上的权利本身并不包含有倾听其他声音的需要。它会让人误以为文明对话就是让各文明的代表都有登台表演、受到公众瞩目的机会，甚至简单地将它看作争夺话语权的竞争。

也许更加恰当的是以"医疗模式"，即把文明对话看作是为当今这个世界治病，来作为对舞台模式的补充。医疗模式的优点至少有如下四个方面：首先，当代的文明对话具有强烈的实际问题意识。世界文明对话高潮的到来恰恰与"911事件"发生在同一年度，绝不是偶然的巧合。整个文明对话在现代的兴起，就是对各种愈来愈尖锐的全球性问题的回应。它好比是世界各文明的"医生"对患有重症的世界进行会诊。用医疗模式正可以突出问题意识，增加人们对文明对话的意义的认识和进行对话的紧迫感。

其次，文明对话不仅是会诊，而且它本身就代表了一种治疗方案、药方或者是疗法，而且这是中医式的处方和疗法！它标志着人类对重物质轻精神的生活方式和用强制的物质手段去压抑症状、头痛医头脚痛医脚那种治标不治本的手段的警惕，标志着人类开始用整体性的思维来看待世界，把它看作一个动态有机联系的整体，标志着人类开始用调理"精气神"的手段，来从根本上解决人类的生存危机。苏格拉底对话的发源地罗德岛和孔子的诞生地尼山就像是地球上的两个关键穴位，其地理位置就代表着特定的传统文明的能量。这两个论坛的交流以及世界各文明对话机制的广泛联系，犹如打通人体的经络，调节气血的流通，对从根

---

① 当然，文明对话的舞台的特点，在于它们并非为了演出自己的独家专场而设。比如尼山论坛就不能搞成只是儒家学者自己探讨儒学的论坛，哪怕你里面涉及很多世界范围的内容。它必须要邀请其他文明的代表来参加、来对话，才能名副其实。这有点像奥运会。确实，奥运会的主办国总是会占些优势。不仅主办国的代表团能在开幕式上第一个出场，事实证明，奥运会的主办方总能取得比它在别国参赛时更好的成绩。但如果没有世界范围的广泛参与，而只有主办国自己的选手在那里表演，当然不能算是奥运会。其他国家的代表，也决不能只是观摩者，或者当作嘉宾出席一下开幕式，帮着哄抬一下气氛，当陪衬。文明对话的成功，根本上在于是否能有真正的对话。无论是"世界公众论坛"还是"尼山论坛"，都需要注意这一点。

本上恢复整个机体的健康可以起到关键的作用。用针灸穴位来比喻各个不同的对话论坛，能够既突出不同穴位的特殊性，又允许我们理解它们之间的呼应和合作的必要性。

第三，正如中医治疗的目的是恢复健康和体能，而不只是得到一些头脑里的认识，文明对话的目的也不局限于得到相互的理解和达到一些原则上的共识。用语言进行的交流探讨固然是文明对话的主要方式，但它能达到的共识还只是抽象的原则。毕竟，文明对话不能仅靠语言，世界的和谐也不能只靠抽象的共识。用医疗模式看待文明对话有助于我们看到现代特殊意义上的文明对话形式与其他文明交流形式的联系。

第四，中医疗法的特点之一是其功效缓慢，但通过调理身体的整体机能，它能从根本上解决问题。这一点也适合于理解文明对话。在解决种种全球危机的时候，文明对话的优点是能够从各文明的基本思想方法和价值观念这个根子上来作出反思和调整，而不是暂时地压抑一些局部的症状。但它与中医一样，在对付急性症状方面，显然不如政治手段、经济制裁手段或者武力震慑手段那么立竿见影。对许多紧迫的问题，还是需要运用其他必要的手段，就像医疗上需要中西医结合一样。但我们也看到，那些其他手段不仅没法从根子上解决问题，而且它们往往本身就导致更深刻的危机。正如许多人否定中医的价值一样，文明对话的阻力也很大。现在大多数的人还是迷信那些快速压抑症状的手段，目光短浅，看不到文明对话的价值。①

"病来如山倒，病去如抽丝。"过去的十年，文明对话无疑已经成为一个世界性的潮流和呼声，而且毋庸置疑它代表了人类的希望。但迄今为止它对世界的进程究竟已经产生了多少实际作用，还很难作出具体的估计。能够确定的是，任重

---

①　比如2009年10月28日美国国会通过了纪念孔子诞辰2560年的决议案，承认孔子在哲学和社会政治思想方面对全人类的贡献，但这个议案也遭到一些人的反对。亚利桑那州的共和党议员杰夫·弗雷克以嘲讽的口吻，模仿孔子的语气说："费时于为琐事立法者，或无暇研读医改法案也。"来自犹他州的共和党众议员杰森·查费兹说："我们喜欢孔子，但为此投票是一个笑话。"从美国网民对这个议案的评论中可以看到上述两位议员的想法代表了相当多的美国人的看法。许多人说他们的国会是吃饱了撑的，放着美国这么多的社会问题不去解决，却投票去纪念一个中国古人。西方现在掀起的中文热，其实主要来自于和中国做生意或者向中国人传播他们的思想的动机。真正对中国传统文化感兴趣、希望与中国文明对话，把中国传统文明作为一个资源来对待的，还是少数。这个情况在中国也同样很严重。许多人还是迷信政治、经济和军事实力能够解决一切，认为简单地接受西方启蒙理性的价值才是中国的方向。尽管现在中国到处都在开发中国传统文化遗产，但其实这背后的动机，多数是利用中国的历史文化资源去获取经济效益。

而道远，在这条道路上，需要有"知其不可而为之的"精神。①

作者简介：

倪培民：复旦大学哲学学士、硕士、美国康涅狄格大学哲学博士、美国密西根格兰谷州立大学哲学系终身教授、纽约全球学术出版社"中国哲学与比较哲学丛书"主编。曾任夏威夷大学和香港大学客座教授、北美中国哲学家协会和国际亚洲哲学与比较哲学协会会长。学术研究方向主要是中西哲学对话。著述包括《孔子：人能弘道》（英文版 2010，中译本 2012）、《论孔子》（2002）等 6 部著作及中英文哲学论文 60 余篇。曾多次应邀参加世界公众论坛"文明对话"会议，在其罗德论坛和巴黎、渥太华会议上作大会主题演讲，其中数篇讲稿被收入论坛"文明对话"的论文集中。关于文明对话的代表性观点是用整体论取代普世主义、用"礼"扬弃"权"、用丰富的人际交流方式补充理性语言的对话方式，以及用文明对话的"医疗模式"更替"丛林模式"、"动物园模式"和"舞台模式"。

---

① 《论语》中有将孔子描述为"知其不可为之者"的说法。（见《论语》宪问 14.38）

中华文明对欧美文明的挑战

谭明舟

随着中国在全球的经济和政治影响力增强，越来越多的欧美学者和政客开始关注中国的未来走向。特别是自 2007 年以来，欧美的大学开始增加他们研究中国的预算，开设更多的课程来教授中国语言和文化，派遣更多的留学生到中国学习。为了方便研究中国，他们将其中文图书的索引全部由威氏注音改成汉语拼音。特别地，中国问题在 2012 年首次成为美国总统大选的独立辩论主题。"中国制造"和中国人也遍及全球的各个角落。于是，一些西方学者开始重新审视中国文化，认为中国文化可以弥补西方文明的不足。例如，卜松山说："与儒家的相遇至少可以让我们认识到西方模式中的盲点。它甚至可以给我们提供另一种现代化概念，一种并非建立于自利和冲突，而是以中庸之道达到社会和谐的现代化。"[①] 但是，另一批学者则是站在对立和冲突的角度来看中国文化的。例如，Halper 认为中国在削弱西方的影响力（Halper 2010: preface），亨廷顿则认为会加剧文明间的冲突（Huntington 1993）。但是不管是补充或是威胁，中华文明对西方文明的主导地位构成相对的挑战是其共同的前提。在下文中，我将分析中华文明如何对西方文明构成挑战，这种挑战能否持续下去。

在进入主题之前，我们需要澄清一下文明的含义。不同的学者对文明有不同的定义，但是一个共同点是，它是一个文化实体，是一个民族或种族的整体生活方式，包括价值、制度、思维模式和行为规范等后代给予极大重视的东西。（Huntington 1996: 41）Ferguson 进一步将文明当作"文化领地"，可以具体到房屋的材料和风格、弓箭特色、方言、饮食、具体的技术、信仰结构、做爱方式、

---

①   Pohl, Karl Heinz.*Ethics for the 21st Century-The Confucian Tradition*. http://www.uni-trier.de/fileadmin/fb2/SIN/Pohl_Publikation/ethics_for_the_21st_century.pdf.

指南针、造纸和印刷术。（Ferguson 2010: preface）简言之，文明包括一个民族或人群的物质和精神生活方式及其技术技能。以这个界定为准，我将探讨中华文明如何在经济、政治和文化上对西方文明构成挑战。

一、经济上的挑战

欧美学者无一例外地相信，一个国家的经济强势必将导致其军事、文化和人种的优越地位，进而按照其自身的文化和利益来重塑世界秩序。自从工业革命后，世界的经济中心一直掌握在欧美手里。目前，美国仍然是世界上最大的经济体，中国如何在经济上对其发起挑战？

经过对西方学者的观点的梳理，其所谓的中国经济上的挑战主要是中国以其庞大的外汇储备削弱 IMF 和世界银行的地位，中国以其独特的发展模式动摇了华盛顿共识——民主加自由市场的资本主义发展模式。特别是 2008 年世界金融危机之后，中国成了美国的债权国，使西方人认为中国人会重塑世界金融秩序。

自从 1979 年改革开放以来，中国以其渐进的改革方式获得了成功，变成了全球的加工业中心，"中国制造"成了大众消费品的代名词。到 2006 年，中国已经生产全世界的三分之二的复印机、鞋子、玩具和微波炉；一半的 DVD 播放器、数码相机和纺织品；三分之一的 DVD—ROM 驱动器和台式电脑，四分之一的汽车、电视和汽车音响。中国的外汇积累高达 1.8 万亿美元。这种成功的经验和巨大的财力后盾使中国在国际舞台上的声音越来越受到重视。

首先，它使美国在肆意指责中国时有所顾忌。2009 年，希拉里·克林顿号召一个更深更广的中美伙伴关系，说："对中国在人权和西藏等问题上的施压，不应当干涉对全球经济危机的处理。"（Halper 2010: 26）

其次，它大大削弱了美国主导的金融机构，像 IMF 和世界银行等的国际地位。自从这些机构的诞生，其决策就掌握在西方人手里。通过这些机构，西方人基于自身利益的考虑，把一些经济政策强加于别的国家。（Huntington 1996: 6）随着中国经济强大，中国却提出了改革这些机构的要求。2008 年，温家宝提出，像 IMF 等全球机构应当给发展中国家更多的发言权，应当监督美国的金融机构和美元体系。（Halper 2010: 5）同时，中国还拒绝了 IMF 所要求的自由汇率政策，认为那是国家主权，不可割让。

更令美国担忧的是中国以其无附加条款式的经济援助对世界银行和 IMF 等

机构釜底抽薪。中国以其 1.3 万亿的贷款储备使 IMF 的 350 亿相形见绌。它使许多国家不需要忍受西方人的说教和冒着自身政府崩溃的危险，就可以获得想要的资助。例如，2007 年安哥拉政府不能忍受 IMF 的附加条款，断然拒绝了它的援助，而从中国得到 20 亿的软贷款。（Leonard 2008: 120）同样，当 2008 年世界银行撤回对乍得的资助时，中国人欣然接手。类似的例子不胜枚举。结果，一些美国学者慨叹："（由于中国的资助），世界上最严重的人权践踏者和武器扩散者、种族清洗者以及各种其他不满者都找到了一个新的甜爹。"（Halper 2010: 212）但是，第三世界的人们却不如此看，他们认为中国的资助使他们获得了自由和尊严。对此，乌干达总统有一段精彩的评论，说："西方统治者傲慢，自我，不顾我们的条件，将别人的事当作他们自己的事来经营。中国人则与代表你的国家的人打交道，他们只代表其自己的利益，而你做你自己的事。"（Halper 2010: 100）毫无疑问，随着这种形势的发展，西方的影响会被进一步削弱，更多的政府会将发扬民主搁置起来。

再次，最令美国和西方焦虑的是中国的经济发展模式广泛地为第三世界所效法。按照西方学者的观点，这种模式严重地削弱或取代了华盛顿共识所制定的发展模式，从而大大地削弱了美国的民主和自由市场的价值观的传播。

华盛顿共识于 1989 年由 John Williamson 提出，其核心概念在于自由市场和民主政体，认为民主政治改革是经济发展的前提。与 IMF、WTO，世界银行等机构一起，西方国家向贷款的穷国施加压力，要求其进行政治改革，实行民主体制。结果是像印尼、柬埔寨和孟加拉国等国家民主化后，国家更加混乱和贫穷。以至于超过半数的拉美人回答，我们不在乎政府民主不民主，只要它能解决经济问题就行。（Halper 2010: 133）

反观历史，所有欧洲列强在经济腾飞时都不是民主政体，而是君主、专制或立宪制。因为经济腾飞和现代化需要集中社会或国家的资源以达到经济复苏和摆脱贫困，而集权政体正好能满足这个要求。（Jacques 2009: 212—214）即使美国的盟友——英国国际发展部也承认，并没有什么明确证据说明民主能够带来经济发展。（Halper 2010: 125）换句话说，民主市场模式可能适用于美国特殊的国情，但并不是普遍有效。

既然如此，美国人为什么还要强行推行其华盛顿模式呢？用约翰·达尔文的话说，这是美国的单边主义和普世思想在作怪。长期以来，美国人认为自己是世界规则的制定者，却不愿被所制定的规则束缚。美国人认为自己的民主制度是世界上最好的，别的制度都是封建制度的残余。而且，美国人认为适用于美国的也适用于世界，美国的民主、市场经济和商业文化将保证社会的富裕和稳定。（Darwin 2008: 482）当然，在单边主义和普世思想背后还有欧美人长期以来享有的文明优越感及其连带的巨大利益。一旦欧美的文化和发展模式失去影响力或为别的模式所代替，势必造成其在全球的利益的巨大损失。明白这个道理，就不难理解欧美人为何对中国的崛起惴惴不安了。用"北京共识"这一名词的缔造者Joshua Cooper Ramo 的话说，在一个被强大的引力中心（指美国）主宰的世界中，中国不仅为发展中国家找到了一条发展的道路，而且还指出了如何在保持自身独立和生活方式的情况下融入世界秩序。（Peerenboom 2007: 7）简单地说，中国为第三世界指出了逃脱欧美控制的方法，阻碍了西方自由民主的普及，削弱了其在全球的利益。

中国的集权市场模式很快为巴西、俄罗斯和越南等效法。更多的非洲国家直接邀请中国去开设经济特区。其原因很简单，虽然中国的集权市场模式限制言论自由或者说不够民主，但是，它保证了高速发展、社会稳定、生活水平的提高。在众多温饱问题尚未解决的国家，有多少人有闲暇关注美国的民主和自由？总之，中国的发展促进了世界走向多极，破坏了美国 1991 年所设想的车轴—轮辐式的世界体系，即：所有国家都要通过美国（美元）来与另一国交往。同时，它也说明了这样一个事实：美国的民主加自由市场的发展模式在其他国家并非唯一有效的模式。

二、政治上的挑战

伴随经济的发展，中国一方面在现有国际秩序内谋求最大的活动空间，一方面则建立自己主导的国际组织，捍卫自己的利益。用 Halper 的话说，越来越多的非洲和拉美国家拥抱中国，人们看到北京模式在西方之外指明了一条道路，使西方在世界事务中越来越显得无足轻重。结果是，中国在蚕食西方。（Halper 2010: preface）

中国并没有直接与美国对抗，而是采取巧妙而实用的外交政策，积极地在联合国、WHO 和 WTO 等组织中扩大自己的影响。但是，中国始终坚持尊重主权、不干涉别国内政和不颠覆别国政权的原则。不到不得已，不会投否决票；其做法是，站在别人背后，阻止某些事件而不被埋怨。例如，对成立新的人权理事会一事，北京让伊斯兰联盟去打头阵。对苏丹达富尔事件，中国同意进驻联合国维和部队，但是前提是必须征得苏丹政府的许可。这种巧妙的外交使美国在国际舞台上的欢迎度大打折扣，从1995年在联合国大会上50.6%的得票率降到2006年的23.6%；在人权事务上，则由57%降至22%。相应地，同期的中国得票率则由43%飘升至82%。据此，Mark Leonard得出结论说，联合国正在成为中国世界观的扬声器。(Leonard 2008: 129—130)

同时，中国也开始建立自己主导的国际组织，包括东亚峰会、中非合作论坛、上海合作组织等。这些组织不邀请美国加入。例如，在2009年金砖四国峰会上，中俄在讨论如何在没有美国的情况下进行贸易和资助。俄罗斯总统梅德韦杰夫称之为"建立一个多极世界秩序，走出单极的世界体系"。美国要求以观察员身份参会，却被淡然拒绝。(Halper 2010: 29) 不同于NATO和欧盟，这些组织体现出中国在尊重主权、避免对抗的基础上重建世界秩序的意愿。

这里需要谈一下为什么中国始终坚持要尊重主权。自从1860年以来，西方列强瓜分世界，制定国际法，拒绝承认他国主权，以自己设定的文明标准强加于他国。(Darwin 2008: 298—299) 一旦认为别的国家没有达到其标准，就进行武力干涉，甚至颠覆。虽然殖民时代已经过去，但美国奉行的单边主义政策和所谓普世价值，实际上仍然是这种殖民思维的继续。因为，首先，美国不愿意被任何原则束缚。正如Mahbubani所言："当它的利益与全球利益一致时，就没有什么问题。……可是，当它的利益与全球利益冲突时，它在安理会的优势地位就造成许多扭曲。美国有效地利用其力量来违背国际社会的愿望。"(Mahbubani 2008: 113) 其次，它认为，它的文明是普遍适用的，对美国好的肯定对世界也是好的，拒绝美国价值观就等于挑战和平与进步。(Darwin 2008: 482) 近来发生在埃及、叙利亚和利比亚的颠覆正是这种思维的具体实现。由此看来，中国人捍卫主权，倡导国际间平等乃真正代表了第三世界或弱势文明的价值观。

总之，通过奉行聆听和微笑外交，中国在以非对抗的方式推行自己的价值观。从短期或中期的角度来看，越来越多的国家会接受中国的尊重主权和国际间民主的诉求，特别是中国的发展模式。这一点是显然的，一个国家只有摆脱别人的操纵和干涉后，才能发展起来。在目前全世界大多数国家还处于贫穷状态的情况下，美国所推行的民主和人权注定不会太受欢迎。当然，从长远角度上看，等到人们的生活水平小康之后，所谓的言论、选举等自由问题才会成为关注。即使如此，如何在实践上解决这些关注仍然是各国人民自己的事。就目前而言，美国应该做的是，抛弃其独霸世界政治和资源的旧梦，帮助世界共同富裕。如此，它才能获得世界的拥护。

三、文化上的挑战

自从 19 世纪西方列强统治世界后，欧美文明就风靡世界，成了现代化和文明的代名词。西化被认为是现代化的唯一途径，西化的程度乃是进步的指标。结果是啼笑皆非的：先是英国的礼帽和文明棍风靡民国时代；后是麦当劳、肯德基等快餐店在中国遍地开花。时至今日，好莱坞电影、美国牛仔裤和留学欧美还是中国和世界各国中产阶级的主流爱好。可以说，世界文化正在欧美化。正如 J. M. Roberts 所说："很清楚，西方文明的故事已成为人类的故事；它的影响力如此广大，使其对手——别的文明显得毫无意义。"（Jacques 2008: 45）

但是，不论西方文化影响力多么强，它并不能将儒家、伊斯兰和印度等其他文明彻底替代。相反，随着这些文化圈的经济发展，这些文明变得更加强势。这个比较也许是恰当的：20 世纪 80 年代广东经济快速发展；进入 90 年代后，广东经济发展走在全国的前面。于是，广东话一度风靡全中国。现在，儒家文化和印度文明在世界上的影响也变得越来越强。最近几年来，汉语普通话和武术在北美变得越来越受欢迎，这也是一个很好的说明。

一些西方学者认为，中华文明的崛起首先是儒家思想对西方价值观的挑战。西方文化，特别是美国的民主制度，其核心是个人主义。个人享有足够的尊重、人权和自由。儒家思想则强调集体主义。家庭或社会成员之间相互负责和互惠，必要时要牺牲个体的利益以成全集体的利益。个体始终处于一种社会关系网中；家庭和社会和谐乃是其共同的追求。例如，《礼记·礼运》就要求"父慈子孝、兄悌弟恭、君仁臣忠、夫义妇顺"。《孟子》也谈到，统治者不善，民可以造反。这种关系式的民主不是美国个人主义式的民主。但是，其中的平等或民主成分是显然的。据此，温家宝在 2007 年曾说，"从孔子到孙中山，中国传统文化有着许多宝贵的东西，许多关于民主和民生的积极成分。例如，它强调仁爱、和谐和共享等。"（Jacques 2009: 218）换言之，中国的关系式民主如果得到发扬光大，其表现方式必然具有浓厚的中国特色。据此，Bergsten 有一个大胆的预言，说"中国很有可能发展一种新的政治模式，也叫做民主，但不包含美国所认为的民主体制的多元主义、竞争和直选等核心元素。"（Bergsten 2008: 11）

其次，是对现代化的诠释和如何实现现代化。长期以来，主张全盘西化的人（如陈独秀和土耳其的 Kamal Maturk）和大多数西方人都将现代化和西化看作一回事。其论断是，"要想成功，你们必须像我们；我们的道路是唯一的道路。"其

56

论证是，"西方社会以外的价值观、道德律令和社会结构都无关、甚至敌对工业化的价值和实践。"（Huntington 1996: 73）可是，自 1860 年的洋务运动以来，中国的学者和政客的主流却总是把现代化和西化分开。中国人的"中学为体、西学为用"的宗旨显示出他们试图将西方的科学技术嫁接在中国的传统之上。虽然洋务运动失败，但是日本明治维新文化嫁接的成功更坚定了中国人的信念。到了 20 世纪末期，诸多西方学者认为，现代化不等同于西化的观点更证明了中国人的选择。（Darwin 2008: 14, Huntington 1996: 69, Cohen 1984: 72）为此，Fareed Zakaria 正确地指出，"变成一个现代社会意味着工业化、城市化、识字、教育和财富的普遍提高。相对地，将一个社会变成西方社会只是一种个案。"（Zakaria 2011: 87）

毫无疑问，现代化与西化的分离势必对美国价值观的扩张构成新的障碍。这个观察推翻了美国的普世主义思想，即：并不是对美国好的一定对其他国家也好；美国化不是现代化的前提。结果，别的国家将按照自己的文化所引导的方向和步伐走进现代化进程，不再完全遵从欧美国家开出的现代化药方。西方的影响势必受到进一步削弱。我想，许多欧美学者和政客对北京模式或黄河资本主义做出过分的反应，这也是情理之中的。

再次，是中国人积极地向全球推行自己文化的活动。1993 年，崔志远就提出中国知识分子要从盲目崇拜西方资本主义中解放出来。（Leonard 2008: 14）同时许多学者如蒙培元等，也反对以西方思想为框架来诠释中国文化。中国人应当基于自身的文化、历史和经验发展自己的现代化，而不是照抄西方。[①] 中国必须向西方学习；但是，西方也需要了解东方。伴随这种呼声就是李长春开展的外宣工作。李长春认为，在 21 世纪，全球信息空间成了最关键的战场。通讯能力决定影响力。一个通讯最强的国家，其文化和核心价值就会传播得越广，对世界产生最强的影响。（Leonard 2008: 9—10）这个项目投入 45 亿元人民币，计划在全球各国建立传媒办公室和 100 所孔子学院，介绍中国文化和发展模式。同时，中国也增加对外国留学生的奖学金名额，希望留学生将中国文化带向世界。虽然，中国文化在世界范围内还不足以与美国文化竞争，但是，它无疑为世人在欧美文明之外提供了一项新的选择。

---

① Meng, Peiyuan, *My Exploration in Chinese Philosophy*（《我的中国哲学研究之路》），http://www.confuchina.com/xuezhe% 20wenji/meng% 20peiyuan.htm。

四、中国挑战的潜力

中国对西方构成挑战的优势可以罗列如下：我们拥有 1.8 万亿的外汇储备；中国成了世界的加工厂，"中国制造"充斥世界的每个角落；中国价格具有最强的竞争优势；中国两位数的增长速度抬高世界商品价格，使所有资源国受利；中国有用不尽的廉价劳动力。

但是，我们却有很难在短时间内改变的致命劣势：一是技术瓶颈；二是资源匮乏；三是我们的经济增长严重依赖对欧美的出口。

首先，中国要保持持续发展，就必须进行技术升级。历史也多次证明谁掌握了一个时代最先进的技术，谁就会成为世界霸主。在 18 世纪，英国以其织布机轻松地击败中国和印度的纺织业对手，将他们变成原料供应地。20 世纪 80 年代，美国又一次利用计算机和互联网等新技术将日本抛开。现在，虽然中国成了世界加工厂，但生产的都是劳动密集型的低技术含量产品，如衣服、玩具等，并没有先进的技术来支撑起经济。对稍微高技术含量的产品，中国工厂充当的只是欧美跨国公司的承包商，只起到组装和包装的作用，至于设计、开发等核心技术仍然为西方国家所垄断。而且，随着制造在整个商品链条中占的比重越来越少，中国就会失去廉价劳动力的优势。（Jacques 2009: 174）所以，一旦中国挑战发达国家的经济利益，其世界制造中心的地位就会很容易被瓦解。实际上，亨廷顿等学者一直坚持西方国家通过技术垄断来维持其经济、军事和技术优势。（Huntington 1993）因此，随着欧美对中国崛起的忧虑，技术封锁势必更严。这就使中国处于很脆弱的地位，一旦跨国公司撤出，西方实行贸易保护，中国的经济必然下滑。

其次，中国的工业多数乃强资源消费型。然而，中国却是一个资源匮乏的国家。中国对原材料的需求不断抬高其价格；这反过来使中国产品的成本也越来越高。而且，中国对原材料日益增长的需求也引起欧美的戒备。从 1990 年海湾战争起，美国就把中东的能源看得越来越紧。近来，又分裂苏丹、颠覆利比亚，并试图颠覆叙利亚和攻打伊朗，都显示出石油已经成为中国与欧美竞争的首要商品。总之，用雅克得出的结论说，中国不可能利用美国的资源消费型工业赶上美国。（Jacques 2009: 170）这里给我们的提示就是，技术升级以降低资源消费已经成为中国的首要任务。

如果说前两项我们还有一定的自主性，中国经济对出口的严重依赖则使我们极度被动。在 2008 年经济危机之前，欧盟占中国出口的 22%；而美国占 18%。如果加上日本，这个比例还会更高。经济危机后，为振兴经济，中国提出扩大内需的号召。可是，2012 年前三个季度的增长率都低于预期的 8%。如果欧美经济持续低迷，其低于 7% 的可能性将会很大。到时候，一方面国内失业率增高会导致社会动荡；一方面欧美会采取更严厉的贸易保护。[①]（Jacques 2009: 164）中国将自顾不暇，很难从经济上挑战欧美。

那么，中国是否能通过技术升级解决这些瓶颈？在不远的将来，似乎很难。其原因在于大多数中国人常常追求眼前利益，而很少能专心地坐下来搞技术创新。中国社会是一个权力占主导地位的社会，各行各业的名人都会自觉不自觉地变成官僚。一旦一个科学家成名，他很快就退化为技术官僚，其创新精神也江郎才尽。所以，中国对西方的挑战只是暂时的。

五、西方的回应

尽管中国的挑战只是暂时的，西方国家特别是美国，也变得非常敏感。用马丁·雅克的话说："我们如此地习惯于世界是西方或美国的，以至于我们很少想到过其反面。在这个按照西方的形象塑造的世界中，西方人有着巨大而多元的隐形利益。所以，无论从利益或思维定势上，西方和美国都很难接受一个他们的影响力日益消退的世界。"（Jacques 2009: 45）正像当年中国的朝贡制度被西方列强击垮之时，中国人拼命地捍卫其在朝鲜、越南和蒙古的利益。中国人失去的不仅是领土，而且是优越感和自豪感。因此，可以理解，即使中国显示出微弱的挑战苗头，欧美都会积极捍卫其文明的强势地位。因为金融体系的挑战会威胁美元的世界货币地位，从而导致美国再不能盗用世界的财富巩固其军事和经济霸权。发展模式和价值观念的挑战会使其在联合国发号施令的地位受到质疑或不理睬。Halper 抱怨的在国际组织中新来者组成俱乐部，置欧美等老成员若陌生人，（Halper 2011: 212）正是这种现象的反应。要改变这种处境，不同的西方学者提出不同的对策，其主要趋势在于对中国进行围堵和破坏。

---

① 其实，在经济危机之后，美国国会就要求对中国采取贸易保护，并部分地付诸实施。如，控告中国不遵守 WTO 条款，使用反倾销法案为借口抵制中国货物；逼迫人民币升值；指控中国商品如食品、玩具等不安全。

亨廷顿认为，为保护西方的利益，在短期内，西方应当加强自己文明内的团结和合作，特别是欧美国家，促进与俄罗斯和日本的合作关系，限制儒家和伊斯兰国家的军事力量的扩张，激化儒家和伊斯兰国家内部的差异和冲突，加强代表西方利益和价值的国际机构。在长期上，非西方文明仍然需要西方的财富、技术、机器和武器以现代化；这就要求西方必须保持经济和军事力量来保护自己的利益。（Huntington 1993）简言之，亨廷顿要求短期上连横以包围中国，长期上通过技术封锁保持经济、军事优势。

Bergsten 的建议是亨廷顿的观点的具体化。他要求充分利用儒家文明和伊斯兰世界的不同和冲突来瓦解二者的联合。他也要求美国与中国内地的基层政府建立联系，了解他们的文化、政策和思维。（Bergsten 2008: 85）

Halper 在合纵连横方面与亨廷顿大同小异；但他同时也要求美国利用中日、中印、印巴等矛盾拆散亚洲，防止亚洲经济一体化。他更强调利用中国内部的权力斗争、民族分裂势力、中国领导者与民众间的张力以瓦解中国。对于美国自身，他呼吁美国节省能源，实现能源独立、吸引外资和增加民间存款。但是，他认为最重要的，能起到一弹击中双鸟的在于高科技和工程项目的投资和研发。

在国际舞台上，Halper 要求美国效法中国在非洲成功的经验。要缓和华盛顿共识的要求，承认各个国家可以按照其自身的特殊环境发展经济；支援非洲国家的基础建设，与中国争夺非洲的资源，成立美非峰会；削减对农产品的补贴，对贫穷小国放开西方市场；利用非洲内部的不同声音削弱中国的影响；同时，激活东南亚国家对美国的好感和依赖，改革安理会常任理事国成员，吸纳日本、德国、印度、南非等国家，以增强美国的同盟。（Halper 2010: 237—247）

不难看到，中国的崛起导致了西方精英阶层的普遍忧虑。他们认为，到 21 世纪中叶，中国就会在国民生产总值上超过美国。马丁·雅克等则预言，中国将会以其儒家文化传统重塑世界新秩序。中国希望有自己的新秩序，而且要坐上座。（Jacques 2009: 318, Bergsten 2008: 12, Leonard 2008: 115）作为对其学者的建议的回应，美国不失时机地将其战略中心转移到了东亚，加强对中国的包围。美国的全球战略是要保持绝对军事优势，防范别人建立与其相当的军事力量，以捍卫其全球经济霸权。

面对美国的围堵，中国的反应将很难预测。但是，战争的爆发总是依赖于交战双方的耐心和判断。如果美国发现对中国的围堵不奏效，或者中国的经济繁荣导致其日益削弱，它很可能会像 1840 年的英国以鸦片输入的方式破坏中国的经济。但是，如果中国不能容忍美国的围堵，像德国对英国 1909 年的围堵的反应那样，战争也会爆发。不管怎样，中国必须做出最坏的打算，以防范美国的攻击。托克维尔1835年冷血的声明还萦绕在世人的脑际。在他访问过美洲之后，托克维尔曾如此宣称："如果依据世界上过去的事来推理，我们几乎可以说，欧洲人之于其他种族就像人类之于动物：他可以使他们为自己服务；当他不能控制他们时，就把他们消灭。"（Darwin 2008: 24）结果，美国白种殖民者很快将他的话付诸实践，清洗了美洲的印第安人。美国人后来的行为也证明了这一论点。20世纪80年代，当美国不能控制日本的经济挑战时，就逼迫日元升值，搞垮日本经济。当萨达姆·侯赛因和卡扎菲挑战美国的霸权时，美国人就毫不犹豫地将他们消灭。所有这些事例都证明，美国人只要有机会，绝对不会放弃击败它的对手。

可是，美国人似乎对中国的崛起显得格外容忍。其原因可能是，1. 用Moritz Schularick和Naill Ferguson的话说，中国和美国已经结成了"中美国（Chimerica）"，中国耽于美国的消费，而美国耽于中国的廉价物品和信贷。（Ferguson 2010: preface）如果中国抛售美国债券，美元大幅贬值，就会影响到中国的美元储备。（Jacques 2009: 360）但是，如果美国攻击中国，中国真的抛售美债，美元体系就会解体，美国的世界霸权将会终结。因此，中国和美国已经进入了一种共生关系。2. 中国已经尽量地容纳美国的存在和利益。在朝鲜和伊朗的问题上，中国积极地与美国合作，向二者施压。在达尔富尔和缅甸的事务上，中国听从了西方人的意愿。而且，中国也逐步地将人民币升值，帮助美国缓解美元的压力。3. 中国还有足够的防御力量以抗击美国的袭击。特别地，中国有战略性武器，可以报复美国的核攻击。所有这些因素都导致两个国家不得不坐下来协商。

六、和平对话的可能性

"中美国"这种共生关系决定中美之间和平对话的可能。但是，保持对话的和平进行还需要双方具有一种平等的心态，认可对方的文化价值。

首先，美国或西方应当放弃他们自殖民时代养成的霸道的对话风格。特别地，美国人应当尊重其对话对象，放弃其"只有我们能如此做，你们却不能"的蛮横态度。（Leonard 2008: 93）由于西方人已经习惯于做世界的主人，很难一下子让他们屈尊，平等地与其他人种对话。但是，困难并不意味着不可能。正如19世纪的美国人不愿接受与黑人平等一样，其后代却于2008年选出了一位黑人总统。正如乾隆时代的中国人不愿承认蛮夷有更好的东西，他们的后代却全部接受了西方的科学和技术。其实，即使欧美人的优越心态也只是一种近期才有的现象。早在文艺复兴时代，欧美人的先驱，如康德、莱布尼兹和伏尔泰等，都高度认可中国文化，并认为可以用来弥补西方传统的不足。因此。欧美人在历史上和现实中都是可以真正地接受"他者"，并认可人类发展渠道的多元性的。这里的关键点是，欧美人必须放弃欧美至上主义的心态——这种心态只会导致对人类整体的伤害。（Mahbubani 2008: 125）

西方人还应当放弃他们在人权问题上所持的双重标准。正如 Ron Wheeler 尖锐地指出，在联合国人权委员会，西方国家很少被指控。实际上，欧美人已经将之变成了一个审判发展中国家的法庭。（Wheeler 1999）具体到中国，美国和其他西方国家应当纠正他们的偏见：对发生在他们的盟友（诸如哥伦比亚、沙特阿拉伯、乌干达、印度等）的严重违反人权的事件视而不见，而对中国却吹毛求疵；尽管他们已经看到中国人民享有了更多的自由和更高的生活水平。（Peerenboom 2007: 164）依 Peerenboom 看来，中美双方都应该花更多的精力自我批判，而不是指责对方。（Peerenboom 2007: 277）

其次，中国人应当跳出"受屈辱"的情结或自卑心态。自从鸦片战争被击败，中国人从上到下曾一度失去方向。逐渐地，他们不但接受了西方科技的先进性，而且也开始怀疑自己的传统文化，特别是儒家文化。对普通民众来说，他们将西方社会当作秩序、富裕和优越地位的象征。这也是中国人到欧美留学的热潮变得越来越热的原因。这种对西方社会的崇拜心态，当然不利于中美或中欧之间的和平对话。

尽管如此，中国作为一个民族或国家却从没有完全丧失对其自身文化的信心。从某种意义上，"中学为体、西学为用"的哲学从来都是以西方的科技来嫁接中国文化。马克思主义的引入也不例外。随着中国经济和外交上的成功，屈辱时代导致中国人对西方文化的开放心态反而成了一笔宝贵的财富。我们看到，它导致中国人以一种开放平常的心态认真地研究和吸收西方文化。相比之下，很少有西方人以同样的心态认真地研究中国文化。为此，Paul A. Cohen 批评说，"西方人步入了古代中国人的老路。当其他文化的代表们被迫吸收大量西方文化，有意识地对其进行分析组合以便其本族文化生存时，西方人却从不将别人对我们的看法当回事。"（Jacques 2009: 100）因此，可以看到，中国的未来文化形态将是中西文化的混合体，就像宋明理学是儒家和佛教的组合物一样。中国人有足够的智慧和信心将中美之间的对话和平地开展下去。

此外，其他因素也导致美国人向世界各国让出更多的权力和空间。虽然欧美人以技术和财富称霸世界，可是到了 21 世纪，财富却慢慢地向世界各地散开。上海、孟买和迪拜相继成为国际金融中心。而且，西方对财富的垄断进一步被 2008 年的金融危机削弱。同时，科学技术也被成功地嫁接到其他文明之上，许多非欧美国家出现了顶级的科学家和发明家。这就导致欧美对技术的垄断越来越难。虽然美国仍然在耗费巨额军费进行武器升级和换代，可是其新的技术很容易被模仿或破解。这说明保持一个独霸的而不受挑战的军队已经变得越来越不现实。一个更为现实的考虑就是美国人坐下来和平地商议。

引证材料：

Bergsten, C. Fred [et al.]（2008）: *China's Rise: Challenges and Opportunities*, Washington, DC: Peterson Institute for International Economics: Center for Strategic and International Studies, 269 pp.

Cohen, Paul（1984）: *Discovering History in China: American Historical Writing on the Recent Chinese Past*, New York: Columbia University Press, 296 pp.

Darwin, John（2008）: *After Tamerlane: The Global History of Empire since 1405*, New York: Bloomsbury Press: Distributed to the trade by Macmillan, 1st 574 pp.

Ferguson, Niall（2010）: *Civilization: The West and Rest*, New York: the Penguin Press, 402 pp.

Halper, Stefan（2010）: *The Beijing Consensus: How China's Authoritarian Model Will Dominate the Twenty-first Century*, New York: Basic Books, 296 pp.

Huntington, Samuel P.（1993）: "The Clash of Civilizations?" *Foreign Affairs*, 72.3, pp.22+.

Hungtington, Samuel P.（1996）: *The Clash of Civilizations and the Remaking of World Order*, New York: Simon and Schuster Paperbacks.

Jacques, Martin（2009）: *When China Rules the World: The Rise of the Middle Kingdom and the End of the Western World*, London: Allen Lane, 550 pp.

Kristof, Nicholas D.（1993）: "The Rise of China", *Foreign Affairs*, 72.5, pp.59+.

Leonard, Mark（2008）: *What Does China Think?* London: Fourth Estate, 164pp.

Mahbubani, Kishore（2008）: *The New Asian Hemisphere: the Irresistible Shift of Global Power to the East*, NewYork: Public Affairs, 314pp.

Meng, Peiyuan, *My Exploration in Chinese Philosophy*（《我的中国哲学研究

之路》），http://www.confuchina.com/xuezhe% 20wenji/meng% 20peiyuan.htm.

Peerenboom, Randall（2007）: *China Modernizes: Threat to the West or Model for the Rest?* NewYork: Oxford University Press，406pp.

Pohl, Karl Heinz: *Ethics for the 21st Century-The Confucian Tradition*, http://www.uni—trier.de/fileadmin/fb2/SIN/Pohl_Publikation/ethics_for_the_21st_century.pdf.

王夫之：《船山全书·礼记章句》，岳麓书社 1998 年版。

Wheeler, Ron（1999）: "The United Nations Commission on Human Rights，1982–1997: A Study of 'Targeted' Resolutions", *Canadian Journal of Political Science*, 32: 75.

杨伯峻：《孟子译注》，中华书局 1988 年版。

Zakaria, Fareed（2011）: *The Post-American World: Release 2.0*, New York: W. W. Norton & Co., Updated and expandeded., 314pp.

作者简介：

谭明冉：北京大学和加拿大多伦多大学哲学博士，现为山东大学哲学与社会发展学院副教授，研究方向为中国哲学和比较哲学。

东方的努力：尼山世界文明论坛

高述群

尼山世界文明论坛，简称尼山论坛，由中国第九届、第十届全国人大常委会副委员长许嘉璐于 2008 年倡议发起，宗旨是响应联合国开展文明对话决议精神，在孔子故乡致力于开展世界不同文明对话，维护世界文化多样性，推动建设和谐世界。按照许嘉璐的说法，在尼山建立"世界文明论坛"，意在秉承孔子"和为贵"、"和而不同"、"三人行必有我师"的教诲，通过促进不同文明间的对话交流，增进不同文明间的相互尊重、相互理解、相互包容与和睦相处。尼山是孔子诞生地，原名尼丘山，后因避讳孔子之名（孔子名丘）而改为尼山，《史记》载"孔子父母祷尼山而生孔子"。尼山位于泰山东南的泰沂山区，是泰沂山系向西延伸的余脉，尼山之西既是开阔的曲阜平原。孔子 3 岁前随父母生活在尼山南麓的鲁源村，鲁源村被后世儒家尊为孔子的原始故里。孔子 3 岁时，父亲去世，母亲便携带孔子离开故居地来到阙里定居下来。阙里是举世闻名的孔子故里。孔子去世后，葬在鲁国城北的泗河南岸，即现在的孔林，他住居的阙里老宅成为祭祀孔子最早的场所，后世在这个基础上扩建为现在的孔庙。后人为在尼山祭祀孔子，把孔子降生的山洞尊为"夫子洞"加以保护，又在尼山东坡建起尼山孔庙和尼山书院，作为祭祀孔子和传承其学说的专用场地。千百年来，尼山与曲阜孔庙、曲阜孔林并称为儒教三大圣地，每年来这里凭吊祭祀孔子的人络绎不绝。2007 年，百位儒家名家联合在尼山东麓的树林里建起一座古式书院，取名尼山圣源书院，首任院长牟钟鉴，首任名誉院长杜维明，首任院高级顾问许嘉璐。这座书院就是"尼山世界文明论坛"的永久会址地。这里也是中国大陆和中国台湾、香港多所高等院校研究生的实习基地。

一、尼山论坛的组织建制与前期工作

尼山论坛是一个民间平台。在许嘉璐领导下，由尼山论坛组委会、中国人民外交学会、中国联合国协会、中国国际友好联络会、中华宗教文化交流协会、孔子学院总部、山东大学、中国人民大学、北京师范大学、中华文化学院联合发起并作为常设主办单位。尼山论坛组委会主席由许嘉璐担任，副主席由邢贲思、李肇星、赵启正、叶小文、汝信、吴建民、陈健、胡占凡、刘长乐、杨文昌、许琳、学诚（佛教）、张继禹（道教）、纪宝成、刘川生、钟秉林、朱正昌、徐显明、陈秋途担任，秘书长由徐向红担任。邢贲思、庞朴担任学术委员会主任。山东大学儒学高等研究院和该校犹太教与跨宗教研究中心、北京师范大学人文宗教高等研究院、中国人民大学宗教研究院等为学术研究基地。中国联合国教科文组织全国委员会为指导单位。凤凰卫视、中新社、光明日报社、山东卫视等为媒体战略合作单位。从上述组织情况看，尼山论坛实际是一个文明对话的自由联合体，"文明对话"是把大家联系起来的纽带。

尼山论坛具有鲜明的学术性、民间性与开放性的特色。从更严格的意义上讲，尼山论坛是一个思想、哲学、艺术论坛。它更多侧重于从思想学术甚或艺术的高度为不同文明间的沟通理解提供一个家庭式的和睦对话场景：大家坐在孔子故乡的书院里，共同欣赏着美妙的音乐，交流着各自对经典的认识、对世界的看法、对生活的感悟和对未来的畅想。尼山论坛之所以没有设在繁华的大都市，而是设在了远离现代城市社区的原野——尼山河谷，所想追求的就是一种返璞归真的精神。许嘉璐主席说，这样可能会有助于不同文明在一起思考和解决人类面临的共同问题。尼山论坛在设计上是每两年在尼山举办一届论坛活动，称为双数年论坛活动；在两届之间，尼山论坛还将在世界各地举办各种内容不一、形式不同的活动，称为单数年论坛活动。这样做的目的，是希望拉近尼山论坛与世界各地的距离，拉近不同文明间和睦交往的关系。"和而不同"、"己所不欲，勿施于人"是尼山论坛的伦理法则。

为了做好尼山论坛工作，许嘉璐主席进行了一些初步的对话尝试。他还利用出国访问和会见外宾的机会，征询世界各地人士的意见，看怎样才能把尼山论坛办好。后来他把这些活动汇集成一本书于 2010 年 9 月由华艺出版社出版，书名定为《为了天下太平》。这个书名道出了他致力于推动开展不同文明对话的心声，可视为他对尼山论坛宗旨的通俗解说。2009 年 1 月，他来到大洋彼岸的美国洛杉矶，与水晶大教堂创始人罗伯特·舒乐（Robert H. Schuller）进行了真诚友好的对话。他们俩一见如故，成了真挚的朋友。许嘉璐邀请舒乐博士出席首届尼山论坛，舒乐欣然应允并履行了诺言。次年9月舒乐来尼山时，身体状况非常不好，医生建议他不要来中国，但他还是坚持要来，演讲时我们不得不为他专门准备了一把椅子。许嘉璐在洛杉矶演讲时说过这样一段话："站在这个透明的水晶大讲堂的讲台上，我感到没有任何的拘束和压抑，仿佛我就处在大自然的怀抱中，温暖的阳光洒遍每个角落，洒在每个人的身上和每个人的心灵里，仿佛大自然在净化着我们每个人的心灵。"他进一步说："中国文化和西方文化是存在差异的。我认为，这种差异不应该成为我们之间和睦相处的障碍，相反，应该是我们增进沟通和交流的动力。中国和美国刚好在地球的两端，如果我们不来往，就很难了解对方。"①他的演讲赢得了经久不息的掌声。透过这番演讲我们可以了解到许嘉璐为什么会倡导发起尼山论坛。

在尼山论坛组委会团队中，不乏参与文明对话的前卫人物。譬如汝信，中国社科院前副院长，他是中国学者中参与世界文明对话最早的学者之一。美国"9·11"之前，他应邀出席了许多重要的文明对话国际会议。但据他介绍，在国际学术领域，中国学者的声音一直非常的微弱。再譬如赵启正，原国务院新闻办公室主任，曾经和美国宗教领袖路易·帕罗（Luis Palau）进行过著名的"江边对话"。②还有一位叶小文，曾连续14年担任国家宗教局局长，是一位学者型的官员。其他如前外长李肇星、前联合国副秘书长陈建、前驻法大使吴建民等，他们都具有非常丰富的国际交往经验，对西方文化和世界不同文明的状况比较了解。学诚是中国佛教协会副会长，张继禹是中国道教协会副会长，他们是中国宗教界的代表。刘长乐被誉为"太平绅士"，作为凤凰卫视总裁，一直活跃于世界媒体和文化舞台。许琳，是通过汉语与世界交往的文化使者。尼山论坛组委会是一个富有国际交往经验和文明对话经历的专家型团队，他们整体地推动世界不同文明间的对话交往，很好地表明了中国人期盼和平、期盼化解人类危机的愿望。

---

① 许嘉璐：《为了天下太平》，华艺出版社2010年版，第9—11页。
② 本书全名为《江边对话——一位无神论者与一位基督徒的友好交流》。

二、尼山论坛开创文明对话新局面

进入 2010 年，许嘉璐开始带领尼山论坛团队正式登上文明对话的前台。许嘉璐为此作了一个颇具深意的选择：在 5 月 21 日——"联合国世界文化多样性促进对话与发展日"（简称"世界文明对话日"）前夕的 5 月 17 日，由尼山论坛组委会主办，在北京主持召开了庆祝"世界文明对话日"的高层学术座谈会。①许嘉璐的想法是首先做一个启蒙：让中国的公众更多了解这个世界性节日。会议请了 12 位文化名家到会发言，尼山论坛组委会还特地邀请光明日报社一起举办这次座谈会。在这次会议上，许嘉璐发表了题为《长期的博弈伟大的任务》的重要讲话，旗帜鲜明地阐述了关于文明对话的认识与主张。他说："不同文明间的对话是当前世界文明一元化与多元化两种主张和趋向之间博弈的产物。"在作了深入阐述后他说："在今天，不同文明间的对话是人类良知、人性之善的体现，而妄自尊大、以我为准、君临天下、排除异己，从本质上看是人类之恶的体现；唤醒人类古老的愿望与睿智、解剖当下、尽力运用人类幸福和平的必要条件以达到有力地遏制乃至消除邪恶，为人类幸福和平准备充分条件，则是进行不同文明对话的职责。"②他还就中华文明要积极参与世界文明对话进行了论述。这篇讲话连同其他学者的发言由《光明日报》刊发，国学版主编梁枢特地加了一个颇具象征意义的题目："世界文明对话日：来自中国的声音"。这是尼山论坛向外界发声的开始。8 月 26 日，尼山论坛组委会在国务院新闻办公室新闻发布厅举行了首届尼山论坛新闻发布会，许嘉璐请赵启正、叶小文、吴建民三位副主席以及常务理事黄星原、秘书长徐向红 5 人同时出席发布会。这是尼山论坛面向国内外的第一次亮相，引起了各国媒体的关注。

2010 年 9 月 26 日上午 9 时，在阳光明媚的尼山河谷，首届尼山论坛开幕式隆重举行，来自亚欧美三大洲 13 个国家和地区的思想家、政治家、宗教家、教育家、艺术家、媒体记者及各界人士齐集一堂，开启了一次别开生面的文明对话

---

① 2002 年，联合国大会通过决议把每年的 5 月 21 日确定为"世界文化多样性促进对话与发展日"，这个节日通常也被简称为"世界文明对话日"或"世界文化发展日"，自那以来，联合国教科文组织每年都要为这个节日举行庆祝活动，但民间组织的庆祝活动却很少见，在中国，这样一个国际性节日甚至还没有完全进入公众的视野。

② 尼山论坛秘书处：《世界文明对话日——来自中国的声音》，五洲出版社 2010 年版，第 10—12 页。

聚会。开幕式之前,主办方特意邀请与会者参观了尼山孔庙、尼山书院和夫子洞。许多与会者之前没有来过尼山,甚至少数人还不知道有尼山这个地方,参观让大家增加了对尼山对孔子的直观感悟。开幕式前,由许琳主持,在尼山圣源书院广场举行了"世界文明论坛碑"落成仪式,由许嘉璐与中国著名书法家欧阳中石亲自揭幕。① 首届尼山论坛的开幕式由美妙的中国民乐演出开始。② 山东歌舞乐团和山东老年合唱团的精彩演出让与会者忘记了旅途的疲劳和相互间的差异,大家共同沉浸到音乐的世界里。音乐演出后,开幕式由吴建民主持。首先请联合国前副秘书长陈健宣读法国前总统希拉克和联合国副秘书长沙祖康的贺信。希拉克在贺信中说:"今天的世界面临着民族主义上升、各国自身特点减弱,我很高兴看到中国主办文明对话的论坛。""今天的世界正承受着许多动荡的煎熬,在这种情况下,中国的智慧和对和谐的追求是富有教益的。尼山论坛从孔子那里汲取了灵感。孔子告诉我们,没有对多样性的尊重,就不可能追求和谐,这个思想为我们指明了前进的道路。"接着请联合国教科文组织官员蓝琴女士宣读伊琳娜·博克娃总干事的贺信。博科娃总干事在贺信中说:"众所周知,在伟大的中国思想家孔子去世约 500 年以后,儒家思想对基督教产生了很深的影响。事实上,无论是儒家思想还是基督教,都倡导中庸之道和互惠伦理,同时,二者都倡导世界人民的和谐共存。'和而不同'的理念与联合国教科文组织的主要任务是完全吻合的,即确保对多种不同文化的保护和传播。我衷心希望此次论坛成果丰厚,同时我也希望此次论坛所产生的影响广泛而深远,远远超出孔子的诞生地。"接着请印尼前总统梅加瓦蒂、匈牙利前总理迈杰希、著名儒学家杜维明等学者发言,最后请许嘉璐代表尼山论坛组委会致辞。开幕式后,第一场对话是许嘉璐与舒乐,由赵启正主持。他们的对话真诚而热烈。这是儒家与基督教在尼山的历史性对话,开创了先例。

首届尼山论坛的主题是"和而不同与和谐世界——儒家文明与基督教文明对话",两天共举行 18 场对话,有些对话是应学者自己要求的,对话形式灵活

---

① "尼山世界文明论坛碑"由许嘉璐撰文,欧阳中石书写,泗水县工匠制作,陈洪夫监制,安放在尼山圣源书院的正门内。这体现了尼山论坛组委会的一个理念,即争取从首届开始,每届论坛都要在会址地留下物质文化遗产,记载在这里发生的每一件关于"文明对话"的大事。

② 尼山论坛组委会特地请中国民乐家刘文金为首届尼山论坛创作了《尼山圣诞曲》和《孔子颂》,演出时刘文金亲自担任指挥,近百人参加的演出让台下观众如痴如醉,演出取得了巨大成功。美国学者白诗朗在演出后说,能够在尼山听到这样美妙的音乐,真是太荣幸了!当有人介绍孔子就是有名的音乐家时,许多人更是发出了由衷的赞叹声。

多样，既有学术全会，也有一对一、二对二的对话，还有凤凰卫视举办的电视论坛。26日晚间，还特别举行了以"孔子与耶稣"为主题的自由式对话。美国牧师亨利·贺理在对话中说："我很尊重孔子，但不信仰儒学，因为我的宗教信仰是基督教，我们在一起探讨爱、宽容、友谊、礼仪等。我很高兴能有机会参加这样的讨论。"学者们很喜欢这样的对话。还有一个对话场景也非常受学者喜爱，就是在古色古香的尼山书院门前草坪上进行对话，两把椅子，二人对坐，开谈。杜维明与美国神学教授德怀特·霍普金斯就在这个位置足足谈了2.5小时。德怀特·霍普金斯表示："尼山论坛为不同文明间交流和儒家思想的对外传播提供了一个平台。"① 首届论坛于27日闭幕，会议通过了世界上首个《人类和谐宣言》，许嘉璐发表了重要的闭幕致辞。他说："与会学者高度认同这次论坛的口号——仁爱、诚信、包容、和谐。儒家文明和基督教文明是当今世界两个影响力巨大的文明，开展这两大文明的对话与交流在今天具有突出的意义和时代紧迫性，今后应该进一步加强沟通和了解，在新的基点上建立起彼此相互尊重、欣赏而又和睦通融的新型文明关系。"最后他加重语气呼吁："希望主张对话、反对冲突的话语能成为我们这个时代的最强音！希望人类的智慧之光能够穿透物质与贪欲所构成的笼罩于人类自身之上的迷雾，让人类能够看到湛蓝湛蓝的天空！"

首届尼山论坛后，正好赶上国庆节长假，到尼山旅游的人比上一年同期增长了5倍。

第二届尼山论坛于2012年5月21—23日在尼山举行。继续开展"儒家文明与基督教文明对话"，主题确定为"信仰·道德·尊重·友爱"八个字。与首届尼山论坛相比，第二届尼山论坛有了一些新的创意：

——**隆重庆祝"世界文明对话日"。**② 2012年5月21日适逢该节日10周年（2002—2012），尼山论坛组委会为此进行了精心的准备。首先是邀请联合国教科文组织、联合国文明联盟共同举办这次活动，得到这两个组织积极热情的回应。联合国教科文组织原本由总干事亲自出席，后因事委派副总干事汉斯·道维勒代表总干事出席。联合国文明联盟则派高级顾问克里斯托弗·贝斯和两位大使一同出席，一位大使是坎迪·门德斯，另一位是潘光。其次，尼山论坛组委会和山东

---

① 尼山论坛秘书处：《尼山：聆听世界多元声音——首届尼山世界文明论坛实录》，五洲出版社出版，2011年版，第109页。

② 这是为庆祝"世界文明对话日"特意做的安排，而且从第二届开始，今后每届尼山论坛的举办时间都固定在这个时间。许嘉璐主席说，这是对联合国倡导文明对话最好的响应，也是对"世界文明对话日"最好的庆祝方式，目的就是让大家记住这个节日。

省为庆祝活动特别制作了一尊"文明对话纪事鼎"①，用以纪念联合国确定"世界文明对话日"10周年。该鼎在开幕式当日隆重安放，许嘉璐主席与中华人民共和国文化部副部长兼国家文物局局长励小捷、山东省省长姜大明、墨西哥前总统福克斯、联合国教科文组织副总干事汉斯·道维勒、联合国文明联盟高级顾问克里斯托弗·贝斯等中外嘉宾一起出席了隆重的安放仪式。该项活动同时宣布"我为多样性和包容性做一件事"活动在尼山起步。②其三，安排了一系列学术活动，包括本报告写作组的国际研讨会。大家共同回顾总结过去世界10年文明对话的做法与经验，展望未来10年全球文明对话的发展趋向。这使得尼山、尼山论坛与联合国、与世界文明对话更加紧密地联系在一起，强化了各文明参与对话的责任意识。论坛期间，尼山论坛组委会分别与联合国教科文组织、联合国文明联盟举行了工作会谈，就未来合作进行了深入商讨，在许多方面达成了共识。

——首次举办**"世界青年博士生论坛"**。这是本届论坛的一项开创性工作。许嘉璐主席对于青年参与文明对话非常重视。此前联合国秘书长潘基文曾专门就此发表讲话，指出现在是到了青年人走向文明对话前台的时候了。尼山论坛对此予以率先响应，专门委托山东大学儒学高等研究院和北京师范大学人文宗教高等研究院负责这项组织工作。各地学生积极踊跃报名，美国有20多位学生专程自费赶来参加这项活动，台湾国民党副主席蒋孝严得知此事后也专程从台湾赶来出席这场青年论坛。青年博士生论文质量高，讨论积极活跃，成为本届论坛的一大亮点。闭幕式上，两位青年代表走向讲台，宣读他们共同起草、民主通过的宣言——《青年人走向文明对话前台倡议书》。这是世界上第一份代表青年人参与文明对话的倡议书，在文明对话史上具有里程碑的意义。

——首次召开**"世界古文明国家文化遗产保护与促进文明对话国际会议"**。这是由尼山论坛组委会、中国国家文物局、山东省文物局共同举办的一次活动。文明对话与文明古国密切相关。文明古国是人类文明的重要发祥地与哺育地，是现代世界各大文明的渊源。文明古国不仅拥有不可再生的古代文化遗产，而且拥

---

① "文明对话纪事鼎"由中央美术学院教授刘家本设计并制作。鼎的形制采用中国古代方鼎的形制，鼎的图案则充分体现了世界文化多样性的精神，表达了人与自然的和谐；鼎耳上是两只和平鸽，象征文明对话的和平与和谐精神，鼎的正面文字是"庆祝联合国世界文明对话十周年"，背面的文字是《人类和谐宣言》(摘要)。山东青年美术家尹铭参与了设计工作。泗水县和尼山圣源书院对鼎的设计、制作、安放给予了全面支持。

② "我为多样性和包容性做一件事"是联合国文明联盟发起的一项全球活动，尼山论坛组委会积极响应并参与，为此在山东的一些大学校园组织了采访，并把采访图像直接发送到文明联盟指定的网站上供全球浏览。

有文明发展的丰富历史经验，积累有文明历经磨难、化解磨难的历史智慧。在今天的文明对话中，文明古国拥有重要发言权。现代文明的发展，很大方面是以牺牲古代文化遗产为代价，在许多国家和地区，因为战争、冲突甚至饥饿而毁掉的物质的和非物质的文化遗产不计其数，而且这种悲剧几乎每天还在世界各地上演。文明古国多数是发展中国家，他们是当今世界文明大家庭中的弱者，因而更加需要保护，更加需要国际团结与国际合作。本次古文明国家合作会议是一个尝试，由于筹备较晚，所以许多方面显得仓促和多有疏漏，尽管如此，本次活动仍然得到了大多数古文明国家专家与学者的积极响应，特别是得到了这些国家驻华使馆的大力支持，为了弥补时间仓促、来不及邀请有关组织与人员的不足，在各国使馆支持下，由国家文物局专门组织了一个驻华使节走进孔孟世界遗产地的活动，这使得这项活动更加丰满起来，不仅如期召开了合作会议，而且在中央电视台支持下，还由山东卫视录制了一场电视论坛，中央电视台一线主持人劳春燕到场主持。尤其重要的是，这项活动得到了联合国教科文组织的积极肯定，汉斯·道维勒副总干事专门到会致辞，世界遗产界多位一线专家出席会议并发言。会后共同发表了《世界古文明国家文化遗产保护与促进文明对话——尼山共识》。山东省还举行了88项重点文物保护工程集中开工仪式，为这项活动添彩。这是世界文明古国第一次因文明对话而走到一起。

第二届尼山论坛无论在规模、层次、代表性诸方面都远远超过了首届：对话时间扩大为3天，参加范围覆盖五大洲22个国家和地区，对话活动扩展为52场次，参与人群扩大到各阶层各领域，仅列席、旁听的人员就达到1.16万人次。到会外国学者包括：联合国秘书长潘基文，信仰与环境高级顾问彭马田，国际社会科学委员会主席坎迪·门德斯，世界公众论坛执行主席达梅尔，国际哲学联合会联盟副主席金丽寿，美国葛培理布道团副总裁亨利·贺理，法国前总统希拉克文化顾问戴哈诺娃，世界宗教对话与精神中心主任布莱恩特，德国前歌德学院中国区总院长阿克曼，墨西哥古迹遗址保护协会主席奥尔加·奥利弗，联合国教科文组织特别顾问卡鲁索，英国爱丁堡大学神学院院长斯图尔特·布朗等。墨西哥前总统福克斯说："我之所以不远万里来到中国，就是希望坐在一个智者的旁边，坐在尼山这样优美的环境下，感受着孔子的思想。""我最大的愿望就是希望尼山论坛能够攀过高山、跨过河流，走遍世界的各个角落，让人们通过论坛彼此加深了解。"世界公众论坛执行主席弗莱德·达梅尔说："我非常高兴地看到，文明对话的理念在中国，尤其是在尼山论坛已落地生根。""更让我高兴的是，我注意到尼山论坛的举办地与孔子诞生地相邻。这是世界文明论坛最好的选址。因为在我的脑海里，孔子完美地诠释了什么是文明。"美国著名福音派牧师亨利·贺理说："我非常荣幸，尤其是在我 85 岁的时候，能够获得在尼山论坛再次发言的机会。本届论坛的主题意义重大，关乎中国的未来以及世界所有民族包括美国的未来。愿尼山论坛利用自己独特的影响力，给人类社会带来和平与和谐。"

第二届尼山论坛还有一个重要的经验是吸收当地大学参与办论坛，开放式办论坛，让各界尽可能都有机会参与进来。山东大学、曲阜师范大学、济宁学院、尼山圣源书院发挥了骨干作用，老师和学生们踊跃参与，组成了庞大的志愿者队伍，青年学生是亮丽的风景线。当地农民、工人和公务员也围拢过来观看，论坛组委会特为他们设立了专场学术讲座，请著名学者给大家做报告。上海交响乐团还专门为与会者举行了一场免费的演出，山东友谊出版社为与会者举行了专场图书展，并在尼山论坛会址地设立了"尼山书屋"。第二届尼山论坛呈现的情景是：文明对话，说什么已经不那么重要，人与人之间近距离的感情交流，这才显得最为重要。5 月 23 日，许嘉璐主席作了闭幕总结。他说："作为论坛主席，我无法也不可能对这次论坛做出全面、细致和周密的总结，我只能用尽量简洁的语言概述两天来的基本情况。这次论坛的内容比上一届更为丰富和多元，信仰、宗教、经典、文化遗产保护、传媒、经济、企业、环境保护、医疗养生等等都成为讲演与发言对话的内容，涉及的学科自然也是众多的，但是大家都始终没有离开和而不同与世界和谐的总主题，以及这次论坛'信仰·道德·尊重·友爱'的议题，这一事实提醒我们任何一种文化都是丰富的、复杂的，不同人民间对话的空间是无限广阔的，因而对话应该是全方位的、无限期的。""论坛的热烈程度是我未料到的，老友相逢自然格外的愉快，新朋相识也大有相见恨晚之感。是什么把相隔遥远的我们连到了一起呢？我想是对人类的热爱，是对现实的思考，是对理智的信心。"对于如何做好下一步的文明对话工作，许嘉璐主席说：

近十几年来世界各地的智者已经在呼吁文化多样性和不同文明对话方面做了很多实实在在的事情，其中也包括了许多在座的朋友。不断呼吁的一个显而易见的结果是在学术界和大学的课堂上力主文化单极化的声音越来越小了。但是我们不能停留在论证不同文明对话的"应该"和"可以"的阶段，似乎应该朝着"怎样"来前进，也就是研究不同文明怎样和谐相处，实际上在提供给这次论坛的论文中和论坛期间举行的对话有些已经涉及这个问题，我的意思是对话应该逐步深化。例如在这次论坛期间，中外学者对今后论坛应该讨论些什么问题、如何讨论这些问题提出了不少建议，在这里我也想试着提出以下这些问题供大家参考。

如何促进各国教育机构、宗教组织间的对话？现在也并不乏这类的交流，但是似乎更多的是仅限于各方教育与宗教组织状况的交换，而并没有深入到各国是如何对学生、对信众进行全人教育，各自教育、宗教背后的文化动因以及教育、宗教如何应对当前世界危机这类问题的层次上来。

如何促进人民与人民之间的对话？旅游、留学等等都是人民与人民广泛接触的机会。但是似乎旅游只关注山水名胜，或者再加上购物。留学生主要关注科学技术和经济金融方面的知识和技能。如果有越来越多的游客和留学生关注他国的文化、历史、宗教等人文现象，有越来越多的留学生想成为研究他国文化的学者，情况就大不一样了。公共外交就真的成为现实了，一个开放的国家人人都是外交家。

如何促进媒体之间的对话？这一领域的对话尤其需要超越业务和技术范围，需要直言不讳，包括像新闻自由、新闻道德等问题都可以成为对话的内容。

如何促进不同语言之间的无障碍沟通？技术领域的语言是最容易翻译的，一涉及信仰、道德，其难易的程度为一般人所难想象。而有障碍的沟通是似通而未通，因为一进入到对方的内心深处就被一层隔膜阻碍住了。这项工作需要各国的哲学、社会学、宗教学、文学、史学等等学者的帮助，促进相关学者就这一问题的研究展开合作是很重要的。

最后，还应该想一想，如何促进政府间开展文明对话？我们都知道自古以来政府间只就眼前的事务进行交流，就具体事务谈具体事务，不涉及包含在事务中的文化，很容易纠缠而难解。历史已经进入到21世纪，为什么不能突破常规，请各国政府的首脑也成为不同文明对话的成员？

我这番话可能被有些朋友看成是"乌托邦式的奇想"，我承认我是个理想主义者，但是人类不是一直就是在想象和理想中生活的？中国古人想象中的大同世界，傅立叶、欧文所实验的"乌托邦世界"至今还在激励着中国人。在西班牙安多露西亚地区马力马来达村3000多村民至今还幸福地生活在村长胡安·马努艾尔·桑切斯哥的威尔按照乌托邦所建构的社会中。关于不同文明如何和谐相处的一些想法和前人对未来社会的想象相比只是一件小事，也只是一个例子，我举这些例子为的是说明，我坚信只要有人和人面对面不仅谈事、谈物，而且谈各自的心才是严格意义上的沟通，才能彻底了解对方和睦相处、幸福的生活。不管是家庭内部还是族群之间、国家之间都是如此。

第二届尼山论坛后，世界公众论坛邀请尼山论坛组委会出席于当年10月3—7日在希腊举行的罗德文明论坛，副主席刘长乐代表尼山论坛出席并发表演讲。联合国文明联盟邀请尼山论坛组委会出席于当年11月29—30日在上海举行的"亚洲及南太平洋地区磋商会议"，高述群代表尼山论坛出席会议并代表中国大陆地区作大会发言，提出了尼山论坛组委会与联合国文明联盟在尼山开展文明对话工作的具体建议。

三、尼山论坛走进联合国总部大厦

2012年4月16日，应联合国教科文组织邀请，"巴黎尼山世界文明论坛"在联合国教科文组织总部——法国巴黎举行。[①] 这次活动由孔子学院总部与联合国教科文组织共同举办，主题是"儒家思想与全球化世界中的新人文主义"，来自法、德、英、美、西班牙、保加利亚、匈牙利、突尼斯、斯里兰卡、马里等国家的高级官员与专家学者，各国常驻教科文组织使节、官员，法国学术界、教育界200多人出席。联合国教科文组织总干事伊琳娜·博科娃在开幕式上致辞，她着重指出："全球化使人类的关系前所未有地紧密，全球化不仅仅是经济的融合，更是文化的融合，而文化的融合需要新人文主义的支撑。用孔子的思想重新考虑国家之间的关系，人与自然的关系，这应该成为新人文主义的重要内涵之一。今天，在教科文组织讨论儒家思想与新人文主义意义非凡。新的世界需要新人文主义，它将促进世界的进步。"法国前总理拉法兰在致辞中说："儒家思想与新人文主义不仅仅是一个哲学命题，也是一个政治话题。只有人与人之间相互尊重，才能达到一种平衡与和谐。孔子的思想具有现代性，它可

---

① 吴建民曾任中国驻法大使，在法国和欧洲享有很高的声誉，巴黎尼山论坛在法国的举行，首先得益于他的推动。曾任其助手的徐波，现供职于 UNESCO，出任副总干事汉斯·道维勒的助手，他为此也做出了很大的努力。吴建民在法国的老朋友，原希拉克总统文化顾问戴哈诺娃女士，是此次活动的重要推手，正是她首先建议尼山论坛组委会到教科文组织总部举行文明对话活动。巴黎尼山论坛后，戴哈诺娃应邀出席了第二届尼山论坛活动，并与吴建民一起参加了首场对话。她在对话中诚恳地表示，中国已经长成了大象，不应该也不能再躲在大树之后。她的这个形象比喻给与会者留下了深刻的印象。

以构成新人文主义的核心，而人类正需要一种更广泛意义的新人文主义。"许嘉璐主席在发表演讲时说："人文主义，作为催生工业化和现代社会的理念，为人类的进步作出了极大贡献。但是在近300年的历史进程中，人文主义发生了蜕变，或者说发生了异化，自由、平等、博爱，已经和当年启蒙思想家所期望的有了巨大差距。眼前的事实证明，我们需要在历史经验的基础上，思考新人文主义问题，这或许是人类疗治心灵创伤所必需的，是地球未来希望之所在。"尼山论坛组委会副主席吴建民、许琳，秘书长徐向红、中国社科院美国研究所所长周弘、北京师范大学教授曹卫东、华东师范大学教授童世骏等7位中国学者出席并作大会发言。

巴黎尼山论坛取得了巨大成功，会场之热烈可谓空前。论坛期间，有50多国常驻联合国教科文组织的大使和官员全程参加，兴致盎然，争相提问，现场从始至终座无虚席，四周站满听众。活动在晚间结束后，许多人还在热烈地讨论，不愿离去，孔子、儒家思想、和而不同、新人文主义，这些词语成为与会者津津乐道的热门话语。会后，埃及、匈牙利、斯里兰卡、阿富汗、贝宁、巴基斯坦、伊拉克、加蓬、丹麦、斯洛伐克、保加利亚、葡萄牙、巴西、印度、洪都拉斯等国使节纷纷祝贺论坛成功。梵蒂冈常驻联合国教科文组织观察员致函中国常驻团，评价"论坛提供了聆听来自世界各国关于儒家思想和新人文主义的不同观点的机会"，要求得到所有发言人的稿件。联合国教科文组织副总干事汉斯表示："教科文组织总部开展类似活动比较多，但能引起如此高度关注，实不多见。论坛主题倡导世界文化多样性，交汇人类历史与现实。中外演讲者学术造诣深厚、国际视野宽阔、发言内容理论联系实际，对深层次思考当今世界面临的问题与挑战具有启迪意义。"联合国教科文组织前执行局主席、贝宁常驻代表约瑟夫认为，"教科文组织现在最需要的就是这种类型的思想实验，你可以同意或不同意演讲者的观点，但是他们提出的问题和启发人们思考这些问题本身就是极其重要的"。中国常驻联合国教科文组织代表尤少忠说，"巴黎尼山论坛的成功举办充分说明，在复杂多变、局势动荡的当今世界，国际社会更加重视来自新兴国家特别是中国的声音"。

巴黎尼山论坛打开了尼山论坛走向欧洲、走向美洲、走向联合国的大门。

2012年11月10—11日，应联合国经济与社会事务部邀请，"纽约尼山世界文明论坛"在美国纽约联合国总部大厦举行，中华能源基金委员会与联合国经济与社会事务部共同主办，主题是"超越国度，不同信仰，共同价值——儒家与基督教文明对话"。中华能源基金委员会副主席兼秘书长何志平主持对话。①两天共开展 5 场学术对话与交流，就哲学、宗教、和谐等话题展开讨论，探索不同文明间的对话方式与和睦相处之道。许嘉璐主席，联合国副秘书长吴红波，联合国大会主席武克·耶雷米奇，中国驻联合国副代表王民，中国驻纽约总领事孙国祥，联合国非政府组织宗教与信仰自由委员会原主席、美国天主教华盛顿总教区荣休大主教西奥多·麦卡里克，美国跨宗教、跨文化、跨国对话研究所主席列奥纳德·斯维德勒，美国华盛顿国际宗教与外交中心主席道格拉斯·钟斯顿，美国达拉斯联邦储备银行原主席詹姆斯·哈科特，原梵蒂冈宗教对话委员会顾问约翰·伯莱利，天主教国际基督和平运动联合主席玛丽·邓尼斯，美国未来学家马可·斯达哈尔曼，凤凰卫视董事局主席刘长乐，中国佛教协会副会长学诚，中国道教协会副会长张继禹，中国人民外交学会副会长张平，尼山论坛组委会常务理事谢治秀，尼山论坛组委会常务副秘书长高述群，以及来自联合国各有关机构、中美两国著名学府和研究机构的学者和研究生逾百人出席了这次盛会。许嘉璐主席以《反思源头，构建人类伦理》为题发表了主旨演讲。他说：

> 今天，我们在联合国总部举行儒耶对话，具有很好的象征意义。联合国在人类历史上最为残酷的大战后成立，宗旨是保障人权，维护和促进世界和平。半个多世纪以来，多少各国政要、专家在这里发出呼吁和解、追求和平的声音，影响了全世界。这次多国学者和宗教家在这里对话，也正是为了消除文化隔膜，促进人类和谐，实现从史前时期至今没有过的永久和平。政要们讲政治，我们讲文化，都是为了同一个目标。用中国话形容这种情况，就是"异曲同工"。而且我认为，我们所做的事情和发表的意见，虽然不能马上进入各国政府的决策，但是却比各国政要在这里所发表的声明更为深刻，因为国家与国家、民族与民族间的和睦或对立，其最根本的原因是对于他人文化和自古传承至今的文化理念的正确理解或者相反。即使如此，文化还是沟通不同国家、不同民族、不同信仰最好的内容和渠道。因为文化是各个民族的灵魂，是每个历史时期选择未来道路的根基和土壤。了解了、理解了别的民族的文化，可以增进彼此的感情，拓宽对话的范围，

---

① 香港中华能源基金委员会是纽约尼山论坛的主要赞助和组织单位，该会行政总裁陈秋途此后当选为尼山论坛组委会副主席。该会美国分会会长张武及全体同人承担了全面组织与接待工作。何志平曾在美国留学和工作 16 年，两天对话都由他主持。他说，儒家文明和基督教文明是全球最重要的两大文明，在联合国总部大厦讨论儒家文明与基督教文明的关系，对于建设和谐世界至关重要，这将为两大文明开展对话开辟一条新的道路。

加深相互的信任。而政治，只是文化的一个组成部分，而且是受文化的核心——宇宙观、价值观制约的文化形式。

不同文明应该对话而不要动不动就打架，这种必要性和可能性已经为近年来的事实所证明。自联合国于2002年一致通过决议，以每年5月21日为世界不同文明对话日以后，在不少国家先后举办了多种形式、多种内容的对话活动，增进了学者和公众对不同文明的理解，增进了友谊。今年5月21日在中国山东孔子诞生地尼山举行第二届尼山世界文明论坛是专门举办了纪念联合国作出这一决议10周年的一系列活动。对这些活动社会的反应是好的，这就鼓励了我们应该继续这样做下去。我认为，在经过了10年以上的努力，不同文明之间的对话应该超越论述"需要对话"、"可以对话"的阶段，进一步提升其内涵，把许多学者已经进入的领域——面对危机重重的当今世界，人类应该怎么办？不同文明应该承担起什么样的责任？——变为自觉的目标。

在这里，我想从一个特定的角度谈谈我的建议。这就是我的演讲题目所示："反思源头，构建人类伦理"。

所谓"反思源头"，就是回顾不同文明起始时的文化根本理念；对于宗教而言，就是重温先知初创时的本意。我之所以这样想是因为，如果仅仅着眼于残酷的现实和充满血泪的人类成长之旅，我们常常会深陷苦闷与彷徨，因为人类自己所造成的种种恶果至今还没有找到解决的办法；文化的多元性和眼前文化冲突的状况，似乎增加了人类前途的不可知性。但是，如果用彻底的历史主义剖析不同信仰的元点，则可以在不同文化中发现"人"的共同期盼，而这就是解决问题的开始。由这一点，我们可以通过思考、辩论、探索而达至轴心时代伟人的初衷：天下太平，世界大同。

首先，我想叙述中国文化的情况。

直到今天，世界上还有很多人认为中国人是没有信仰的。这种误解甚至影响了对中国的看法和态度。因为一个没有信仰的人是可怕的人，一个没有信仰的民族当然也是可怕的民族。

可是，中国人是有信仰的。中国文化的骨干为儒家、佛教和道教。在这三家中，儒家又是影响最大的。佛教徒信佛，道教徒信仰众多的神，这都是大家所知道的。儒家呢？崇拜其创始人孔子，信仰他所确立并倡导的"仁"和"礼"，即以"爱人"、"泛爱众而亲仁"为最高准则，以"仁"的外在形式，"礼"区分和调节人际关系和天人关系。孔子在中国人眼里是"至圣先师"，而不是神。大多数中国人虽然没有一个统一的创造了包括人在内的一切的人格神，但在崇拜孔子、信仰"德"的同时也各自有自己的神，例如老子、妈祖等。因为孔子说过"敬鬼神而远之"，所以中国人，包括无神论者一向对所有合法宗教都抱着尊重、包容、平等的态度，历代执政者，也都采取了和民众态度相应的政策。

其次，我想介绍一下也许大家都知道的古代情况。中国从汉代（前206—220）起，更确切地说，从公元前1世纪开始，直至现在，中国对先后传入中国的景教（基督教的聂斯托利派，Nestorius，亦即于17世纪才被马丁·路德认定并非异端的东方亚述教会）、印度佛教、犹太教、伊斯兰教、天主教、基督教都是接纳的，并给予和中国人同样的待遇：居住、旅行、经商、就学、传教、建教堂等自由。历史沧桑，这些宗教进入中国和在中国境内传播的情况，虽然还有许多遗存文物可以让我们略知大概，但是已经不能做出详细的描绘。引起世界许多历史学家和传教人士注意的是宋代（960—1279）首都开封市的犹太社区。1163年，开封的闹市区建成了第一座犹太教堂。犹太教当时被称为"一赐乐业教"（"一赐乐业"即Israel的音译）。犹太人以其杰出的经营能力，在当地处于社会的中上层；他们还可以经考试进入政府任职。据中国学者研究，在元代（1271—1386），一位名为珠笏氏亦思哈的犹太人，还在中央政府担任高官（参见潘光、王健《犹太人与中国》）。

关于中国与其他外来宗教的关系，时间不允许我在这里一一叙述，有一点我想提到：自古以来，儒家、佛家和道家之间，在很多时候有过理论的争辩——其实，在这三家各自内部也一直存在着宗派间的争论——但从来没有发生过宗教战争。中国有句俗语："君子动口不动手"，恰好可以用来形容中国宗教间的情况。三家争辩的结果是，彼此互相吸收对方教理教义乃至祭祀祈祷仪轨的长处，以补自己的不足，于是各自都得到了空前的提高。例如，佛教加快了中国化的进程，儒家加强了形上学和"德"内化过程的研究，道教的仪轨得益于儒、佛，并形成了自己的理论体系。特别是在唐（618—907）、宋、元三朝，佛学、儒学和道学都达到了极高的水平。其中儒家的哲学成就尤为杰出，至今仍然是世界各国中国学和哲学研究的热点。

古代和今天的中国之所以如此，是因为中国人看出了不同信仰在伦理观上有着共性，求同存异，于是获得了共存共荣的结果。

我之所以要提到中国对外来宗教的包容、吸纳的历史事实，是想说，中国的这一传统决定了中国人在当前这个纷乱的世界里，身处文明冲突环境中，由衷地主张大家多点对话，少点争吵，更不赞成用武器说话。

现在，请允许我回到我的演讲题目《反思源头，构建人类伦理》上来。

在各个文明的伦理无例外地遭到前所未有的摧残的今天，在事实上不同文明正在发生不同程度、不同方式冲突的今天，不同文明间的误会太多了。原因之一是人们常常着眼于文明的表层，例如信仰对象的差异、对待世俗生活的态度、各自艺术的表现形式等等，而忽略了自己和对方文明的核心，而这一核心，最完整、最集中地含蕴在所有文明的初始定型阶段。

例如，所有文明，起始都是关心人的生与死，今世与来世。印度文明在婆罗门教正式形成之前，已经有世界和人类生于"梵"的观念。（例如《爱多利亚奥义书》第一章）而"梵"则是"自我"，也就是神灵、精神，是真，是智，是乐（例如《金刚针奥义书》）。这些已为后来的婆罗门教和佛教所吸取。希伯来文明，关于神的认识集中于《圣经·旧约》中。虽然摩西见到过上帝，听到过他口授戒律，而且上帝按照自己的形象塑造了人，但是实质上，上帝也是代表了全能、至善的一种精神。儒家所崇信的"德"，以"仁"为核心，是极高的目标，人人都达不到最高点，想象中的最高境界即为"圣"。孔子说自己到了 70 岁，即"从心所欲，不逾矩"，就含有了这种境界的精神。环顾其他信仰，也无不是以追求"善"、"爱"为终极目标，而且无论是出于对神的敬畏，还是对死后堕入地狱的恐怖，都使得人重视自律，遵守他律，节制自己的物欲和肉欲。由此可见，在宗教发生时期，人们对解决生死和来世问题的期望可以说既简单又难以满足。

相对于古代，现在越来越多的人只关心现世的物质享受，和对某种精神的信仰比起来，这样肉体要舒适得多，简单得多，容易得多，也肤浅得多。唯其如此，所以无所畏惧，自律已经付诸东流，他律也已置若罔闻，追求物质利益不择手段，并诡称这是上天的意志。现在各国种种社会问题、环境问题、国家间的冲突问题，无不由此而生。

如果各个民族都能理性地回顾自己的民族史、思想史或宗教史，将能够体验到自己原初的信仰包涵着人生和宇宙的真理，沿此以往才能有真正的幸福，就会有越来越多的人向往真正的"善"，拒绝现在这种紧张、疲劳、空虚、危机四伏的生活。这是基于人的本性必然要走的路。

现在的世界，伦理的不同几乎不是以民族或宗教，而是按照财富的多寡区分的。富人有富人的伦理，穷人有穷人的伦理，强者有强者的伦理，弱者有弱者的伦理。不同标准的伦理相遇，自然就要发生亨廷顿教授所说的文明冲突。因此，现在到了各国的智者一起研究构建人类共同伦理的时候了。因为伦理是所有国家、所有民众所关心的也是最无争论的问题，所以我相信，构建人类伦理的议题一定会得到世界性的积极响应。

既然"善"是各个民族的信仰中共同的内容——尽管古今学者对本民族心中的"善"有多种不同解释——就应该成为未来人类共同伦理的内容。原哈佛大学教授杜维明先生就在 10 天前，在北京大学成立了"世界伦理中心"，我有幸参加了中心的揭牌仪式。到会的各国学者都很赞赏北京大学的这一举措，我相信，这个信息也会让今天到会的一些朋友们感兴趣，因为这反映了世界思想界的一种动向，而研讨、构建世界伦理的重任只能由各国智者，即公共知识分子来承担。我认为，在这个领域，中国人几千年的经验是可以供世界参考的。回想斯宾诺莎、康德等伟大的哲学家，当年就曾为研究人类的伦理和道德理性殚精竭虑，现在到了 21 世纪，总会有人奋起为了人类的和平和幸福再次作出贡献。

构建人类伦理，先由交流开始，这是必然的。亚欧之间，亚洲大陆不同国家之间，在很原始的农耕时代和游牧时代，就有先行者用马蹄和双脚开辟出多条人类交流的道路，那时亚欧之间、亚洲国家之间是和睦的，友好的；现在交通和通讯如此便利，实现了，甚至远远超过了当年先行者们的想象和人们创造的神话，人们的交流更应该注重内涵和质量。时代变了，但是交流的本质依旧。希望构建人类伦理成为今后智者对话交流的突出主题。我对此是十分乐观的。

人类总会有一天厌弃那种把民族抛进相互攻讦、威胁、厮杀的伦理和政治，创造耶稣基督、释迦牟尼和孔子所理想的新世界。

纽约尼山论坛的成功举办在联合国和美国各界引起了重要反响。联合国大会主席武克·耶雷米奇出席论坛闭幕酒会并发表重要讲话，指出"纽约尼山论坛"在联合国总部的成功举办是中国尼山论坛组委会对联合国开展文明对话工作的有力的支持，代表了这个时代的文明发展趋势，称赞这样的对话有助于消除隔阂，促进世界和平。中国驻联合国副代表王民评价说，尼山论坛在纽约联合国总部的成功举办，实现了几个第一：这是第一次由中国人到美国纽约主办的儒家与基督教文明对话；这是第一次由非政府组织进入联合国总部主办文明对话活动，而且是第一次由中国的非政府组织实现了这个在联合国历史上的第一次突破。纽约各界普遍认为，中国的尼山论坛进入纽约和联合国总部开展儒家文明与基督教文明对话，"是一个奇迹"。

纽约尼山论坛表明，直接面对面的对话有助于消除偏见、误解与误判，而且还能建立起新的友谊。美国天主教华盛顿宗教区资深元老大主教西奥多·麦卡里克枢机，以80多岁高龄到会发表演讲，许嘉璐即时回应，取得了意想不到的良好对话效果。开始麦卡里克枢机提出天下是一个大家庭、大家都是兄弟姐妹的观点；许嘉璐接着说，这正好与儒家的天人一体、民胞物与思想相暗合。麦卡里克枢机提到自己布道、传教的时候主要进行三种对话——慈爱、合作与宽恕；许嘉璐认为这正好与仁者爱人、和而不同、忠恕之道等儒家思想不谋而合。麦卡里克枢机最后总结时指出，对话通常需要通过谈话、交谈、理解、欣赏与合作五个步骤展开；许嘉璐惊叹这是历史的巧合、天意的安排，因为他曾在今年5月尼山论坛闭幕式上谈到，不同文明、不同信仰的民族进行对话的时候，需要了解对方、理解对话、欣赏对方、学习对方，然后携手共进。两人在对话中多次握手互致敬意。纽约尼山论坛举办期间，正赶上"桑迪"飓风袭击美国，纽约是飓风重灾区，许嘉璐等中国学者不避危险按时赶到纽约出席对话活动，给美国人留下了良好印象。

四、儒家文明重返世界文明中心舞台

在尼山建立"世界文明论坛"，在世界范围，包括到联合国开展儒家文明与基督教文明对话，标志着儒家文明在沉寂百年后开始大步重返世界文明中心舞台。其切入点就是参与世界文明对话。正如许嘉璐主席所反复强调的那样，西方文明（主要是指基督教文明）在经历过数百年的扩张发展后，作为世界上的唯一强势文明也为当今世界和人类未来发展带来了深重的危机。王义桅在其新著《海殇？——欧洲文明启示录》中指出，欧洲文明的一个鲜明特征是"过度扩张"及其特有的"原罪"："开放而不包容、对内多元与对外普世的双重标准、进取与破坏相伴生。"[①]这一评判是十分精到的。放眼全球，当今世界上几乎所有的深层次危机问题，都可以追溯到西方文明。这真是成也萧何败也萧何。而除了西方文明，世界上所有的其他文明，几乎都难以与西方文明平等对话，唯一有的就

---

① 转引自陈昕《改造我们的欧洲文明观》，《文汇报》2013年5月6日。

是西方文明自说自话。儒家文明差一点被打入死牢。但是在百年之后，儒家文明又奇迹般地生还和站立起来。2000 年中国加入 WTO 是一个转折点，2008 年北京举办奥运会又是一个抬升点，2010 年中国经济总量超过日本成为世界仅次于美国的第二大经济体又是一个升华点。这些都显示了儒家文明历史性的力量。早在 20 世纪 70 年代英国历史学家汤因比就对此作出过预测，到了 90 年代美国学者亨廷顿在提出"文明冲突论"时，再次把儒家文明、伊斯兰文明与基督教文明相并列，认为前两者有可能向后者提出挑战并由此引发文明冲突。这种担忧论扩展到全球并引发共鸣。此后美国"9·11"危机爆发，此后中国快速崛起，这种担忧论更加在全球弥漫开来。这实际上仍然是西方式的文明思维。但是这在全球却很有市场。因为儒家文明，或者说是中华文明，早在 1840 年就开始失去话语权了。世界对儒家文明疏离已久。即使在中国本土也是如此。但是，世界的智者，仍然看好儒家文明。因为儒家文明是历史最悠久的文明，儒家文明有处理复杂问题、多元问题、危机问题的丰富的历史经验。当西方文明对眼下的世界危机问题感到无能为力时，世界把目光转向了东方，转向了孔子和儒家文明。天人合一、和而不同、己所不欲勿施于人等等，这不正是当今世界所急切需要的文明智慧吗？而这些，早在 2500 多年前孔子就提出来了，而中国人同样地践行了 2500 多年。许嘉璐主席敏锐地捕捉到世界的需要，毅然由大都市来到尼山这个偏僻之地，举起"世界文明论坛"的大旗，发起并组织儒家文明与基督教文明的多场次对话。当然，这样的对话将是长期和持续的。儒家文明走向世界文明中心舞台，不是要试图压倒西方文明或世界其他文明，不是这样的，而是要把儒家文明的思考问题和处理问题的方式带给世界，试图告诉世人，或许我们换一种相处的方式，换一种解决危机问题的方式，我们人类的共同未来就不会那样糟。正如美国学者安靖如所说："中国文化的崛起，意味着我们理解这个变化的世界的方式，有了更多的可能性。"①

儒家文明走向世界文明中心舞台不是要回归过去，而是要面对未来、走向未来。许嘉璐指出："近几十年来，西方学术界不断提出对自身文化的质疑、批判和重构，并且这一思潮已经逐渐成为西方思想界的主流；与此同时，其中不少人开始注意东方文化，尤其是中国文化中惊人的智慧；其后，恰好中国也开始了一个重新认识自己的过程，当前所谓国学热、儒学热就是这一过程的学术表现。西方思想界的反思和对于东方文化的关注，以及中国自身对精神遗产的反刍，这三

---

① 引自安靖如《理解"中国文化的崛起"》，《人民日报》2010 年 9 月 29 日。

者将要或者已经、正在会合成一体，成为中国的和世界的思想界的最活跃的洪流，因为这是世界未来的需要，是人类摆脱人造的神话和由此而生的缠缚着人类的梦魇、争取永世和平幸福的需要，是符合人类成长、文化发展之道的历史必然。"[1] 这实际是清楚地指出了我们文明前行的方向。人类是一个大家庭，人类面临的危机就是各文明共同的危机。作为世界上历史最悠久的文明，儒家文明回归世界文明中心舞台，就是要与其他文明一道，着力于缓解人与人、人与社会、人与自然紧张到极点的关系，进而探求一种人类与自然、文明与文明之间可以和睦相处的新的文明关系，建构一个"和而不同"的和谐世界。

作者简介：

高述群：清华大学工学毕业，经济学教授，多年在孔子故乡从事儒家文明的研究与传播工作。现任山东省文物局副局长、山东省中华文化标志城规划建设办公室副主任、山东大学跨文明对话研究中心副主任。2008 年至今，在尼山世界文明论坛秘书处担任常务副秘书长，是《人类和谐宣言》的主要起草者。

---

[1] 引自许嘉璐于 2010 年 4 月 21 日在山东大学儒学高等研究院成立大会上的致辞，原文收录于《为了天下太平》，华艺出版社 2010 年版，第 190—195 页。是时起许嘉璐受聘为该院院长。

文明对话的动态与趋势

高述群

起源于 20 世纪末、发展于 21 世纪初的"文明对话"在本质上是人类文明自觉意识的普遍觉醒。"文明对话"是"文明自觉"的表达与展开。文明自觉程度越高，对话越会充分和越有实效。从这个意义上讲，本世纪勃兴的"文明对话"正在预示着一个全球性文明自觉时代的到来。换言之，21 世纪将是一个文明自觉的世纪，文明自省与文明自觉正变得越来越常态化和具有普遍性。

"文明对话"与"文明自觉"进一步昭示着另一个重要的事实：人类文明行进程式正在发生深刻的转折。"文明对话"实际已宣告：强势文明凌驾于其他文明之上的历史行将终结。因为"对话是平等的对视"①，是首先承认文明之间存在一个平等的关系，一方不可再凌驾于另一方之上；其次，对话还意味着文明之间是相互尊重的关系，没有尊卑、大小、强弱之分；其三，对话是双向的沟通，不是说教，不是单向的传输。这样的状况发展下去，无疑会结束西方文明数百年来在全世界的文明霸权地位，代之而起的是多文明平等平视的新文明时代。

互联网的快速发展、人口的快速洲际流动、全球多元势力的崛起，使得文明对话和文明自觉正在消解文明间出现对抗的危险，文明对话正在变得生活化而非学术化，文明对话不再是相互说理的博弈，而是相互包容的生活体验——因不同而包容，因不同而相互欣赏，因不同而需要对方。世界正出现一种新的文明趋向：不同文明之间正在学习如何和睦相处。

10 年反恐博弈表明，战争和恐怖行为均不能解决文明间的根本问题，世界日益需要通过文明间关系的平衡来重塑国家和民族之间的关系。文明间的关系——正在上升为重要的双边或多边关系，"文明对话"正在成为国际关系的新

---

① 杜维明做客中央电视台语。

兴范式。文明间的问题再也不能听之任之地发展下去，联合国正在把更多的精力从处理国家之间的关系转向处理文明之间的关系。

10年文明对话是一次组织性较强的有序文明对话。这一特点十分明显。这主要得力于20世纪成立的联合国。在联合国的程序里超级大国已不可能为所欲为。譬如在教科文组织，美国先是宣布退出，之后又不得不宣布进入。这表现了美国的无可奈何。在联合国主导下，全球文明对话正在表现为三个重要的态势：

第一个态势是联合国教科文组织开始致力于通过推动新人文主义来推动文明对话。在教科文组织主导的文明对话的第一阶段，即在松浦晃一郎担任总干事的10年间（1999—2009），教科文组织推动联合国为"文明对话"采取了一系列重要举措。在第二阶段，即在伊琳娜·博克娃于2009年11月担任总干事以来①，教科文组织开始把文明对话引向深入，致力于通过高扬新人文主义来推动文明对话。

第二个态势是联合国文明联盟开始把战略重心移向亚洲。2012年11月底联合国文明联盟在上海召开"亚洲及南太平洋地区磋商会议"，正式宣布文明联盟扎根亚洲开展工作。时任中国外交部副部长的崔天凯代表中国政府到会致辞，表示欢迎文明联盟扎根亚洲。文明联盟本由西班牙与土耳其联合发起，主要用于处理西方与伊斯兰之间的紧张关系。但在2007年奥特兰会议时，文明联盟就已启动了转向亚洲的程序。

第三个态势是儒家文明开始由边缘逐步走向中心舞台。"文明对话"原本导源于西方基督教文明与伊斯兰文明之间的紧张关系，当年（1998）伊朗总统哈塔米在联大提出文明对话的建议时，也是主要着眼于推动开展伊耶两大文明之间的对话。但是结果，21世纪最重要的文明对话却逐步把儒家文明推向了前台，儒家文明正在成为世界文明对话的主角。②

以上三个态势正共同指向一个方向：教科文组织推动的新人文主义，实际与儒家思想日趋接近；或者新人文主义的发展还需要儒家思想作为助力。③文明联盟推动的进入亚洲行动，实际就是进入儒家文明的腹地。而儒家文明的复

---

① 伊琳娜·博克娃任期4年，可连选连任。
② "9·11"之后，反恐牵扯了美国和西方的主要精力，使得伊耶之间的对话难以深入进行。同期，由于中国经济力的快速增长，使得美国及西方越来越把中国作为主要的竞争对手，文明之间的角力也随之展开。
③ 新人文主义的思想渊源可能在儒家这里更为深厚，当年欧洲人文主义思潮形成时就曾借力于儒家思想。

苏与复兴正好与上述两个趋向相吻合相呼应，这反过来又会进一步助推儒家文明的快速复兴。所以，趋势与走向十分明显：趋向亚洲和亚洲的多元文明。过去 10 年中，尽管世界其他地区的文明，如北欧、南美和非洲，都对文明对话表现出了浓厚的兴趣，但是在可预见的将来，世界文明对话将会主要集中在亚洲和亚洲的多元文明之间。而中国和儒家文明会不可避免地迎来更多的机会和更大的挑战。

面向未来，儒家文明无疑具有举足轻重的地位。但是迄今为止，世界各国，包括在中国国内，并没有对儒家文明在 21 世纪会扮演什么样的角色做出过认真的评估。美国、日本和西方国家，对于中国经济与军力的兴趣远远超过了对于儒家文明的兴趣。而真正改变世界的力量，必是中国的儒家文明。儒家文明重返世界舞台，将会给世界文明的发展带来根本性的影响。

历史地看，儒家文明在相当长时间内可以说是置身世外。在西方基督教文明与中东伊斯兰文明长达上千年的较量中，儒家文明几乎浑然不知。地球的第三极，喜马拉雅高原，挡住了儒家文明向西参与西方与伊斯兰纷争的视线。高原、大海、荒漠的屏障，使得儒家文明基本说来是一个相对封闭的文明。儒家文明的特殊禀赋，使得这一文明在历史的大多数时间内都不得不为生计而抗斗。主要的战争也是发生在游牧人群与农耕人群之间（期间也有倭寇长时间在沿海地区的骚扰）。影响文明发生和发展的主要因素是干旱、洪涝、地震、疾病和外敌入侵。如无上述大灾大难发生，儒家文明社会多呈现为和睦升平的安定繁荣气象。然而，儒家文明所处的自然地理环境，使得这一文明注定只能在"忧患中"过活。其中，"水患"是铸就儒家文明特质的重要因素之一。在一定意义上，儒家文明实际就是一个"治水"的文明。中国早期科学、哲学、宗教的发展，多数都与"治水"有关。战争，对于儒家文明社会是一个不得已而为之的事情。"和亲"这种柔弱的政治外交政策，代替军事，在中国实行了上千年。汉唐两个盛世，也是中国"和亲"最多的朝代。通往西域、中东和欧洲的"丝绸之路"从来都是"和平之路"而非"战争之路"。儒家文明的内敛性格在世界史的大部分时间内不为外人所知。但是在西方文明势力席卷全球之后，情况发生了根本的改变。欧洲基督教文明走向世界的历史，对于弱势文明而言，无疑是一段不堪回首的灾难史，许多文明遭遇灭顶之灾。在西方列强将要灭亡儒家文明中国的时候，不想在中国的最底层，却爆发出了数亿中国人前赴后继形成的"救亡图存"历史洪流，他们怀着儒家文明"舍生取义"的牺牲精神，毅然用 3000 多万人的生命而保全了一个文明的延续。妇女、儿童都走上了救亡的战场。儒家文明的顽强生命力再一次得到了淋漓尽致的验证。面对这段历史，"一些西方学者甚至将毛泽东称为'新的摩西'、将红军长征比作'走向应许之地'"①。这是对中国在共产党人领导下走向新的文明史的西方式诠释与认可。同样得到认可的是在第二次世界大战期间蒙难的犹太民族，他们把在二战期间救助犹太人的中国人统称为"中国的辛德勒"，以色列前总理埃胡德·奥尔默特曾说："我们很幸运，我们在两种文化——犹太文化和中华文化熏陶之下成长。犹太文化教导我们如何选择人生，中华文化教导我们如何在人生路上勇往直前。"②这就是与西方文明迥异的富有仁爱、谦恭、礼让、包容与进取精神的儒家文明。因而，一旦儒家文明出手解决世界性文明问题，问题可能会变得较为容易。礼之用，和为贵；先王之道，斯为美。何谓先王之道？即礼让之道、和睦相敬之道也。只需尊重、只需理解、只需包容，也许一切便会迎刃而解。儒家文明的天下观，在古代，只是一小局；儒家文明再次回来，其新的天下观，就是面向全球的大局了。

在 10 年文明对话中，有三方力量在推动儒家文明快速回归与复兴。第一方力量来自中国政府。中国领导人不仅使用儒家文明应对"文明对话"，使用儒家思想向世界阐明国家文明本质，而且采取多种举措把民本、和谐等儒家思想用之于政治纲领和对外政策。2003 年 12 月 11 日，温家宝在哈佛大学演讲时指出，"中华民族具有极其深厚的文化底蕴，历来酷爱和平。'和而不同'，是中国古代思想家提出的一个伟大思想。和谐而又不千篇一律，不同而又不彼此冲突；和谐以共生共长，不同以相辅相成。用'和而不同'的观点观察、处理问题，不仅有利于我们善待友邦，也有利于国际社会化解矛盾。"2005 年 9 月 16 日，胡锦涛在联合国成立 60 周年演讲中鲜明提出了"坚持包容精神，共建和谐世界"的文化主张。2010 年 2 月 27 日，温家宝与网友在线交流，集中阐述了儒家式的道德观。他说："什么是道德？其实最重要的：第一是爱人。仁者人也，仁者爱人。每个企业家或者社会的每个成员都要知道热爱群众、热爱国家。第二，要有同情心。己所不欲，勿施于人。同情是道德的基础，这在儒家哲学里头很明确地讲过。孟子说过，人无恻隐之心，非人也。他把恻隐之心作为人之端。我们的企业如果只考虑自己的利益，甚至见利忘义，把自己挣的钱建立在别人的痛苦甚至生命上，那是可悲的，也是法律不允许的。"2011 年 4 月 15 日，胡锦涛在亚洲博鳌论坛上

---

① 杨慧林：《汉学及其"主义"中的身份游移》，《读书》2012 第 2 期，第 3 页。

② 张迎辉：《一个杰出犹太家族的中国情缘——为中以建交 20 周年献礼》，《世界知识》2012 年 4 月 1 日（总 1578 期）。

提出了建立"国际文明新秩序"的主张，他阐释说："当今世界，有200多个国家和地区，2500多个民族，6000多种语言。正是这些不同民族、不同肤色、不同历史文化背景的人们，共同创造了丰富多彩的世界，就如同有了七音八调的差异，才能演奏出美妙动听的音乐。不同文明之间的对话、交流、融合，汇成了人类文明奔流不息的长河。世界文明的多样性，不仅是一种客观存在，而且有益于世界文明的进步。所以，世界上的人们，都要尊重世界文明的多样性，在多样中求同一，在差异中求和谐，在交流中求发展。这样的世界，才能赢得长久和平与发展。"同年6月27日，温家宝在英国皇家学会发表演讲时重温了社会学家费孝通"各美其美，美人之美，美美与共，世界大同"的名言，表示"费老先生的这一人生感悟，生动反映了当代中国人开放包容的胸怀"。第二方力量来自海外，这其中杜维明等发挥了关键性作用。10年文明对话期间，杜维明等活跃于世界各地，他们向世界介绍儒家文明，向世界传播儒家思想和中华文化，恢复了儒家文明与基督教文明、与伊斯兰文明对话的尊严与地位。第三方力量来自中国的民间，包括大陆和港、澳、台地区。各方力量积极活跃，初步促成了百家争鸣、学术繁荣的景象，使儒家文明迅速回归中国本土。这其间许嘉璐在尼山领导的儒家文明与不同文明对话具有标志性意义，联合国各机构对尼山论坛的欢迎实际是迎接儒家文明重返世界文明中心舞台的文明自觉表现。

未来10年的文明对话无疑会以亚洲为中心舞台向世界各地展开。教科文组织关于新人文主义的推动将会在亚洲取得深入。联合国文明联盟在亚洲的发展将会把亚洲诸文明进一步联系起来。儒家文明在其中将会扮演文明对话轴心的作用。世界其他文明地区，如非洲、拉丁美洲、北欧等地区也会不同程度地加入进来。世界各文明古国、世界各文明主体也会加速向亚洲聚拢，并最终促成"和而不同"的文明大联盟，胡锦涛阐述的"世界文明新秩序"有可能在这个进程中得以孕育与形成。这其中的关键还是要看儒家文明如何作为。儒家文明在亚洲发挥建设性作用具有深厚的历史基础，不仅在本土有儒释道的结合，在亚洲各区域，如韩国、新加坡、泰国、越南等地，也具有"儒家文化圈"的历史联系。儒家文明可能会与联合国等多方面力量合作，以孔子、曲阜、儒学为纽带，向东跨越太平洋、大西洋与美洲、欧洲各文明建立更加密切的联系，向西跨越喜马拉雅高原与印度和阿拉伯文明发展传统友谊，向文明古国和世界其他文明，如非洲文明，寻求建立全新的文明关系。新的对话可能会从亚洲以外的诸文明入手，在取得经验和累积成果后，再推动亚洲诸文明形成共识与发展。但是主要的对话空间，无疑会集中在亚洲和周边的广大地区。

跋

徐向红

在尼山世界文明论坛组委会与孔子学院总部筹备在法国巴黎联合国教科文组织总部举行"巴黎尼山世界文明论坛"时，本报告即在酝酿之中。因为在 10 年前，正是在教科文组织的积极推动下，本世纪才出现了蔚为壮观的几乎波及全球各大文明的不同文明对话行动。许嘉璐主席及尼山世界文明论坛各位副主席对这项十分艰难的学术工作给予期许。在这个过程中，本报告得到了山东大学儒学高等研究院的鼎力支持，进而又得到杜维明、沈清松、孔汉思等国际学术大师的指导。这是本报告得以面世的重要基础。尤其，在炎热的夏季，许嘉璐主席为本报告撰写了长篇序言，这令我们十分地钦敬。在研究过程中，山东大学的谢文郁教授发挥了主要作用，他和高述群教授共同完成了本报告的学术组织工作。在谢文郁教授主导下，刘铁娃、张贵洪、倪培民、谭明冉、高述群完成了各章的撰写工作，前后历时一年有余。山东大学的一些学生参与了本报告的研究工作，附录部分主要是他们的辛劳与贡献。

诚如许嘉璐主席所说，"对文明对话的研究，是全新的课题"。在本报告将要付梓出版之际，作为尼山世界文明论坛的高端学术智库，山东大学跨文明对话研究中心即将在泉城济南挂牌成立，这将掀开尼山世界文明论坛组织学术研究的新的一页。我们会继续跟踪研究全球性的跨文明对话行动，并祝愿这样的行动能够掀开人类文明发展的新的篇章。

限于我们的能力，本报告在材料上或观点上难免会有纰漏和错谬之处，敬请读者批评指正。

2013 年 8 月
于尼山世界文明论坛秘书处

附　录

附录一:

世界文化多样性宣言

*(2001 年 11 月 2 日联合国教育、科学及文化组织大会
第三十一届会议通过)*

　　大会重视充分实现《世界人权宣言》和 1966 年关于公民权利和政治权利及关于经济、社会与文化权利的两项国际公约等其他普遍认同的法律文件中宣布的人权与基本自由,忆及教科文组织《组织法》序言确认"……文化之广泛传播以及为争取正义、自由与和平对人类进行之教育为维护人类尊严不可缺少的举措,亦为一切国家关切互助之精神,必须履行之神圣义务",还忆及《组织法》第一条特别规定教科文组织的宗旨之一是,建议"订立必要之国际协定,以便于运用文字与图像促进思想之自由交流",参照教科文组织颁布的国际文件中涉及文化多样性和行使文化权利的各项条款,重申应把文化视为某个社会或某个社会群体特有的精神与物质,智力与情感方面的不同特点之总和;除了文学和艺术外,文化还包括生活方式、共处的方式、价值观体系,传统和信仰,注意到文化是当代就特性、社会凝聚力和以知识为基础的经济发展问题展开的辩论的焦点,确认在相互信任和理解氛围下,尊重文化多样性、宽容、对话及合作是国际和平与安全的最佳保障之一,希望在承认文化多样性、认识到人类是一个统一的整体和发展文化间交流的基础上开展更广泛的团结互助,认为尽管受到新的信息和传播技术的迅速发展积极推动的全球化进程对文化多样性是一种挑战,但也为各种文化和文明之间进行新的对话创造了条件,认识到教科文组织在联合国系统中担负着保护和促进丰富多彩的文化多样性的特殊职责。

　　宣布下述原则并通过本宣言:

特性、多样性和多元化

第 1 条:文化多样性——人类的共同遗产

　　文化在不同的时代和不同的地方具有各种不同的表现形式。这种多样性的具体表现是构成人类的各群体和各社会的特性所具有的独特性和多样化。文化多样

93

性是交流、革新和创作的源泉，对人类来讲就像生物多样性对维持生物平衡那样必不可少。从这个意义上讲，文化多样性是人类的共同遗产，应当从当代人和子孙后代的利益考虑予以承认和肯定。

第2条：从文化多样性到文化多元化

在日益走向多样化的当今社会中必须确保属于多元的、不同的和发展的文化特性的个人和群体的和睦关系和共处。主张所有公民的融入和参与的政策是增强社会凝聚力、民间社会活力及维护和平的可靠保障。因此，这种文化多元化是与文化多样性这一客观现实相应的一套政策。文化多元化与民主制度密不可分，它有利于文化交流和能够充实公众生活的创作能力的发挥。

第3条：文化多样性——发展的因素

文化多样性增加了每个人的选择机会；它是发展的源泉之一，它不仅是促进经济增长的因素，而且还是享有令人满意的智力、情感、道德精神生活的手段。

文化多样性与人权

第4条：人权——文化多样性的保障

捍卫文化多样性是伦理方面的迫切需要，与尊重人的尊严是密不可分的，它要求人们必须尊重人权和基本自由，特别是尊重少数人群体和土著人民的各种权利。任何人不得以文化多样性为由，损害受国际法保护的人权或限制其范围。

第5条：文化权利——文化多样性的有利条件

文化权利是人权的一个组成部分，它们是一致的、不可分割的和相互依存的。富有创造力的多样性的发展，要求充分地实现《世界人权宣言》第27条和《经济、社会、文化权利国际公约》第13条和第15条所规定的文化权利。因此，每个人都应当能够用其选择的语言，特别是用自己的母语来表达自己的思想，进行创作和传播自己的作品；每个人都有权接受充分尊重其文化特性的优质教育和培训；每个人都应当能够参加其选择的文化生活和从事自己所特有的文化活动，但必须在尊重人权和基本自由的范围内。

第6条：促进面向所有人的文化多样性

在保障思想通过文字和图像的自由交流的同时，务必使所有的文化都能表现自己和宣传自己，言论自由，传媒的多元化，语言多元化，平等享有各种艺术表现形式，科学和技术知识——包括数码知识——以及所有文化都有利用表达和传播手段的机会等，均是文化多样性的可靠保证。

文化多样性与创作

第 7 条：文化遗产——创作的源泉

每项创作都来源于有关的文化传统，但也在同其他文化传统的交流中得到充分的发展。因此，各种形式的文化遗产都应当作为人类的经历和期望的见证得到保护、开发利用和代代相传，以支持各种创作和建立各种文化之间的真正对话。

第 8 条：文化物品和文化服务——不同一般的商品

面对目前为创作和革新开辟了广阔前景的经济和技术的发展变化，应当特别注意创作意愿的多样性，公正地考虑作者和艺术家的权利，以及文化物品和文化服务的特殊性，因为它们体现的是特性、价值观和观念，不应被视为一般的商品或消费品。

第 9 条：文化政策——推动创作的积极因素

文化政策应当在确保思想和作品的自由交流的情况下，利用那些有能力在地方和世界一级发挥其作用的文化产业，创造有利于生产和传播文化物品和文化服务的条件。每个国家都应在遵守其国际义务的前提下，制订本国的文化政策，并采取其认为最为合适的行动方法，即不管是在行动上给予支持还是制定必要的规章制度，来实施这一政策。

文化多样性与国际团结

第 10 条：增强世界范围的创作和传播能力

面对目前世界上文化物品的流通和交换所存在的失衡现象，必须加强国际合作和国际团结，使所有国家，尤其是发展中国家和转型期国家能够开办一些有活力、在本国和国际上都具有竞争力的文化产业。

第 11 条：建立政府、私营部门和民间社会之间的合作伙伴关系

单靠市场的作用是做不到保护和促进文化多样性这一可持续发展之保证的。为此，必须重申政府在私营部门和民间社会的合作下推行有关政策所具有的首要作用。

第 12 条：教科文组织的作用

教科文组织根据其职责和职能，应当：

（a）促进各政府间机构在制定发展方面的战略时考虑本宣言中陈述的原则；

（b）充任各国、各政府和非政府国际组织、民间社会及私营部门之间为共同确定文化多样性的概念、目标和政策所需要的联系和协商机构；

（c）继续在其与本宣言有关的各主管领域中开展制定准则的行动、提高认识和培养能力的行动；

（d）为实施其要点附于本宣言之后的行动计划提供便利。

保护和促进文化表现形式多样性公约

(2005 年 10 月 20 日联合国教育、科学及文化组织
第三十三届会议通过）序言

联合国教育、科学及文化组织大会于 2005 年 10 月 3 日至 21 日在巴黎举行第三十三届会议：

（一）确认文化多样性是人类的一项基本特性；

（二）认识到文化多样性是人类的共同遗产，应当为了全人类的利益对其加以珍爱和维护；

（三）意识到文化多样性创造了一个多姿多彩的世界，它使人类有了更多的选择，得以提高自己的能力和形成价值观，并因此成为各社区、各民族和各国可持续发展的一股主要推动力；

（四）忆及在民主、宽容、社会公正以及各民族和各文化间相互尊重的环境中繁荣发展起来的文化多样性对于地方、国家和国际层面的和平与安全是不可或缺的；

（五）颂扬文化多样性对充分实现《世界人权宣言》和其他公认的文书主张的人权和基本自由所具有的重要意义；

（六）强调需要把文化作为一个战略要素纳入国家和国际发展政策以及国际发展合作之中，同时也要考虑特别强调消除贫困的《联合国千年宣言》(2000 年)；

（七）考虑到文化在不同时间和空间具有多样形式，这种多样性体现为人类各民族和各社会文化特征和文化表现形式的独特性和多元性；

（八）承认作为非物质和物质财富来源的传统知识的重要性，特别是原住民知识体系的重要性，其对可持续发展的积极贡献及其得到充分保护和促进的需要；

（九）认识到需要采取措施保护文化表现形式连同其内容的多样性，特别是当文化表现形式有可能遭到灭绝或受到严重损害时；

（十）强调文化对社会凝聚力的重要性，尤其是对提高妇女的社会地位、发

挥其社会作用所具有的潜在影响力;

（十一）意识到文化多样性通过思想的自由交流得到加强，通过文化间的不断交流和互动得到滋养;

（十二）重申思想、表达和信息自由以及传媒多样性使各种文化表现形式得以在社会中繁荣发展;

（十三）认识到文化表现形式，包括传统文化表现形式的多样性，是个人和各民族能够表达并同他人分享自己的思想和价值观的重要因素;

（十四）忆及语言多样性是文化多样性的基本要素之一，并重申教育在保护和促进文化表现形式中发挥着重要作用;

（十五）考虑到文化活力的重要性，包括对少数民族和原住民人群中的个体的重要性，这种重要的活力体现为创造、传播、销售及获取其传统文化表现形式的自由，以有益于他们自身的发展;

（十六）强调文化互动和文化创造力对滋养和革新文化表现形式所发挥的关键作用，他们也会增强那些为社会整体进步而参与文化发展的人们所发挥的作用;

（十七）认识到知识产权对支持文化创造的参与者具有重要意义;

（十八）确信传递着文化特征、价值观和意义的文化活动、产品与服务具有经济和文化双重性质，故不应视为仅具商业价值;

（十九）注意到信息和传播技术飞速发展所推动的全球化进程为加强各种文化互动创造了前所未有的条件，但同时也对文化多样性构成挑战，尤其是可能在富国与穷国之间造成种种失衡;

（二十）意识到联合国教科文组织肩负的特殊使命，即确保对文化多样性的尊重以及建议签订有助于推动通过语言和图像进行自由思想交流的各种国际协定;

（二十一）根据联合国教科文组织通过的有关文化多样性和行使文化权利的各种国际文书的条款，特别是 2001 年通过的《世界文化多样性宣言》，于 2005 年 10 月 20 日通过本公约。

第一章　目标与指导原则

第一条　目　标

本公约的目标是:

（一）保护和促进文化表现形式的多样性;

（二）以互利的方式为各种文化的繁荣发展和自由互动创造条件；

（三）鼓励不同文化间的对话，以保证世界上的文化交流更广泛和均衡，促进不同文化间的相互尊重与和平文化建设；

（四）加强文化间性，本着在各民族间架设桥梁的精神开展文化互动；

（五）促进地方、国家和国际层面对文化表现形式多样性的尊重，并提高对其价值的认识；

（六）确认文化与发展之间的联系对所有国家，特别是对发展中国家的重要性，并支持为确保承认这种联系的真正价值而在国内和国际采取行动；

（七）承认文化活动、产品与服务具有传递文化特征、价值观和意义的特殊性；

（八）重申各国拥有在其领土上维持、采取和实施他们认为合适的保护和促进文化表现形式多样性的政策和措施的主权；

（九）本着伙伴精神，加强国际合作与团结，特别是要提高发展中国家保护和促进文化表现形式多样性的能力。

第二条　指导原则

一、尊重人权和基本自由原则

只有确保人权，以及表达、信息和交流等基本自由，并确保个人可以选择文化表现形式，才能保护和促进文化多样性。任何人都不得援引本公约的规定侵犯《世界人权宣言》规定的或受到国际法保障的人权和基本自由或限制其适用范围。

二、主权原则

根据《联合国宪章》和国际法原则，各国拥有在其境内采取保护和促进文化表现形式多样性措施和政策的主权。

三、所有文化同等尊严和尊重原则

保护与促进文化表现形式多样性的前提是承认所有文化，包括少数民族和原住民的文化在内，具有同等尊严，并应受到同等尊重。

四、国际团结与合作原则

国际合作与团结的目的应当是使各个国家，尤其是发展中国家都有能力在地方、国家和国际层面上创建和加强其文化表现手段，包括其新兴的或成熟的文化产业。

五、经济和文化发展互补原则

文化是发展的主要推动力之一，所以文化的发展与经济的发展同样重要，且所有个人和民族都有权参与两者的发展并从中获益。

六、可持续发展原则

文化多样性是个人和社会的一种财富。保护、促进和维护文化多样性是当代和后代的可持续发展的一项基本要求。

七、平等享有原则

平等享有全世界丰富多样的文化表现形式，所有文化享有各种表现形式和传播手段，是增进文化多样性和促进相互理解的要素。

八、开放和平衡原则

在采取措施维护文化表现形式多样性时，各国应寻求以适当的方式促进向世界其他文化开放，并确保这些措施符合本公约的目标。

第二章　适用范围

第三条　公约的适用范围

本公约适用于缔约方采取的有关保护和促进文化表现形式多样性的政策和措施。

第三章　定　义

第四条　定　义

在本公约中，应作如下理解：

（一）文化多样性

"文化多样性"指各群体和社会借以表现其文化的多种不同形式。这些表现形式在他们内部及其间传承。

文化多样性不仅体现在人类文化遗产通过丰富多彩的文化表现形式来表达、弘扬和传承的多种方式，也体现在借助各种方式和技术进行的艺术创造、生产、传播、销售和消费的多种方式。

（二）文化内容

"文化内容"指源于文化特征或表现文化特征的象征意义、艺术特色和文化价值。

（三）文化表现形式

"文化表现形式"指个人、群体和社会创造的具有文化内容的表现形式。

（四）文化活动、产品与服务

"文化活动、产品与服务"是指从其具有的特殊属性、用途或目的考虑时，体现或传达文化表现形式的活动、产品与服务，无论它们是否具有商业价值。文化活动可能以自身为目的，也可能是为文化产品与服务的生产提供帮助。

（五）文化产业

"文化产业"指生产和销售上述第（四）项所述的文化产品或服务的产业。

（六）文化政策和措施

"文化政策和措施"指地方、国家、区域或国际层面上针对文化本身或为了对个人、群体或社会的文化表现形式产生直接影响的各项政策和措施，包括与创作、生产、传播、销售和享有文化活动、产品与服务相关的政策和措施。

（七）保　护

名词"保护"意指为保存、卫护和加强文化表现形式多样性而采取措施。动词"保护"意指采取这类措施。

（八）文化间性

"文化间性"指不同文化的存在与平等互动，以及通过对话和相互尊重产生共同文化表现形式的可能性。

第四章　缔约方的权利和义务

第五条　权利和义务的一般规则

一、缔约方根据《联合国宪章》、国际法原则及国际公认的人权文书，重申拥有为实现本公约的宗旨而制定和实施其文化政策、采取措施以保护和促进文化表现形式多样性及加强国际合作的主权。

二、当缔约方在其境内实施政策和采取措施以保护和促进文化表现形式的多样性时，这些政策和措施应与本公约的规定相符。

第六条　缔约方在本国的权利

一、各缔约方可在第四条第（六）项所定义的文化政策和措施范围内，根据自身的特殊情况和需求，在其境内采取措施保护和促进文化表现形式的多样性。

二、这类措施可包括：

（一）为了保护和促进文化表现形式的多样性所采取的管理性措施；

（二）以适当方式在本国境内的所有文化活动、产品与服务中为本国的文化活动、产品与服务提供创作、生产、传播、销售和享有的机会的措施，包括规定上述活动、产品与服务所使用的语言；

（三）为国内独立的文化产业和非正规产业部门活动能有效获取生产、传播和销售文化活动、产品与服务的手段采取的措施；

（四）提供公共财政资助的措施；

（五）鼓励非营利组织以及公共和私人机构、艺术家及其他文化专业人员发展和促进思想、文化表现形式、文化活动、产品与服务的自由交流和流通，以及在这些活动中激励创新精神和积极进取精神的措施；

（六）建立并适当支持公共机构的措施；

（七）培育并支持参与文化表现形式创作活动的艺术家和其他人员的措施；

（八）旨在加强媒体多样性的措施，包括运用公共广播服务。

第七条 促进文化表现形式的措施

一、缔约方应努力在其境内创造环境，鼓励个人和社会群体：

（一）创作、生产、传播、销售和获取他们自己的文化表现形式，同时对妇女及不同社会群体，包括少数民族和原住民的特殊情况和需求给予应有的重视；

（二）获取本国境内及世界其他国家的各种不同的文化表现形式。

二、缔约方还应努力承认艺术家、参与创作活动的其他人员、文化界以及支持他们工作的有关组织的重要贡献，以及他们在培育文化表现形式多样性方面的核心作用。

第八条 保护文化表现形式的措施

一、在不影响第五条和第六条规定的前提下，缔约一方可以确定其领土上哪些文化表现形式属于面临消亡危险、受到严重威胁或是需要紧急保护的情况。

二、缔约方可通过与本公约的规定相符的方式，采取一切恰当的措施保护处于第一款所述情况下的文化表现形式。

三、缔约方应向政府间委员会报告为应对这类紧急情况所采取的所有措施，该委员会则可以对此提出合适的建议。

第九条 信息共享和透明度

缔约方应：

（一）在向联合国教科文组织四年一度的报告中，提供其在本国境内和国际层面为保护和促进文化表现形式多样性所采取的措施的适当信息；

（二）指定一处联络点，负责共享有关本公约的信息；

（三）共享和交流有关保护和促进文化表现形式多样性的信息。

第十条 教育和公众认知

缔约方应：

（一）鼓励和提高对保护和促进文化表现形式多样性重要意义的理解，尤其是通过教育和提高公众认知的计划；

（二）为实现本条的宗旨与其他缔约方和相关国际组织及地区组织开展合作；

（三）通过制定文化产业方面的教育、培训和交流计划，致力于鼓励创作和提高生产能力，但所采取的措施不能对传统生产形式产生负面影响。

第十一条　公民社会的参与

缔约方承认公民社会在保护和促进文化表现形式多样性方面的重要作用。缔约方应鼓励公民社会积极参与其为实现本公约各项目标所作的努力。

第十二条　促进国际合作

缔约方应致力于加强双边、区域和国际合作，创造有利于促进文化表现形式多样性的条件，同时特别考虑第八条和第十七条所述情况，以便着重：

（一）促进缔约方之间开展文化政策和措施的对话；

（二）通过开展专业和国际文化交流及有关成功经验的交流，增强公共文化部门战略管理能力；

（三）加强与公民社会、非政府组织和私人部门及其内部的伙伴关系，以鼓励和促进文化表现形式的多样性；

（四）提倡应用新技术，鼓励发展伙伴关系以加强信息共享和文化理解，促进文化表现形式的多样性；

（五）鼓励缔结共同生产和共同销售的协定。

第十三条　将文化纳入可持续发展

缔约方应致力于将文化纳入其各级发展政策，创造有利于可持续发展的条件，并在此框架内完善与保护和促进文化表现形式多样性相关的各个环节。

第十四条　为发展而合作

缔约方应致力于支持为促进可持续发展和减轻贫困而开展合作，尤其要关注发展中国家的特殊需要，主要通过以下途径来推动形成富有活力的文化部门：

（一）通过以下方式加强发展中国家的文化产业：

1. 建立和加强发展中国家文化生产和销售能力；

2. 推动其文化活动、产品与服务更多地进入全球市场和国际销售网络；

3. 促使形成有活力的地方市场和区域市场；

4. 尽可能在发达国家采取适当措施，为发展中国家的文化活动、产品与服务进入这些国家提供方便；

5. 尽可能支持发展中国家艺术家的创作，促进他们的流动；

6. 鼓励发达国家与发展中国家之间开展适当的协作，特别是在音乐和电影领域。

（二）通过在发展中国家开展信息、经验和专业知识交流以及人力资源培训，加强公共和私人部门的能力建设，尤其是在战略管理能力、政策制定和实施、文化表现形式的促进和推广、中小企业和微型企业的发展、技术的应用及技能开发与转让等方面。

（三）通过采取适当的鼓励措施来推动技术和专门知识的转让，尤其是在文化产业和文化企业领域。

（四）通过以下方式提供财政支持：

1. 根据第十八条的规定设立文化多样性国际基金；

2. 提供官方发展援助，必要时包括提供技术援助，以激励和支持创作；

3. 提供其他形式的财政援助，比如提供低息贷款、赠款以及其他资金机制。

第十五条　协作安排

缔约方应鼓励在公共、私人部门和非营利组织之间及其内部发展伙伴关系，以便与发展中国家合作，增强他们在保护和促进文化表现形式多样性方面的能力。这类新型伙伴关系应根据发展中国家的实际需求，注重基础设施建设、人力资源开发和政策制定，以及文化活动、产品与服务的交流。

第十六条　对发展中国家的优惠待遇

发达国家应通过适当的机构和法律框架，为发展中国家的艺术家和其他文化专业人员及从业人员，以及那里的文化产品和文化服务提供优惠待遇，促进与这些国家的文化交流。

第十七条　在文化表现形式受到严重威胁情况下的国际合作

在第八条所述情况下，缔约方应开展合作，相互提供援助，特别要援助发展中国家。

第十八条　文化多样性国际基金

一、兹建立"文化多样性国际基金"（以下简称基金）。

二、根据教科文组织《财务条例》，此项基金为信托基金。

三、基金的资金来源为：

（一）缔约方的自愿捐款；

（二）教科文组织大会为此划拨的资金；

（三）其他国家、联合国系统组织和计划署、其他地区和国际组织、公共和私人部门以及个人的捐款、赠款和遗赠；

（四）基金产生的利息；

（五）为基金组织募捐或其他活动的收入；

（六）基金条例许可的所有其他资金来源。

四、政府间委员会应根据缔约方大会确定的指导方针决定基金资金的使用。

五、对已获政府间委员会批准的具体项目，政府间委员会可以接受为实现这些项目的整体目标或具体目标而提供的捐款及其他形式的援助。

六、捐赠不得附带任何与本公约目标不相符的政治、经济或其他条件。

七、缔约方应努力定期为实施本公约提供自愿捐款。

第十九条　信息交流、分析和传播

一、缔约方同意，就有关文化表现形式多样性以及对其保护和促进方面的先进经验的数据收集和统计，开展信息交流和共享专业知识。

二、教科文组织应利用秘书处现有的机制，促进各种相关的信息、统计数据和先进经验的收集、分析和传播。

三、教科文组织还应建立一个文化表现形式领域内各类部门和政府组织、私人及非营利组织的数据库，并更新其内容。

四、为了便于收集数据，教科文组织应特别重视申请援助的缔约方的能力建设和专业知识积累。

五、本条涉及的信息收集应作为第九条规定的信息收集的补充。

第五章　与其他法律文书的关系

第二十条　与其他条约的关系：相互支持，互为补充和不隶属

一、缔约方承认，他们应善意履行其在本公约及其为缔约方的其他所有条约中的义务。因此，在本公约不隶属于其他条约的情况下：

（一）缔约方应促使本公约与其为缔约方的其他条约相互支持；

（二）缔约方解释和实施其为缔约方的其他条约或承担其他国际义务时应考虑到本公约的相关规定。

二、本公约的任何规定不得解释为变更缔约方在其为缔约方的其他条约中的权利和义务。

第二十一条　国际磋商与协调

缔约方承诺在其他国际场合倡导本公约的宗旨和原则。为此，缔约方在需要时应进行相互磋商，并牢记这些目标与原则。

第六章　公约的机构

第二十二条　缔约方大会

一、应设立一个缔约方大会。缔约方大会应为本公约的全会和最高权力机构。

二、缔约方大会全会每两年一次，尽可能与联合国教科文组织大会同期举行。缔约方大会作出决定，或政府间委员会收到至少三分之一缔约方的请求，缔约方大会可召开特别会议。

三、缔约方大会应通过自己的议事规则。

四、缔约方大会的职能应主要包括以下方面：

（一）选举政府间委员会的成员；

（二）接受并审议由政府间委员会转交的缔约方报告；

（三）核准政府间委员会根据缔约方大会的要求拟订的操作指南；

（四）采取其认为有必要的其他措施来推进本公约的目标。

第二十三条　政府间委员会

一、应在联合国教科文组织内设立"保护与促进文化表现形式多样性政府间委员会"（以下简称政府间委员会）。政府间委员会由缔约方大会在本公约根据其第二十九条规定生效后选出的 18 个本公约缔约国的代表组成，任期四年。

二、政府间委员会每年举行一次会议。

三、政府间委员会根据缔约方大会的授权和在其指导下运作并向其负责。

四、一旦公约缔约方数目达到 50 个，政府间委员会的成员应增至 24 名。

五、政府间委员会成员的选举应遵循公平的地理代表性以及轮换的原则。

六、在不影响本公约赋予它的其他职责的前提下，政府间委员会的职责如下：

（一）促进本公约目标，鼓励并监督公约的实施；

（二）应缔约方大会要求，起草并提交缔约方大会核准履行和实施公约条款的操作指南；

（三）向缔约方大会转交公约缔约方的报告，并随附评论及报告内容概要；

（四）根据公约的有关规定，特别是第八条规定，对公约缔约方提请关注的情况提出适当的建议；

（五）建立磋商程序和其他机制，以在其他国际场合倡导本公约的目标和原则；

（六）执行缔约方大会可能要求的其他任务。

七、政府间委员会根据其议事规则，可随时邀请公共或私人组织或个人参加就具体问题举行的磋商会议。

八、政府间委员会应制定并提交缔约方大会核准自己的议事规则。

第二十四条 联合国教科文组织秘书处

一、联合国教科文组织秘书处应为本公约的有关机构提供协助。

二、秘书处编制缔约方大会和政府间委员会的文件及其会议的议程，协助实施会议的决定，并报告缔约方大会决定的实施情况。

第七章 最后条款

第二十五条 争端的解决

一、公约缔约方之间关于本公约的解释或实施产生的争端，应通过谈判寻求解决。

二、如果有关各方不能通过谈判达成一致，可共同寻求第三方斡旋或要求第三方调停。

三、如果没有进行斡旋或调停，或者协商、斡旋或调停均未能解决争端，一方可根据本公约附件所列的程序要求调解。相关各方应善意考虑调解委员会为解决争端提出的建议。

四、任何缔约方均可在批准、接受、核准或加入本公约时，声明不承认上述调解程序。任何发表这一声明的缔约方，可随时通知教科文组织总干事，宣布撤回该声明。

第二十六条 会员国批准、接受、核准或加入

一、联合国教科文组织会员国依据各自的宪法程序批准、接受、核准或加入本公约。

二、批准书、接受书、核准书或加入书应交联合国教科文组织总干事保存。

第二十七条 加 入

一、所有非联合国教科文组织会员国，但为联合国或其任何一个专门机构成员的国家，经联合国教科文组织大会邀请，均可加入本公约。

二、任何经联合国承认享有充分内部自治，并有权处理本公约范围内的事宜，包括有权就这些事宜签署协议，但按联合国大会第 1514（XV）号决议没有完全独立的地区，也可以加入本公约。

三、对区域经济一体化组织适用如下规定：

（一）任何一个区域经济一体化组织均可加入本公约，除以下各项规定外，这类组织应以与缔约国相同的方式，完全受本公约规定的约束；

（二）如果这类组织的一个或数个成员国也是本公约的缔约国，该组织与这一或这些成员国应确定在履行公约规定的义务上各自承担的责任。责任的分担应

在完成第（三）项规定的书面通知程序后生效，该组织与成员国无权同时行使公约规定的权利。此外，经济一体化组织在其权限范围内，行使与其参加本公约的成员国数目相同的表决权。如果其任何一个成员国行使其表决权，此类组织则不应行使表决权，反之亦然。

（三）同意按照第（二）项规定分担责任的区域经济一体化组织及其一个或数个成员国，应按以下方式将所建议的责任分担通知各缔约方：

1. 该组织在加入书内，应具体声明对本公约管辖事项责任的分担；

2. 在各自承担的责任变更时，该经济一体化组织应将拟议的责任变更通知保管人，保管人应将此变更通报各缔约方。

（四）已成为本公约缔约国的区域经济一体化组织的成员国在其没有明确声明或通知保管人将管辖权转给该组织的所有领域，应被推定为仍然享有管辖权。

（五）"区域经济一体化组织"，系指由作为联合国或其任何一个专门机构成员国的主权国家组成的组织，这些国家已将其在本公约所辖领域的权限转移给该组织，并且该组织已按其内部程序获得适当授权成为本公约的缔约方。

四、加入书应交存联合国教科文组织总干事处。

第二十八条　联络点

在成为本公约缔约方时，每一缔约方应指定第九条所述的联络点。

第二十九条　生　效

一、本公约在第三十份批准书、接受书、核准书或加入书交存之日起的三个月后生效，但只针对在该日或该日之前交存批准书、接受书、核准书或加入书的国家或区域经济一体化组织。对其他缔约方，本公约则在其批准书、接受书、核准书或加入书交存之日起的三个月之后生效。

二、就本条而言，一个区域经济一体化组织交存的任何文书不得在该组织成员国已交存文书之外另行计算。

第三十条　联邦制或非单一立宪制

鉴于国际协定对无论采取何种立宪制度的缔约方具有同等约束力，对实行联邦制或非单一立宪制的缔约方实行下述规定：

（一）对于在联邦或中央立法机构的法律管辖下实施的本公约各项条款，联邦或中央政府的义务与非联邦国家的缔约方的义务相同；

（二）对于在构成联邦，但按照联邦立宪制无须采取立法手段的单位，如州、成员国、省或行政区的法律管辖下实施的本公约各项条款，联邦政府须将这些条款连同其关于采用这些条款的建议一并通知各个州、成员国、省或行政区等单位的主管当局。

第三十一条 退 约

一、本公约各缔约方均可宣布退出本公约。

二、退约决定须以书面形式通知，有关文件交存联合国教科文组织总干事处。

三、退约在收到退约书十二个月后开始生效。退约国在退约生效之前的财政义务不受任何影响。

第三十二条 保管职责

联合国教科文组织总干事作为本公约的保管人，应将第二十六条和第二十七条规定的所有批准书、接受书、核准书或加入书和第三十一条规定的退约书的交存情况通告本组织各会员国、第二十七条提到的非会员国和区域经济一体化组织以及联合国。

第三十三条 修 正

一、本公约缔约方可通过给总干事的书面函件，提出对本公约的修正。总干事应将此类函件周知全体缔约方。如果通知发出的六个月内对上述要求做出积极反应的成员国不少于半数，总干事则可将公约修正建议提交下一届缔约方大会进行讨论或通过。

二、对公约的修正须经出席并参加表决的缔约方三分之二多数票通过。

三、对本公约的修正一旦获得通过，须交各缔约方批准、接受、核准或加入。

四、对于批准、接受、核准或加入修正案的缔约方来说，本公约修正案在三分之二的缔约方递交本条第三款所提及的文件之日起三个月后生效。此后，对任何批准、接受、核准或加入该公约修正案的缔约方来说，在其递交批准书、接受书、核准书或加入书之日起三个月之后，本公约修正案生效。

五、第三款及第四款所述程序不适用第二十三条所述政府间委员会成员国数目的修改。该类修改一经通过即生效。

六、在公约修正案按本条第四款生效之后加入本公约的那些第二十七条所指的国家或区域经济一体化组织，如未表示异议，则应：

（一）被视为经修正的本公约的缔约方；

（二）但在与不受修正案约束的任何缔约方的关系中，仍被视为未经修正的公约的缔约方。

第三十四条　有效文本

本公约用阿拉伯文、中文、英文、法文、俄文和西班牙文制定，六种文本具有同等效力。

第三十五条　登　记

根据《联合国宪章》第一百零二条的规定，本公约将应联合国教科文组织总干事的要求交联合国秘书处登记。

附　件：

调解程序

第一条　调解委员会

应争议一方的请求成立调解委员会。除非各方另有约定，委员会应由5名成员组成，有关各方各指定其中2名，受指定的成员再共同选定1名主席。

第二条　委员会成员

如果争议当事方超过两方，利益一致的各方应共同协商指定代表自己的委员会成员。如果两方或更多方利益各不相同，或对是否拥有一致利益无法达成共识，则各方应分别指定代表自己的委员会成员。

第三条　成员的任命

在提出成立调解委员会请求之日起的两个月内，如果某一方未指定其委员会成员，联合国教科文组织总干事可在提出调解请求一方的要求下，在随后的两个月内做出任命。

第四条　委员会主席

如果调解委员会在最后一名成员获得任命后的两个月内未选定主席，联合国教科文组织总干事可在一方要求下，在随后的两个月内指定一位主席。

第五条　决　定

调解委员会根据其成员的多数表决票做出决定。除非争议各方另有约定，委员会应确定自己的议事规则。委员会应就解决争议提出建议，争议各方应善意考虑委员会提出的建议。

第六条　分　歧

对是否属于调解委员会的权限出现分歧时，由委员会作出决定。

附录三：

"文明联盟"高级名人小组报告

(2006 年 11 月 13 日)

一、弥合世界鸿沟

1.1 我们这个世界严重失衡，已经到了令人惊恐的程度。对许多人而言，20世纪带来了前所未有的进步、繁荣、自由，而对其他人来说，20世纪却标志着一个征服、屈辱、被剥夺的时代。我们这个世界充满了巨大的不平等和矛盾性。在这一世界上，最富有的三个人的收入超过了世界最不发达国家的总收入；虽然现代医药每天创造着奇迹，可是有 300 万人每年死于可预防的疾病；虽然我们比以往任何时候都更加了解遥远的宇宙，但仍有 1.3 亿个儿童无法获得教育机会；虽然存在着各种多边的公约与机构，然而，国际社会在面对冲突和大屠杀时经常显得无能为力。对于人类中的大多数来说，免于饥饿、免于恐惧依然是遥不可及的梦想。

1.2 我们也生活在一个日益复杂的世界中，在这里，两极对立的看法在不公正和不平等的催化下，往往酿成暴力和冲突，威胁着国际的稳定。以往数年中，战争、占领及恐怖行为加剧了各个社会内部和各个社会之间的猜疑和畏惧。除了激进团体之外，某些政治领导人及部分媒体利用了这种环境，向世人描绘了一种似是而非的景象，好像这个世界上的文化、宗教、文明互相排斥，历来截然不同，注定要走向对抗。

1.3 令人遗憾的是，由"文明冲突"论所带来的忧虑和混乱扭曲了对于该世界面临困境之实质的讨论话语。文化之间的关系史并非只是战争和冲突的历史，它同时也是建设性交流、相互启迪、和平共处的历史。况且，用一成不变的文明分界线来概括内部不断变化、千差万别的不同社会，妨碍了人们以更有启发性的方式去理解身份、动机、行为这类问题。与这种公式化的文化框框相比，有权势者与无权势者之间的裂痕，富有者与贫穷者之间的裂痕，不同政治团体、阶级、职业、民族之间的裂痕，会具有更大的解释力。事实上，文化框框只会强化已经两极对立的看法，更糟糕的是，它们会助长一种错误的观点，似乎不同文化处于某种不可避免的冲突的轨道上，因此会把本可协商解决的争端变为看来无法克服的、基于身份的冲突，而且还会挑起大众的绵绵想象。故此，很有必要反对这些公式化的偏见和错误理念，因为它们加深了不同社会间的对立与不信任。

1.4 以此观之，在不同社会之间架起桥梁，促进对话和理解，并且形成一个处理全球失衡问题的集体政治意志，这种必要性在今天比以往任何时候都更为迫切了。这个急迫的任务构成了"文明联盟"行动的政治理由。该行动先由西班牙和土耳其的总理联合倡议，2005 年由联合国秘书长正式发起。它强调在不同国家、文化、宗教之间应有的一种广泛共识，即所有社会都是人类大家庭中的成员，大家在寻求稳定、繁荣及和平共处的征程中，相互依赖、命运相连。

1.5 "文明联盟"力图关注不同社会之间日益扩大的裂痕，重申具有不同文化与宗教传统的民族应当互相尊重这一规范，并愿促使各方为此而采取共同的行动。这一努力反映了绝大多数民族要求摒弃任何社会中的极端主义、尊重宗教和文化多样性这样的意愿。为了指导这一举措，联合国秘书长建立了由著名人士组成的"高级名人小组"，本文件便是小组的报告。① 该报告以分析为基础，评估了不同社会之间的关系，考察了当今正在出现的滑向极端主义的趋势，特别关注西方社会与穆斯林社会之间的关系——当然，我们深知，这样的特点描述并未反映各自内部巨大的差异。报告向行政当局（包括国家、地区和基层各层次）、国际组织和公民社会提出了务实的行动方案建议，希望借此有助于减少世界各民族和文化之间的敌意，促进其相互间的和谐。

二、指导原则

2.1 "文明联盟"从本质上说，必须立足于一个多极的视野。因此，有一些原则指导了名人小组的思考，这些原则确立了倡导一种对话文化、倡导所有民族和文化互相尊重这样的框架。《联合国宪章》、旨在将人类从恐惧和苦难中解放出来的 1948 年《人权普遍宣言》，以及其他有关文化和宗教权利的基本文件② 为下列这些原则提供了基本的参照。

2.2 一个日益互相依赖和全球化的世界只能通过以联合国体系为核心的法治和有效的多边体制来加以管理。这要求遵守国际法和国际公约，包括遵守比如

---

① 本报告反映了高级名人小组成员的共识，但并不意味着在所有问题上大家都完全一致。

② 参见"文明对话"网址 www.unaoc.org 列出的参考文件。

《国际人道法》(尤其是《日内瓦公约》) 所载明的规范战争行为的所有权利和责任，也要求尊重确立这些法规的机构，并要求支持那些对违规行为进行裁决的机制。

2.3 对人权标准充分地、始终如一地恪守构成了稳定的社会及和平的国际关系的基石。这些标准包括禁止身体和精神上的酷刑、有权自由信仰宗教、有权自由表达和自由结社。这些权利的神圣性体现于其普遍性和无条件性，因此，这些权利应当被视为不可侵犯的，在任何情况下，所有政权、国际组织、非国家行为体、个人都必须恪守这些标准。

2.4 文明和文化的多样性是人类社会的一个基本特征，也是人类进步的一股推动力量。文明和文化反映了人类的巨大财富和遗产，其本质就是彼此交叠、相互影响、不断演化。各个文化都对人类的进化作出了贡献，它们相互之间没有高低等级之差。文明的历史实际上是一段互相借鉴、彼此不断取长补短的历史。

2.5 贫困导致绝望，导致不公平感，导致被排斥感，当与政治悲情相结合时，会助长极端主义。消除贫困可以减少那些与经济边缘化和被排斥相关联的因素，所以，就如联合国"千年发展目标"所要求的那样，必须全力推进消除贫困的事业。

2.6 恐怖主义永远都没有为自己开脱的理由。为了成功地促使国际机构和各国政府制止恐怖主义，我们需要关注一切有利于恐怖主义滋长的条件，要看到在和平、安全、社会与经济发展、人权之间的相互联系。就此而言，最近批准的"联合国反恐战略"代表了一个重要的里程碑。

2.7 民主治理代表了公民的意志，并且会对公民的需要和诉求做出反应，它为个体充分实现其潜力提供着最为有效的渠道。为了保证其成功，民主制度必须从每个社会自己的文化土壤中有机地成长起来，体现出该社会中人们的共同价值，并适应其公民的需求和利益。只有当人民拥有自由，而且感到自己在掌握自己命运的时候，才能做到这一点。

2.8 宗教是许多社会中日益重要的一个方面，也是个体价值观念的重要源泉。在促使人们尊重其他文化、宗教和生活方式并使之和谐相处方面，宗教扮演着关键的作用。

三、全球背景

概　述

3.1 20世纪的政治和技术进步展示了希望和可能，可望在国家之间维持前所未有的长期和谐，同时大幅度地改善全球的福利状况。事实上，也的确取得了许多成就。多边合作，加之公民社会的主动参与，为国际关系中的众多积极的进展创造了条件，禁止使用地雷、建立国际刑事法庭、开启旨在消除疾病或者消除贫困的广泛合作行动，便是积极进展中的若干例子。然而，尽管取得了这些成就，在世界现状的许多方面，依然可以感觉到一种总体的失调现象。人们普遍察觉到，主要由于缺乏大多数强国的支持，本来为了推行普遍原则和改善总体福祉而建立的多边机构效力不彰；同时，人们切实地担忧，为当今年轻人创造一个更加和平、稳定和繁荣未来的前景面临着危险。在某些情况下，这种悲观看法起源于某种特定的当地的、国家的或者区域的事态变迁，但是，也的确存在着某种更为广泛的全球背景，这种全球背景必须予以关注。

3.2 从社会、政治、经济的角度观察，西方既在推动着全球化，又似乎受到全球化的某些趋势的威胁。西方强国在世界上维持着压倒性的政治、经济和军事力量，包括在多边政治和经济机构中拥有不成比例的影响力。同时，漏洞百出的边境，从穷国向富国节节上升的人口流动，未能融入主流社会的移民群体，经济、环境、健康，甚至是实物性的安全威胁的跨境扩散，都昭示着不同社会既互相依存、相互间差异又在持续拉大这一事实。

3.3 就经济福利而言，收入上的不平等在近几十年中继续扩大，目前的研究表明，世界经济进一步的一体化实际上加剧了国家间在经济增长方面的差距。因此，全人类的一半以上仍然过着穷困潦倒的日子，国家内部以及国家之间的贫富分化似乎在难以避免地继续发展。发展中国家的健康和教育体系依然满足不了需求，对于环境的破坏还在恶化，核武器、生物和化学武器的扩散似乎脱离了有效的控制，包括官方和非法的全球武器销售也在失去监控。

3.4 就政治福祉而言，人们越来越感到，人权和民主治理这些普遍原则只在被某些国家认为符合其自身利益时才会得到它们的有力捍卫，这种有选择的方式削弱了相关多边组织的合法性，因为它们肩负着表达、促进、倡导这些原则的使命。当民主选出的政府被强国绕开，或有时被强国颠覆时，那些支持民主制的博文鸿辞随即黯然失色、无足轻重。

3.5 族群之间用于互相沟通的机制和技术发展迅速，似乎快于我们借此来谋取人类共同福利而应有的集体政治意志的成长。这一环境使以族群的身份认同为基础的政治获得了生长的沃土，而这种政治反过来又会导致各族群之间的暴力性紧张关系，催生各族群之间的敌对关系。

身份认同与感知

3.6 特点各异的文化身份认同是丰富的人类经验中不可分割的一部分，因而

114

必须得到尊重和光大。在现代身份认同的发展与传播中，传统和习俗尤其扮演着关键的角色。但是，难以抵挡的"全球化"趋势在世界的许多地区，包括拉美、非洲和亚洲，对集体性身份认同形成挑战。20世纪后期的进步开启了新的可能性，让不同的民族和文化在保持其各自特有身份认同与信仰体系的同时，能够更加容易地交流，以更加平等的地位协商其利益，并且追求其共同的目标。可是，许多人感到，实际出现的却是这样一种国际体系：它展现了让部分群体改善经济福利的前景，作为交换，却要求各文化更大程度地遵从和同质化；同时，家庭和社区因城市化而轰然解体，传统的生活方式被否定或抛弃，自然环境则走向衰败和退化。在任何地方，只要有关群体感到面临着被边缘化的处境，感到未来无望，甚至只感到受压抑和被排除，部分人必然会做出反应，更加有力地来宣示其基本的身份特征。

3.7 在民主社会，当共同遭受歧视或迫害的群体起来要求平等权利和政治参与时，可以通过诸如平权运动这样的方式来和平地回应其要求。但在那些没有提供渠道让苦难得到倾听的政治体制中，经常会出现政治和军事团体，它们会倡导使用暴力来实现利益的调整。有些人会将它们视为解放运动，而另有人则将其视为对国家安全的威胁。在这一空间的最极端，那些角逐经济和政治利益的激进分子会利用受屈辱和被剥夺的情绪，为其按宗教和民族分野组织起来的政治党派和军事团体吸引和招募人员。虽然媒体上时有客观的分析，但经常充斥肤浅的、简单化的言辞，加之不公正的报道，会强化人们相互间的负面看法。

极端主义的抬头

3.8 唯意识形态分子极力说服人们接受并支持其事业，他们对于宗教的利用造成了一种错觉，好像宗教本身是跨文化冲突的一个根本原因。故此，很有必要消除误解，客观并准确地评估宗教在当代政治中的作用。事实上，在我们时代，宗教与政治之间可能在呈现一种互利共生、相互影响的关系。历史上也不乏此种例子，如貌似世俗的殖民事业曾打着"文明拓展使命"的旗号，也即19世纪时人们所相信的"天定命运论"，实际上就有深刻的宗教根源。反过来，当代某些表面上以宗教为纲领的运动则掩盖了其借用宗教来服务于意识形态目的的政治野心。

3.9 从19世纪中叶到20世纪中叶，许多知识分子和政治精英曾以为，现代化将会瓦解宗教的活力。根据他们的理论，随着人们经济上更加富有，政治上自由度更大，受教育程度更高，世俗化和世俗主义作为一条法律和政治原则，也将向前发展，从而在世界事务中将宗教降低到一个不那么重要的地位。但是，在最

115

近几十年里，几乎每一个主要的世界性宗教都在挑战这一理论，反而在政治中确立了其新的地位。在某些社会中，支持宗教在公共事务中发挥更大作用的呼声在不断增大。多数人以和平的方式表达这一愿望，但在世界范围内，也有一小部分基于宗教动机的团体在参与暴力活动。

3.10 在此紧要关头，澄清我们对于某些常用术语的理解是颇为重要的。"原教旨主义"是基督教新教徒杜撰的一个西方术语，直接用于其他群体是不合适的。它经常被用来描述某些不安于宗教在世俗社会中的边缘化，试图重新恢复宗教中心地位的运动。实际上这些运动具有高度的创新性，甚至还是非正统的，但它们往往呼吁回到宗教传统的本源，不顾历史因素而原原本本地恪守基本的文本和原则。尽管"原教旨主义"一词经常被滥用，但值得指出的是，这些运动在大多数信仰传统中都确实存在，而且它们并非天然倾向暴力。一般来说，它们都怀有一种对于世俗现代性的深深的失望和畏惧。在它们的经验中，世俗现代性具有侵犯性和不道德性，而且缺乏深层意义；另一方面，由于极端主义倡导采取激进措施以追求政治目标，在某些情况下，它们可利用原教旨主义和极端意识形态来证明暴力行为、甚至针对平民的恐怖主义袭击是合理的。

3.11 必须认识到，世界上没有哪个宗教可以宽恕或者准许对平民的杀戮，所有宗教都崇尚同情、公正、敬重生活的尊严。然而，在世界不少地方近来持续发生的冲突中，宗教被用来证明不宽容、暴力，甚至杀人都是有理的。最近，极端主义团伙搞的许多暴力和恐怖活动都是打着穆斯林社团的旗号进行的。由于这些活动，伊斯兰教正被某些人视为一个天然崇尚暴力的宗教。诸如此类的看法往好说是错误的，往坏说则是居心叵测，它们加深了各社团之间的裂痕，并且强化了其相互间危险的敌意。

3.12 极端主义和恐怖主义并非纯粹由宗教排他主义所挑起，也不是只由非国家行为体实施。事实上，世俗的政治动机曾经导致的最为骇人的恐怖罪行在人们的脑海中仍然记忆犹新，如纳粹大屠杀、苏联时期斯大林的大清洗，以及更近些在柬埔寨、巴尔干和卢旺达的种族屠杀，所有这些罪行都是由国家政权犯下的。简言之，随便浏览20世纪便可发现，没有哪个社团、文化、地区或政治主张可以特别地与极端主义或恐怖主义行为画等号。

3.13 在任何地方，只要一些群体相信自己正面临以种族、宗教或者其他身份特征为基础的持续不断的歧视、屈辱或者边缘化，那么它们就可能更加激烈地张扬其身份。只要愤怒的源头依然如故，特别是如果正常政治进程中进一步的羞辱或者失意加强这种愤怒的情绪，温和的领导人总会不遗余力地去争夺激进领导人的光芒，而后者总是挑动集体愤怒的情绪，并且通过排他主义的意识形态、对立性的政治和暴力，来提供本群体一家的感情和调整现状的手段。有效的应对之策不能单靠攻击这些意识形态的追随者，实际上，此类战术反而可能进一步煽起本欲消灭的那些情绪。唯一持久的解决方案是消除怨恨和愤怒的根源，因为它们使极端主义的、暴力的意识形态显得魅力十足。排他主义的意识形态、敌对性的感受、文化上的傲慢、媒体的模式化宣传，与脱胎于不公正（主观认为的和客观存在的）的冲突往往危险地结合在一起，没有哪里比在西方与穆斯林的关系中可以更加明显地看到这种危险的结合了。

四、政治方面

历史叙述

4.1 "文明联盟"是以此前有关"文明对话"①的努力及其他相关倡议为基础的②，它必须以一种多视角和综合的方法来考察当今不同社群之间关系的现状，以及塑造这些关系的世界观和相互感受。这里的分析集中于考察西方社会和穆斯林社会之间的关系，当然，名人小组对于这个问题的考察和见解，将会对于一般意义上的跨越鸿沟提供借鉴作用，从而会有助于建设和平与和谐。

4.2 虽然在世界三大"一神教"——基督教、伊斯兰教和犹太教的信徒之间曾经有过紧张和对抗的历史，但是他们之间的冲突往往更多地出于政治原因而非宗教原因。重要的是，应当看到和平共处、互惠贸易和相互学习是这三大宗教从古至今关系中的主要特点。在中世纪，伊斯兰文明曾经是善于创新、知识积累、科学进步的重要源泉，为欧洲文艺复兴和启蒙运动的兴起作出了贡献。历史上，在穆斯林统治下，犹太教徒和基督教徒基本上可以自由地从事其宗教活动，其中很多人还曾晋升至较高的政治职位。特别是，犹太人在历史上不同的时期都曾在穆斯林帝国中寻求庇护，以逃离歧视和迫害。同样的，在最近的数个世纪中，西方的政治、科学、文化和技术的进步，也影响了穆斯林社会生活中的很多方面。许多穆斯林也试图移民到西方社会，部分地是因为在那里可以找到政治自由和经济机会。

---

① 参见"文明对话全球议程"（A/60/259）。
② 尤其是"建设和平文化宣言与行动方案"，此文件随同"文明对话与文明联盟"，在"联合国大会 2005 年世界峰会成果"第 144 段中得到提及。

西方社会与穆斯林国家的关系

4.3 激进势力利用古代史中的历史片段来描绘一幅不祥的画面，好像各个宗教团体历史上就是泾渭分明的、相互排斥的，并且注定要走向对抗的。我们必须反对这种扭曲的历史叙述。对于本报告而言，最为重要的是这样的事实，久远的历史并不能为当今的冲突提供解释，也不能为西方社会与穆斯林社会之间敌意的上升提供解释。相反，当今这些现象的根源，存在于19世纪和20世纪的那些发展。那时，先出现了欧洲的帝国主义，此后便导致了反殖民主义运动，进而形成了相互对抗及其遗产。

4.4 1947年，联合国同意巴勒斯坦分治时，曾经设想建立两个国家——巴勒斯坦国和以色列国，同时给予耶路撒冷以特殊的地位。这后来导致了1948年以色列国的建立，并从此开启了一系列的事件。至今，这些事件还是西方社会和穆斯林社会关系中最为困扰人的问题。以色列持续占领巴勒斯坦和其他阿拉伯领土，耶路撒冷这个穆斯林、基督教徒、犹太教徒心目中的圣城至今一直未能确定其地位，人们认为这是得到了西方政府的默许。因此，这成为穆斯林世界对西方世界抱有怨恨和愤怒的主要原因。这种占领在穆斯林世界中被看作是另一种形式的殖民主义，使许多人相信，不管他们的看法是对是错，以色列跟"西方"在进行着共谋。这些怨恨和感受由于以色列最近在加沙和黎巴嫩过分的报复行动而进一步加剧。

4.5 在另外一个关键的方面，中东作为一个对繁荣和权力具有关键意义的重要石油产地而崛起。冷战时期的大国在这一地区的战略重地和石油资源丰富的国家进行角逐，经常采取军事和政治的干预行动。这导致一些国家的发展受到阻碍，最后反过来还使干涉这些国家的强国引火烧身，其后果至今还能够感受到。1953年伊朗的政变就是这些事件中的一个，这一事件的后果充分展示了外国对于一国政治进程的干预既具有局限性，又充满危险性。

4.6 1979年，苏联对阿富汗的侵略和占领开辟了另一条战线上的对抗。作为支持宗教抵抗组织遏制共产主义的西方政策的一部分，美国及其盟国（包括该地区的某些穆斯林政府）为阿富汗的抵抗组织（圣战者游击队）撑腰，最终迫使苏联在1989年撤离。经过一段时间的不稳定之后，塔利班政权控制了阿富汗，并且支持基地组织，由此而挑起了针对西方的敌对情绪，同时也开始了一系列使新千年开端蒙上血腥的事件。

4.7 2001年9月，由基地组织对美国实施的恐怖袭击，几乎招致了全球范围不分宗教信仰、不分政治立场的同声谴责。袭击也展示了这个极端组织敌对情绪的深度。恐怖袭击引发了对于阿富汗塔利班政权的强力报复,后来这些袭击又被当作侵略伊拉克的正当理由之一。实际上,伊拉克与这些袭击的联系从来都没有得到证实,这使穆斯林社会觉得对伊拉克的入侵是西方进行的又一场非正义侵略战争。

4.8 在穆斯林与西方社会的关系方面尤其让人感到尖锐的问题是,人们认为在国际法应用和对人权的保护方面存在着双重标准。有关集体惩罚、定点清除、严刑拷打、任意拘禁、高压引渡,以及对于独裁政权的刻意支持等等报道,导致全球各地、尤其是穆斯林国家深感自己易受外来攻击,也导致了人们对于西方双重标准的反感。西方某些政治和宗教领导人关于伊斯兰天性暴力及其他相关的言论,包括使用像"伊斯兰恐怖主义"和"伊斯兰法西斯主义"这样的词汇,引起了"恐伊斯兰情绪"的急剧上升,反过来又进一步加深了穆斯林世界对西方的畏惧。

4.9 在另一方面,针对西方平民的暴力袭击,包括自杀性爆炸、人质劫持、严刑拷打,也造成了西方社会的怀疑、不安和恐惧气氛。西方的许多人也感到穆斯林领导人身上也有双重标准。事实上,虽然穆斯林世界普遍指责西方的军事行动,但是,对于穆斯林内部的冲突,大家却闭口不言。比如,某些穆斯林国家中什叶派和逊尼派之间的暴力冲突,以及针对苏丹达尔福尔地区平民的暴行等,都没有遭到穆斯林世界的普遍谴责。

4.10 双方各自感受到对方的双重标准,也造成了一种猜疑和不信任的气氛,破坏了穆斯林社会与西方社会之间的关系。

穆斯林社会中的趋势

4.11 在殖民时代后期,许多穆斯林思想家敦促他们的社会应该顺应时代、与时俱进。获得独立之后,一些穆斯林领导人开始实施现代化计划,以促进自己国家的发展。这些政策经常被宗教派别视为在走一条世俗化道路。最近几十年里,人们却看到了五花八门的宗教政治运动的崛起,大家把它们笼统地称为"伊斯兰主义"运动。这些运动赢得了可信度和民众支持,部分是因为它们向社会中的被剥夺群体提供了急需的社会服务,特别是在医疗卫生和基础教育方面。这些运动与统治当局形成了鲜明的对照,因为人们普遍认为当局未能为其国民提供足够的经济和社会福利。

4.12 在评估西方社会与穆斯林社会关系的时候,应当看到,伊斯兰主义运动并非必然地在伊斯兰社会中制造伊斯兰主义好战情绪,也并非自然地导致与西方的暴力对抗。西方军事力量对于某些穆斯林国家的侵略,以及它们在这些国家中持续的存在，加上穆斯林世界中对于政治运动的压制，才是暴力活动出现的原因。正如历史上在许多国家中所见到的那样，长期占领和政治压制会激起暴力抵抗。这一视角让我们看到了穆斯林世界正在发生的内部变化，它们才影响着穆斯林社会与外部世界的关系。

4.13 目前大部分穆斯林国家所遭遇的困境并不能简单地归咎于外来干涉。在穆斯林社会内部，进步派和保守派之间的争论正在展开，除涉及对于伊斯兰教法及传统的解释外，还涉及整个穆斯林世界的社会和经济问题。用简单而明了的话说，几个穆斯林国家对于变化的抗拒才是他们目前处境不妙的根源，这种不妙处境是相对于当今正在迅速进步的其他社会而言的。在穆斯林中似乎有一种越来越明显的认识，在以往数个世纪中，随着世界日益一体化和相互依存，他们社会中的威权主义和高压求同构成了进步的严重障碍。似乎显而易见的是，如果穆斯林社会能够加强对话和讨论，以看清妨碍其社会充分融入到全球政治、经济和思想群体中的那些内部障碍，并就如何克服这些障碍进行探讨，将会给所有穆斯林社团都带来益处。

4.14 在某些情况下，一些自封的宗教人物利用了民众寻求宗教指导的愿望，对伊斯兰教义进行狭隘的、扭曲的解释。这些人歪曲性地描述某些习俗，把为名誉而杀、肉体惩罚、迫害妇女当作其宗教所要求的内容。这些习俗不仅仅违背了国际间达成共识的人权标准，而且在受尊敬的穆斯林学者眼中也毫无宗教基础。这些穆斯林学者认为，如对伊斯兰经文和历史进行恰当的解读，应当让人们革除而不是延续这些习俗。

4.15 很多这些习俗与妇女的地位直接相关。在某些穆斯林社会中，孤陋寡闻的宗教人士与一些思想僵化的保守政治政权结为一体，成功地严格限制妇女参与政治和职业生活，从而妨碍了她们自我实现的前景和潜力。所造成的结果是，对于整个社会以及对于未来子孙后代而言，民主多元主义被扼杀、经济和社会进步被妨碍。这一问题只能通过法律来加以克服，即法律应依据国际达成共识的人权标准来保障性别平等。如果得到宗教教育的支持，而这种教育又是以对宗教教义作恰当解释为基础的话，那么，这些措施有可能取得成功。不过，必须指出的是，在世界的许多地方，包括西方社会在内，有关改善妇女地位的问题，尚有待于更多的努力。

4.16 谁将从这些穆斯林的内部斗争中获胜，不仅对于穆斯林社会的未来是至关重要的，而且对于穆斯林与外部世界的关系也是至为关键的。故此，我们要在这里讨论这一问题。显然，上述紧张关系只能由穆斯林社会自己来加以解决。

在此过程中，非穆斯林世界并没有一个特别的角色要扮演。西方的活动分子和政府尤其应当避免采取一些会对穆斯林社会正在进行的辩论具有负面影响的行为。西方媒体和官方经常作一些简单化的解释，或者对整个伊斯兰宗教进行一番指责，或者不恰当地挑起世俗主义者和宗教分子之间的对立，这种言行都是具有危害性的。例如，我们看到媒体只把时间和空间给予那些伊斯兰世界中最为激进的宗教势力以及西方社会中最为反穆斯林的意识形态分子。同样，穆斯林世界制作的某些媒体产品也主要地或者完全地对其他群体进行负面报导，这也强化了舆论的两极化对立。有些用语，比如西方世界所谓的"穆斯林恐怖主义"和穆斯林世界所谓的"现代十字军远征"，都增加了双方的敌对情绪。

4.17 在穆斯林内部的讨论中，直接影响到与西方社会关系的一个问题就是"圣战"这一概念。"圣战"概念非常丰富，包含很多层意思，既可以指每一个个体内心善与恶之间的斗争（经常在伊斯兰中被称为"大"圣战），也可以指拿起武器捍卫自己的社会（所谓"小"圣战）。现在这个术语却越来越多地被激进分子用来证明他们的暴力是正确的，而很少考虑其相应的历史条件及宗教条件。大多数穆斯林学者都认为，使用该词时应当附加这些条件。当媒体和西方政治领导人捕捉并放大激进团体对于暴力的这种呼吁时，"圣战"的概念便丧失了对穆斯林所具有的多层含义和正面内涵，只成为跟暴力或者负面意义连在一起的一个词。然而，这些负面意义本来就是错误地强加给它的。

4.18 对于许多穆斯林而言，在以往30年中，能感受到的摆脱西方国家占领和政治主导的成功，都是由那些宗教政治军事合一的运动和非国家行为体所领导的。西方国家的力量不管在军事上、经济上还是政治上，都远远超出这些团体。但是，这些团体通过非对称战争，成功地抵制了侵略和占领。这种获胜的能力让人感到一种同仇敌忾和同心协力的力量。人们对于西方占领的担忧是如此的尖锐和普遍，以至于某些温和领导人也不得不支持抵抗运动。这些领导人本来并不赞成上述团体更广泛的政治和宗教方面的意识形态，他们更担心这些团体势力的上升会对政治自由和社会自由带来长远的影响。因此，出现这样的现象就不奇怪了：在穆斯林社会中，那些最感到被排斥、最体会到沮丧的群体中，无能为力感和受迫害感越强烈，激进宗教军事运动的革命言辞就越能得到响应和支持。

4.19 更主要的是，这些团体都是在政治反对派的背景下崛起的，它们的行为与许多伊斯兰国家当局所遭遇的失败形成了鲜明的对照。实际上，这些当局都被视为未能抵制西方的干预，或者与西方国家站在一起来支持占领穆斯林国家或压迫穆斯林兄弟。

4.20 有鉴于此，在伊斯兰社会内部以及更大的范围内，出现了一种日益强烈的认识，认为应将那些抵制外来占领的民族运动与那些具有全球野心的恐怖主义团体区分开来。国际社会中并不是所有人都赞成这种看法。对于那些抵抗组织，应当鼓励它们通过非暴力地参与政治进程和民主化过程，来寻求实现其目标。对于全球性的恐怖主义团体，"文明冲突"论正好是一个可资利用的口号，可以帮助吸引和调动松散网络中的行动分子和支持者。我们必须清楚地表明，在我们看来，没有任何政治目标，不管是基于历史上的不公正还是现实中的挑衅，也不管是由抵抗组织所为、由全球好战团体所为，还是由国家所为，可以把枪口对准平民或者非战斗人员，此种行径必须得到毫不含糊的谴责。

五、走向"文明联盟"：总体政策建议

中 东

5.1 就伊斯兰社会与西方社会的关系而言，我们必须承认造就了数以百万计穆斯林之观点的当今现实，那就是由来已久的以色列与巴勒斯坦的冲突、阿富汗境内的武装冲突，以及伊拉克内部日益激烈的暴力冲突。

5.2 我们必须强调，解决巴勒斯坦问题日益迫切，这是伊斯兰社会与西方社会裂痕加深的一个主要因素。就此而言，我们有责任表达我们集体的看法，即，没有一个代表了这场冲突中所有各方意志的公正的、有尊严的、民主的解决方案，一切试图弥合鸿沟、化解敌意的努力，包括本报告中所提建议在内，都只能取得有限的成功。

5.3 我们强调巴以冲突，并不是说它就是伊斯兰与西方社会所有紧张关系中唯一的原因。其他因素也在酿成怨恨和不信任，比如，伊拉克境内日渐上升的危机、阿富汗持续的不稳定、穆斯林社会中的内部问题，以及许多国家里针对平民的恐怖袭击。然而，在我们看来，巴以问题，已具有一种象征意义，它影响着三大宗教信徒之间跨文化的和政治的关系，已经远远超出其有限的地域范围。

5.4 对于这样一场冲突，寻求一个公正的和可持续的解决方案，将需要以色列人、巴勒斯坦人和所有能够影响局面的国家拿出勇气，大胆地对未来进行构想。我们坚信，这方面的进步，将有赖于同时承认巴勒斯坦人和以色列人的国家诉求，有赖于建立两个充分具有主权、并肩生活在和平与安全中的独立国家。

5.5 实现这一目标将要求以色列不仅仅接受，而且要努力推动建立一个可维持的巴勒斯坦国，包括以色列、埃及和约旦在内的和平协定表明，符合国际法的

这种建设性步骤是可行的。况且，1991 年马德里会议上各方所达成的有关条件、2000 年克林顿总统所推动的和平倡议、2002 年在黎巴嫩贝鲁特会议上阿拉伯联盟所提出的和平建议都表明，一个广泛的协定框架的确存在，政治意志是可以形成的。

5.6 在这方面最为重要的是，冲突双方应当认识到，在以色列国建立之后，出现了相互抵触的两种说法。在大多数犹太人和以色列人的眼中，以色列建国是犹太人建立家园这一长期诉求的结果，可是随后却受到了毗邻阿拉伯国家的攻击。然而，对于巴勒斯坦人和穆斯林世界中的大多数人而言，以色列的建国是一个侵略性举动，导致了数十万巴勒斯坦人的被驱逐及自己土地的被占领。值得注意的是，这些相互抵触的说法，也反映在他们对最近历史各不相同的解释上，双方都以相异的方式来描述冲突、占领，以及和平谈判的努力。

5.7 巴以冲突白皮书。巴勒斯坦人和以色列人相互抵触的说法不能得到充分的调和，但是，两种说法必须得到共同的认可，如此方可奠定持久解决方案的基础。为此，我们建议制定一份白皮书，以冷静的、客观的方式来分析巴以冲突，倾听双方互相矛盾的说法，回顾并且诊断以往和平举措的成功和失败，清晰地界定为摆脱危机必须要实现的条件。这样的一份文件可以为参与这一冲突解决的关键决策者的工作提供一个坚实的基石。平衡的和理性的分析将让巴勒斯坦人清楚地看到，他们几十年被占领、被误解、被丑化的代价现在正在得到充分的承认。与此同时，此份文件又有助于消除以色列人的担忧。这样的努力将会对那些寻求公正解决这一危机的人们给予有力的帮助，同时又可削弱各方面的极端势力，因为他们将再也无法误导这一进程。本来由于没有人去讲述这一事实，或者由于这一事实被国际社会有意地漠视，这些人一直在利用这一点谋取私利。

5.8 恢复多边和平进程的活力。为解决处于中东危机核心的问题，作为重新努力的进一步步骤，名人小组呼吁再次开启政治进程，包括尽快召开有关中东和平进程的国际会议。所有相关方面都应当参与该会议，其目的是要达成一个广泛的和平协定。

5.9 与伊拉克和阿富汗达成国际约定①。国际社会应该以高度的责任感来关

---

① "与伊拉克国际约定"由伊拉克政府、联合国、世界银行倡议，在 2006 年 9 月 10 日阿布扎比筹备会上发起，参见 www.iraqcompact.org。"与阿富汗国际约定"由阿富汗政府、联合国及国际社会磋商后制订，在 2006 年 1 月 31 日至 2 月 1 日伦敦阿富汗会议上发起，参见 www.fco.gov.uk。

注伊拉克境内的政治和人道主义危机。名人小组表示充分支持阿拉伯联盟在伊拉克内部寻求国内政治共识的努力，也表示充分支持实施"与伊拉克的国际约定"。同样，当然是在不同的一个区域范围内，名人小组表示充分支持最近所倡导的"与阿富汗的国际约定"。

5.10 伊斯兰国家中的政治多元化导致穆斯林社会与西方社会两极对立，并且导致其关系中出现激进主义情绪的原因之一，就是穆斯林世界对于政治运动的压制。因此，穆斯林世界的执政当局应当为非暴力的政治党派（不管是宗教的还是世俗的）提供充分参政的空间。这符合穆斯林社会和西方社会的利益。为此，外国政府应当前后一贯地支持民主进程，当有关结果并不符合自己的政治议程时，也不应加以干预。对政治多元化的这一呼吁，不仅适用于中东国家或者更大范围内的穆斯林世界，而且适用于所有的国家。

其他的总体政策建议

5.11 重新致力于多边主义像本报告通篇指出的那样，国际社会所面对的很多问题，只有在一个多边的框架下才能得到有效的解决。因此，各国都有义务来强化多边的机制，尤其是联合国，大家也有义务来支持那些旨在强化这些机制能力和效率的改革努力。

5.12 充分地、一贯地尊重国际法和人权。当人们只是有选择地捍卫或者所谓"捍卫"普遍人权时，群体之间的两极对立情绪就会增长。因此，在各民族之间进行真正的对话，就要求对于国际人权原则，对于充分地和始终如一地应用这些原则有一个共同的理解。特别是，这一对话必须建立在对人权尊重的基础上，也建立在对于国际刑事法庭权威尊重的基础上。这里的人权包括良心的自由、表达的自由、免予拷打和其他非人道酷刑的自由。这些人权原则已由《人权普遍公约》、《日内瓦公约》和其他基本文件加以规定。

5.13 与人权标准相适应的协调性移民政策。移民问题要想得到最为有效的管理，必须要求相关的政策在移出国、中途国和目的国之间得到协调，也要求有关政策符合国际人权法、国际人道主义法和其他为保护难民和内部流离失所人员提供指南的国际协定。

5.14 扶贫与经济不平等"文明联盟"，只有在一个包括所有国家都致力于实现"千年发展目标"的框架下才能得到实现。这个问题的迫切性，再强调也不过分。全球的不平等正在以令人发指的速度加剧。在非洲，一半的人口每日生活费不足 1 美元；虽然非洲人口占世界人口的将近1/6，它只占世界贸易的不足 3%；而且，在包括投资、教育和健康在内的其他领域中，非洲也明显落后。^① 必须只争朝夕地处理这些问题，因为贫富日益扩大的差距，对于挑起怨恨、腐蚀全球团结，会具有很大的影响力。

5.15 保护宗教信仰自由。宗教自由和信仰自由是所有国家和宗教团体都加以保障的基本权利，为此，必须尤其关注对于宗教纪念场所和神圣地点的尊重问题，因为其意义直接关涉个人和集体宗教身份的核心。冒犯和损坏宗教信仰场所会严重地破坏不同群体之间的关系，并且增加诱发大规模暴力的危险。因此，依照2001年联合国大会所采纳的决议案^②，我们相信，各国政府应该采取有力措施，反对污损神圣地点和信仰场所，并且肩负起保护这些地方的责任。我们同时也呼吁公民社会和国际组织，帮助弘扬一种宽容的文化和尊重所有宗教和宗教场所的风气。

5.16 发挥负责任的领导作用。很多导致群体间紧张关系的问题实际上都出现在政治和宗教交汇的地方。这些问题中的一个就是，有时候政治和宗教领导人使用煽动性的言辞会带来不良影响，这些语言通过媒体传播更可造成破坏性的影响。此类语言会挑动仇恨和不信任，使之扩散开来，导致"恐伊斯兰情绪"、"恐外症"和反犹主义。在目前遍及世界各国的恐惧与猜疑气氛中，公众舆论的领导者和影响者肩负着特别的责任，他们应当在不同文化当中致力于促进理解，促进不同宗教信仰和传统之间的互相尊重。由于他们拥有影响力，拥有人们的尊重，他们有责任来防止使用一些涉及他人信仰或者神圣象征的暴力性或者挑衅性语言。

5.17 公民社会积极参与的关键作用。要实现上述的每一项政策建议，政治步骤固然必要，但是，如果没有公民社会的支持，政治行动往往会无法形成长期的效果。名人小组因此呼吁，在推进这些政策建议的过程中，尤其是在和平解决冲突的过程中，公民社会应发挥更大的作用，应能够更深地介入。

5.18 建立推进"文明联盟"的伙伴关系。名人小组建议，应当跟那些赞成其目标的国际组织在"文明联盟"的框架下建立伙伴关系。同时，应当强化其与联合国体系的互动与协调，特别应当关注那些作为联合国大家庭一部分的国际组织，以及那些已经与"文明联盟"名人小组进行合作的组织。这些组织有：联合

---

① 根据联合国发展计划署《2005 年人类发展报告》，在 2003 年，非洲获得的外国直接投资为 130 亿美元，与之相对照，欧洲联盟为 2160 亿美元，亚洲为 1470 亿美元，北美为 950 亿美元。而且在 1990 至 2003 年期间，非洲大陆 53 个国家中有 18 个遭遇了生活水准的下降。

② 参见 2001 年 5 月 31 日联合国大会通过的联合国关于"宗教场所保护"的决议（A/RES/55/254）。

国教育科学和文化组织、欧洲联盟、欧洲安全与合作组织、伊斯兰会议组织、阿拉伯国家联盟、伊斯兰教育科学和文化组织、联合城市和地方政府组织、世界旅游组织，以及其他官方或民间的国际与国家组织。

5.19 本报告第一部分所作分析的目的，不管是就全球角度而言，还是就穆斯林社会与西方社会关系这一具体角度而言，是要确定一个基础，是要为建设跨文化和谐、增加全球稳定而在机构层面和公民组织层面采取联合行动，奠定基石，并确认其道德基础。本报告的以下部分，即第二部分主要是行动领域和主题建议，将探讨可以采取这些行动的主要途径，分析教育、青年、移民、媒体目前在不同社会之间的关系方面所扮演的关键角色，并就这些领域可以采取的改善关系的行动提出建议。

附：高级名人小组的成员

联合倡议者

1. 双主席之一 Mehmet Aydi 教授（土耳其）：土耳其国务部长、哲学教授

2. 双主席之一 Federico Mayor 教授（西班牙）：联合国教科文组织和平文化基金会主席、前秘书长

中 东

3. Seyed Mohamed Khatami 先生（伊朗）：伊朗前总统

4. Sheikha Mozahbint Nasseral Missned 陛下（卡塔尔）：卡塔尔国埃米尔夫人、卡塔尔教育学与社区发展基金会主席

5. Ismail Serageldin 博士（埃及）：亚力山大图书馆馆长

北 非

6. Mohamed Charfi 博士（突尼斯）：突尼斯前教育部长

7. Andre Azoulay 先生（摩洛哥）：摩洛哥国王陛下顾问

西 非

8. Moustapha Niasse 先生（塞内加尔）：塞内加尔前总理

南部非洲

9. Desmond Tutu 大主教（南非）：开普顿大主教

西 欧

10. Hubert Vedrine 先生（法国）：法国前外交部长

11. Karen Armstrong 女士（英国）：宗教史学家

东　欧

12. Vitaly Naumkin 教授（俄罗斯）：莫斯科国立大学院长兼国际战略与政治研究中心主任

北　美

13. John Esposito 教授（美国）：乔治顿大学穆斯林与基督教徒理解中心创始主任、牛津伊斯兰世界百科全书主编

14. Arthur Schneier 拉比（美国）：呼吁良知基金会主席、纽约东园犹太会堂拉比

拉　美

15. Enrique Iglesias 先生（乌拉圭）：伊比利亚美洲组织秘书长暨前主席

16. Candido Mendes 教授（巴西）：拉丁学院秘书长

南　亚

17. Nafis Sadik 博士（巴基斯坦）：联合国秘书长特别顾问

18. Shobhana Bhartia 女士（印度）：印度议会议员、新德里印度斯坦时报副总裁兼编辑主任

东南亚

19. Ali Alatas 先生（印度尼西亚）：印度尼西亚前外长

东　亚

20. Pan Guang（潘光）教授（中国）：上海社会科学院所长兼教授

人类和谐宣言

首届尼山世界文明论坛通过
（2010 年 9 月 27 日于尼山）

2010 年 9 月 27 日，出席首届尼山论坛的中外专家学者，共同发出尼山宣言——《人类和谐宣言》。这是世界第一个关于人类和谐的主题宣言，对推动不同文明对话交流、建设和谐世界产生了重要影响。全文如下：

公元 2010 年 9 月 27 日，中国古代伟大的思想家、教育家孔子诞辰 2561 周年之际，我们重温 2500 年前那个需要智者并产生智者的时代的人类智慧，借尼山世界文明论坛，共同发出和谐宣言：
怀着对人类现实命运的忧伤，
怀着对人类共同未来的焦虑，
面对战争、杀戮、冲突的残酷现实，
面对日趋恶化的地球生存环境，
人类的灵魂感受到了前所未有的孤独和恐慌。
汲取 2500 多年来人类精神导师们的伟大智慧，
我们倡导和谐，
我们倡导仁爱，
我们倡导宽容，
我们倡导礼让，
我们倡导信义，
我们倡导己所不欲，勿施于人，
我们倡导民胞物与，天人合一，
我们倡导各美其美，美美与共，
我们倡导四海之内，皆兄妹也，
我们倡导和谐世界，和而不同。

为了建设一个和谐的世界，

为了守护一个共同的地球，

我们呼吁理解尊重，化解积怨；

我们呼吁对话交流，避免冲突；

我们呼吁节俭低碳，呵护家园；

我们呼吁团结合作，共创未来。

我们祈愿——我们的倡导和呼吁能够得到全世界的响应！

我们祈愿——我们的倡导和呼吁能够变成全人类的共同行动！

附录五：

青年人积极参与世界文明对话倡议书

第二届尼山世界文明论坛通过

（2012 年 5 月 23 日）

有位哲人说过，青年者，人生之王也。青年人，朝气蓬勃，勇于进取，乃今日之主人，明日之栋梁，寄托着人类的希望。

我们倡议：全世界青年不分种族、不分性别、不分信仰，共同行动起来，担当起人类文明永续发展的重任，主动走向世界文明对话的前台。

我们倡议：全世界青年以平实之眼光，以天地之胸怀，了解、对待一切样式的人类文明，一切文化上的或信仰上的他者。我们有责任像保护地球生物多样性一样，保护人类文明的多样性。

我们倡议：全世界不同宗教信仰、不同文明形态陶冶出的青年人，应相互尊重、相互包容、相互理解，反对一切种族的傲慢与文化歧视，反对任何形式的文化的妄自尊大。

我们倡议：全世界不同民族、不同信仰的青年人，将深入研究本民族之文化视为自己的责任与义务，承担起传承和发展民族文化的重任。

我们倡议：全世界的青年人以开放之心灵，学习之态度，聆听不同文明的声音，学习其他文明的长处，促进本民族文明的发展，实现人类文明的共同繁荣。

我们的宗旨是，加强不同文明对话、促进人类和谐发展；化解人类文明冲突，达到人类文明的和睦相处。文化与宗教信仰的多样性以及它们之间的差异不应是文明冲突的根源，而应是文明交流与合作的动力与起点。一枝独秀不是春，百花齐放春满园。一种文明独盛不是人类之福，多种文明共同发展才是人类之大幸！西哲赫拉克里特有言："不同音调造成最美的和谐。"孔子也曾指出："和而不同。"我们正视人类不同文明差异，因为这些差异恰恰是人类文明生生不息的动力！

亲爱的朋友们，让我们不分种族、不分性别、不分信仰，手牵着手，昂然走上世界文明对话的前台。以青春之我，创造青春之文明；以我之青春，永褒人类文明之青春！以青春对话之旋律，奏出人类不同文明和谐之乐章！

附录六：

世界古文明国家文化遗产保护与促进文明对话尼山共识

第二届尼山世界文明论坛通过
(2012 年 5 月 23 日)

2012 年 5 月 21 日，第二届尼山世界文明论坛隆重开幕。时逢联合国"世界文明对话日"10 周年，来自中国、印度、墨西哥、意大利、美国等国家的专家学者共聚孔子的诞生地——曲阜，围绕"文明古国的合作与文明责任"这一时代主题展开对话和交流。达成如下共识：

一、彼此尊重。文化遗产是全人类共同的财富。在漫长的历史进程中，世界各民族以其聪明才智创造了光辉灿烂、多姿多彩的文化，这些宝贵的文化遗产凝聚着人类共同的智慧，是人类历史发展的见证。

民族的即是人类的，多样性是世界文明的一个基本特征。尊重彼此的历史文化传统是维护文化多样性的基本原则。文明古国在人类文明的起源和发展进程中曾经作出过巨大贡献，新的历史时期，有责任承担起不断丰富和推进全球遗产事业的历史使命。

二、增强合作。世界的发展为文化遗产保护带来前所未有的机遇，但全球化也使文化遗产面临着更严峻的压力与挑战，实现文化遗产的可持续发展已成为国际社会刻不容缓的任务。

国际合作是保护遗产、实现人类文明延续的根本途径。人类历史发展的过程是各种文明不断交流、融合创新的过程。加强文明古国之间以及文明古国与各国、各民族的文明对话，积极参与文化遗产保护的国际多边交流与合作，对于保护文化遗产，传承民族文脉，构建国家之间、民族之间尊重包容、和谐发展的人类文化生态，促进世界和平与进步具有十分重要的意义。

三、面向未来。文化遗产属于历史也属于未来。文化遗产作为人类与自然共同创造的杰作，是人类永恒的历史记忆和精神家园，是当代人传承历史、继往开来的文化渊源。

文化遗产保护要融入人类的发展，引领文明的进步，为民众带来新生活。为了今天和未来，我们要更好地保护各民族的悠久历史和赖以生存、发展的文化根基。我们今天所做的一切，是使世界各民族的精神和情感的载体能够传承下去。

文明古国呼唤世界各国、各民族共同努力，推动文化遗产的可持续发展，实现人类文明的永续流传！

附录七：

十年文明对话大事记

（2002—2012）

1998 年 9 月 21 日　在联合国第 53 次全体会议上，伊朗总统赛义德·穆罕默德·哈塔米呼吁将对话制度化，"用话语和理解来取代敌意和对抗"。哈塔米特别地邀请国际社会扩大和鼓励不同文明间在环境、和平与安全方面的对话。这项提议的要点是呼吁人类认识到在全球范围内真正的对话，涉及所有利益相关者，为保证有意义和有效的国际合作提供了唯一的可行办法。1998 年 11 月 4 日，联合国大会 53/22 号决议，宣布 2001 年为联合国不同文明之间对话年。它呼吁各国政府、联合国系统，包括联合国教育、科学及文化组织和其他有关国际组织和非政府组织规划和执行适当的文化、教育和社会方案，促进不同文明之间对话的构想，包括组织会议和讨论会以及传播关于这个问题的材料和信息。

2000 年 12 月 11 日至 12 日　联合国教科文组织在巴黎召开了第二届国际文化部长圆桌会议，其主题为"2000 至 2010 年的文化多样性：市场挑战"。这届圆桌会议既分析了全球化带来的挑战又分析了联合国教科文组织在这个背景下扮演的角色。会议得出的结论是：各国文化产业的发展既要适应市场经济的发展，利用全球广阔的市场空间，又要着重保护文化多样性，避免对经济利益的追逐侵蚀文化的多样性。

2001 年 6 月 18 日至 20 日　由立陶宛共和国、波兰共和国和联合国教科文组织共同主办的文明对话国际会议在立陶宛的维尔纽斯举行。这次会议是庆祝联合国不同文明之间对话年的一件大事。汇集来自世界不同地方的领导者、决策者、著名学者和艺术家，会议的辩论在影响不同文化和文明之间的关系的复杂议题上呈现出"复调"的声音。会议的结尾通过了维尔纽斯宣言。

2001 年 6 月 18 日至 20 日　由伊朗伊斯兰共和国主办以及在联合国（UN）和联合国环境计划署（UNEP）的积极合作下，"环境，宗教和文化"国际研讨会在德黑兰举行。研讨会通过了"德黑兰环境、宗教和文化宣言"，其中要求与会者推动宗教的环保内容方面的教育和鼓励对环境负责的行为。

2001 年 7 月 31 日至 8 月 3 日　文明对话国际会议在东京和京都举行。来自学术界、政界和社会各界的专家齐聚一堂来共同解决联合国文明对话项目的核心问题：什么是有意义的对话的先决条件？我们如何最好地促进文明对话？有着来自 23 个不同国家超过 40 位的发言人参会，会议就一个有意义的文明对话所涉及的许多方面给出了一个清晰的图景。会议表明，即使对于那些经常参与到对话议题中的人来说，讨论也并不总是一件容易的事，特别是在当他们谈及具体的价值观和行为准则的时候。然而，这也非常清楚地证明了，只要参与的各方之间有一个共识：对话要比互相对抗好，那么对话就有可能并且实际上也会带来人类面临的共同问题的新的创造性的解答。

2001 年 9 月 11 日　全国政协外事委员会在京举办"21 世纪论坛——不同文明对话"研讨会，邀请国内外知名人士和专家学者，就不同文明对话问题进行多方面的交流与探讨。全国政协副主席、中国工程院院长宋健在研讨会上致开幕词。本次研讨会为期两天，议题涉及"不同文明间交流对人类历史发展的推动作用"、"不同文明对话对国际关系发展的影响"以及"联合国在推动不同文明对话中所起的作用"等三大方面，来自中国、埃及、希腊、美国等国的代表在研讨会上阐述了各自的观点。

2001 年 11 月 2 日　联合国教科文组织（UNESCO）第 31 届大会在巴黎总部通过了《世界文化多样性宣言》，主张将文化多样性作为一种有生命力、因而能不断发展的财富加以保护。从这个意义上说，文化多样性是人类的共同遗产，应当从当代人和子孙后代的利益考虑，予以承认和肯定。

2002 年 6 月 7 日至 10 日　由北美华人基督教学会与西敏寺神学院联合主办的"第七届北美华人基督教与其他宗教学者学术研讨会"在费城西敏寺神学院成功举行，来自美国、加拿大、中国及中国香港地区、台湾地区和英国的华人学者 70 多人参加了这次学术大会。这次大会的主题为"基督教与中国文化的对话"，会议共收到学术论文 45 篇，内容涵盖基督教与中国文化对话、中国基督教史、中国基督教现状等诸多方面。

2002 年 8 月 8 日至 10 日　由南京大学与美国哈佛大学哈佛—燕京学社共同发起的"文明对话学术研讨会"在南京召开，共有来自海内外各大学、研究机构等单位 50 余人参加了此次会议。与会代表就文明间的对话与冲突、融合和对立、尤其是回儒之间的对话等诸多方面的话题从历史和现实两个维度空间中展开了"智慧"的对话，在不同层面上都有所收获。

2002 年 8 月 26 日至 9 月 4 日　可持续发展世界首脑会议在南非约翰内斯

堡举行。这次会议通过了两个主要文件:《约翰内斯堡可持续发展宣言》和《约翰内斯堡执行计划》。《约翰内斯堡执行计划》指出:和平、安全、稳定和尊重人权与基本自由,包括发展权以及尊重文化的多样性,是实现可持续发展的关键。《约翰内斯堡执行计划》包含有时间限制的目标,在以下几个方面实施可持续发展:基本卫生设施、化工、水资源综合管理、海洋和鱼类资源、臭氧层消耗物的替代品、减缓目前生物多样性流失的速度、小岛屿发展中国家、非洲粮食安全和能源通道。

2002 年 9 月 19 日至 22 日 以"没有边界的世界——亚欧青年对全球化的回应"为题的首届亚欧会议(ASEM)青年对话在丹麦的哥本哈根举行,这次对话创造了新的友谊、共同的看法以及继续对话的愿望。这是来自 24 个亚欧会议成员国的 62 个参与者和观察者表达的共同心声。根据主题,这次对话由亚欧基金会和丹麦青年理事会共同举办。在 3 天的相聚中,与会者对四个和全球化有关的重要问题进行了深入探讨,也就是移民;青年参与的良好治理;全球形象和身份;青年就业、教育和终身学习。会议成功地发布了亚欧会议青年关于全球化的宣言,这份宣言抓住了与会者的共识并且指出面对全球化挑战的建议。

2002 年 10 月 20 日至 22 日 为期 3 天的第九届法语国家首脑会议在黎巴嫩首都贝鲁特落下帷幕,并通过了《贝鲁特宣言》。会议强调在联合国决议框架内通过和平途径解决巴勒斯坦问题和伊拉克问题,即奉行"对话"不是"对抗","和平"不是"战争","民主"不是"独裁","多极"不是"单极"的"文明对话"的原则。

2003 年 8 月 10 日至 17 日 以"面向世界问题的哲学"为主题的第二十一届世界哲学大会在土耳其伊斯坦布尔会展中心隆重举行。此次盛会吸引了世界各国的大批学者,大会正式代表达 2000 多人,当代德国著名哲学家哈贝马斯也欣然与会并作专题演讲。这次会议旨在强调在新世纪开初之际,需要用哲学知识研究解决重大的全球性问题,使哲学在创造一个"没有恐惧与贫困"的世界方面发挥重要作用。

2003 年 9 月 7 日至 10 日 以"寻求新视角"为题的国际文明对话部长级会议在印度新德里举行。透过文化和文明间对话和互动的镜头,会议被看成是定义 21 世纪的全球互动的一大贡献。它聚焦于联合国教科文组织的核心使命所关注的问题:(1)教育作为一种对话的工具;(2)科学技术(包括信息技术)作为全球团结和连通的新前沿;(3)在全球化时代保护文化多样性和精神价值。会议通过《新德里宣言》。与会代表请求"各国政府和公民社会积极支持文明和文化内部以及它们之间的对话，这样对话才会成为一个改革的有效工具，一个和平与宽容的尺度和一个多样性和多元主义的机会"。

2003年9月3—6日　第一届世界公共论坛"文明对话"年会在希腊罗得岛举办。这次会议在面对复杂的国际形势下举行，从而证明了广泛的国际讨论，致力于达成代表不同文明之间的相互理解的必要性。罗德论坛在2003年成为最有代表性的公共论坛，从那时起它每年举行一次。在首届论坛上代表们通过了题为"为了促进文明秩序的文明对话"的《罗德岛宣言》，宣言呼吁继续讨论人类的命运并且宣布把论坛建成一支国际舞台上的生力军的目标。

2003年9月22日至24日　首届世界宗教大会在哈萨克斯坦首都阿斯塔纳举行，有18个有关国家和国际宗教组织的代表共150余人出席此次大会。这次世界宗教大会的主题是"和平、宽容与对话"，倡导宗教间的和睦相处，以此消除暴力和仇恨，一定意义上可以看作是当今世界宗教对话潮流的具体反映。

2003年11月6日至8日　由中国社会科学院世界文明比较研究中心、南京师范大学外国语学院、澳门基金会共同举办的"世界文明国际论坛"第一次国际学术研讨会在南京召开。研讨会讨论议题包括"文明理论"、"通过文明差异进行文明对话和交流"、"在国际关系和国际政治中文化的作用"等。来自世界各地20多个国家和我国部分高校、研究机构的代表出席了研讨会，共提交论文30多篇。

2003年12月3日　为期两天的亚欧会议——文化与文明会议上午在北京开幕。亚欧会议26个成员及各界代表近200人出席会议。与会者以文化多样性和统一性为主题，就亚欧在文化、种族及社会经济等多样性中存在的共同价值展开对话。

2004年1月8日至12日　"全球正义与文明对话国际学术研讨会"在华东师范大学举行。会议代表来自中国、美国、澳大利亚、新加坡、挪威等国家。华东师大副校长陈群、挪威科学院院士希尔贝克、卡内基委员会项目负责人卡勒出席开幕式并致贺词。校长助理童世俊主持研讨会。

2004年2月10日至11日　联合国教科文组织在也门萨那举办"文化与文明间对话"专题讨论会。讨论会的出发点在于：阿拉伯穆斯林文化对世界其他文明的贡献理应根据有科学依据的途径得到仔细和准确的评估。讨论会主要从下列5个角度探讨文化与文明间对话：全球化与对话；教育对对话的贡献；阿拉伯文化对其他文化的贡献；对话在遏制恐怖主义的过程中发挥的作用；东西方的对话。

2004年8月23日至25日　由北京大学主办的首届北京论坛在北京举行。

论坛的主题是"文明的和谐与共同繁荣"。来自世界五大洲 32 个国家的 200 多位著名学者参加了会议。大陆和港澳台地区有 225 位著名学者参加了会议。论坛致力于推动全球人文社会科学问题的研究，促进世界的学术发展和社会进步，从而为全人类的发展与繁荣作出贡献。论坛相信，不同文明在和平环境中的交汇始终是人类社会进步的动力源泉和根本保证。自这时起，北京论坛每年举办一次。

2004 年 9 月 7 日至 8 日 由中国社会科学院日本研究所、甘肃省人民政府外事办公室、日本未来工学研究所和韩国世宗研究所共同主办的"第二次中日韩新世纪文明国际学术讨论会"在兰州举办。本次研讨会围绕"创建和谐文明，推动东亚发展"的主题，就未来的世界文明、文明的多样化以及和平亚洲的作用等重大问题进行深入讨论。来自中国、日本、韩国的近 70 名政治家和学者就如何创建新世纪和谐文明展开讨论。

2004 年 10 月 12 日至 13 日 由中国社会科学院世界宗教研究所与日本东洋哲学研究所共同主办的"现代文明与宗教对话"中日学术会议在中国社会科学院学术报告厅举行。北京各高校、各科研院所及相关机构专家学者约 100 人参加了这次会议。这是由中日双方共同举办的第一次关于"宗教对话"的学术会议，会上中日双方学者从不同的角度展开宗教对话，丰富和深化了对宗教对话的理解。

2004 年 11 月 12 日至 14 日 中国社会科学院历史研究所和福建师范大学社会历史学院联合在武夷山举办了"中西文明交融与兴衰国际学术研讨会"。会议共收到 51 篇学术论文或论文提纲。3 天来，50 多位来自海内外高等院校、科研机构的代表分别就东西文明的交融与兴衰进行了多方面和多层次的探讨与分析，取得了丰硕的学术成果。

2004 年 12 月 3 日至 5 日 "儒学思想在世界的传播与发展"国际学术研讨会在中国人民大学召开。此次研讨会由中国人民大学和韩国高等教育财团主办，中国人民大学孔子研究院和中国人民大学亚洲研究中心承办。参加本次国际学术研讨会的有来自 10 多个国家的 130 多位专家学者，大会收到学术论文 70 余篇。会议主旨，一是沟通中西文化，推动儒家思想的传播与发展；二是了解海外儒学发展现状，为当代中国汲取儒学文化资源提供借鉴和参考。

2004 年 12 月 20 日至 22 日 由越南和联合国教科文组织联合举办的"为了和平与可持续发展的文化和文明之间的对话"亚洲太平洋区域会议在越南河内召开。本次区域会议寻求提供一个论坛为致力于不同文化和文明间对话的各机构和个人进行直接和公开的对话，在不同层次和交叉领域里讨论政治行动的方向、策略和措施。参会者被要求突出促进不同文化和文明之间对话，特别是那些和教育、文化相关的示范方法和创新战略。巩固、推进和沟通区域联合进路的意见和建议被确定是未来在这一领域的行动的最终政策导向结论所采用的观点。

2005年3月4日　由南京大学历史系、英国考文垂大学宽恕与和解研究中心、澳门基金会和爱德基金会联合主办的"和平研究国际学术研讨会"在南京国际会议中心隆重开幕。来自中国大陆、澳门地区以及国外的50多名专家学者参加了会议，他们将围绕"人类历史上的对抗、冲突与化解"这一主题进行为期3天的讨论。

2005年3月27—30日　"文明对话"世界公众论坛（WPF）在古巴举办了题为"拉丁美洲在21世纪：普遍性和独创性"的国际会议，本次会议的主题是拉丁美洲当前形势，因为这个地区正在经历一场文明的自决进程。本次会议的主要成就之一是在国际背景下审视最重要的拉美问题。与会者表示要维护社会选择的自由和国际社会的多极化。

2005年4月5日　"文明、文化和民族对话"国际会议在巴黎的联合国教科文组织总部召开。在这次会议上，伊朗总统哈塔米极力主张把文明间的公开对话作为改善国际关系和发展的必要条件，并呼吁建立一个全球论坛来促进不同文明和文化间的对话。

2005年5月9日至10日　"环境、和平、文化与文明对话"国际会议在伊朗首都德黑兰举行。这次会议由伊朗的环境部门、联合国环境规划署承办，并由联合国大学和教科文组织协办。来自世界20多个国家、国际组织、宗教团体以及非政府组织的20多名部长、100多名政府官员、研究人员、学者出席了本次会议。会议的目的是研究在多边文明对话的背景下，环境、和平与安全之间的相互作用，并讨论进行对于多边主义有意义的对话的需要。

2005年5月30日至31日　山东大学犹太教与跨宗教研究中心在山东大学东校区举办了题为"跨宗教对话：儒教、犹太教、基督教"的国际研讨会，来自国内外20多所高校和研究机构的近40名犹太文化与跨宗教研究方面的专家、学者齐聚山大，共商学术。

2005年6月20日至21日　由中国外交部和欧盟委员会共同举办的"中欧人权对话研讨会·表达自由"和"中欧人权对话研讨会·死刑"两个会议，在北京好苑建国商务酒店同时举行。这是8年来中欧召开的第十三次人权对话研讨会。

2005年6月30日至7月3日　由宁夏社科院和伊朗伊斯兰共和国驻华大使馆文化处主办的"郑和下西洋与文明对话国际研讨会"在银川召开。此次国际研讨会的主题是"郑和下西洋与文明传播"、"波斯——阿拉伯伊斯兰文明与中国伊斯兰文明的关系"、"重振丝绸之路,促进中国与伊斯兰国家经贸关系发展"、"文明对话"等。来自伊朗、巴基斯坦、日本、保加利亚等国和我国各地的120多名专家学者参加研讨会。此次研讨会共收到国内外学者提交的中英文论文78篇,得到中伊两国政府有关部门和媒体的高度重视。

2005年7月14日 联合国秘书长科菲·安南在纽约的联合国总部的一份声明中宣布了推出"文明联盟"的倡议。这个倡议意图回应国际社会——不管是在机构还是市民社会的层面上——在弥合分歧,克服那些可能会威胁和平的偏见、误解和对立方面做出坚实努力的需要。该联盟将致力于解决来自煽动暴力的敌对观念带来的新兴威胁,并带来消除这种分歧的多方面努力之间的合作。文明联盟的成立是西班牙首相何塞·路易斯·罗德里格斯·萨帕特罗发起的,并且由土耳其总理雷杰普·塔伊普·埃尔多安共同提案。两国政府作为共同提案国会继续提供支持。

2005年7月21日至22日 第一届亚欧会议不同信仰间对话在印度尼西亚巴厘岛召开。印尼、英国、泰国等28个亚欧国家的174名代表参加了此次对话会议。与会代表通过《构建不同宗教信仰间和谐的巴厘宣言》,呼吁国际社会中的不同宗教和信仰之间相互理解与尊重,和谐共处。

2005年9月9日至12日 由武汉大学、台北东方人文学术研究基金会、台北鹅湖杂志社和台湾"中央"大学哲学研究所联合举办的第七届当代新儒学国际学术会议在武汉大学召开。出席会议的有来自国内外学者近150人,提交论文120余篇。本次大会的主题为"儒学、当代新儒学与当代世界"。学者们就现当代新儒学三代代表人物的学术思想、儒学在当代的作用与意义、当代新儒学如何深入发展等问题展开了热烈的讨论。

2005年9月19日至20日 中国社会科学院世界文明比较研究中心分别与深圳大学、电子科技大学中山学院、澳门基金会及澳门理工学院联手举办"第二届世界文明国际论坛",精心策划了三场各有特色的主题研讨会:《世界文明与公民社会理论国际研讨会》、《亚洲与世界文明国际研讨会》、《当代世界与世界文明研究新动向》。这是继2003年"首届世界文明国际论坛"之后的第二届国际论坛,会议分别在深圳、中山、澳门三地召开。

2005年11月18日至21日 由南京大学、哈佛大学哈佛—燕京学社、宁夏社会科学院联合主办的"文明对话国际学术研讨会"在宁夏召开,来自海内外各大学、研究机构等单位的100多位专家、学者及宗教界人士参加了研讨会。哈佛大学哈佛—燕京学社主任杜维明教授作主题演讲。此次研讨会的主题为"文化对话与文化自觉"，在为期4天的研讨会上，与会专家深入探讨了"回儒对话"的世界意义与哲学意蕴，多层次阐释、发掘了不同文化之间相互学习、相互理解、平等对话的时代意义。

2005年12月7日至10日　由中国社会科学院基督教研究中心主办的"基督宗教与跨文化对话"学术研讨会在北京宝辰饭店举行。来自全国各地的100余位专家、学者参加或旁听了此次研讨会，其中，近50位学者提交了会议论文并作了大会发言。本次会议围绕着"基督宗教与跨文化对话"的基本理论、宗教间比较与对话、文化视域与思想比较、思想史上的反思、基督宗教与儒家思想、社会政治与社会研究、基督宗教与中国处境等主题展开了广泛交流和深入研讨。

2005年12月9日至11日　由中国人民大学和韩国高等教育财团主办、中国人民大学孔子研究院和中国人民亚洲研究中心承办的"儒学与亚洲人文价值"国际学术研讨会在北京举行，来自10多个国家和地区的150多位专家学者参加会议，并提交论文100多篇。大会围绕儒学及其传统、儒学的人文价值、儒学与文明对话、儒学与东亚文化、儒学与和谐社会、儒家思想的现代转换等议题展开了热烈讨论。

2005年12月10日　为期两天的伊斯兰国家特别首脑会议在伊斯兰圣地麦加闭幕。伊斯兰会议组织的57个成员国全部派代表参加会议，多数国家还是元首或政府首脑亲自与会。会议发表了最后声明，通过了《麦加宣言》和《未来10年行动纲领》。为此，与会领导人讨论了宗教、政治、经济和社会等问题，并达成了不少共识，取得了积极成果。他们认为，极端主义和恐怖主义绝不是伊斯兰教，反对任何打着宗教旗号的极端思想和行为，主张在互相理解的基础上进行平等的文明对话，让世人更好地理解伊斯兰教等。

2006年1月12日至13日　东亚宗教领袖论坛在印尼首都雅加达举行，来自东亚国家的200多名宗教界代表出席了论坛。本次论坛的主题是：贫穷、文盲、失业；宗教在构建安全、防止恐怖主义和极端主义等方面所起的作用以及纪念中国的伟大航海家、和平使者郑和。

2006年6月20日至21日　"文明、文化和民族对话"非洲区域会议在尼日利亚的阿布贾举行。本次会议由联合国教科文组织和尼日利亚联邦政府联合主办，尼日利亚总统奥卢塞贡·奥巴桑乔酋长和教科文组织总干事松浦晃一郎先生共同主持，并且松浦晃一郎先生还参加了会议。本次会议特别关注教育和科学在促进对话、彼此间更好地理解和相互了解方面的潜力。

2006 年 6 月 26 日至 28 日　由中华美学学会、中国社会科学院哲学研究所和四川师范大学共同主办的"美学与多元文化对话"国际学术研讨会在四川成都召开，来自国际美学协会的 20 余位理事和国内 40 余位学者参加了会议。与会学者围绕会议的主题展开了充分的讨论和交流，并形成共识：今日全球美学面临着"文化间性"转向的问题。

2006 年 8 月 1 日至 3 日　"丝绸之路与文明的对话"学术讨论会在新疆喀什召开，会议由中国中外关系史学会、新疆社会科学院、暨南大学文学院、西北民族大学历史文化学院、新疆师范大学、喀什师范学院共同发起主办，由新疆社会科学院、喀什师范学院具体承办。共逾百位代表参加了会议，与会者多为国内对丝绸之路研究颇有建树的专家、学者。大会共收到 79 篇论文，涉及的研究领域非常广泛。此次学术讨论会注重把丝绸之路的历史与现实结合起来进行研究和探讨，对于推进新世纪丝绸之路研究事业的发展具有重要的意义。

2006 年 8 月 26 日至 29 日　世界宗教和平会议第八届大会在日本京都召开，约 100 个国家和地区的代表约 1500 人与会，其中包括 500 多名宗教界人士。本次会议围绕"抵制暴力，共享安全"的主题，又分为"化解矛盾"、"构建和平"、"促进可持续发展"三个专题，进行了大会发言及分组讨论。最后会议通过了《京都宣言》，呼吁各宗教加强对话与合作，共同抵制暴力，维护和平，促进发展，保护地球这一人类共同的家园。

2006 年 9 月 22 日至 25 日　由南京大学、哈佛—燕京学社和苏州工业园区管委会共同主办的哈佛—燕京第六届国际学术研讨会在苏州工业园区举行。来自国内各重点大学和科研机构以及美国、日本、韩国和中国台湾地区的哈佛、燕京校友共计 80 余人与会。本次会议以"文化自觉与文化认同：东亚视角"为主题，是前三届文明对话学术研讨会的继续与深入。2000 年、2002 年和 2004 年在苏州召开的前三届会议的主题分别为："文明对话：本土知识的全球意义"、"文明对话：东亚现代化的含义"和"文明对话：全球化与文化多样性"。

2006 年 10 月 17 日至 18 日　由中国现代文学研究会、北京鲁迅博物馆和绍兴市人民政府联合主办，中共绍兴市委宣传部、绍兴文理学院、上海鲁迅纪念馆等单位承办的纪念鲁迅诞辰 125 周年、逝世 70 周年暨"鲁迅：跨文化对话"国际学术研讨会在鲁迅故里、国家历史文化名城绍兴市顺利举行，来自日本、德国、俄罗斯、澳大利亚和中国台湾、香港与大陆等国家和地区的 120 多名专家学者出席了会议。

2006 年 11 月 24 日　"文化多样性与当代世界"国际学术研讨会在中山大

学举行，本次会议由中山大学人类学系承办，吸引了来自 20 多个国家和地区的 500 余名专家学者以及政府官员。本次大会代表来自人类学、民族学、社会学、民俗学、考古学、博物馆学、政府部门和非政府组织，人员众多、议题广泛。

2006 年 12 月 24 日　中国首届文明论坛暨《文明》杂志创刊 5 周年纪念在中国社会科学院学术报告厅举行，这次文明论坛的思想主题是"文明传播，和谐中国"。首届文明论坛发表了《丙戌文明宣言》，阐明了对文化、文明与传播关系的认识，表达了对人类文明需要和谐传播、对话与交流的美好意愿。

2007 年 3 月 13 日至 14 日　"文明对话"世界公众论坛（WPF）在联合国教科文组织的支持下举办了一次国际研讨会，这次会议在法国巴黎的联合国教科文组织总部举行。此次研讨会的主题是"文化与文明对话：人权和道德价值观之间的桥梁"，来自 30 多个国家的与会者参加了这次活动。

2007 年 3 月 26 日至 28 日　"世界汉学大会 2007：文明对话与和谐世界"在北京隆重举行。"世界汉学大会 2007"由国家汉语国际推广领导小组办公室与中国人民大学共同主办，并由中国人民大学汉语国际推广研究所、中国人民大学文学院、中国人民大学国学院承办。大会旨在通过世界汉学界主要学者的深入对话和讨论，促进当代国际汉学研究领域的交流与合作，进一步凸显中国传统文化对于建构和谐世界的价值。会议共邀请了国内外的 200 余位专家学者出席，其中包括许多世界汉学界顶级的专家。大会分为"作为文明对话的汉学研究"、"'中国形象'在汉学研究中的变迁"、"中国传统文化：诠释和影响"、"汉学家与汉学史"以及"汉语国际推广与跨文化交流"5 个主题进行了集体和分组发言与讨论。大会共收到论文 100 余篇。

2007 年 4 月 13 日至 14 日　由西安交通大学丝绸之路国际法研究所和人文社会科学学院主办的"多边文化与国际法"国际研讨会在西安建国饭店举行。参加会议的有中国、中国香港、加拿大、美国、法国、德国、日本、乌拉圭、奥地利、罗马尼亚、尼日利亚等国家和地区的近 20 位知名的国际法专家。

2007 年 4 月 17 日至 19 日　由浙江大学主办的"文明和谐与创新国际论坛"在杭州召开，来自中国、美国、英国、德国、法国、瑞士、意大利、埃及、土耳其、西班牙、日本等 15 个国家和地区，代表了当今世界主要文明区和文化系的跨文化研究学者 50 余人出席了会议。会议围绕世界多元文化的和谐、合作与发展、世界文明间的历史关系与未来展望、中华文明的现代价值与自主创新等问题，展开了广泛交流与深入研讨，取得了若干重要的成果。

2007 年 4 月 20 日至 22 日　"跨文明对话——视界融合与文化互动"国际

学术研讨会在西南交通大学举行。此次国际学术研讨会由西南交通大学比较文学与当代文化研究中心、艺术与传播学院主办。100余名中外知名学者、专家参会，其中包括国际比较文学协会名誉会长佛克马先生、伦敦大学东方学院讲席教授赵毅衡等。研讨会围绕"跨文明对话"这一主题进行了热烈的讨论。

2007年5月24日至25日 第二届"全球化和文明对话"国际论坛在格鲁吉亚的第比利斯举行。筹办这次论坛的组织机构有：格鲁吉亚的外交部；教育科学部；文化、古迹保护和体育部；支持商业活动中的教育和团结国际基金会；"亚欧对话平台"国际基金会。大约30位著名政界和宗教界人士、政治学家、学者和代表参加了这次论坛。与会者分析了文明对话对于和平的贡献。

2007年5月30日到6月2日 "当代语境下的儒耶对谈：思想与实践"国际研讨会在香港浸会大学举行。来自中国大陆、香港和台湾地区、北美的华人学者40余人进行了3天的对谈。这次对谈的定位是"寻找共同关心的问题"。这次对谈是由山东大学（济南）和浸会大学（香港）共同组织的。

2007年6月4日至5日 "文明对话"世界公众论坛（WPF）在芬兰坦佩雷举办了国际区域会议"欧洲文明的空间：波罗的海对话"，超过200人参加了会议。与会者专注于创新、能源和运输领域的合作前景。

2007年6月4日至6日 第一届"宗教对话与和谐社会"学术研讨会在兰州举行，这次会议由兰州大学哲学社会学院、兰州大学基督教文化研究中心、兰州大学伊斯兰文化研究所主办。来自30个宗教学研究学术单位的近50位专家学者参加了此次会议。与会专家学者主要围绕四个议题展开讨论：（一）宗教对话与和谐社会；（二）多元宗教与和谐社会；（三）宗教对话；（四）西北基督教与伊斯兰教的历史与现状。会议由加拿大文化更新研究中心协办。

2007年6月19日至21日 第三届亚欧会议不同信仰间对话会议在中国南京举行，来自37个亚欧会议成员和4个观察员的约200名代表齐聚一堂。会议围绕"深化不同信仰对话，实现和平、发展与和谐"主题，讨论了如何发挥不同信仰对话在应对全球化、维护和平、促进社会融合及发展、推动文化和教育合作等方面的作用等问题。会议呼吁亚欧会议成员尊重社会制度、发展道路和文化的多样性，共同应对全球化挑战；强调及时、全面实现千年发展目标对消除贫困、促进发展、实现共同繁荣的重要性；呼吁亚欧会议成员在文化交流和教育合作领域加强合作。

2007年6月25日至27日 第15届国际中国哲学大会在武汉大学隆重举行。本次大会由国际中国哲学学会（ISCP）、中国哲学史学会、中华孔子学会、武汉大学哲学学院、中国传统文化研究中心、孔子与儒学研究中心等单位主办。来自美国、加拿大、德国、英国、丹麦、西班牙等 14 个国家及我国台湾、香港和大陆 20 个省、市、自治区的 200 多位学者应邀出席大会。本届国际中国哲学会会长郭齐勇教授担任本次大会主席。会议紧扣大会主题——"21 世纪中国哲学与全球文明的对话"而展开。

2007 年 8 月 25 日至 26 日　由中国中东学会、上海社会科学院欧亚研究所、上海世界史学会和上海国际问题研究中心联合举办的"文明对话与中东发展"学术研讨会在上海成功举行。作为中国中东学会年会及上海国际关系学会建立 50 周年的重要学术活动之一，20 多家单位的近 60 名专家学者参加了这次会议并且围绕中东问题展开了深入讨论。与会单位分别是外交部、中国社会科学院西亚非洲研究所、中国现代国际关系研究院、西北大学、云南大学、西南大学、河南师范大学、上海国际问题研究所等等。

2007 年 9 月 9 日至 10 日　由南开大学和日本大东文化大学主办，日本国际交流基金协办，南开大学世界近代史研究中心、日本研究院承办的"近代化过程中东亚三国的相互认识"国际学术研讨会在南开大学召开。70 余名专家学者出席了本次研讨会。会议的成功召开，加深了东亚各国的学术交流，促进了各国学者对各国近代化道路的认识。

2007 年 10 月 26 日至 28 日　"世界宗教与文明对话会议"在马其顿文化名城奥赫里德市举办，来自 20 多个国家的 200 多名宗教界人士和学者出席了会议。此次会议由马其顿共和国文化部与联合国教科文组织联合举办，主题为"宗教与文化对和平的贡献，互敬与共存"。此次"宗教与文明对话会议"为首届会议，以后将每三年召开一次。大会通过了大会宣言，呼吁各宗教与文明加强对话，放弃偏见，尊重宗教与文明的多样性，谴责宗教暴力，加强宗教教育，尊重女权。

2008 年 1 月 15 日至 16 日　由西班牙政府主办的"第一届文明联盟全球论坛"在马德里召开，会议召集了政治领袖、国际和区域机构的代表、宗教领袖、青年、企业高管、民间社会团体以及旨在减少国家之间的两极分化和在全球采取联合行动促进跨文化理解的基金会。超过 900 名参与者和 89 个官方代表团在马德里的出席证明了文明联盟在世界各地发展的重要性。全球论坛这两天的行程围绕着三次全体会议和八个工作会议来举行。来自 78 个国家的与会者讨论了媒体在跨文化对话中的作用、宗教领袖作为和平倡导者所面临的挑战和要求、多元文化主义可以提供给商界的机会等不同的问题。全球论坛以务实的态度给政府机构、国际组织和公民社会的代表提供了一个独特的国际平台，使得他们能在跨文化和跨宗教对话领域，特别是在文明联盟的诸如教育、青年、移民和媒体等重点领域，建立伙伴关系和制定具体措施。

2008 年 4 月 18 日至 21 日　由叶圣陶研究会、中华宗教文化交流协会、中华炎黄文化研究会、中华文化交流协会（澳门）合办的首届文明对话暨论坛在澳门举行，来自中国内地和香港、澳门、台湾地区的专家学者以及佛教界、道教界人士等共百余人参加了此次活动。活动主题为"中华文明与社会和谐"，希望通过高层次的名家对话及各专家参与论坛的模式，引领社会对中华文化进行更深层次的思考；借此审视中华文化在传承与发展过程中的积极影响与其变革之路，同时思考中华文化与当代社会现代化发展的关系，为中华文化在华人社会的进一步传承和保持更长久的影响作出贡献。

2008 年 7 月 16 日　由穆斯林世界联盟（MWL）组织的国际宗教研讨会在西班牙首都马德里举行，会期 3 天，有近 300 多位世界各国宗教领袖参加大会，他们来自伊斯兰教、犹太教、基督教、印度教、佛教等世界各大宗教团体。这次会议寻求世界各宗教共同的价值观，营造世界和平的精神，从而探索和平共处、互相谅解和彼此合作的途径。

2008 年 7 月 30 日至 8 月 5 日　第 22 届世界哲学大会在韩国首尔的首尔大学举行，总主题为"反思当今的哲学"。这是世界哲学大会首次在亚洲举行。

2008 年 10 月 11 日至 13 日　"登州与海上丝绸之路"国际学术研讨会在山东蓬莱召开。此次会议由鲁东大学和联合国泛丝绸之路·系列活动组委会、中国中外关系史学会、山东师范大学齐鲁文化研究中心、蓬莱市人民政府联合主办，鲁东大学和蓬莱市人民政府承办。国内外著名学者及《光明日报》、《当代韩国》记者 60 余人出席了研讨会。本次会议围绕古登州与海上丝绸之路、山东半岛与海上丝绸之路、山东半岛在中韩日关系史中的作用与地位等论题，展开深入而广泛的研讨交流。

2008 年 11 月 10 日　"文明对话"世界公共论坛在联合国教科文组织的赞助下召开了一个高级专家会议，在维也纳霍夫堡宫讨论当今世界面临的最紧迫的社会文化问题。本次会议汇集了来自世界各地的约 40 名专家、政要，专注于目前世界面临的经济金融形势恶化以及由于全球化而加剧的当前问题。

2008 年 11 月 10 日至 12 日　由西北大学中东研究所和沙特阿拉伯沙特国王大学联合主办、西安外国语大学阿拉伯语系协办的"中国—沙特阿拉伯王国学者论坛"在西北大学举行。来自沙特国王大学、盖西姆大学的 4 位沙特学者和西北大学中东研究所、西安外国语大学、中国社会科学院西亚非洲研究所、中国社会科学院世界宗教研究所、上海国际问题研究院等国内单位的代表共 30 余人与会。会议开幕式由西北大学中东研究所所长王铁铮教授主持，西北大学副校长任宗哲教授和沙特阿拉伯的穆罕默德·阿里谢博士分别在开幕式上致辞。会议就"伊斯兰中间主义"思潮做了深入交流。

2009 年 4 月 6 日至 7 日　联合国文明联盟的第二次全球论坛在土耳其的伊斯坦布尔举行。该论坛是一次旨在促进跨文化理解的全球盛会。超过 1000 位参与者在伊斯坦布尔聚首，其中包括一些政府领导人，50 余位部长，同时还有来自全世界的决策者、基金会、媒体和基层领袖，为的是建立新的伙伴关系和产生出旨在为不同社会间建立信任和合作的想法。这个论坛也是盘点文明联盟的倡议及企业伙伴协作的可行项目的一次机会。

2009 年 5 月 18 日　澳门大学社会科学及人文学院及澳门特区政府高等教育辅助办公室联合举办的《冲突对话与文明建设国际学术研讨会》于当天上午在澳门开幕，40 余名来自中国内地，台、港、澳地区以及日本的专家学者出席。

2009 年 10 月 16 日至 18 日　由浙江大学和香港中文大学共同发起，浙江大学基督教与跨文化研究中心承办的"文明对话与对话文明——21 世纪佛耶相遇"国际学术研讨会在杭州灵峰山庄举行，共有来自国内外大学、研究机构等单位的总计 43 位代表出席了会议。此次召开的是第三届学术研讨会，前两届分别由陕西师范大学和香港中文大学举办。

2009 年 11 月 6 日　由北京大学、北京市教育委员会和韩国高等教育财团联合主办的北京论坛第六届年会——北京论坛（2009）在北京隆重召开。此次论坛为期 3 天，以"文明的和谐与共同繁荣——危机的挑战、反思与和谐发展"为主题。联合国秘书长潘基文先生特为本届论坛的召开发表视频讲话。来自 40 多个国家和地区的 300 余位海内外知名专家学者参会，他们从理论和实践两个方面探寻规律，研究化解危机的政策和走出危机的途径，为全球的和谐发展贡献智慧和力量。

2009 年 11 月 12 日至 13 日　为进一步推动中加文化交流，增进中加两国人民之间的相互了解，中国人民对外友好协会与加拿大国际文化基金会合作在北京举办了第一届"中国—加拿大文化对话"会议。会议期间，中加双方代表围绕"转变"、"多样性"、"伙伴关系"、"沟通交流"、"文化外交"、"创意城市"、"引领下一代"等主题深入探讨，分享传统文化，交流当代文化。

2009 年 12 月 12 日至 13 日　"传统与当代世界：走向多元文化、思想与价值的对话"国际学术研讨会在北京举行。会议由北京师范大学价值与文化研究中心、北京师范大学哲学与社会学学院、中国社会科学院哲学研究所《世界哲学》编辑部联合主办，来自国内外的100多名专家学者参加了此次研讨会。与会学者围绕"传统与当代世界"这一主题，对文化多样性与当代世界、哲学与伦理学视野下的现代生活、儒学的阐释及其当代价值、当代社会秩序与政治哲学等热点问题展开了深入的交流与探讨。

2010年4月16日至17日　由中国社会科学院世界文明比较研究中心、上海社会科学院思想文化研究中心、南京师范大学外国语学院、澳门基金会联合举办的"世界文明国际论坛"第四届国际学术研讨会在中国社会科学院举行。此次研讨会的主题是"当代世界文明进程的新特征和文明研究的新进展"，来自德国、加拿大、俄罗斯、日本、韩国等有关外国专家及来自国内大学等70余位专家学者与会。话题指向均聚焦于当今世界文明面对的重要问题。

2010年4月27日至28日　中国中山大学比较宗教研究所、云南大学西南边疆少数民族研究中心和越南社会科学院宗教研究所，在越南河内市合作举办了第四届"越南与中国宗教生活状况"国际学术研讨会。与会的中越两国学者在回顾和总结前三届合作研究的基础上，针对中越两国面临的新的宗教问题，深入交换了意见。

2010年5月6日至7日　由开罗大学孔子学院和开罗大学中文系联合主办的"中阿文明对话——语言文化国际研讨会"在开罗举行。研讨会上，与会者围绕汉语、阿拉伯语教学的思想与观念、东西方文化差异和融合、中阿文化交流、中阿语言文化对比、中阿语言翻译等题目进行深入研讨与交流。

2010年5月21日　与联合国教科文组织有业务往来的中国民俗摄影协会，协助开展了"联合国教科文组织周和国际文化和睦年走进中国活动"，来自中国10多个省市的文化官员出席了该活动。在国际文化和睦年的主题下，中国的许多省份都举办了一系列国内和国际文化活动，其中包括甘肃省的全国摄影大赛。

2010年5月24日　武汉大学欧美宗教文化研究所、武汉大学哲学学院和武汉大学孔子与儒学研究中心联合举办了"儒学与基督教会通"国际学术会议，三位美国学者和国内多所高校的学者与会。学者们从儒学、基督教、当下中国人的精神状态、美国政教分离的发展史等角度论述了儒家与基督教的相关学说及其关联，并展开了激烈的学术争鸣。一致认为儒学和基督教思想并不存在着根本的对立和冲突，相反，存在着对话和会通的可能性。

2010年5月27日至29日　联合国文明联盟第三次论坛在里约热内卢举行。拥有来自世界各地的几千名注册参与者，其中包括政界和商界领袖、市长、青年、记者、基金会、国际组织以及宗教领袖等，里约论坛表明联合国文明联盟已经坚定地成为联合国进行全球对话的主要稳固平台，而这次会议旨在在跨文化和宗教的国家和民族之间改善理解和合作关系。关注于"沟通文化，缔造和平"，联合国文明联盟第三次论坛是一个建立关系、获得世界上最紧迫的跨文化挑战的洞察以及将想法付诸行动的特殊地方。

2010 年 6 月 11 日至 14 日　由南京大学和哈佛—燕京学社发起的"第四次文明对话国际学术会议"在南京召开。此次大会的主题是"文化理解与文化对话的百年进程"，共有来自美国、日本、意大利以及国内著名大学和研究机构的 84 位正式代表参加了大会。会议讨论的核心问题是"回儒对话"，即伊斯兰教与中国传统儒家思想的对话。大会共收到 43 篇论文。

2010 年 7 月 5 日　首届郑和国际研讨会在马来西亚著名旅游城市马六甲举行，此次研讨会由国际郑和学会、马六甲州政府、马六甲博物管理局及郑和文化馆联合举行，研讨会的主题是"郑和与亚非世界"。来自中国、新加坡、马来西亚、美国、澳大利亚、新西兰等国家和地区的近百名专家和学者出席研讨会。

2010 年 8 月 10 日至 12 日　"2010 海峡两岸西域文化学术研讨会"在塔里木大学召开，来自港澳台与大陆的 50 多家单位、90 多位专家提交了高质量论文，130 余位专家积极与会。丝绸之路风云变幻与西域文化系统阐述是这次学术会议的主题，综合性研究突出了会议宗旨，丝绸之路与文明对话、中华文明史上的西域、西域屯垦戍边两千年、环塔里木文化多样性、古今中外西域探查史、西域文化的现代转型等六个宏观专题则揭示了边疆史地研究的新方向。

2010 年 10 月 15 日　为期一天的"伊斯兰教和基督教友好对话"国际会议在叙利亚首都大马士革举行。与会代表呼吁中东地区伊斯兰教和基督教和平共处，进行友好对话，反对各种形式的恐怖主义。来自 30 多个国家的代表团出席了会议。会议讨论了加强伊斯兰教和基督教团结与合作以应对各种挑战和威胁的重要性。

2010 年 10 月 21 日至 23 日　"文明的交融：第二届伊斯兰教与基督教对话"学术研讨会在北京召开。此次研讨会由中国社会科学院世界宗教研究所、宁夏社会科学院回族伊斯兰教研究所、建道神学院基督教与中国文化研究中心共同主办，共有百余位代表与嘉宾出席会议，其中既包括部分高校、研究机构相关领域的学者，也有政界和宗教界的专家和代表。会议历时两天，共有 40 多位学者和专家围绕议题发表了演讲。

2010 年 12 月 4 日至 5 日　由北京外国语大学阿拉伯语系主办的第六届"中

阿文明对话"国际学术研讨会在北京外研社国际会议中心举行。来自中国和阿拉伯国家的 80 多位专家、学者围绕"中阿文明对话"的相关议题展开了深入而广泛的研讨。"中阿文明对话"国际学术研讨会自 2005 年开始，每年举办一次。

2010 年 12 月 7 日　由新加坡炎黄国际文化协会、中华炎黄文化研究会和新加坡国立大学中文系联合主办的"21 世纪中华文化世界论坛"在新加坡举行，本届论坛以"文化共生：中华文化与东南亚文化的交流、会通和发展"为主题，将分三大部分和 20 多个议题以展开小组讨论。议题包括"中华文化与世界文明的多元共处"、"华族文化的演变和内涵与东南亚族群"、"文化和社会的关系"，以及"中华文化与新马的社会发展"。会议由中华炎黄文化研究会于 1998 年倡议成立，旨在推动中华文化与世界各民族文化的对话和交流。

2011 年 4 月 7 日至 9 日　由联合国文明联盟与阿塞拜疆政府联合主办的第一届世界跨文化对话论坛在阿塞拜疆的巴库举办。大约 500 名来自世界五大洲的 102 个国家、许多国际组织、非政府组织以及媒体的代表、专家学者等参加了这次论坛。这次论坛围绕着"因共同价值观而团结，因文化多样性而丰富"的口号进行。

2011 年 5 月 6 日至 13 日　在土耳其基金会和研究机构的合作下，世界进步组织在土耳其筹办了一系列关于宗教在当今社会的作用的讲座和研讨会。来自奥地利、法国、德国、希腊、意大利、巴基斯坦和美国的研究者和学生，他们分别代表了哲学、宗教学、政治科学、国际法和国际关系等不同学科，和来自土耳其本土的学者与学生一块讨论了"多元文化主义"、"跨宗教对话"以及"穆斯林和西方的关系"等议题。

2011 年 5 月 18 日至 19 日　由太湖文化论坛、中国文联、江苏省人民政府、中国人民外交学会共同主办的太湖文化论坛首届年会在江苏苏州举办。国务委员刘延东出席开幕式并致辞。来自国内及世界各地的国家政要、官员、专家学者等约 500 人出席了论坛。本届论坛以"加强文明对话与合作，促进世界和谐与发展"为主题，旨在汇聚各国政要、知名专家学者进行对话，重点研讨当前国际社会面临的人类文明发展、文化交流与合作等最紧迫的问题，寻求解决这些问题切实可行的全球合作机制。会议期间，进行了"不同文明的历史启示和现实价值"、"中华文明与世界文明"、"文化多样性与人类文明进步"、"共建世界和谐：政府与民间力量的作用" 4 场分论坛。

2011 年 6 月 25 日　由云南大学和伊朗穆斯塔法国际大学联合主办，云南大学伊朗研究中心承办的首届"回儒文明对话论坛"国际学术研讨会在云南大学开幕。会议旨在推动中—伊两大文明的交流，促进两国人民的传统友谊，服务于两国政治、经济、文化关系的全面健康发展，服务于和谐世界的构建。本次会议将集中探讨伊斯兰文明与儒家文明中的和平、和谐、公正思想价值等。

2011 年 7 月 28 日至 29 日　由中国先秦史学会、中国中外关系史学会、四川师范大学巴蜀文化研究中心、四川师范大学历史旅游学院、三星堆博物馆等单位联合主办的"三星堆与南方丝绸之路：中国西南与欧亚古代文明国际学术研讨会"在广汉市三星堆博物馆隆重召开。来自国内外 30 余所高校和科研机构的专家学者共 70 余人出席了研讨会，会议收到学术论文 40 余篇。

2011 年 10 月 5 日至 13 日　第九届世界公共论坛"文明对话"年会在希腊罗得岛举办。此次论坛有来自 70 个国家的 600 多名代表参加，来自国际组织以及各国政府部门、非政府组织、研究机构、宗教组织的与会代表，就"文明的未来展望与未来挑战的应对之策"、"对当前世界不均衡发展的新的社会回应"、"国际社会交互作用的对话模式"、"跨文化的国际制度与法律"、"当前经济发展与社会发展挑战"、"宗教和传统文明对和平的意义"、"媒体对全球化的影响"等议题展开了积极坦率的对话与交流，发表了许多有价值的见解和建设性建议，形成了该论坛第九届年会的"罗德岛宣言"，增进了不同文明之间的相互理解与沟通。

2011 年 10 月 10 日至 20 日　由中国对外友协和希腊雅典孔子学院、弗雷展会集团、意大利罗马大学孔子学院、瑞中文化交流协会共同主办的孔子文化行暨中欧文明对话系列活动分别在希腊雅典、意大利罗马和瑞士苏黎世举行。山东文化代表团出席上述活动并开展了内容丰富的交流与访问活动。10 月 18 日，中欧文明对话交流大会在雅典举行。大会的主题是：孔子和苏格拉底思想的传播及其现实意义。来自中国、希腊、意大利、英国等国家文化、教育、新闻领域的 100 多名代表出席了会议。与会者对孔子和苏格拉底的哲学思想，特别是他们关于"仁"、"德"、"信"、"正义"、"天人合一"等理念进行了广泛热烈的探讨。

2011 年 10 月 19 日　第 19 届"中国、中国文明及世界"国际学术会议在俄罗斯科学院隆重开幕。"中国、中国文明及世界"国际学术会议由俄罗斯科学院远东研究所主办。为了纪念辛亥革命 100 周年，主办方把今年会议的主题定为"中国走向进步和现代化的百年历程"。俄罗斯、中国及欧洲学者近 200 人出席了研讨会。学者们从历史、哲学、经济和中国发展道路等各个角度探讨了中国走向进步和现代化的百年历程。

2011 年 12 月 11 日至 13 日　联合国文明联盟在卡塔尔的多哈召开了它的第四届全球论坛。超过 2000 名代表，其中包括政治和企业领导人、民间社会活动家、青年团体、宗教团体和研究机构、基金会和记者，共聚一堂并同意采取共同行动来改善跨文化的关系，消除偏见和建立持久的和平。多哈论坛召集了在这个问题下工作的不同行动者网络，使得他们能够分享观念，相互学习并且倾听全世界不同社会里的一般民众的需求。

2011年8月1日至2日 "生态智慧：草原文明与山地文明的对话"学术研讨会在呼和浩特市举行。国家民委专家团以及来自全国35所高等院校、科研机构的80余位专家学者应邀参加本次研讨会。研讨会从"生态理论与生态哲学"、"地方知识与生存智慧"、"生态实践与生态对策"三个方向进行相关问题的研究与交流。

2011年12月3日至6日 由中山大学广州口岸史重点研究基地举办的"海陆交通与世界文明"国际学术研讨会在中山大学举行，28位来自中国、美国、俄罗斯、伊朗等国的学者们提交了出色的研究成果，分别围绕"中古摩尼教"、"中俄关系史"、"中古中国与西域文明"、"中古中国与南海文明"和"清代广州与西洋文明"等五个专题，展开了深入的学术讨论，内容涵盖了通过陆路和海路所发生的中外关系的历史，体现了"海陆交通与世界文明"的会议主旨。从2006年以来，中山大学连续举办了多次以广州口岸的世界联系为主要内容的国际学术研讨会。

2012年4月16日 以"儒家思想与全球化世界中的新人文主义"为主题的巴黎尼山论坛在联合国教科文组织总部举行。驻联合国教科文组织的各国使节、法国政界、教育界、文化界人士200多人出席活动。此次巴黎尼山论坛设有"和而不同与全球化世界的迫切需求"、"和而不同与文化对话"、"和而不同与新人文主义"3个分议题，邀请来自中国、法国、英国、美国、西班牙、突尼斯、匈牙利、斯里兰卡和马里9个国家的20多位国际组织官员、社会学家和历史学家展开高端对话。

2012年5月21日至23日 以中国古代伟大的思想家、教育家孔子诞生地尼山命名的论坛——第二届尼山世界文明论坛，在山东泗水尼山圣源书院隆重开幕。来自20多个国家和地区的嘉宾、思想家、教育家及各界人士聚集在尼山脚下，展开世界不同文明之间高层次、高水平的对话交流。在短短3天时间里，尼山论坛共进行了中外儒学和基督教专家学者之间的40多场高端对话、专题演讲、学术分会、博士生论坛，收到近百篇论文，列席、旁听的人员达到万人次。论坛发布了《文化遗产保护与促进文明对话尼山共识》。本届尼山论坛把"信仰·道德·尊重·友爱"作为主题，借此向世界发出"要对话不要对抗"的呼声。

2012 年 5 月 31 日至 6 月 1 日　应土耳其总理埃尔多安的邀请，联合国文明联盟首届合作伙伴论坛在伊斯坦布尔举办。这次重要活动汇集了各国政府、政府间组织、企业、基金会和个人。他们做出郑重的承诺，要实现一个摆脱跨文化冲突和分裂的世界愿景，文化多样性在其中是资产而不是债务。论坛由联合国秘书长潘基文共同主持。

2012 年 6 月 28 日至 29 日　"中国与伊斯兰文明"学术研讨会在中国社会科学院召开。此次会议由中国社会科学院与伊斯兰合作组织（OIC）下属的伊斯兰历史、艺术与文化研究中心（IRCICA）联合举办。参加此次会议的外方代表来自土耳其、沙特阿拉伯、埃及、卡塔尔、美国、英国、马来西亚、巴基斯坦等国。与会代表围绕"中国与穆斯林世界的历史联系"、"中国与穆斯林世界的艺术交流与互动"、"文献与语言"、"科学、宗教与思想"、"当代世界与穆斯林世界的关系"以及"全球化背景下的中国与穆斯林世界"等六个主题展开热烈讨论。

2012 年 10 月 5 日　由文化部和山东省人民政府主办的第五届世界儒学大会暨 2012 年度孔子文化奖颁奖典礼，在孔子故里山东曲阜的孔子研究院隆重举行。来自海内外十余个国家及地区的百余名专家学者出席了此次国际学术盛会，共同探讨儒家思想的当代意义，期待通过不同文明间的平等对话促进人类社会的和谐发展。与会专家学者围绕"儒家思想的当代意义"的大会主题和"儒家伦理与市场伦理"、"中华元典与现代文明"、"儒学与国民教育"等重大现实议题进行了深入研讨和广泛对话。

2012 年 11 月 3 日至 5 日　第三届世界汉学大会在北京召开。"世界汉学大会"由国家汉办和中国人民大学共同主办，中国人民大学文学院、汉语国际推广研究所承办。本次会议主题为"汉学与当今世界"，意在推进中国主流学术与海外汉学的沟通，探讨世界对中国的阐释以及"中国道路"对世界的意义，使"文明对话"与"文化交流"的主题得到进一步深化。同时，大会还设有"中外文学大奖获奖者论坛"、"孔子学院与世界多元文化交流"两个专题论坛，共有来自海内外的一百多位专家学者参加。

2012 年 8 月 25 日　"纪念韩中建交二十周年"之"第四届韩中日汉字文化国际论坛"在韩国济州岛济州大学盛大召开。本届会议由华东师范大学中国文字研究与应用中心、韩国庆星大学韩国汉字研究所、济州大学人文学院联合举办。会议主题为"汉字文化圈古代汉字文献数据之数字典藏建设和共享以及东西方之汉字文化新谈"。本届会议共有来自韩国、中国、日本、美国、德国、法国、挪威、中国台湾等国家和地区的近 90 位专家学者出席，提交会议论文 60 余篇。

2012 年 10 月 4 日　第十届"文明对话——世界公众论坛"年会在希腊东南部的罗德岛举行了全体会议。为期 5 天的本届论坛汇聚了近 80 个国家的 500 多位专家学者和各界代表。他们将围绕世界政治变革、国际经济秩序、生态保护、不同文明对话、未来教育发展等广泛议题进行深入的交流与探讨。"文明对话"世界公众论坛创立于 2003 年，倡导各种文明间的建设性对话，以共同应对全球性挑战。目前该论坛已成为具有国际影响的非官方对话机制。

2012 年 11 月 10 日至 11 日　"纽约世界文明论坛"在美国纽约联合国总部举行。"纽约世界文明论坛"由中华能源基金委员会承办，主题为"超越国度，不同信仰，共同价值：儒家与基督教文明对话"，旨在为儒家文明与基督教文明之间提供一次重要的沟通机会，增进两大文明的交流和了解。

2012 年 11 月 29 日至 30 日　"联合国文明联盟亚洲南太平洋磋商会议"于上海国际会议中心隆重举行。此次会议由联合国文明联盟（UNAOC）、中国联合国协会（UNA-China）共同主办。来自中国、印度、澳大利亚、新西兰、马来西亚、泰国、菲律宾、印度尼西亚、日本、韩国、中国台湾等数十个国家和地区的代表、国际和地区组织的代表、私人机构和非政府组织领袖、媒体代表等约 150 人应邀与会。会议的主题是"通过对话和多样性促进和谐"。

2012 年 12 月 1 日至 2 日　由中华炎黄文化研究会与炎黄国际文化协会等联合主办的"21 世纪中华文化世界论坛"第七届国际学术研讨会在澳大利亚墨尔本举行。许嘉璐先生在开幕式上致辞，来自中外 120 多位学者围绕"文明对话与中华文化精神"这一主题进行了学术研讨，并且呼吁中西文明进行更多的交流和互动。

编撰：许　欢

十年文明对话名人录

(2002—2012)

　　阿部正雄（Masao Abe，1915—2006）　日本佛教徒和宗教研究的教授。他因佛教和基督教之间跨宗教对话的工作而广为人知。他以佛教的"空"改造基督教的上帝观念，引起了众多西方基督教学者的广泛讨论，为 20 世纪耶佛对话的经典案例。他的写作还有关于禅的体验。

　　阿富汗尼（Jamal ad-Din al-Afghani，1838—1897）　伊斯兰哲学家、政治活动家，泛伊斯兰主义的创始人。他还是阿拉伯国家现代复兴运动的先驱。他终生致力于社会和宗教改革。他号召伊斯兰国家在统一的哈里发管辖之下，团结一致，共同抵抗欧洲帝国主义的侵略和从事民族的复兴。他利用集会和报刊积极宣传自己的主张，激发东方各国穆斯林的宗教感情和爱国主义热情。

　　阿诺德·约瑟夫·汤因比（Arnold Joseph Toynbee，1889—1975）　是英国著名历史学家。他的两部最主要的代表作是《历史研究》和《人类与大地母亲》。他的 12 册巨著《历史研究》讲述了世界各个主要民族的兴起与衰落，被誉为"现代学者最伟大的成就"。汤因比治史，一反国家至上的观念，主张文明才是历史的单位；他把世界历史划分为 21 种文明，并以人的生老病死的现象，来解释文明的兴衰与死亡。

　　阿忒纳哥拉一世（Athenagoras I，1886—1972）　自 1948 年到 1972 年间，担任君士坦丁堡第 268 任牧首。1964 年其与教皇保罗六世在耶路撒冷会晤，促成了在历史上意味着东西方教会分裂的 1054 年逐出教会决定的撤销，这是天主教和东正教关系的转变的重大转折点。

　　奥　托（Rudolf Otto，1869—1937）　德国神学家，比较宗教学家。曾先后在哥廷根、布雷斯劳和马堡大学担任教授。研究领域包括西方哲学、系统神学、新约和旧约宗教史学、印度学等，曾潜心探讨宗教本质与真理、宗教情感与体验、哲学认识论、神圣观念和神秘主义等问题。代表作为《论神圣：关于神灵观念的非理性现象和它与理性的关系》，还写有《自然主义与宗教的世界观》、《东西方神秘主义》、《印度的恩典宗教与基督教》等重要著作。其对"神圣"这一宗教范畴的研究影响深远，曾为宗教现象学的发展创造了条件。

巴尔多禄茂一世（Patrik I. Bartolomeos，1940—　）　自1991年9月2日起担任君士坦丁堡的总主教（普世牧首），为正教会名义上地位最高的神职人员。自1977年他开始推动与犹太教团体间的跨宗教对话、1986年与伊斯兰教团体的跨宗教对话。1994年以来他为加深与犹太教徒、基督徒及穆斯林间的对话，举办了一系列国际会议。

白诗朗（John Berthrong，1946—　）　1989年至今任波士顿大学比较神学副教授。白诗朗博士致力于不同信仰间的对话项目和活动，他的教学与研究兴趣在于宗教间对话、中国宗教与哲学以及比较哲学与神学等领域。代表作品有：《普天之下：儒耶对话中的范式转化》、《儒家之道的转型》等。

班　纳（Hassan al-Banna，1906—1949）　埃及苏菲派学者、原教旨主义的代表、穆斯林兄弟会创始人。班纳是一名学校教师、社会运动家、逊尼派伊玛目，致力于推动埃及的社会改革以及伊斯兰世界的政治革新运动。他最著名的事迹是在20世纪30年代创立并领导穆斯林兄弟会。它是在20世纪中最大和最富影响力的穆斯林复古主义政治团体，直到今天仍然活跃在伊斯兰世界。

保罗六世（Pope Paul VI，1897—1978）　意大利籍罗马教皇（1963—1978年在位），本名乔瓦尼·巴蒂斯塔·蒙蒂尼（Giovanni Battista Enrica Antonia Maria Montini）。1963年6月登基，立王号为保罗六世。1963年9月29日至12月4日，他领导召开了第二次梵蒂冈大公会议第二期会议。在长达25年的统治生涯中，他积极参与国际事务，发挥了独特的作用。

本尼迪克特（Ruth Benedict，1887—1948）　美国人类学家和民俗学家。她师从美国人类学之父博厄斯，后者的教学和观点在她的作品中的影响显而易见。本尼迪克特的大部分研究涉及美国印第安文化的起源问题。她注意到任何一种文化都是其他许多文化成分的集合体。本尼迪克特除了对没有文字的小社会进行研究以外，还从事日本文化的研究，以便帮助西方人了解日本社会的文化。本尼迪克特的主要著作有：《文化模式》（1934）、《菊与刀》（1946）等。

布　伯（Martin Buber，1878—1965）　奥地利裔以色列籍犹太人哲学家、翻译家、教育家，他的研究工作集中于宗教有神论、人际关系和团体。马丁·布伯是一位文化锡安主义者，他活跃于德国和以色列的犹太人团体和教育团体。他还是一位坚定的在巴勒斯坦实施一国解决方案（与两国解决方案相对）的支持者。他的影响遍及整个人文学科，特别是在社会心理学、社会哲学和宗教存在主义领域。布伯以对话哲学而著称，《我与你》是他最重要的著作。在这本书里，布伯提出了一种人本主义的哲学思想。

蔡元培（1868—1940）　中国近代教育家、革命家、政治家。中华民国首任教育总长，1916 年至 1927 年任北京大学校长，革新北大，开"学术"与"自由"之风；1920 年至 1930 年，蔡元培同时兼任中法大学校长。北伐时期，国民政府定都南京后，他主持教育行政委员会，主导教育及学术体制改革。1928 年至 1940 年，他帮助成立中央研究院并成为第一任院长，贯彻对学术研究的主张。

陈　明（1962—　）　中国社科院儒教研究中心秘书长，信孚国学院院长。1992 年中国社科院研究生院宗教系博士毕业。出版有《儒学的历史文化功能》，创办思想学术性辑刊《原道》并任主编，追求在当代语境中为儒家寻找一种恰当的表达。

成中英（1935—　）　美籍华人学者，现为美国夏威夷大学哲学系教授，被认为是"第三代新儒家"的代表人物之一。他是著名管理哲学家，是"国际中国哲学会"荣誉会长、国际《易经》学会主席、国际易学导师资格评审委员会主席。作为海外儒学研究代表人物的成中英，长年致力于在西方世界介绍中国哲学。

池田大作（Ikeda Daisaku，1928—　）　国际创价学会会长，这个佛教协会在 192 个国家和地区拥有超过 1200 万成员，同时他还是一些教育、文化和和平研究机构的创始人。迄今，池田大作被誉为世界著名的佛教思想家、哲学家、教育家、社会活动家、桂冠诗人、国际人道主义者。

达　斯（Bhagwan Das，1869—1958）　印度哲学家，吠檀多派哲学的改革者。曾任中印度学院教授。他反对商羯罗关于"世界是幻"的说法，并从唯心主义的立场出发，把印度古代的瑜伽派的心理学说和西方实证论的心理学联系起来，企图建立一套新的心理学体系。著作有《自我的科学》、《社会组织的科学》等。

道　森（Christopher Dawson，1889—1970）　英国著名的文化哲学家、历史学家。道森被认为是"二十世纪最伟大的英语天主教历史学家"。但他的主要兴趣却在文化哲学，尤其是在宗教信仰与文化变迁的关系方面。其主要著作有《神抵时代》(1928)、《进步与宗教》(1929)、《基督教与新时代》(1931)、《中世纪宗教》(1934)、《宗教与现代国家》(1936)、《宗教与西方文化的兴起》(1950)、《理解欧洲》(1952) 等。

德日进（Pierre Teilhardde Chardin，1881—1955）　法国哲学家，古生物学家，地质学家和耶稣会教士。在中国生活 20 余年。他的所有著作已收入《德日进全集》，其中具有代表性的是《人的现象》、《人的未来》和《神的氛围》等。

蒂里希（又译作"田立克"，Paul Tillich，1886—1965）　德裔美籍基督教存在主义哲学家和神学家。蒂里希被广泛认为是 20 世纪最有影响力的神学家之一。他最出名的是他的主要作品三卷本《系统神学》（1950—1963）。他的神学观点和哲学观点在美国和第二次世界大战以后的联邦德国的新教神学家中间颇有影响。

丁光训（1915—2012）　中国基督教新教三自爱国运动和现代派神学的代表人物之一。在 20 世纪 40 年代和 50 年代是圣公会主教。历任中华人民共和国政府支持的中国基督教三自爱国运动委员会主席和名誉主席、中国基督教协会会长和名誉会长，中国人民政治协商会议全国委员会副主席（1989—2008），全国人大常委会委员。

杜维明（1940—　）　伦理学家和新儒家。曾任哈佛大学东亚语言与文明系中国历史哲学与儒学研究教授，哈佛燕京学社社长，夏威夷东西中心文化与传播研究所所长。现任哈佛大学亚洲研究中心研究教授和高级研究员，美国人文社会科学院院士。杜维明将儒家文化置于世界思潮的背景中来进行研究，直接关切如何使传统文化与中国的现代化问题接轨，勾画了当代新儒学理论的基本构架，在东亚和西方世界产生了相当的影响。杜维明在 2001 年被科菲·安南任命为联合国"知名人士小组"一员以促进"不同文明之间的对话"。他于 2004 年在联合国教科文组织执行局就文明间对话作陈述。

多勒米尔（Fred R. Dallmayr，1928—　）　美国圣母大学哲学系和政治学系的帕奇·迪伊教授。他一直担任德国汉堡大学和纽约社会研究新学院的客座教授、牛津大学纳菲尔德学院的研究员。自 1978 年以来，他一直任教于圣母大学。在他最近出版的著作中有：《实现我们的世界：走向全球和多元民主》（2001）、《文明对话：一些示范的声音》（2002）、《完整的多元主义：超越文化战争》（2010）。他曾任亚洲与比较哲学学会会长，现任"文明对话—世界公众论坛"的联席执行主席。

费孝通（1910—2005）　中国著名社会学家、人类学家、民族学家、社会活动家，因对中国族群的研究而著称，中国社会学和人类学的奠基人之一，第七、第八届全国人民代表大会常务委员会副委员长，中国人民政治协商会议第六届全国委员会副主席。

弗雷德里克（James L. Fredericks，1951—　）　美国罗耀拉—玛丽蒙特大学教授，长期从事佛教研究，从事佛教和基督教之间的对话实践和理论研究。他是当代比较神学的代表人物之一。主要著作有：《诸信仰中的信仰：基督教神学与非基督宗教》、《佛教徒与基督徒：通过比较神学走向宗教团结》。他于 2002 年获得美国 Frederick J. Streng 图书奖。

福　山（Francis Fukuyama，1952—　）　日裔美籍学者、政治学家和政治经济学家，现任斯坦福大学民主、发展与法治中心高级研究员。福山著有《历史的终结与最后的人》、《信任：社会美德与创造繁荣》、《后人类未来——基因工程的人性浩劫》、《跨越断层——人性与社会秩序重建》。在《历史的终结与最后的人》一书中他认为最后的历史是自由民主的历史，在自由民主阶段，人类获得了平等的认可，历史也就终结了。关于伊斯兰世界的问题，他认为这不是文化冲突，而实质上是政治激进主义，与文化无关。

福特·D.（David Frank Ford，1948—　）　出生于都柏林，是一名学者和公众神学家。自1991年以来任剑桥大学皇家神学教授。他的研究兴趣包括政治神学，普世神学，基督教神学和神学家，神学和诗歌，大学和大学内的神学和宗教学领域的塑造，诠释学以及跨信仰的神学和关系。他是剑桥大学跨信仰项目的创始主任和经文辨读学会的共同发起人。

傅有德（1956—）　山东大学犹太教与跨宗教研究中心主任、宗教学系主任、山东省"泰山学者"特聘教授。兼任全国外国哲学学会和宗教学学会常务理事、山东省哲学学会会长、《犹太研究》主编。拥有众多著述，获过多项奖项，一直致力于在中国语境中的犹太教研究。

甘　地（Mahatma Gandhi，1869—1948）　印度民族解放运动的领导人和印度国家大会党领袖。他是现代印度的国父，是印度最伟大的政治领袖，也是现代民族资产阶级政治学说——甘地主义的创始人。他的精神思想带领印度迈向独立，脱离英国的殖民统治。他的"非暴力"（ahimsa）的哲学思想，影响了全世界的民族主义者和争取能以和平变革的国际运动。

奥罗宾多·高斯（Aurobindo Ghose，1872—1950）　印度民族主义者、哲学家、印度民族独立运动的领导人。他的精神进化论哲学，在印度现代思想史上占有重要的地位。奥罗宾多·高斯写有一百多篇著作，主要有《神圣人生论》、《人类循环》、《最后的诗篇》等。在印度他被称为圣哲或精神大师，他的名字与圣雄甘地、诗圣泰戈尔并列，合称为"三圣"。

海　姆（S. Mark Heim）　安杜佛牛顿神学院的塞缪尔·阿博特基督教神学教授。海姆热衷于研究宗教多元论、基督教普世主义、神学和科学的关系等问题，为当代研究宗教多元论的主要学者之一，著有《拯救：宗教中的真理和差异》、《丰盛的恩典》等。

亨廷顿（Samuel Phillips Huntington，1927—2008）　当代颇有争议的美国保

守派政治学家，哈佛大学教授。亨廷顿因在《文明的冲突与世界秩序的重建》一书中提出"文明冲突"观点而闻名。亨廷顿认为在冷战后的世界，文化和宗教的差异而非意识形态的分歧将导致世界几大文明之间的竞争和冲突。

弘一法师（俗名李叔同，1880—1942）　中国佛教徒，卓越的艺术家、教育家、思想家，是中国传统文化与佛教文化相结合的优秀代表，是中国近现代佛教史上最杰出的一位高僧，又是国际上声誉甚高的知名人士。他在美术、音乐、戏剧、书法、篆刻、诗歌诸方面均有创造性发展。

胡　适（1891—1962）　中国哲学家、散文家、外交家。因提倡文学革命而成为中国新文化运动的领袖之一，曾担任国立北京大学校长。胡适兴趣广泛，在文学、哲学、史学、考据学、教育学、红学等诸多领域都有深入的研究。1939年还获得诺贝尔文学奖的提名。胡适深受赫胥黎与杜威的影响，毕生宣扬自由主义，是中国自由主义的先驱。毕生倡言"大胆的假设，小心的求证"、"言必有证"的治学方法，以及"认真作事，严肃做人"的做人之道。

季羡林（1911—2009）　中国语言学家、印度学家、文学翻译家、教育家和社会活动家，精通 12 国语言。曾历任中国科学院哲学社会科学部委员、中国社科院南亚研究所所长、北京大学副校长。季羡林通晓梵语、巴利语、吐火罗语等语言，是世界上仅有的几位从事吐火罗语研究的学者之一。

金克木（1912—2000）　中国著名文学家、翻译家、学者。历任湖南大学、武汉大学、北京大学教授。他曾将一些古印度文学和哲学作品翻译成中文。代表作品有：《梵语文学史》、《印度文化论集》、《比较文化论集》等。

净　空（俗名徐业鸿，1927—　 ）　中国佛学大师，他不仅熟通佛教各派经论，对于儒学、道家和伊斯兰教等其他宗教学说也广泛涉猎。于众多典籍中，他对佛教净土宗着力最多，成就也最为辉煌。净空大师因用现代科技来传播佛陀教诲而为人所熟知。

卡尔·拉纳（Karl Rahner，1904—1984）　德国传教士和神学家。他被认为是 20 世纪最有影响力的罗马天主教思想家之一。拉纳作为罗马天主教指定的官方神学顾问在"梵二会议"上发挥了巨大的作用，不仅启迪了几代神学家，而且影响到自那以后整个天主教思想的发展。为了因应世俗化和现代化对天主教形成的挑战，拉纳倡导并积极从事基督教内外的对话，著述几乎涉及神学和相关思想的所有领域，其中包括卷帙浩繁的《神学论集》（德文原本 16 卷）。

卡尔·西奥多·雅斯贝尔斯（Karl Theodor Jaspers，1883—1969）　德国存在主义哲学家、神学家、精神病学家。他在《历史的起源与目标》中提出"轴心时代"理论，认为公元前800年至前200年之间，尤其是公元前600年至前300年间，是人类文明的"轴心时代"。这段时期是人类文明精神的重大突破时期。在轴心时代里，各个文明都出现了伟大的精神导师——古希腊有苏格拉底、柏拉图、亚里士多德，以色列有犹太教的先知们，古印度有释迦牟尼，中国有孔子、老子。

卡普尔（Jagdish Chandra Kapur，1917—2010） 印度哲学家、公众人物。他是"文明对话—世界公众论坛"的联合创办人和联席主席。曾任印度卡普尔苏里亚基金会主席、《世界事务》杂志主编。他出版的著作有：《印度，一个不受约束的社会》、《人类今天的处境：一些新的视角》和《我们的未来：消费主义或人文主义》。他是2010年的帕德玛·普山奖获得者之一。

康有为（1858—1927） 中国清末民初学者、政治思想家、改革家。他的思想启发了被称为"戊戌变法"的改革运动。他信奉孔子的儒家学说，并致力于将儒家学说改造为可以适应现代社会的国教，曾担任孔教会会长。主要著作有《新学伪经考》、《孔子改制考》、《日本变政考》、《俄大彼得变政记》、《大同书》等。

科 布（John B. Cobb，1925— ） 美国当代过程神学家和过程哲学家，他在过程神学的发展中发挥了至关重要的作用。科布已经出版几十部重要著作，代表作有：《多元化时代的基督》、《过程神学》、《可持续性：经济、生态和正义》和《改造基督教和世界：超越绝对主义和相对主义的方式》等。

科尼特（Paul F. Knitter，1939— ） 美国神学家、社会活动家。他是宗教多元论的主要倡导者之一，致力于社会正义、信仰对话和全球生态关怀等领域的理论研究和社会实践活动。他的主要著作有：《走向新教诸宗教神学》、《没有别的名？》、《一个地球多种宗教：多信仰对话和全球责任》、《耶稣与其他的名：基督徒的使命和全球责任》等。另外，他还是奥比斯图书出版社（Orbis Books）"信仰遇见信仰"（*Faith Meets Faith*）丛书的主编，至今已经出版近50部著作，在宗教对话、全球神学、社会正义等领域产生了广泛的影响。

克里希那穆提（Jiddu Krishnamurti，1895—1986） 印度佛学家，被公认为20世纪最伟大的灵性导师。他一生走访全球70多个的国家演讲，他的演讲被辑录成超过80本书，并被翻译成超过50个国家的语言。在现今全球包括美国、欧洲、印度和澳洲都设有克里希那穆提基金会及学校，致力推广克氏慈悲与当世解脱的理念。

克鲁尼·F. X.（Francis X. Clooney，1950— ） 哈佛大学神学院教授和世界宗教研究中心主任，是当代比较神学的代表人物。主要作品有：《吠檀多之后的神学》、《通过文本理解》、《印度教的上帝和基督教的上帝》和《神母与圣母》等。

他于 2010 年 7 月当选为英国科学院院士。

孔汉斯（Hans Küng，1928— ） 瑞士天主教神学家，德国图宾根大学基督教神学教授。自 1995 年以来，他一直担任全球伦理基金会主席。孔汉斯倡导一种崭新范式的基督教思想，致力于推动神学在所谓后现代处境中的范式转换。在其倡导下，1993 年世界宗教会议通过了他起草的《走向全球伦理宣言》。

库比特（Don Cupitt，1934— ） 英国杰出的宗教哲学家和基督教神学家，剑桥大学客座教授、圣公会牧师。他以非实在论的宗教哲学观点而著称。至今出版 36 部作品。其代表作有：《告别上帝》、《信仰之海》、《上帝之后》、《现代性之后的神秘主义》、《最后的哲学》等。他提出"非实在论的上帝"，旨在探索把宗教当作一件人类杰作的含义，同时推广这种宗教观，进而肯定宗教思想的持续有效性以及赞美精神与社会价值的修道活动的持续有效性。

邝雅各（James H. Cone，1938— ） 协和神学院教授，黑人神学的代表。著作《黑人解放神学》和《黑人神学与黑人权力》。他主张在神学意义内寻找黑人的身份，指出黑人权力不单是与耶稣基督的福音吻合，它本身就是耶稣基督的福音，并非与基督教敌对。

拉达克里希南（Sarvepalli Radhakrishnan，1888—1975） 印度哲学家、政治家。曾担任迈索尔大学和加尔各答大学的哲学教授、牛津大学斯波尔丁东方宗教和伦理学讲座教授。印度独立后，他担任第一任印度共和国副总统，并于 1962 年当选为第二任印度总统。作为印度最有影响力的比较宗教学和哲学家，拉达克里希南通过展示不同传统的哲学系统在各自的概念下可以相互理解，建立了一个沟通东西方的桥梁。他的代表作品有：《印度哲学》、《印度教的人生观》、《唯心主义的人生观》、《东方的宗教和西方的思想》。

赖品超（1963— ） 香港中文大学文化及宗教研究系教授。学术兴趣包括：现代基督教思想、宗教对话、基督教与中国文化、环境伦理、宗教与自然科学。在发表了数本关于基督教神学的专著以及编著一些有关耶佛对话及耶儒对话的论文集后，近几年出版了数本专著，一本关于大乘基督教神学（2011，获第三十三届汤清基督教文学奖），另一本有关神学与文化（2011），还有一本则涉及宗教与科学（合著，2012）。

李炽昌（1950— ） 香港中文大学文化及宗教研究系教授，国内经文辨读的主要倡导者之一，代表作品有《生命言说与社群认同：希伯 圣经，五小卷研究》、《文本实践与身份辨识：中国基督徒知识分子的中文著述》等。

李泽厚（1930— ） 中国哲学家、美学家、中国思想史学家。曾担任中国社会科学院研究员，德国图宾根大学、美国威斯康星大学、密歇根大学、科罗拉多学院客席教授、客席讲座教授，台北"中央研究院"客席讲座研究等职。1988年当选巴黎国际哲学院院士，1998年获美国科罗拉多学院荣誉人文学博士学位。

梁启超（1873—1929）　中国清末民初学者、记者、哲学家和改革家。1894年，梁启超提倡变法，于上海主撰《时务报》。他将政治理念刊布报端，启发国人之革新思想。梁启超与谭嗣同等6人同参新政，变法失败后逃亡日本。中华民国成立后，梁启超返回中国，并参与了反对袁世凯称帝的斗争。晚年远离政治，专以著述讲学为务，又深研佛学。著有《墨子学案》、《清代学术概论》、《饮冰室文集》、《中国近三百年学术史》等。

梁漱溟（1893—1988）　中国著名的思想家、哲学家、教育家。他是乡村建设运动的领袖，主要研究人生问题和社会问题。他还是现代新儒家的早期代表人物之一，有"中国最后一位儒家"之称。主要著作有《中国文化要义》、《东西文化及其哲学》、《乡村建设理论》、《印度哲学概论》等，今编有八卷本的《梁漱溟全集》。

林贝克（George Lindbeck，1923—　）　美国路德会神学家，生于中国洛阳，现为耶鲁大学路德教授。林贝克因作为叙事神学的创始者之一和泛基督教主义者而著称。他曾以世界信义会联合会的官方观察员身份参与第二次梵蒂冈大公会议。林贝克最出名的著作是1984年出版的《教义的本质：后自由主义时代的宗教及神学》。

铃木大拙（D. T. Suzuki，1870—1966）　日本佛教学者、禅学思想家，也是因向西方介绍禅学而著称的世界文化名人。主要著作有《禅的研究》、《禅的诸问题》、《中国古代哲学史》、《佛教与基督教》、《华严的研究》等。全部著作收于《铃木大拙全集》。

刘小枫（1956—　）　中国人民大学文学院教授，香港中文大学中国文化研究所研究员，北京大学比较文化研究所兼任教授。1993年瑞士巴塞尔大学神学博士毕业。自20世纪80年代以来，刘小枫教授致力于对现代性问题与中西文明的重新认识，先后在国内引入基督教思想、社会理论、政治神学、古典政治哲学、古典学等学术资源，推进了汉语学界对西方思想传统的深度理解。

罗宾德拉纳特·泰戈尔（Rabindranath Tagore，1861—1941）　印度诗人、哲学家和印度民族主义者。1913年他成为第一位获得诺贝尔文学奖的亚洲人。泰戈尔的诗在印度享有史诗的地位，代表作有《吉檀迦利》、《飞鸟集》。他的作品反映了印度人民在帝国主义和封建种姓制度压迫下要求改变自己命运的强烈愿望，描写了他们不屈不挠的反抗斗争，充满了鲜明的爱国主义和民主主义精神，同时又富有民族风格和民族特色，具有很高的艺术价值，深受人们喜爱。

马丁·路德·金（Martin Luther King, Jr., 1929—1968）　著名的美国黑人民权运动领袖。1963 年 8 月 28 日在林肯纪念堂前发表《我有一个梦想》的演说。1964 年获诺贝尔和平奖。1968 年 4 月 4 日，马丁·路德·金前往孟菲斯市领导工人罢工被人刺杀，时年 39 岁。1986 年起美国政府将每年 1 月的第三个星期一定为马丁·路德·金全国纪念日。

马　坚（1906—1978）　中国穆斯林学者与翻译家，阿拉伯语言学家，通晓汉、阿两种语言文化，兼通波、英两种语言。1945 年后，先后任云南大学东方语言系、北京大学东方语言系教授。马坚是中国伊斯兰教协会的发起人之一。主要成就为翻译《古兰经》以及《阿拉伯通史》。

马克斯·韦伯（Max Weber，1864—1920）　德国社会学家、哲学家和政治经济学家。他系统地阐释了东西方宗教伦理差异对于社会现代性以及现代资本主义发展的影响。他和迪尔凯姆被认为是宗教社会学的开创者。他的著作《新教伦理与资本主义精神》是对宗教社会学最早的研究。韦伯在这本书中主张，宗教的影响是造成东西方文化发展差距的主要原因，并且强调新教伦理在资本主义、官僚制度和法律权威的发展上所扮演的重要角色。其他代表作有《中国的宗教：儒教与道教》、《印度的宗教：印度教和佛教社会学》和《古犹太教》。

麦奎利（John Macquarrie，1919—2007）　苏格兰神学家和哲学家、牛津大学"荣誉教授"。他著有《实存主义神学：海德格尔与布尔特曼比较研究》、《二十世纪宗教思想》、《基督教实存主义研究》、《谈论上帝——神学的语言与逻辑之考察》、《基督教的统一与差异》、《基督教的希望》、《探求人性》、《探求神性》、《现代思想中的耶稣基督》、《所有基督徒的马利亚》等大量著作。麦奎利在退休后一直保持着活跃的写作和讲学活动。

曼德拉（Nelson Rolihlahla Mandela，1918—2013）　南非反对种族隔离的革命家和政治家，于 1994 年到 1999 年担任南非总统。他是南非首位黑人总统，被尊称为南非国父。1994 年 5 月 11 日，曼德拉及首届南非民族团结政府内阁成员宣誓就职，这标志着 3 个多世纪的种族隔离制度和白人种族主义统治终于走到了终点。曼德拉曾在牢中服刑 27 年，在其 40 年的政治生涯中获得了超过一百项奖项，其中最令人瞩目的是 1993 年的诺贝尔和平奖。

梅里诺，G. G.（Gustavo Gutiérrez Merino，1928—　）　秘鲁神学家，多明我会教士。他被看成是解放神学的创始人，对拉丁美洲的社会、历史及神学有深入的见解与批判，著有《解放神学的各种视角》（1973）、《我们喝自己的井水：一个民族的灵修旅程》（1983）、《福传与站在穷人的立场》（1987）。

牟宗三（1909—1995） 中国现代学者、哲学家、哲学史家，现代新儒家的重要代表人物之一，被称为当代新儒学的集大成者。主要著作有《心体与性体》、《道德的理想主义》、《历史哲学》、《佛性与般若》、《才性与玄理》、《圆善论》等28部；有《康德的道德哲学》、《康德〈纯粹理性之批判〉》（译注）、《康德判断力之批判》等3部译作。其哲学成就代表了中国传统哲学在现代发展的新水平，其影响力具有世界水平。英国剑桥哲学词典誉之为"当代新儒家他那一代中最富原创性与影响力的哲学家"。

南怀瑾（1918—2012） 中国学者，诗人，中国传统文化的积极传播者。1949年春赴台湾后，相继任文化大学、辅仁大学、政治大学等教授。其著作多以演讲整理为主，内容往往将儒、释、道等思想进行比对，别具一格。代表著作有《论语别裁》、《楞严大义今译》、《如何修正佛法》等。

南乐山（Robert Cummings Neville，1939— ） 他是一位具有广泛的国际性影响的美国哲学家和神学家，同时也是近年崛起的"波士顿儒家"学派的最重要的代表人物。现为波士顿大学宗教学院哲学、宗教学与神学教授，国际中国哲学会执行委员会主席。南乐山也相当注重中国哲学，特别是儒家哲学，并一直积极推动国际儒学的发展。他长期以来的研究领域是比较哲学、宗教哲学等，出版了大量的学术著作，其中有两部著作已被译为中文。

尼赫鲁（Jawaharlal Nehru，1889—1964） 印度民族独立运动领导人，印度共和国首任总理，不结盟运动的创始人之一。印度将尼赫鲁的生日11月14日定为儿童节，以纪念他对儿童的关怀。1954年6月，尼赫鲁与中国总理周恩来共同提出著名的和平共处五项原则。1955年尼赫鲁发起并参加了在印度尼西亚举行的万隆亚非会议。

倪柝声（1903—1972） 福州人，是一位教会领袖和基督度教师，整个20世纪上半叶都在中国工作。在30年的牧师生涯里，倪柝声出版了许多阐释《圣经》的著作，包括《正常的基督徒生活》和《教会的正统》。他是地方教会的创始人，其基督教神学思想在中国文化语境中找到了一种系统的表达，在当今大陆以及华人基督教文化圈里广有影响力。

潘尼卡（Raimundo Panikkar，1918—2010） 西班牙罗马天主教神父、跨宗教对话先驱、比较宗教学家。他试图在不同宗教和思想体系传统的各自内在哲学结构层面建立起联系。他不仅努力去分辨某个传统的内在秩序和奥秘基础，而且是在此传统的哲学自我理解光照下进行的。经过这种批判性筛选，他阐明了不同传统间的结构性类似以便它们能彼此对话。其结果事实上成了三方对话：基督宗教与印度教或佛教，以及当代多元化的社会—政治—宗教思想体系。

任继愈（1916—2009） 中国著名哲学家、宗教学家、历史学家，国家图书馆名誉馆长。毕业于北京大学哲学系。曾任北京大学教授，中国哲学史学会会长，中国无神论学会理事长。他致力于用唯物史观研究中国佛教史和中国哲学史，并曾多次在国外讲学并进行学术访问。

瑟德尔布罗姆（Nathan Soderblom，1866—1931） 瑞典著名的神学家、宗教历史学家。他一生从事宗教事业，积极倡导各国基督教会的团结，始终不渝地为世界和平而努力，因而于1930年获得诺贝尔和平奖。瑟德尔布罗姆是宗教界第一个获得诺贝尔和平奖的人。他的活动对20世纪世界性基督教运动有着很大的影响。

圣严法师（1930—2009） 中国佛学大师、教育家，也是禅宗曹洞宗的第50代传人、临济宗的第57代传人、台湾法鼓山的创办人。法师于1985年创办中华佛学研究所，并于1989年创办国际法鼓山文教基金会。他以中、日、英三种语言在亚、美、欧各洲出版的著作近百种。他的著作之中发行量最多的是《正信的佛教》，已超过300万册，译本最多的是《信心铭》，已有10种，系列册数最多的是《寰游自传》及《禅修指引》，这些著述均受到广大读者的欢迎。

施舟人（Kristofer Schipper，1934— ） 荷兰汉学家，是欧洲三大汉学家之一。1979年来到中国专门从事文化研究，于2003年在福州大学建立了福州大学世界文明研究中心。尤以研究中国道教而驰名于国际汉学界，同时在中国古代思想史、文化史研究领域和宗教人类学方面颇有建树，出版著作有《道体论》、《道藏通考》等。

史密斯·W.C.（Wilfred Cantwell Smith，1916—2000） 加拿大比较宗教学教授，曾于1964年至1973年间在哈佛大学担任"世界宗教研究中心"主任。他在1962年的著作《宗教的意义和终结》中极具争议地质疑了宗教概念的有效性。史密斯一生著作甚丰，其中包括《现代历史中的伊斯兰》(1957)、《宗教真理问题》(1967)、《信念与历史》(1979)、《信仰与信念》(1987)、《走向一种世界神学》(1989)、《何为圣经?》(1993)等。

释太虚（1890—1947） 中国近代著名高僧、活动家和思想家，他主张改革和复兴中国佛教。曾任世界佛学苑苑长、中国佛教学会会长、中国佛教整理委员会主任。释太虚是一位使中国乃至世界佛教起到历史性转折的佛教伟人。1928

年，太虚赴欧美诸国宣讲佛学，并应法国学者建议，在巴黎筹设世界佛学苑，开中国僧人跨越欧美弘传佛教之先河。

释星云（俗名李国深，1927— ） 中国佛教徒，佛光山开山宗长、国际佛光会世界总会会长。星云大师在佛教教育、文化、慈善、弘法事业方面作出了卓越贡献，为促进两岸关系作出积极努力，并在政治、文化等领域交流中具有巨大影响力。他创立的人间佛教影响遍及80多个国家，超过500万人接受其思想。释星云著作等身，他的著作被翻译成多国语言于欧美、东亚、非洲等地区发行。

司徒雷登（John Leighton Stuart，1876—1962） 美国基督教长老会传教士、外交官、教育家。1876年6月生于杭州，父母均为美国传教士。1904年开始在中国传教，曾参加建立杭州育英书院（即后来的之江大学）。1919年1月起任燕京大学首任校长。1946年任美国驻华大使，1949年8月离开中国。

斯宾格勒（Oswald Spengler，1880—1936） 德国著名历史学家、历史哲学家、历史形态学的开创人。斯宾格勒的历史哲学被称之为"文化形态学"。它是对以往历史学研究中以西方的历史为中心的线性进化模式的一种反叛，强调每一种文化的独立地位和独立价值。他在《西方的没落》一书中提出文明是一个包含着从出生到成长、从衰老到死亡的有机过程，我们已经目睹了古代文明的没落，而西方文明没落的征兆也已经预示出来了。

斯马特（Ninian Smart，1927—2001） 加利福尼亚和兰卡斯特大学的比较宗教和宗教学荣誉退休教授。他被看成是世界上在宗教学方面最重要的学者之一，2000年任美国宗教学会主席。他写作了许多广受好评的书，包括《宗教体验》、《神圣的维度》和《世界宗教》。

斯威德勒（Leonard Swidler，1929— ） 美国天普大学天主教思想和宗教间对话教授，长期研究和促进不同宗教和文化之间的对话。1991年，他发出一份呼吁书，号召起草全球伦理宣言，并主张宣言应汇聚对全球伦理及相关问题的各种研究和思考成果，然后散发到所有宗教和伦理团体的各种不同的讨论会上，去进行适当的修改，以便最终能被世界上所有的宗教和伦理团体所接受。

谭嗣同（1865—1898） 中国近代革命先驱，著名的"戊戌六君子"之一。其慷慨赴死的壮烈一幕，是中国革命的重要精神资源。其代表作《仁学》，对封建君主专制制度进行了强烈的抨击。他的诗感情真挚，志趣豪迈，境界恢弘。有《谭嗣同全集》遗世。

汤用彤（1893—1964） 中国哲学家、教育家、国学大师。毕业于清华学堂。留学美国，回国后历任国立东南大学、南开大学、北京大学、西南联大教授。

1951 年后任北京大学副校长。汤用彤是现代中国学术史上少数几位能会通中西、接通华梵、熔铸古今的国学大师之一。学术著作有《汉魏两晋南北朝佛教史》、《印度哲学史略》、《魏晋玄学论稿》等。

唐君毅（1909—1978） 中国现代学者、哲学家、哲学史家，现代新儒家的代表人物之一。曾任教于华西大学、中央大学、金陵大学，任过江南大学教务长。1949 年赴香港，与钱穆等创办新亚书院，并兼任教务长、哲学系主任等职。1958 年与徐复观、牟宗三、张君劢联名发表现代新儒家的纲领性文章《为中国文化敬告世界人士宣言》。

特蕾莎修女（Mother Teresa of Calcutta，1910—1997） 印度人，是世界著名的天主教慈善工作者，主要替印度加尔各答的穷人服务。因其一生奉献给消除贫困，而于 1979 年得到诺贝尔和平奖。2003 年 10 月，她被教皇约翰·保罗二世列入了天主教宣福名单（Beatification），被称为真福德雷莎修女（Blessed Teresa）。

图　图（Desmond Tutu，1931—　） 南非著名黑人主教，也是南非圣公会首位非裔大主教。图图是南非领导黑人反对种族压迫的坚强斗士，他一贯反对南非种族歧视和种族隔离政策，为黑人的解放进行勇敢的斗争。1984 年，他被授予诺贝尔和平奖。2012 年，他荣获教科文组织授予的毕尔巴鄂奖，以表彰他在国内和国际上促进人权所作的贡献。

王志成（1966—） 浙江大学教授，国内关于宗教对话的主要倡导者之一。代表著作有：《解释与拯救：宗教多元哲学论》、《宗教、解释与和平：对约翰·希克宗教多元论哲学的建设性研究》等。

希　克（John Harwood Hick，1922—2012） 英国当代宗教哲学家、神学家。在神学上，他对自然神学、末世学和基督论的研究作出了贡献。在宗教哲学上，他则致力于宗教认识论和宗教多元论。1991 年，他获得了著名的宗教格威文美尔奖。

谢和耐（Jacques Gernet，1921—　） 法国 20 世纪下半叶著名的汉学家、历史学家、社会学家。他专事中国社会和文化史研究，著述等身，代表著作以《中国社会史》（1972）和《中国和基督教》（1982）两部著作获国际汉学界好评。1979 年 6 月 8 日，谢和耐当选为法兰西文学院院士。

熊十力（1885—1968） 中国著名哲学家，新儒家开山祖师。著有《新唯识论》、《原儒》、《体用论》、《明心篇》、《佛家名相通释》、《乾坤衍》等书。其学说影响深远，在哲学界自成一体，"熊学"研究者也遍及全国和海外，《大英百科全书》称"熊十力与冯友兰为中国当代哲学之杰出人物"。

徐复观（1904—1982） "现代新儒家"的代表人物之一。其一生中就儒家思想与中国传统、文化问题，中国知识分子的性格及历史、命运问题发表大量论著，为研究、传播中国传统思想、文化作出重要贡献，成为名扬海内外的"现代大儒"。著书十余种，主要有《两汉思想史》三卷、《学术与政治（甲、乙集）》、《徐复观杂文》六集、《中国艺术精神》、《中国思想史论集》及续集、《石涛之一研究》等。

许嘉璐（1937— ） 尼山论坛组委会主席、全国人大常委会原副委员长。长期从事训诂学、《说文》学、古代文化学、中文信息处理等学科的教学和研究，出版学术专著 9 部，发表论文多篇，主编学术著作及工具书多部，主持完成《文白对照十三经》、《文白对照诸子集成》、《二十四史全译》等大型文化工程及国家 863 项目"中文信息处理应用基础研究"。近年来以推进世界文明对话为己任。

雅库宁（Vladimir Yakunin, 1948— ） 国营俄罗斯铁路集团主席。他一直担任斯德哥尔摩经济学院的客座教授。自从 2010 年以来，他担任莫斯科国立大学政治科学学院的国家政策系主任。他还是"文明对话—世界公众论坛"的创始主席。

严 复（1854—1921） 清末很有影响的启蒙思想家、翻译家和教育家，是中国近代史上向西方国家寻找真理的"先进的中国人"之一。严复系统地将西方的社会学、政治学、政治经济学、哲学和自然科学介绍到中国，他的译著是中国 20 世纪最重要的启蒙译著，主要有《天演论》。

杨庆堃（1911—1999） 华裔美国社会学家。原籍广东南海。1939 年获美国密歇根大学社会学博士学位。1951 年任麻省理工学院国际研究中心研究员。1953 年任匹兹堡大学社会学系副教授、教授。70 年代在香港中文大学创办社会学系。著有《共产党领导下的中国的农村社会及家庭变迁》、《中国社会中的宗教》。

一行禅师（Thich Nhat Hanh, 1926— ） 越南禅宗佛教徒、作家、诗人和和平使者。越美战争时，他是越南佛教和平代表团主席，向美国人民讲述了沉默的越南下层人民在战争中所受的痛苦以及他们的和平愿望。1967 年，一行禅师被马丁·路德·金（Martin Luther King, Jr.）提名诺贝尔和平奖。他已经出版了 100 多本书，其中包括 40 多本英文著作。他现在还活跃在和平运动中，推动非暴力的冲突解决方案。

余英时（1930— ） 当代华人世界著名历史学者，被认为是第三代新儒家的代表人物之一。曾任密西根大学、哈佛大学、耶鲁大学教授，香港新亚书院院长兼中文大学副校长、普林斯顿大学讲座教授、台湾"中央研究院"院士。余英时治学自史学起，其对儒家思想及中国道统文化的现代诠释自成一体。他的中、英文著述多达数十种，包括《汉代的贸易与扩张》、《士与中国文化》、《历史与思想》、《史学与传统》、《中国文化与现代变迁》、《现代儒学论》等。2006年11月，余英时获得美国国会图书馆颁发的有"人文诺贝尔奖"之称的克鲁格人文与社会科学终身成就奖。

约翰二十三世（Pope John XXIII，1881—1963）　意大利籍罗马教皇（1958—1963年在位），原名安吉洛·朱塞佩·隆卡利（Angelo Giuseppe Roncalli）。登位时已77岁，在位不到5年，但他所开创的天主教新变化意义深远，他在位时期堪称天主教会史中新时代的开端。

赵紫宸（1888—1979）　中国基督教神学家、学者。赵紫宸是中国20世纪最具影响力的神学家之一，是中国处境化神学的早期缔造者，也是"中国系统神学"的最早倡导者。他在西方基督教界享有较高声誉，被誉为"向东方心灵诠释基督教信仰的首席学者"。

证严法师（俗名王锦云，1937—　）　中国佛教徒和慈善家。她在花莲建成了第一所慈济医院，还把慈济事业扩展到全球。30多年来一共筹集了上百亿台币的善款，台湾几乎五分之一的人口也就是说有400多万人都或多或少地参与了她的慈善活动。在全球有1000多万她的志愿者。人们称她为"东方特蕾莎"、"人间观世音菩萨"。

赵敦华（1949—　）　北京大学哲学系教授、博士生导师。比利时卢汶大学哲学博士，全国优秀教师，北京大学"十佳教师"，教育部教学指导委员会副主任、中华外国哲学史学会理事长、中国现代西方哲学学会副理事长、中国宗教学会副会长，在学术界具有重要的学术地位和威望。著有《基督教哲学1500年》、《人性和伦理的跨文化研究》、《圣经历史哲学》等著作，致力于中国文化语境中圣经学建设。

卓新平（1955—　）　享誉海内外的宗教学专家，我国基督宗教研究领域的著名学者及领军人物。德国慕尼黑大学哲学博士。现任中国社会科学院世界宗教研究所所长、研究员，中国宗教学会会长。代表著作有《世界宗教与宗教学》、《宗教理解》、《基督宗教论》等。2006年当选为欧洲科学艺术研究院院士。

编撰：许　欢、李建宇、谢一批

A RESEARCH REPORT ON
THE WORLD CIVILIZATION DIALOGUE

(2002–2012)

Adivisory Board: (CHN)Xu Jialu, (GER) Kvng Hans, (USA)Tu Weiming, (CAN)Shen Vincent

Organizing Committee of Nishan Forum on World Civilization

People's Publishing House

CONTENTS

Preface .... Xu Jialu   1

Review and Prospect:Momentum and Principle of World
   Civilization Dialogue .... Xie Wenyu   1

Dialogues among Civilizations: UNESCO's Endeavors .... Liu Tiewa   15

Dialogues among Civilizations: Alliance
   of Civilizations .... Zhang Guihong   Yang Rujia   34

World Public Forum "Dialogue of Civilizations" (Rhodes) .... Ni Peimin   53

Challenges Imposed by ChineseCivilization .... Tan Mingran   67

The Eastern World's Endeavor: Nishan Forum
   on World Civilizations .... Gao Shuqun   87

The Momentum and Trends of Civilization Dialogues .... Gao Shuqun   117

Postscript .... Xu Xianghong   126

Appendices

   Appendix 1: UNESCO Universal Declaration on Cultural Diversity 131

Appendix 2: Convention on the Protection and Promotion of the Diversity of
Cultural Expressions... 138

Appendix 3: Alliance of Civilizations (Part I) Report of High Level Group 158

Appendix 4:The Nishan Declaration of Human Harmony (2010)........................ 180

Appendix 5: A Proposal for Young People to Take an Active Part
in Dialogues among World Civilizations (2012) 182

Appendix 6:Nishan Consensus (2012).. 184

Appendix 7:Chronicle of Civilization Dialogue 186

Appendix 8:Who is Who in Civilization Dialogue 219

Preface

Xu Jialu

In today's world, conducting dialogue between different civilizations and underlining the diversity of human culture have formed a neither too big nor a too small trend. Not too big is meant for its still being basically remained in the small circle of scholars, theologians and some former state dignitaries; to say it's not too small is because the voice for the dialogues between different civilizations and advocating diversity of human culture is huge, thanks to the efforts by UNESCO and NGOs from all countries, which has nurtured the concept of "public diplomacy". Further, it has shaken the empire which, for the past century, by any means considers only certain values as universal; and makes it admit that dialogues between different civilizations and cultural diversities should be promoted and protected. Although there are confrontations between what is said and what is done, we believe that "public diplomacy" will ultimately become the main theme in international affairs accompanied by the rational awareness of the people from all over the world.

UNESCO has played a significant and irreplaceable role in the initiative to promote cultural diversity. The independence and rise of the ex-colonial countries are the supporting powers behind it. After the ex-colonial countries gained their political independence, they will naturally cry out their cultural independent appeal for recognition, respect and protection of their own cultures and traditions, together with the demands for their economic independence. To respond to this, UNESCO has initiated many effective projects over the last decade, sponsoring and organizing the relevant countries to conduct civilization dialogue activities.

China has been absent, however, in many of the dialogue activities. A nation with

1.3 billion population, boasting with the world's most ancient civilization, now rapidly revitalizing, should be like many of the ex-colonial countries, speak out his opinions in the world arena , make the people of the world know about its past, present and future expectations. In conducting the dialogue with local civilization, Chinese people will also comprehensively touch upon and learn about, as well as absorb the culture and experience of other nations and countries. From another perspective, if you do not see Chinese people in the world civilization dialogues, the diversified cultural arena can hardly be crowned as "the world's" or "global".

Chinese people's say in the world's cultural arena largely depends on Chinese people themselves: Do we have enough awareness of the importance of such different civilization oriented dialogues? Whose side does Chinese culture stand on in this struggle and dialogue between the dominate culture and the weak culture in the modern world? In comparison with other civilizations, do we know the features of our own culture well enough? Are we keen to tell our stories to the people of different backgrounds? Have we learnt about doing this? Obviously, the people of a culture should have a clear understanding of their own culture and other cultures before they are going to engage in dialogues with other civilizations. So far as this is concerned, we are not yet ready.

Our world is controlled by the dominate culture; and the right to say for most countries and nations are subjected to their economic and technological developments, and restrained by three hundred years' cultural bias. However, just like an old Chinese saying says: "Man conducts projects, and the heaven fulfills it," the noble, beautiful, sincere and righteous voices cannot be hindered to become the ictus even if they may not occupy the main stream of international media. When Chinese people talk about "the heaven fulfills it", we actually mean that when water flows, a channel is formed; success will come when efforts are taken. Dominant culture may still be strong, yet, let me cite a saying from the famed Chinese novel *A Dream in the Red Mansions*, it reaches its limit already. Don't you see?

We Chinese people are not fully prepared, and now we are dragged to go into the battle. At this point, the forerunners are usually the "social elites", to name them in an old way, the illuminati. The intellectual elites possess conspicuous advantage in knowledge, language and social network; they are the conscience of society; and the

2

power of a nation's culture largely lies in the people. Generally speaking, scholars and theologians are honest and sincere with each other when encountering their foreign peers, and their understanding of the subjects may reach into the essence. Chinese humanity scholars must shoulder this burden and pave the way!

As the new millennium was around the corner, the voice from Chinese academia and religions was heard in worldwide. They went abroad and invited colleagues to come, participating in international forums held by multi-nations, and organizing forums and seminars by cooperation of multi-agencies, multi-provinces and municipalities. This trend has, in a sense, activated the "Sinology" in many countries where such studies have been relatively dreary. More scholars and theologians from western contraries become attracted to understanding and studying Chinese civilization. This momentum is in full swing and no one can hold it back.

China has her voice and stories to tell the world and we need a long term endeavor to make them heard. To fulfill this endeavor, we must prepare our voices and stories right away, or we may never be prepared. At this point, we should learn about what we have done, domestic and international, in respects of the dialogues between civilizations, as well as what theories we may have created for such a dialogue. In a word, there should be people and agencies engaging in the in-depth study of different civilization dialogues, the diversity of culture, and cross-cultural communication in China. We expect that their research will serve as reference to those people who concern about and participate in the civilization dialogues, and even to those who are committed to international cultural communication activities.

In fact, the Nishan Forum on World Civilizations is such a platform created for China's engagement. We are determined to maintain its features as of international, academic, and non-governmental. For last four years, we have organized five forums, added by this year's "Beijing Nishan Forum". I want point it out that this is a feeling derived from our efforts of preparing and organizing the Nishan Forum. Now, here we have *A Research Report of World Civilization Dialogue* for our readers. This report is a by-product from the Nishan Forum, which is an extensional effort by the organizing committee.

The reader may find seven not very long articles in this book. The contributors are keen in the field of international issues, especially in different civilization dialogues. It is not hard to feel from them, though concise and comprehensive, that the authors have broad vision and strong historical sense. They contain an earnest aspiration to promote the globalization of Chinese culture. This is a momentum of world culture movement. Besides, the book contains eight appendices, serving as references for further research and study in the field. One may notice the *Chronicle of Civilization Dialogue* (2002 – 2012). We try our best in documenting the events. However, since there are so many activities in this field in last decade, we are afraid that we might not have listed all of them. As to those events we may have missed, I want to say that they are not less important, and we will add them on in the revised edition.

Study on civilization dialogue is a brand new subject. This small edition is an explorative attempt. Let me put it in one of the clichés: We hope this book is a brick that may induce a piece of precious stone. We expect readers' criticism. Meanwhile, we sincerely anticipate that experts in the studies of culture, religion, philosophy, and international relations, become concerned with this subject, though small yet significant. It may extend to become a large issue. With your intellectual support, we believe that it will help China to shoulder its due responsibilities in the world cultural communication, with more confidence and inclusiveness, and in a high yet humble self-esteem.

28th July, 2013

In the Reading Room of a Roll a Day

Review and Prospect:
Momentum and Principle of World
Civilization Dialogue

Xie Wenyu

Once two different civilizations come to a direct contact, they react to each other in a mutual way. There are various ways of the interaction, such as of war, oppression, education, or equally dialogue. After the Cold War, we are able to see a particular kind of interaction, which assumes that there are universal values which must be accepted and instituted by any civilization. For those which have not recognized and instituted these universal values, they should be externally forced to realize them and make them to be their own values in transformation. In the domination of western civilization as today, the universal values are seen as the same values as those accepted and instituted by western countries. By setting up them as the destination of all civilizations, it is required that all civilizations be transformed towards the universal values, that is, towards the western values. We call it the model of civilization transformation in universal values.

We will trace this model's history, analyze into it, and demonstrate its impasse. Meanwhile, we will propose a new model, i.e., the model of self-awaking in core values. Principally, we assume that each civilization contains the primary duty consciousness, based on which its core values are nurtured. A civilization is sustained and identified by its primary duty consciousness and core values. In the dialogue among civilizations, it is not the universal values to be promoted; rather, it is their own core values to be awakened, maintained and developed.

1. Origin of the Term of Universal Values

The term *universal values* become popular after the World War II. It is believed that the War brought huge damages to the world and taught us a lesson that a disrespect for human rights is the disrespect for our own existence. In this consideration, UN convened a conference on December 10, 1948, and reached a declaration, called the Universal Declaration of Human Rights. Literally, the document does not mention the term "universal value". However, the listed human rights are interpreted by western scholars and politicians as universally applied to all human beings. We may list some articles from it to display its spirit:

Article 1 : All human beings are born free and equal in dignity and rights. They are endowed with reason and conscience and should act towards one another in a spirit of brotherhood.

Article 2 : Everyone is entitled to all the rights and freedoms set forth in this Declaration, without distinction of any kind, such as race, colour, sex, language, religion, political or other opinion, national or social origin, property, birth or other status. Furthermore, no distinction shall be made on the basis of the political, jurisdictional or international status of the country or territory to which a person belongs, whether it be independent, trust, non-self-governing or under any other limitation of sovereignty.

Article 13: Everyone has the right to freedom of movement and residence within the borders of each state.
Everyone has the right to leave any country, including his own, and to return to his country.

Article 17: Everyone has the right to own property alone as well as in association with others.
No one shall be arbitrarily deprived of his property.

Article 18: Everyone has the right to freedom of thought, conscience and religion; this right includes freedom to change his religion or belief, and freedom, either alone or in community with others and in public or private, to manifest his religion or belief in teaching, practice, worship and observance.

Article 19: Everyone has the right to freedom of opinion and expression; this right includes freedom to hold opinions without interference and to seek, receive and impart information and ideas through any media and regardless of frontiers.

Article 20: Everyone has the right to freedom of peaceful assembly and association.

No one may be compelled to belong to an association.

In each article, it declares "everyone has the right…" When referring to everyone, it must be universal and can be applied to all human beings, anywhere and anytime. In this reading, the declaration is seen as a list of universal human rights and must be accepted and instituted as the universal values by all countries.

In our observation, the document was written under the shadow of western culture and contains a certain ideology approved by certain politicians. A brief analysis of the article 13 may be enough to support this assertion. The freedom of movement in residence is presumed by a Chinese notion of Tianxia, as it has been said: "All lands under the heaven are King's land." For centuries, Chinese were free to move around whenever they were pleased. They did not have the notion of the boarder of the state and country. When the modern idea of dividing countries by border has been introduced, and Chinese government uses the identity of citizenship to impose a strong restriction on movement in residence, the Chinese people lose their right of free movement in residence. The article 13 endorses the right of free movement within the state and the right of leaving the residency country. Yet, the full concept of free movement in residence must include the right of leaving an area and entering another area without any restriction by governments. Currently, Chinese population is too big and the land is too small, while the western countries occupy a large territory with a small population. That the freedom of movement in residence is not fully endorsed as the human right indicates that western scholars and politicians are indeed limited by their own particular consciousness of human rights or so called universal values.

In 1966, UN adopted two more documents relating to human rights: International Covenant on Economic, Social and Cultural Rights and the International Covenant on Civil and Political Rights. In 1976, the above three documents are combined into one title: *International Bill of Human Rights* and authorized it as the official document to supervise related cases and protect human rights worldwide.

Indeed, after the cold war, the term "universal values" becomes a popular term in the international relationship dominated by the western ideology. Although it has played a positive role to promote those civilizations in a weaker position to reflect on their core values and reveal their blind spots, it has brought more troubles to them, as the civilization transformation always causes turmoil in a civil order, and therefore disturbs the direction of the civilization's inner momentum. It becomes necessary for us to learn more about the negative effects from the model of civilization transformation in universal values, so that we may avoid more destruction to the world peace.

Although Chinese government did not participate in drafting these documents, in 1980, PRC agreed to sign the bill in a good will. However, the bill is not an enforced law. The speculation behind this signature is that the enforcement of a law needs an understanding of law, and when different understandings occur, it demands a final authority in interpretation. The issue is of interpretation of law, and requires the sovereignty of the state. Chinese government sees these documents merely as of international politic, but may interpret them when applying them in law. That is to say, the bill must be interpreted in a way conforming to Chinese civil law, and the Chinese government, rather than the UN, reserved the sovereignty in interpretation, as well as the power in law enforcement.

After the fall of the Soviet Union, westerners have assumed the high profile in interpretation of the bill, and insistently claim as the universal rights some articles of the bill, such as democracy in election, freedom of religion, freedom of speech, etc. Only at this time, the term "universal values" emerges as the key issue in international political relationship. Under the umbrella of universal values, some western politicians strongly demand all nations in the world to transform their civilizations to conform to western civilization. In doing so, the term of universal values functions as a way of interfering other nations' internal political affairs. This is the so-called model of civilization transformation in universal values.

In this consideration, Samuel Moyn rightly points it out: "Human rights in this sense have come to define the most elevated aspiration of both social movements and political entities - state and interstate, they evoke hope and provoke actions." [①] Now, it is the time to reconsider this claim.

2. Right and Duty

Generally, a human being must assume a right in making a decision. However, human beings live in a society and do not make decisions in isolation. In making a decision, an individual has to consider what is good to his/her next moment (future), what is good to his/her loved ones, and what is good to the task he/she is assigned. All these considerations are conducted in his/her duty consciousness. That is to say, in existence, an individual makes decisions in his/her duty consciousness. In making a decision, one is using his/her right, and the right is prior. But one makes the decision according to one's consciousness of duty, without which one cannot make any decision. In this consideration, his/her duty consciousness is prior. Conceptually, right and duty cannot be separated in a human existence. [②]

In defending universal rights, some people argue that human rights must be seen in the first place for protection, while duty is only considered as a consequence of choice in using rights. This treatment is in fact to see right as prior to duty. However, no one can make decision in an empty mind. To assume the priority of right is to separate right from duty. Such an assumption has nothing to do with the actual decision - making in human existence. Indeed, an individual makes decisions (employment of rights) based on his/her duty consciousness, which has been fostered in life tim Some analysis of the Universal Declaration of Human Rights may help. In the article 1, it says: "All human beings are born free and equal in dignity and rights. They are endowed with reason and conscience and should act towards one another in a spirit of brotherhood."

---

① Samuel Moyn: *The Last Utopia: Human Rights in History*, Harvard University Press, 2010, p.1.

② See Xie Wenyu: "Liberty and Duty: An Analysis of Political Philosophy," *Journal of Zhejiang University*, January, 2010.1, pp.182 – 195.

The document begins with equal rights, but employs "reason, conscience, and a spirit of brotherhood" to support the declaration of equal rights. Obviously, reason, conscience, and a spirit of brotherhood do not have any sense of right. They are indeed a kind of duty consciousness. For example, someone is in possession of reason, and may use it to design and conduct a plan of murder; but may also use it to do something good to humanity. It completely depends on his duty consciousness. As to "a spirit of brotherhood", it does not come with birth; rather, it must be nurtured in a certain environment of humanity. Therefore, it is a kind of duty consciousness. Different duty consciousness may cause a human being to do differently with reason, conscience, and a spirit of brotherhood.

Historically, a civilization began with a primary duty consciousness, as it wants to survive, moving on to the next moment. But its content may not be easy to trace. In fact, an accidental circumstance may cause a certain primary duty consciousness. For example, when twins were born, the mother may occasionally assign one of them as older brother or sister. This oral assignment is a trivial thing, yet this element may respectively direct the developments of their duty consciousness. Similarly, a civilization may catch something accidentally and came out with a primary duty consciousness. Since then, the direction of the civilization is determined. Once a primary duty consciousness occurs, it provides the foundation of the civilization in her development, in which people living in the civilization will learn and nurture their duty consciousness. And further, certain core values will be formed out from their duty consciousness. Being the foundation of the civilization, the primary duty consciousness cannot be separated from the civilization. Indeed, without it, the civilization cannot continue to exist.

Let us move on a bit. Although the duty consciousness is in development, it must be represented in a certain form, i.e., in forms of values, based on which human beings make decisions. There are many forms of values, such as rights, virtues, norms, examples, and wishes. Among them, we may discern a certain values which represent directly the primary duty consciousness. We call them the core values. When conflicts between two civilizations occur, it usually gets involved with less important values. For example, the greeting manners, the expression of disagreement, and so on. These kinds of conflicts can be solved easily when both sides come to know each other more.

However, when the conflict touches the core values, it becomes violent.

Human beings live in a civilization; and their existential decisions are made according to the core values. Further, core values are nurtured by the primary duty consciousness. The foundation is the primary duty consciousness. To understand a civilization is to understand the primary duty consciousness. In fact, in making a value judgment, if it is in conformation with the primary duty consciousness, people will see it as absolutely correct.

A civilization may exist in isolation. In such a state, the primary duty consciousness is seen as the absolute good and perfect, as no one may challenge it in any way. As the starting point as well as the foundation of the society, the primary duty consciousness align the direction of the development of civilization, fostering those things it sees as good and correcting whatever it judges as bad. Yet, they may have many blind spots, which prevent them from seeing many other things. All actual civilizations have their own blind spots, which may never be revealed when in isolation.

However, when two civilizations come to communicate, and two systems of core values conflict, each side imposes a challenge to the other side. There is a possibility in which a blind spot in one side may be seen by the other side, and then this blind spot is revealed externally. This revelation propels the civilization to respond, based upon its primary duty consciousness, to the issues which was not perceived before. Obviously, the dialogue among civilizations may help reveal blind spots to a civilization and enhance its prospect. This is called a process of self-awaking, or a process of perfection, as people become aware of more the core values of their civilization.

The difference between the above two models lies in this: in practicing the model of civilization transformation in universal values, we have to remove the primary duty consciousness of the civilization and therefore bring the destruction to this civilization and reestablish a new civilization based on that of universal values. Meanwhile, the model of self-awaking in core values will allow the civilization to improve itself by responding to the revealed blind spots.

As removing the primary duty consciousness is destruction to the civilization which has founded on it, if we want to preserve it, we must be very cautious of the destructivity brought by the model of civilization transformation in universal values.

Having considered this, we promote the dialogues among civilizations in the model of self-awaking in core values.

3. Theories of Cultural Dialogues

Under the shadow of universal value presumption, some westerners attempt to find out a conductible forum of dialogue to promote a good inter-cultural relationship. In 1970s, John Hick (1922–2012) proposes the theory of pluralism for cultural dialogues. [1] He creates a term "the Real" to refer to the absolute being, which is the final end for all religions to pursue. However, all existing religions may only touch a part of the Real and so should not claim to have the truth; instead, they should learn from each other. If we all accept this pluralism, according to Hick, we will then establish a platform of dialogue, on which all religions may share their understandings of the Real. In order to build up this platform, it is necessary for each related religion to abandon its exclusivism, which arrogantly places itself above others. With acceptance of pluralism, people in all sides will be able to erase their arrogance and start to dialogue. In his proposal, Hick urges the reader to adopt the consciousness of "the Real" as the foundation for all religions. In fact, he advises the reader to be converted to his religion of the Real. In the name of pluralism, Hick is building a new religion. In practice, to follow him is to fall into a trap, in which a civilization in superior position will be seen as containing more truth about the Real, while those civilizations in inferior position are advised to give up their core values to catch up.

After Hick's pluralism, many scholars endeavor to explore a more concrete way to make it feasible for dialogue among civilizations in practice. The so-called second axial age is the flag for this movement. These scholars include Ewert Cousins, Raimon Panikkar, and Paul F. Knitter. [2] The central theme in this movement is: one can understand an alien religion only through converting to it and practice it in daily

---

[1] See his works: *God and the Universe of Faiths*, Oxford: OneWorld Publications Ltd., 1973; and *Dialogues in the Philosophy of Religion*, Palgrave Macmillan, 2001.

[2] See Paul F. Knitter: *One Earth-Many Religions: Multifaith Dialogue and Global Responsibilities*, Orbis Books, 1995.

life. It is advisable that one may experience many conversions in his life time, with which one is able to dialogue between different religions at a fundamental level. The idea of the second axial age is to promote conversions among religions in contact. Multi-experiences in different religions may help one understand each of them. Theoretically, it may help a scholar in many conversions get a first hand experience of the religions he has been converted to. Practically, however, it is not feasible for ordinary people, who are in their whole life stuck to a certain religion faithfully. Some individual scholars' conversional experience may have no impact on ordinary people at all. Without ordinary people's participation, we cannot found a platform for dialogue among civilizations.

In the summer issue of 1993, an American journal, *Foreign Affairs*, published an article by Samuel P. Huntington: *The Clash of Civilizations?*[①] The article expresses a deep concern about the danger derived from western international policy based on the model of civilization transformation in universal values. According to Huntington, westerners should not see their values as universal; as such an attitude has aroused a world wide anti-American mood. Rather, they should treat them as being particular to the western civilization. To maintain the superior position of the western civilization in the world, it is better for the western politicians to abandon the claim of universal values in handling international relations. Huntington seems more sensitive to the feeling of the people in other civilizations. However, a brief analysis may divulge a strong anxiety in Huntington's covered universalism, as he deeply believes that western civilization is able to maintain its supremacy among world civilizations. His real purpose is to maintain the dominant position of western civilization. We may call it the Huntingdon's stratagem.

In fact, universalism exists in every civilization. We may start with the primary duty consciousness. The primary duty consciousness is to maintain the civilization to subsist and sees its existence as the best for human beings. It contains self confidence sustained by its universalism. When a civilization encounters another civilization, people in the former desire to understand the latter and soon begin to figure out its

---

① The theme of the article later was expanded into a book: *The Clash of Civilizations and the remaking of World Order*, New York: Simon & Schuster, 1996.

goodness and evilness according to their notion of good and evil. The judgment in fact is a rational examination and contains a universal disposition. That is, with their understandings of good and evil, they may absorb what seems good to them and reject evil elements. In doing so, it is natural for them to teach and correct the people in the latter for their impropriety and evilness. Meanwhile, they are happy to offer good things to them, namely, educate them. All civilizations have this trend of universalism. Indeed, this universalism provides momentum to sustain the communications and dialogues among civilizations. The primary duty consciousness has been nurturing values in history; and a set of values constitute a perspective for people to judge and valuate whatever come to them. Since the perspective is limited and so contains blind spots, we will then naturally reject as evils those things which are valuable in other civilizations. Framed by our own primary duty consciousness and blocked by these blind spots, we may never be able to perceive the goodness behind them.

However, blind spots can be revealed when two civilizations come into contact. The exposure of evils by other civilizations in contact, which were concealed in blind spots of one's perspective, is a challenge to one's value system and may arouse a strong emotional resistance. The resistance is so strong that two sides may confront each other in violence and war, especially when both sides do not have a basic trust. The situation may change dramatically, however, when both sides are friendly in trust. When one points out the weakness or bad things his friend fails to know, his friend may respond emotionally at first but will then gradually calm down to reflect, as trust sustains communications. Similarly, to avoid the violent conflicts between two civilizations in confrontation when the blind spots have been revealed, we need a basic trust to sustain our communications. This trust contains a good will to promote the other's primary duty consciousness and its core values, rather than to replace them and so destroy the civilization. When blind spots are revealed, it expands one's perspective. It is profitable for all civilizations in confrontation.

4. The Basic Principles in Civilization Dialogue

In the above analyses, we have dealt with two crucial elements: the primary duty consciousness in a civilization and blind spots in perspective fostered by this consciousness. All civilizations have the trend of universalism and therefore they have momentum to communicate with each other. We also see the fact that a healthy relationship among civilization in contact depends on a basic trust. No trust, no dialogue. Through dialogues in trust, all sides of civilizations in contact will be able to be revealed of their blind spots and then expand their perspectives respectively. To a civilization in an inferior position, people in it should concentrate on their core values and reflect on their primary duty consciousness at a deeper level. In responding to the challenge from other civilization, people in a civilization should base on their primary duty consciousness to improve their value system, erase their blind spots, and move their civilization on. Similarly, to the people of a civilization in a superior position, they should keep in mind that they have blind spots in their perspective too, and needs other civilizations in contact to help reveal their blind spots, and improve their value system, and understand deeper their primary consciousness. In this way, they will make more contributions to the world civilization, and their superiority will be welcome among other civilizations. We call this kind of civilization dialogue the model of self-awaking in core values. We believe this model will bring a harmonious co-existence of plural civilizations in our common earth.

In comparing two models of civilization dialogue, we notice that the model of self-awaking in core values has its root in Chinese thought, which promotes an ideal of harmony in difference. In a Chinese classic, the "Zhongyong", we read these words: "All things are nourished together without their injuring one another. And they can co-exist in their ways without conflict to each other. A small gain makes it a flowing stream; a big gain makes it a transforming power. That is why heaven-earth is great." Each civilization has the way of existence and development in its primary duty consciousness. They can be together without conflict and co-exist without doing harm to each other. This is the harmonious world.

Sticking to this position, we consider the advantage of the model of self-awaking in core values over that of civilization transformation in universal values. We admit the universalism in each civilization, as it provides momentum for dialogue among civilizations. However, we insist that the dialogue should be conducted in a way of respecting the primary duty consciousness and core values of each other, and helping each other erase the blind spots. Practically, the following principles are advised:

First, be respectful to each other's expression in language and behavior. In communication with an alien civilization, we come to recognize its existences. To us, people in this alien civilization are strangers, with different concerns, weird ideas, unpleasant manner of behaviors, improper customs and so on. Usually, this alienage may cause some bad feeling and annoyance. It is not necessary that these bad feeling and annoyance must be destructive. In the beginning, each side may willingly to offer good things in their perspective to the other side, while demand them to abandon and improve their impropriety. Here, bad feelings and annoyance are indeed providing momentum for communication and dialogue. If there is a basic trust between two sides, the offering and demanding can be seen a sign of good will. However, when no good will is perceived, the two sides will run into conflicts and confront each other. Clearly, respectfulness is a bridge.

Secondly, promote self-awaking of its core values through dialogue. A civilization has been sustained by its primary duty consciousness, which further nurtures core values. Each civilization has its history and tradition. Realization of its own primary duty consciousness and recognition of its own core values are essential to maintain the development of a civilization. To remove its primary duty consciousness and core values is to destroy this civilization. Of course, each civilization, whether strong or weak, has its blind spots, and within its perspective it cannot reveal its blind spots. Civilization dialogue, however, provide an occasion for both sides to reveal their own blind spots. The exposure of the blind spot is a huge challenge to a civilization. It may bring down the system of values. However, it will not destroy the core values. In fact, destruction to a system of values makes it possible for reconstruction. A new system of values must be built upon its core values, as well as within the primary duty consciousness. The model self-awaking of its core values in civilization dialogue will improve the civilization, instead of destroying it.

Thirdly, in politic, people in a civilization have sovereignty in choosing a political system acceptable and suitable to their mind-set. Political government is a forcible management of society, involving various social forces in the society. These social forces are connected in a complicated network and can be properly and profoundly understood only by those who are in the net. They have been fostered by the society

12

and contain certain duty consciousness, with which they engage themselves in their concerned political issues. Of course, they have different political positions over various social issues among themselves, as their duty consciousness may differ and even conflict with each other. Now, we are bound to encounter these questions: Whose understanding should be considered or judged as correct? And what solution should we accepted for action as proper? To these questions, one thing is certain, i.e., the answers should come from the people who are the members of the society; and definitely not from outsiders. In the contemporary international political relationship, we observe that the civilizations in superior position holds on to the model of civilization transformation in universal values, and interferes externally the political affairs of the civilizations in inferior position. Such an interfering never brings benefits to both sides. An essential advance in a civilization's political government can be made only on the foundation of its primary duty consciousness. No external interference on other civilization's domestic political affairs should be maintained as the principle of civilization dialogue.

Fourthly, work together to infuse the global economies among world civilizations. There are many tunnels to connect different civilizations, such as geographical neighborhood, the needs of exchanging commercial products, attractive arts, and interesting ideas, and so on. Among these tunnels, internationals commercial exchange or trade imposes a special impact. For a long time in human history, geographical distance blocks the communications among civilizations. In the last century, however, this geographical barrier has been gradually removed by fast developed transportation tools. International commercial trade becomes the neccssity for daily life for all people in different civilizations, and mutual-dependence among civilizations has reached such a level that no civilization can subsist well without others' involvements. This mutual-dependence is an important propelling force for civilization dialogue. Obviously, the infusion of economies among different civilizations demands a deep mutual-understanding of each other. And this can be done through a respectful and trust dialogues among civilizations.

Fifthly, a platform for religion dialogue is urgently needed. Human beings appeal to the absolute concerns in their existence; and religion is the proper way for them to express this absolute concerns. The object of absolute concern cannot be found in this world, but it may lead the believers to move on towards different directions. That is, while religion expresses people's absolute concerns, it guides the direction of their lives. Its theme is transcendent as well as realistic. Each civilization has its own religion. A well treatment on the interaction between religions in civilization dialogue will make dialogue to move smoothly. In this consideration, we call for a platform of religion dialogue.

We propose the above five guiding principles for civilization dialogue, based on the model of self-awaking in core values. We oppose to the model of civilization transformation in universal values, as it brings destruction to the civilization in inferior position, and seals firmly the blind spots of the civilization in superior position. This world needs dialogues among civilizations, and we believe that the model of self-awaking in core values will be a blessing to the world civilizations.

Xie Wenyu received his Ph.D. degree from Claremont Graduate University, Californian, USA, and now is now Professor of Philosophy and Religious Studies at Shandong University. He serves as the director of the Center for Greek Thought. His publication includes *The Concept of Freedom* (2002); *Freedom and Existence* (2007); *The Way and Truth* (2012); and some 90 academic articles. His expertise is in the field of philosophy of religion, Christian thought, and comparative studies.

Dialogues among Civilizations: UNESCO's Endeavors

Liu Tiewa

As one of the major specialized agencies of the United Nations, UNESCO mainly concentrates on education, science, culture and exchanges promotion. It claims: "UNESCO works to create the conditions for dialogue among civilizations, cultures and peoples, based upon respect for commonly shared values. It is through this dialogue that the world can achieve global visions of sustainable development encompassing observance of human rights, mutual respect and the alleviation of poverty, all of which are at the heart of UNESCO'S mission and activities." [1]

Now, the Cold War has ended, and tensions and conflicts among super powers have reduced; yet conflicts among cultures, civilizations, religions, have increased gradually. Some scholars call it the clash of civilizations. [2] UNESCO is of special significance in this regard. There are arguments about diversity of cultures in terms of "universal values" and "relative values". In the process of globalization, we are also able to see a trend of cultural globalization, which advocates universal values or universal ethics, called universalism. Meanwhile, some states maintain the particularity of their own cultures, seeing the importance of the relative values within their civilizations, called particularism, which promotes the so called global diversification

---

[1]   http://unesdoc.unesco.org/images/0014/001473/147330c.pdf.

[2]   Samuel. P. Huntington: *The Clash of Civilizations and the Remaking of World Order*, trans. by Zhou Qi, Beijing: Xinhua Publishing House, 1998. p. 18.

of culture. [1] As one Chinese scholar points out: "On one hand, the enhancement of the cultural diversity awareness has driven people to be bigoted on the cultural values of 'particularism' and 'regionalism', and thus have less confidence in the universal values, ideals and ethics of mankind." "On the other hand, both modern people and the modern world are more aware of the battle of diversified cultures, and are thus more eager to seek for a general consensus, in certain form that is beyond cultural differences." [2]

With the consideration of universalism and particularism in mind, we instead focuses on tracing the role UNESCO has played in promoting cultural diversity and dialogues among civilizations. It is interesting to note that, UNESCO has changed its stand from the advocate of universal values to of cultural diversity. Major resolutions and actions UNESCO has adopted since 2000 may elaborate its endeavors in promoting cultural diversity.

1. Universal Values or Cultural Diversity?

As the major intergovernmental organization in education, science and culture, UNESCO has a strong voice in areas related to cultures and relations among civilizations. However, the organization has undergone an obvious transition period to become an advocate for cultural diversity. In the early post-war period, UNESCO, under the control of the United States, was a major platform to propaganda and spread the Western ideology. But since the middle of 1960s, UNESCO, in opposing cultural colonialism and imperialism, has shifted to emphasize on cultural diversity.

Unlike many other post-war intergovernmental organizations, UNESCO originated in Europe. [3] In 1941, the Conference of Allied Ministers of Education

---

① Fan Hao: "Ecological Dialogue and Ecological Development in the Spirit of Ethics—Rational Notion of Value of Chinese Ethics in Answering to 'Globalization'", *Journal of Graduate School,* Chinese Academy of Social Sciences, 2001, Vol. 6, p. 16.

② Wan Junren: *Seeking Universal Ethnic*, Shangwu Publishing House, 2001, p. 303.

③ Roger A. Coate: "Changing Patterns of Conflict: the United States and UNESCO," in Magaret P. Karns and Karen A. Mingst (ed.), *The United States and Multilateral Institutions: Patterns of Changing Instrumentality and Influence*, London: Routledge, p. 232.

(CAME) [①] was convened under British government's proposal to set up an "International Organization for Education". American Delegation proposed a draft of the Constitution, which was later adopted by the Conference, named *A Proposal of the Conference of Allied Ministers of Education to Promote the Foundation of United Nations Organization for Educational and Cultural Reconstruction*. Through negotiations and compromises, the mission of the new organization was agreed as to "contribute to peace and security by promoting collaboration among the nations through education, science and culture in order to further universal respect for justice, for the rule of law and for the human rights and fundamental freedoms which are affirmed for the peoples of the world, without distinction of race, sex, language or religion, by the Charter of the United Nations." [②] Obviously, UNESCO was originally established based on the political ideology and values of the Western liberalism.

This time was the period of the cold war, and the United States and the USSR were in tension; the battle of ideologies had prevailed. A brief analysis may show that the original principles of UNESCO were actually under the shadow of American values such as individual rights, freedom of the press, etc. To be more specific, UNESCO elaborated its mission to advocate universal values in its Constitution: "That the wide diffusion of culture, and the education of humanity for justice and liberty and peace are indispensable to the dignity of man and constitute a sacred duty which all the nations must fulfill in a spirit of mutual assistance and concern." [③] Therefore, the priority of UNESCO, in its early days of establishment, was to spread universal values such as human rights, democracy, and freedom. And consequently the concept of human rights was inserted in the various projects of many international organizations. In fact, for many years since the establishment of the organization, the United States was behind the projects of UNESCO concerning global human rights. There was a project targeting

---

① CAME was established based on the proposal of the Director of the British Council, and included representatives from governments of the 8 U.N. Member States. The objective of CAME was post-war education reconstruction. The members of the CAME in 1943 were also the members of the London International Assembly, which called for a permanent international organization for education.

② See UNESCO: *Constitution*, Article 1, paragraph 1, at: http://portal.unesco.org/en/ev.php-URL_ID=15244&URL_DO=DO_TOPIC&URL_SECTION=201.html.

③ Roger A. Coate: *Unilateralism, Ideology, & U.S. Foreign Policy: The United States In and Out of UNESCO*, Boulder, Lynne Rienner Publishers, 1988, p. 38.

on the USSR's violation of human rights, which has been seen as part of universal values by the United States. In a newsletter from the department of Social and Human Sciences, UNESCO, it says: "Human rights are central to the very origins of UNESCO. They were massively violated in the tragic backdrop to the Organizations' emergence, and universal respect for them is the ultimate goal set for it by Article I of its Constitution, which was adopted in London on 16 November 1945." [1]

In order to spread the ideology of liberalism, as well as America's values and political system, the United States insisted that UNESCO's mission be expanded to enhance international telecommunication. UNESCO then worked to "collaborate in the work of advancing the mutual knowledge and understanding of peoples, through all means of mass communication and to that end recommend such international agreements as may be necessary to promote the free flow of ideas by word and image" [2]. Actually, communication has been one of the major concerns of the American politicians since the establishment of UNESCO. Early in the 1st Assembly of UNESCO in 1946, Americans proposed to build a broadcast network of the organization to "cover every inch of the earth with intense signals." [3] The role UNESCO played in the Korean War was another typical example of the organization's deep involvement in political events. [4] UNESCO was actually a tool of propaganda of the U.S. government in the Korean War. UNESCO explained the reason why it provided DPRK with assistance in its resolution: "One of the main purposes of UNESCO, as said in Article 1 in the Constitution, is 'to contribute to peace and security by promoting collaboration among the nations through education, science and culture in order to further universal respect for justice, for the rule of law and for the human rights and fundamental freedoms which are affirmed for the peoples of the world, without distinction of race, sex, language or religion, by the Charter of the United

---

[1] See the Official Website of UNESCO, at: http://portal.unesco.org/shs/en/ev.php-URL_ID=8736&URL_DO=DO_TOPIC&URL_SECTION=201.html.

[2] See UNESCO: *Constitution*, Article 1, Section 2, at: http://portal.unesco.org/en/ev.php-URL_ID=15244&URL_DO=DO_TOPIC&URL_SECTION=201.html.

[3] Robert W. Cox and Harold K. Jacobson, *The Anatomy of Influence: Decision Making in International Organization*, New Haven: Yale University Press, 1973, p. 162.

[4] See Agenda item 4 of the 23rd session of the Executive Board in September 1950. See Executive Board document 23 EX/Decisions, p. 2, at: http://unesdoc.unesco.org/images/0011/001139/113905E.pdf.

Nations.'" The Executive Board was also "profoundly moved by the armed attack of which the Republic of Korea has been the victim." [1]

In 1954, the USSR decided not to stay away from UNESCO, and advised its followers to seek actively to join in the organization, including Czechoslovakia, Poland and Hungary which once joined UNESCO but withdrew later. Bulgaria, Romania and Albania became member states soon after the USSR join UNESCO. Also, the Third World countries were gaining substantial strength and increasing influence, which won themselves more advantages in ideological battles. [2] Meanwhile, the US government was witnessing a decreasing interest and influence in UNESCO. The American delegation strongly opposed Romania and the Republic of Bulgaria's joining UNESCO, for America believed that these two countries had severely violated human rights, which is at the heart of the Constitution of the organization. However, while condemning the two countries, America was also challenged by its "selective morality". As is all known, Republic of South Africa, while keeping violating human rights, was not rejected by UNESCO. In the 8th session of the UNESCO General Conference in 1954, delegations from both USSR and Czechoslovakia highly praised Romania's endeavor and achievements in education, science and culture. The USSR delegation also pointed out that America's accusation against Romania's violation of the human rights was rootless, and thus cannot be accepted. Finally, the Conference decided that "this issue needs no further consideration, for the rights Romanian people were endowed with, and the cultural and scientific development have proven all these accusations rootless." [3]

Since the early 1960s, the non-Western member states in UNESCO had been trying to redefine the goal and principle of the organization with their own thoughts which differed from the ideology of liberalism in the Western World. Gradually, UNESCO was changing its way of thinking, working philosophy and political

---

① See Executive Board document 23 EX/Decisions, p. 2, at: http://unesdoc. unesco. org/images/0011/001139/113905E.pdf.

② The number of UNESCO's member states has risen from 27 to 100 in 1960. In 1960 and 1962, 18 and 34 countries joined UNESCO respectively, most of which were African countries.

③ See "Proceedings of the General Conference", 8th session, 3rd Plenary Meeting, Montevideo, 1954, p. 48, also at: http://unesdoc.unesco.org/images/0011/001145/114586E.pdf.

preferences. One good example is that, many of UNESCO's resolutions did adopt non-colonial ideology advocated by the Third World countries. The resolution passed on the General Conference in 1960 was named "The role of UNESCO in contributing to the attainment of independence by colonial countries and peoples", saying that "Colonialism in all its forms and all its manifestations must be speedily abolished, and that accession to freedom and independence must not be delayed on the false pretext that a particular territory has not reached a sufficiently high standard in economic, social, educational and cultural matters", "one of UNESCO's most urgent tasks is to help the newly independent countries, and those which are preparing for independence, to overcome any harmful after-effects of colonialism, such as economic, social and cultural underdevelopment, illiteracy, and the serious shortage of trained personnel." [1]

In the late 1960s, there emerged a hot discussion of anti-cultural imperialism and cultural sovereignty, cooperated by the international political forces opposing the cultural penetration from the western states. In 1972, the USSR proposed a draft of *Mass Media Declaration* which was affirmed in 1974, granting the nation's control over the media. Some representatives from western countries, however, believing that the draft was an attempt to violate the freedom of media, left the conference to lodge a protest against the anti-Israel words. The UNESCO General Conference in 1974 drew the conclusion that "the Non-Aligned Countries and other developing countries are obligated to change the current situation where global information is in extreme unbalance, so as to achieve non-colonialism and express determination in the information field." [2] In 1976, the Intergovernmental Conference on Communication Policies in Latin America was held by UNESCO. The Conference established a fairer standard for information exchange among different countries; allowed global policies to be made based on sovereignty self-determination and preferences on global information flow; acknowledged that the real free flow of information can only

---

① See the Records of 11th session of General Conference in 1960, at: http://unesdoc.unesco.org/images/0011/001145/114583E.pdf, p. 74; also see the records of Executive Board meeting, http://unesdoc.unesco.org/images/0011/001132/113245E.pdf.

② See "Final Report," Tunis, March 26–30, Symposium of the Non-Aligned on Information, 1976.

be achieved when all countries extend equal dialogue, have equal control over all information resources, and use international transmission channels.[1] All these have shown that UNESCO, once dedicated to spreading a certain ideology led by the United States at the beginning of its establishment, has now changed its objectives to affirming and promoting cultural diversity which are more often called for by the Third World countries.

The primary reason was UNESCO's democratic principles in decision-making: each country has only one vote. According to its Constitution, UNESCO can be defined as an open organization, "all countries have equal right to vote on the Conference; based on the original Constitution, the Conference should be held annually. However, it was actually held on a two-year basis since 1948. Members of the Executive Board are selected from the representatives of the Conference."[2] "Each member of the Executive Board has only one vote. And the decision of the Executive Board, despite certain occasions, should be made by the simple majority of the representatives."[3] In the meantime, "Membership of the United Nations Organization shall carry with it the right to membership of the United Nations Educational, Scientific and Cultural Organization."[4] This means that a member state of the United Nations could, if it wills, automatically become the member state of UNESCO. Before 1954, however, a number of socialist countries were still excluded from UNESCO, as well as many Third World countries which hadn't gained national independence yet. In this regard, the openness of UNESCO was not

---

① Herbert I. Schiller: "Decolonization of Information: Efforts toward a New International Order", *Latin American Perspectives*, Vol. 5, No.1, Culture in the Age of Mass Media (Winter, 1978), pp. 35–48.

② Sources come from the official website of UNESCO, http://unesdoc.unesco.org/images/0013/001337/133729cb.pdf#page=7
.

③ When a proposal has been adopted or rejected it may not be reconsidered at the same session of the Board, unless the Board, by a two-thirds majority of the Members present and voting, so decides. (Rule 45); Special consultation by correspondence (Rule 60); Amendment (Rule 66); Suspension (Rule 67); The affirmation on the non-Member States who could send observers to the conference.

See: http://unesdoc.unesco.org/images/0013/001390/139080e.pdf.

④ See: *Constitution of the United Nations Educational, Scientific and Cultural Organization*, Article II, at: http://portal.unesco.org/en/ev.php-URL_ID=15244&URL_DO=DO_TOPIC&URL_SECTION=201.html.

fully installed. [1] From 1945 to 1954, UNESCO was mainly constituted of Western countries, with our three socialist member states: Poland, Czechoslovakia and Hungary. These three countries voted often against the anti-communism political decisions made by the General Conference or the Executive Board. In fact, because their efforts had made little positive result, they withdrew from the organization. At that time, the majority of the Third World countries, having just gained national independence, were in lack of experience and capability in terms of multilateral diplomacy. It is also noteworthy that many member states were Latin American countries deeply influenced by the developed countries in the north. Without certain coordination and cooperation, most of the member states agreed to be led by Western countries, the United States, in particular. [2]

However, with a great number of countries joining the organization, UNESCO has become one of the most open international organizations. Richard Bissell once said that "The expansion of the UN members, and the changes of the characters of the new member states, in particular, has fundamentally changed the organization's major objectives. In organizations as UNESCO, for instance, each member state has the same right to vote, which shifts the attention of the organization from the political interests of the Big Powers to the economic prosperity of the developing countries, including the new World Order of information. Generally, the global society has been attaching more attention to population, food, energy, accommodation and environmental issues, while underlining interdependency instead of unilateral dependency between countries." [3]

This was mainly because of the equal way of decision-making, the "One country, one vote" policy. UNESCO, with numbers of Third World countries joining in, has become ever more open. The United States, as a result, found itself unable to dominate, or even control UNESCO anymore to promote its so-called "Universal Values". Since

---

① Attention: in Article II of the Constitution, "States not members of the United Nations Organization may be admitted to membership of the Organization, upon recommendation of the Executive Board, by a two-thirds majority vote of the General Conference."

② Sagarika Dutt: *The Politicization of the United Nations Specialized Agencies, A Case Study of UNESCO*, Mellen University Press, 1995, p. 44.

③ Richard E. Bissell: "The United States in the UN: Past and Present", *The US, the UN and the Management of Global Change*, edited by Toby Trister Gati, New York University press, 1983, pp. 90–91.

the middle 1960s, the call for opposition against cultural colonialism and for adhering to cultural sovereignty has become ever stronger in UNESCO, resulting in a new objective of the organization, cultural diversity. In 1984, the United States withdrew from UNESCO, for it found that the USSR and the Third World countries had almost controlled the agenda setting, and have adopted many resolutions unfavorable to America. The United States Department of State said that UNESCO "behaves extremely politicized on every subject, and is very hostile to the basic principles of the freedom of society, market and the press." [1]

2. Endeavors in Organizing and Supporting Dialogues among Civilizations

The battle between advocating of universal values and opposing against colonialism still prevailed in UNESCO even after the Cold War ended, bringing UNESCO back to the track of promoting dialogue, harmony and mutual prosperity among civilizations based on the principle of adhering to cultural diversity. In 1998, the UN Resolution 53/22 proclaimed the year 2001 "International Year of Dialogue among Civilizations". In the *World Culture Report: Culture, Creativity and Markets* in 1998, UNESCO stated the seven major reasons for adhering to cultural diversity: (1) cultural diversity, as an expression of our spiritual creativity, is of great value; (2) fairness, human rights and the right to self-determination call for cultural diversity; (3) just like biodiversity, cultural diversity helps people adapt to the limited natural resources and achieve sustainable development; (4) cultural diversity reduces the dependence on politics and economic growth; (5) from an aesthetic point of view, cultural diversity presents a pleasant series of cultures; (6) cultural diversity enlightens our way of thinking; (7) cultural diversity stores knowledge, experience and great ways of doing things. [2] We will mainly focus on the major resolutions and works of UNESCO since

① "US Statement on UNESCO", *New York Times,* Dec. 30, 1983, p. A4.

② UNESCO: *World Culture Report 1998*, Foreword by Lourdes Arizpe, Peking University Press, July, 2000, p.3.

2000 to elaborate its endeavors in pushing forward dialogue among civilizations.

(1) Declarations, Conventions and Activities at the International Level

Since 1999, UNESCO has been organizing Round Tables of Ministers of Culture aperiodically, bringing together culture ministers and representatives from all around the world to discuss various themes. From December 11th to December 12th, 2000, the 2nd Round Table of Ministers of Culture was held, themed "2000–2010 Cultural Diversity: Challenges of the Marketplace". The Round Table mainly discussed how culture should adapt to the market's demand, and how the pursuit of maximum benefit impacts cultural diversity and the due countermeasures. The development of culture industry of each country, as was concluded by the Conference, should both adapt to the global market's demand, and strength protection of culture diversity from being eroded by the pursuit of economic benefit.[1] Meanwhile, UNESCO has been holding "International Mother Language Day" since 2000 to promote awareness of linguistic and cultural diversity, as well as multilingualism. The theme in the year 2000 was "Inaugural Celebration of International Mother Language Day".

From April 23rd to April 26th, 2001, UNESCO held "International Conference on 'Dialogue among Civilizations'" in Vilnius, Lithuania, bringing together heads of state, political decision-makers and diplomats, distinguished scholars, academics and artists to debate about the complex issues of culture and civilizations in the contemporary world. The Conference resulted in *Dialogue among Civilizations: the International Conference in Vilnius, Lithuania, 23–26 April, 2001*. The dialogue, based on the unity of mankind and commonly shared values, recognized the world's cultural diversity and the equal dignity of each civilization, culture and individual, and underlines the need to prevent the emergence and nurturing of new prejudices and stereotypes, laying a solid foundation for the *UNESCO Universal Declaration on Cultural Diversity 2001* Adopted by the 31st session of the UNESCO General Conference on November 2nd, 2001. As in the *Declaration*, "culture takes diverse forms across time and space. This diversity is embodied in the uniqueness and plurality of the identities of the groups and

---

[1] http://www.unesco.org.cn/ViewInfoText.jsp?INFO_ID=94&KEYWORD=.

societies making up humankind. As a source of exchange, innovation and creativity, cultural diversity is as necessary for humankind as biodiversity is for nature. In this sense, it is the common heritage of humanity and should be recognized and affirmed for the benefit of present and future generations." [1] The Global Alliance for Cultural Diversity, an initiative based on the concept of partnership, was launched by UNESCO following the decision of the 31st Session of the General Conference of UNESCO (November 2001), and has entered its active phase in 2002. Supported by the European Union, some 20 pilot projects covering fields as varied as music, publishing, museum originating products, the production of cartoons and small craft enterprises, are presently being developed on the basis of the principle of solidarity and mutual help, in Peru, Algeria, Jamaica, China (Tibet) and in Zimbabwe. [2] On December 20th, 2002, UNESCO declared May 21st to be the World Day for Cultural Diversity for Dialogue and Development, underlining the close connection between the protections of cultural diversity with dialogue among civilizations.

On September 12th, 2002, the then U.S President George W. Bush delivered a speech to the UN General Assembly, saying that "as a symbol of our commitment to human dignity, the United States will return to UNESCO. This organization has been reformed, and America will participate fully in its mission to advance human rights and tolerance and learning." [3] Timothy E. Wirth, director of the United Nations Foundation and Better World Fund, believes that "UNESCO is playing a key role in spreading America's value to the world whether in education, democracy or human rights." [4] Still, it is not easy to coordinate the relation between America's interest and UNESCO's operation. Promoting cultural diversity and dialogue among civilizations remain one of the major goals of UNESCO on the international level. From September 16th to September 17th, 2002, the 3rd Round Table of Ministers of Culture was held in Istanbul, Turkey, themed "Intangible Cultural Heritage-a Mirror of Cultural Diversity". Through full negotiations, member states passed Istanbul Declaration for

---

[1]　See: http://www.fsa.gov.cn/web_db/sdzg2006/adv/BLDPX/DYMB/zhc/jcjy020.htm.

[2]　http://www.ncac.gov.cn/cms/html/205/2094/200401/671932.html.

[3]　"President's Remarks at the United Nations General Assembly," at the website of Whitehouse: http://www.whitehouse.gov/news/releases/2002/09/20020912-1.html.

[4]　http://betterworldfund.org/multimedia/pdf/2004/Congress_Funds_UNESC_030904.pdf.

the protection of intangible cultural heritage. [1] From October 9th to October 10th, 2003, the 4th Round Table of Ministers of Culture was held, themed "Towards Knowledge Societies". The conference believed that "Knowledge societies are about capabilities to identify, produce, process, transform, disseminate and use information to build and apply knowledge for human development. They require an empowering social vision which encompasses plurality, inclusion, solidarity and participation." [2] UNESCO has also been holding "Universal Forum of Cultures" since 2004, and has held 3 forums by 2011: the 2004 Universal Forum of Cultures in Barcelona, Spain; the 2007 Universal Forum of Cultures in Monterrey, Mexico; the 2010 Universal Forum of Cultures in Valparaíso, Chile. The first forum was held from May 9th to September 26th, 2004 in Barcelona, Spain, themed "Cultural Diversity". 50 exhibitions, 56 concerts, 31 dramas, 300 films, street performances and dances gathered on the forum. The forum also showed four major exhibitions, intending to achieve a renewal of ideas and attitudes toward the 21st century, by undertaking a careful analysis of cultural diversity, sustainable development and the conditions for peace: "Voices", "Cities‑Corners", "Inhabiting the World" and "Warriors of Xi'an". [3]

The Convention on the Protection and Promotion of the Diversity of Cultural Expressions set a great example in analyzing the relationship among the United States, UNESCO and the promotion of cultural diversity. On October 20th, 2005, the General Conference of UNESCO adopted the Convention on the Protection and Promotion of the Diversity of Cultural Expressions. The objectives of the Convention included protecting and promoting the diversity of cultural expressions, spreading cultural expressions in an appropriate manner, and providing necessary legal frameworks for the protection and promotion of cultural diversity, etc. [4] According to the Convention, "cultural expressions" are those expressions that result from the creativity of individuals, groups and societies, and that have cultural content. "Cultural diversity" refers to the manifold ways in which the cultures of groups and societies find expression. These expressions are passed on within and among groups and societies.

①   For *Istanbul Declaration*, see: http://www.un.org/zh/.

②   http://www.unesco.org/dialogue/en/publications.html.

③   http://static.chinavisual.com/storage/contents/2006/10/15/8555T20061015132854_1.shtml.

④   http://www.fmprc.gov.cn/chn/pds/ziliao/tytj/tyfg/t311879.htm.

Cultural diversity is made manifest not only through the varied ways in which the cultural heritage of humanity is expressed, augmented and transmitted through the variety of cultural expressions, but also through diverse modes of artistic creation, production, dissemination, distribution and enjoyment, whatever the means and technologies used. The Convention entered into force on March 18th, 2007.

Though unsatisfied with the draft of the Convention, the United States found himself still failed to dominate the negotiation. The American Delegation said, in a stinging rebuke to UNESCO, that "the manner in which the Intergovernmental Meetings have been conducted has inhibited rather than encouraged negotiation and deliberation. The rules of procedure-as well as UNESCO's normal practices-have been inconsistently applied and at time completely ignored…What we have done here in the past week has undermined the spirit of consensus that normally characterizes the work of UNESCO" [①], and vetoed the Convention. [②] However, Israel was the only follower of the United States in the vote. Therefore we can see that in an open organization like UNESCO, each member state has equal right to vote. And despite that some members still paid respect to America, and that some America-preferred values were added in the Convention, America still had to admit that he cannot decide the UNESCO's resolutions single-handedly.

In December, 2007, The Declaration on the Rights of Indigenous Peoples was adopted by the United Nations General Assembly. The Declaration establishes a universal framework of minimum standards for the survival, dignity, well-being and rights of the world's indigenous peoples. It outlaws discrimination against indigenous peoples and promotes their full and effective participation in all matters that concern them. It also ensures their right to remain distinct and to pursue their own priorities in economic, social and cultural development. [③] In September 2009, strategic program objective 10 of document 34 C/4 further specifies the mission of promoting dialogue among civilizations and cultural diversity as: "UNESCO will pursue its concrete and

---

① See "Final Statement of the United States Delegation," at: http://www.amb-usa.fr/usunesco/texts/Cultural_Diversity_Final.pdf.

② About the Convention, please refer to: http://unesdoc.unesco.org/images/0014/001429/142919e.pdf.

③ http://www.un.org/esa/socdev/unpfii/documents/DRIPS_zh.pdf.

practical action in the area of the dialogue among civilizations and cultures, including a specific focus on indigenous peoples and interfaith dialogue, initiatives at the regional and subregional levels, the articulation of a set of commonly shared values and principles, thematic focus building on its five fields of competence, and dialogue as a vehicle for advancing women's human rights." "UNESCO will also promote the potential of dialogue based on music and the arts as a vector for the strengthening of mutual understanding and interaction as well as for building a culture of peace and respect for cultural diversity." "Interfaith dialogue will be strengthened with a view to ensuring that (i) shared values for respect of religious beliefs and tolerance are reflected in curricula and textbooks, and (ii) faith issues are addressed in a secular framework contributing to the objectives of dialogue." [1]

Dialogue among religious constitutes a major part of UNESCO's endeavors to promote cultural diversity and dialogue among civilizations. Pushed by UNESCO, Resolution 60/150 "Combating defamation of religions" was adopted by the 61st United Nations General Assembly, recognizing the valuable contributions of all religions to modern civilization, and showing the strong will of the global society to keep dialogue and cooperation among civilizations for peace promotion. [2] On March 30th, 2006, the resolution "Respect for Freedom of Expression and Respect for Sacred Beliefs and Values and Religious and Cultural Symbols" was adopted by the UNESCO Executive Board on the 174th session of the General Conference [3], underlining global society's concern on peace, tolerance, and various civilizations, cultures, nationalities and religious, and calling for UNESCO's applicable methods to provide due guarantees. The General Assembly, in December, 2006, decided to convene in 2007 a high-level dialogue on interreligious and intercultural cooperation for the promotion of tolerance, understanding and universal respect on matters of freedom of religion or belief and cultural diversity, in coordination with other similar initiatives in this area. [4] In December, 2007, the UNESCO General Conference affirmed that mutual understanding and interreligious dialogue are of great significance in dialogue among

---

① http://unesdoc.unesco.org/images/0018/001836/183612c.pdf.
② See the official site of the United Nations: http://www.un.org/zh/.
③ See Proceedings of the 174th UNESCO Executive Board General Conference.
④ See the official site of the United Nations: http://www.un.org/zh/.

civilizations, and encouraged member states to take into consideration the methods at all levels to promote interreligious and intercultural dialogue, tolerance, understanding and cooperation. The Conference also encourages dialogue among media from different cultures and civilizations. [1]

A great number of actions have been taken at the international level to promote dialogue among civilizations with the religion as the nucleus. The World Conference on Dialogue among Religions and Civilizations, themed "The contribution of religion and culture to peace, mutual respect and cohabitation", which was co-held by UNESCO and Ministry of Culture of Republic of Macedonia from October 26th to October 28th, 2007 in Ohrid, Macedonia. Over 200 religious figures and scholars participated in the conference, ranging from more than 20 countries such as Macedonia, Albania, Bosnia and Herzegovina, the United States, Russia, Germany, Switzerland, Austria, Ireland, Vatican, Jordan, India, Japan, Korea and China. The Conference would be held every three years. 70 representatives were elected as members of the Organizing Committee of the 2nd conference. The Conference also adopted a declaration, calling for dialogue among religions and civilizations to further discard prejudices, respect religious and cultural diversity, condemn religious violence, strengthen religious education and respect women's rights. [2] Other conferences also include: the Special Non-Aligned Movement Ministerial Meeting on Interfaith Dialogue and Cooperation for Peace and Development, held in Manila from May 26th to May 28th, 2009; the Parliament of the World's Religions, held in Melbourne, Australia, from December 3rd to December 9th, 2009; the 3rd Congress of Leaders of World and Traditional Religions, held in Astana on July 1st and July 2nd, 2009.

(2) Promoting Dialogue among Civilizations of Different Countries and Regions

Apart from a great number of Declarations, action plans and dialogue among civilizations at the international level, UNESCO has also been dedicated to pushing forward dialogue among civilizations among different countries and regions,

---

① See: *Proceedings of the UNESCO General Conference 2007.*

② http://www.unesco.org/dialogue/en/events.htm.

contributing greatly to the harmonious cohabitation and mutual learning of these civilizations.

From September 16th to September 17th, 2002, the 3rd Round Table of Ministers of Culture was held in Istanbul, Turkey, themed "Intangible Cultural Heritage-a Mirror of Cultural Diversity". The themes discussed ranged from the spectrum of intangible cultural heritage, the threats it faced, the relationship between cultural diversity and sustainable development, domestic regulations for the protection of such heritage, and global cooperation enhancement. Member states passed *Istanbul Declaration* for the protection of intangible cultural heritage. The Declaration stated the significance of intangible cultural heritage and the urgency to protect such heritage. The Declaration also called on member states to carry out policies and regulations for the protection of such heritage, and enhance exchange and cooperation at the international level. After the Round Table, Convention for the Safeguarding of the Intangible Cultural Heritage was drafted. [1] The Regional Forum on the Dialogue among Civilizations took place in Ohrid, FYR Macedonia from August 29th to August 30th, 2003, bringing together eight Heads of State from the Southeast Europe region-The Former Yugoslav Republic of Macedonia (host country), Albania, Bosnia and Herzegovina, Bulgaria, Croatia, Hungary, Serbia and Montenegro, and Slovenia. The President of the UNESCO General Conference and the Personal Representative of the Secretary-General of the United Nations also attended the conference. *Message from Ohrid*, including details on further cooperation in value education, cultural heritage and science in Southeast Europe, was adopted by the forum, setting a great example of extending dialogue for resolving regional and interregional issues.

The International Symposium on Dialogue among Cultures and Civilizations was held by UNESCO in Sana'a, Yemen from February 10th to 11th, 2004, bringing together around 50 representatives from the Arab World and other countries and regions. The notion of a dialogue among cultures and civilizations was approached from five different angles: globalization and dialogue; the contribution of education to the dialogue; the contribution of Arab culture to other cultures; the role of dialogue in curbing terrorism; and dialogue between East and West. "Curbing terrorism" was

---

[1]   http://www.bjww.gov.cn/2004/7-12/1633.html.

the major theme. *The Sana'a Call for Dialogue among Cultures and Civilizations*, adopted by the Symposium, noted the quest for common values, the indispensible role education plays in nurturing and sustaining dialogue, and the strive for cultural diversity. [1] The Asia-Pacific Regional Conference on Dialogue among Civilizations for Peace and Sustainable Development took place in Hanoi, Vietnam from December 20th to December 21st, 2004, bringing together ministerial-level officials from over 30 countries in the Asia-Pacific region. The Conference adopted the *Hanoi Declaration* to enhance human security in the region; to intensify people-to-people cultural and scientific exchanges and partnerships in the region and to review and renew curricula, textbooks and educational materials so as to adapt educational programs to the exigencies of quality education. The Declaration served, among institutions and individuals from different cultures and civilizations, as a platform for direct and open dialogue on direction, strategy and methods of the political actions at all levels and cross all departments. [2]

From May 20th to May 21st, 2005, Regional Forum on The Cultural Corridors of South East Europe: Common Past and Shared Heritage, a Key to Future Partnership took place in Varna, Bulgaria, bringing together the presidents of Albania, Bosnia-Herzegovina, Bulgaria (host country), Greece, The Former Yugoslav Republic of Macedonia, Turkey and Croatia, as well as Ministers of Culture from Romania and Serbia and Montenegro, representing the two presidents respectively. The Bulgarian Government, UNESCO and the European Committee co-held the Forum. The Forum discussed the cultural heritage and cultural corridor within the region, and committed to promote urgent measures for the protection of cultural heritage at risk within the region, including continuing action to counter the illicit traffic in cultural property. *Address on the occasion of the Regional Forum on the Cultural Corridors of South East Europe: Common Past and Shared Heritage, a Key to Future Partnership* was adopted by the Forum. In the Address, the 9 countries in Southeast Europe committed to join hands in the exploration, protection and spread of the cultural and historical heritage within the region, and would take measures to counter the illicit traffic in

---

① http://www.unesco.org/dialogue/en/conferences.html.

② http://www.unesco.org/dialogue/en/conferences.html.

cultural and historical property, making the Cultural Corridors a "key" to the future partnership among the countries and peoples within the region. ①

UNESCO has also been dedicated to pushing forward dialogues among religious civilizations of different countries and regions. On September, 2000, UNESCO International Congress on Interreligious Dialogue and Culture of Peace was held in Tashkent, Uzbekistan, themed "Spiritual Convergences and Intercultural Dialogue" and "East-West: Intercultural Dialogue in Central Asia". ② The Dialogue focused on the mutual understanding between the Islamic civilization and the Western Christian Civilization, for Islam is the dominant religion in Central Asia. In December, 2004, Regional Summit on Inter-religious and Inter-ethnic Dialogue was held in Tirana, Albania. The Summit adopted *The Tirana Summit Declaration*, underlining that all religious leaders, like other civil society and community leaders, have the potential to exercise a moral and positive influence on how people in society understand each other and interact. ③ Other conferences include: 5th Asia-Pacific Regional Interfaith Dialogue in Australia in 2009, as well as 3rd Global Forum of the Alliance of Civilizations in Brazil in May, 2010, a symposium on friendship among civilizations, themed "Interreligious Dialogue among Youths in Latin America: History and Future", etc.

Conclusion

We have discussed two issues: the transition of the United Nations Educational, Scientific and Cultural Organization (UNESCO)'s endeavors from advocating universal values to advocating cultural diversity; and how UNESCO actually promotes dialogue among civilizations under the guideline of cultural diversity at both regional and international levels since the end of the Cold War, especially since the year 2000. UNESCO, as the thesis points out, is an open organization in policy-making,

---

① http://news.xinhuanet.com/world/2005-05/21/content_2985210.htm.

② http://www.unesco.org/dialogue/en/events.htm.

③ http://gb.cri.cn/3821/2004/07/28/561@246635.htm.

which disenables the United States and other western countries from dominating the agenda and resolution. Promoting cultural diversity, instead of spreading Western ideologies and values, remains UNESCO's major mission, as it continues to engage in promoting dialogue among civilizations. It is seen that UNESCO has been working comprehensively and positively in various fields ranging from language, films, to religious civilization and rights of indigenous people. As the most significant international intergovernmental organization in education, science and culture, UNESCO plays an indispensable role in promoting cultural diversity globally.

Liu Tiewa received her Ph.D. degree from Waseda University, Japan, and Beijing University, China. She has been a lecturer in School of International Relations and Diplomacy at Beijing Foreign Studies University since 2007. Her expertise is in United Nations affairs, International Organizations, and North-East Asian Studies. She has been the Deputy Director of Research Centre of the United Nations and International Organizations since 2010, and serves as the Advisory Board Member and China Program coordinator of Asia Pacific Centre for the Responsibility to Protect in Australia and of the UPEACE Asia Pacific Centre at Sogang University in Seoul.

Dialogues among Civilizations: Alliance of Civilizations

Zhang Guihong   Yang Rujia

As the most universal, representative and authoritative inter-governmental international organization, the United Nations is not only the best place to practice multilateralism, an effective platform for collective response to threats and challenges, but also a typical representative of the diversity of civilizations in the world. It is a forum for the convergence of different civilizations and plays an irreplaceable role in promoting dialogue among civilizations. United Nations Alliance of Civilizations (UNAOC) is an advocator, organizer, participant as well as promoter of dialogue among civilizations.

From Dialogue among civilizations to UNAOC

As an organization of world's highest level to promote dialogue among civilizations, UNAOC is an initiative of former UN Secretary-General Kofi Annan, which aims to improve understanding and cooperative relations among nations and peoples across cultures and religions, and to help counter the forces that fuel polarization and extremism. Working in partnership with governments, international and regional organizations, civil society groups, foundations, and the private sectors, the Alliance is supporting a range of projects and initiatives aimed at building bridges among a diversity of cultures and communities.

The development of UNAOC could be dated back to the beginning of dialogue among civilizations. On November 4, 1998, the 53rd Session of the UN General Assembly unanimously adopted Resolution A/RES/53/22 which decided the year 2001 as the "Year of Dialogue among Civilizations" in order to enhance the understanding and communication between the various civilizations and reduce the conflicts between them. The resolution reaffirmed that "civilization achievements constitute the collective heritage of humankind, providing a source of inspiration and progress for humanity at large". It recognized "the diverse civilization achievements of humankind" and "creative human diversity". What's more, it emphasized "the importance of tolerance in international relations and significant role of dialogue as a means to reach understanding, remove threats to peace and strengthen interaction and exchange among civilizations". [1] Since then, dialogue among different civilizations, including equal dialogue between different faiths and religions developed all over the world.

Both the 54th and 55th Session of the UN General Assembly held in 1999 and 2000 respectively included project entitled as "United Nations Year of Dialogue among civilizations" into the provisional agenda of the General Assembly (see Resolution A/RES/54/113 and A/RES/55/23). In November 2001, the 56th session of the UN General Assembly held a plenary meeting to discuss promotion of dialogue between different civilizations, to enhance the understanding and communication between the various civilizations, and to reduce conflicts between them. Since the meeting was held right after the "911" terrorist attacks, how to prevent and combat international terrorism by promoting dialogue among civilizations became one of the important topics.

UN Secretary-General Kofi Annan issued a report on "United Nations Year of Dialogue among Civilizations", which pointed out that cultural and religious diversity is a source of strength, rather than the cause of division and confrontation. In 2002, the United Nations General Assembly unanimously adopted Resolution A/RES/57/249, which declared 21 May as "World Day for Cultural Diversity for Dialogue and Development".

HE José Luis Rodríguez Zapatero, President of the Government of Spain, called for the creation of the Alliance of Civilizations during the 59th Session of the General Assembly of the United Nations in 2004. Later, HE Recep Tayyip Erdoğan, Prime

---

①   Quote from UN Resolution A/RES/53/22, http://www.un.org/documents/r53-22.pdf.

Minister of Turkey, joined by HE José Luis Rodríguez Zapatero as the co-sponsor of the Alliance of Civilizations initiative. In July 2005, former Secretary-General Kofi Annan announced the launch of the Alliance of Civilizations initiative in the Statement (SG/SM/10004) at the United Nations Headquarters. Nearly two months later, a High-level Group of experts was formed by Kofi Annan to explore the roots of polarization between societies and cultures, and to recommend a practical program of action to address this issue. The report submitted in November 2006 provided analysis of recent West-Islam estrangement, pointed out that the cause of that mainly lay on terrorism and distrust between different civilizations, and put forward practical recommendations that form the basis for the implementation plan of the United Nations Alliance of Civilizations, such as promoting communication and understanding through education, media and migration. The report emphasized that international community should join hands in dealing with all those political issues. The Secretary-General also has established a voluntary Trust Fund for Alliance of Civilizations, as recommended by the Report. On 26 April 2007, former President of Portugal, Jorge Sampaio, was appointed as the High Representative for the UNAOC by Secretary-General Ban Ki-moon to lead the implementation phase of the Alliance.

The UNAOC Secretariat, which is based in New York, works with a global network of partners with States, international and regional organizations, civil society groups, foundations, and the private sector to improve cross-cultural relations between diverse nations and communities. It also works at the grassroots level, promoting innovative projects that build trust, reconciliation and mutual respect.

So far, UNAOC has 134 members of group of friends, including countries and significant UN agencies as well as other international organizations, for instance, UNESCO (United Nations Educational, Scientific and Cultural Organization) and IOM (International Organization of Migration). In addition, there is a UNAOC Research Network, which brings together a small group of institutions from around the world who have interests in the areas of focus for the Alliance-education, media, migration, and youth plus other topics with special reference to cross-cultural understanding, good governance of cultural diversity, conflict resolution such as women and peacemaking, city diplomacy and other areas. Currently, 21 institutions/networks of institutions and research centers from around the world have signed a Memorandum of Understanding with the Alliance, delineating their involvement and participation in the Research Network, including ESEADE (Argentina), Research Center for Islamic History, Art and Culture-IRCICA (Turkey) and so on. The diagram below showed the structure o f UNAOC:

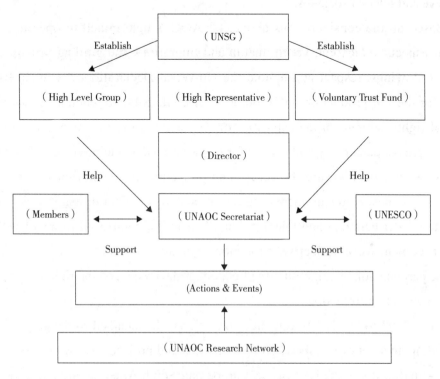

The Structure of UNAOC

While being active on a number of cross-cutting issues, the Alliance works mainly in four priority areas to which it brings a multi-disciplinary and multi-perspective approach: in increasingly multicultural contexts that shape our lives in the 21st century, education is fundamental to address the ignorance and mistrust that are the source of human conflict. Enabling citizens to acquire intercultural competencies and skills is a key to fostering intercultural dialogue. Youth is a key constituency of the Alliance. Roughly one in five individuals of world population is between the ages of 15 and 24. A pool of talent, ideas and energy, young people is key agents for social change, economic growth, development and technological innovation. Meanwhile, traditional media, as well as social media and new information technologies, shape perceptions, narratives and attitudes. They hold the potential to bridge cultural and religious divides and to develop a positive narrative around diversity. Amplifying this constructive role is one of the core tasks of the UNAOC. Migration and mobility of populations shape our diverse societies. They bring potential for development and innovation which must be harnessed, but also create new challenges that need to be addressed in order to build inclusive and tolerant societies.

Based on the considerations above, UNAOC is determined to operate mainly in four aspects: education, youth, media and migration. The guiding principles are as the followings: respect and uphold the Universal Declaration of Human Rights; strive for the full production and promotion of civil, political, economic, social and cultural rights; strengthen the capacities of all countries to implement the principles and practices of democracy and respect for human rights, including minority rights and right to development; ensure respect for and protection of human rights for migrants and their families, eliminate increasing racism and xenophobia in many societies and promote greater harmony and tolerance on all societies; combat all forms of violence against women; work collectively for more inclusive political processes, allowing genuine participation by all; ensure the freedom of the media and the right of the public to have access to information.

From 2007 to 2012, UNAOC has gone global. It managed to develop globally by building up a net of members, group of friends and projects. At the very beginning of the Alliance, it operated mainly in Europe and South America, after five years of rapid development, nowadays it operates in much larger area including North America, Australia, Asia and Africa. Over the past five years the Alliance has managed to: (a) become a well-recognized and credible United Nations platform for intercultural dialogue and cooperation in spite of its *sui generis* nature and status that make it different but complementary to any other United Nations agency, as well as to other intergovernmental organizations; (b)profile itself as an emerging soft-power tool aimed at addressing our growing difficulties of living together, listening to each other and respecting each other by means of fighting against ignorance, deconstructing stereotypes and misconceptions that deepen patterns of hostility and mistrust and developing a culture of dialogue, tolerance, justice, human rights and human dignity; (c) reach out to civil society, grass-roots organizations and ordinary people in addition to the classic stakeholders as a bridge builder, convener and catalyst, helping to give impetus to innovative projects aimed at reducing polarization among nations and cultures through joint pursuits and mutually beneficial partnerships; (d)shape a coherent framework for the Alliance in spite of its growing diversity.

Dialogue among Civilizations: UNAOC in Action

Guided by its missions and principles, UNAOC launched several core projects and had remarkable achievements as the followings:

Annual Forums

So far, the Alliance has held annual forum for four times. In January 2008, the first forum of the United Nations Alliance of Civilizations was held in Madrid, Spain. This forum convened political leaders, representatives of international and regional bodies, religious leaders, youth, corporate executives, civil society groups, and foundations for open dialogue on reducing polarization between nations and launching joint initiatives to promote cross-cultural understanding globally. The main topics of the forum are "Managing Diversity in the Era of Globalization", "Political Challenges to Building Cross-Cultural Understanding" and "From Global Talk to Local Action". In April 2009, the second annual forum was held in Istanbul, Turkey, having discussion on topics, such as, "Shaping the Global Agenda in Times of Crisis-Why Does Good Governance of Cultural Diversity Matter?", "Enhancing Dialogue and Strengthening Cooperation: Connecting Innovative Policies and Initiatives" and "Education for Dialogue: Building Peace in the Minds of People". In May 2010, the third session of the Forum was held in Rio de Janeiro, Brazil, with the theme of "Bridging Cultures, Building Peace." In December 2011, the fourth forum was held in Doha, Qatar, which has the topics of "How Does Cultural Diversity Matter to Development?", "Tolerance and Trust, as Key Conditions for Development and Peace" and "New Strategies for Intercultural Dialogue, Understanding and Cooperation ". What's more, the forum also focused on the relationship between Muslims and the West after the tenth anniversary of "911".The fifth annual forum will be held in Vienna in February 2013. Annual forums not only build a platform for dialogue and exchange among different civilizations, but also provide an opportunity to showcase a large tapestry of initiatives and programs, as well as to launch new forms of cooperation between partners.

National Plans and Regional Strategies

Through encouraging countries to implement National Plans and Initiatives for Intercultural Dialogue and Cooperation, the Alliance helps to generate ownership of its goals at the country level, shape policies conducive to a better living together and establish relevant capacity building. They help develop national agendas for addressing a number of cross-cutting issues, ranging from education to migration, media and youth, as well as introducing a new overall approach to social policies and attitudes. Regional Strategies come to effects in a higher level. Through regional strategies, the Alliance helps to set a framework for joint action and shape a common strategy to tackle shared challenges. Through developing a number of key programs, the Alliance engages a wider public and contributes to ongoing efforts with institutional and civil society partners. So far, two regional strategies have been adopted: the Regional Strategy for South East Europe (adopted in Bosina and Herzegovina in 2009) covers 14 countries, and the Regional Strategy for Mediterranean (adopted in Malta in 2010) encompasses over 40 countries from Europe, including the Balkans, North Africa and the Middle-East. Others are in the pipeline (namely a Regional Strategy for Latin America).

Regional Strategies materialize into Action Plans based on public-private partnerships. Action Plans are made up of three different types of projects: first, UNAOC flagship programs that go regional; second, new actions developed by organizations-partners and/or promoted by UNAOC; third, projects submitted by civil society organizations and selected upon a call for proposals. The practices of these projects help to accomplish the mission of the Alliance, such as reducing conflicts among different civilizations, eliminating racism and xenophobe, increasing understanding of diversity of civilizations.

The Media Program

The core of the media program is a plan of global experts, a network of experts and an online resource of journalists to attain free access to a range of opinion leaders who provide sound analysis on political, social and religious issues. This program helps journalist all over the world find accurate, fair and informed sources of commentary in order to achieve balanced reporting. Global Experts has achieved a number of key milestones over the past three years, including the following: managing an online resource of Global Experts which provides detailed biographies and contact information for roughly 350 individual experts in their fields; generating articles and commentary distributed to editors around the world to increase the quality and diversity of analysis; alerting journalists (and other stakeholders) on significant international crises and developments; developing a mobile application to enable journalists and media professionals to use mobile devices to find experts in real time.

Skill-building Journalist trainings are a second component of the program. They are run by recognized senior journalists and experts to support media professionals in their efforts to report across cultural divides. Workshops have been organized for journalists from Pakistan, Indonesia, as well as from throughout the Arab world, Europe and North America. They are aimed at building journalism skills, reflecting on the role of media in covering conflicts, exploring tools for reporting on political and social issues and reporting on "Muslim-West" relations. Practical outcomes of these trainings have, in the past, included articles, TV and radio interviews, as well as blogs developed by participants.

In a similar spirit, the program provides Media Empowerment Trainings to civil society leaders, particularly voices from stereotyped communities, to enhance their ability to reach out to the media.

Forums for Media leaders are also organized to enable influential media leaders - owners, editors, funders and educators - to strategize new ways of improving news analysis on cross-cultural conflicts. A major gathering of these leaders took place in October 2011 at the Dead Sea.

Finally, the UNAOC's Media Program includes Video and Multimedia Projects jointly conducted with partners, such as top journalism schools, to provide facts and commentary on complex and divisive issues. Two projects have been led thus for around the topics of Islam and identities.

The Youth Solidarity Fund

The Youth Solidarity Fund (YSF) provides small grants of up to 30,000 USD to youth organizations advancing cross-cultural understanding at the local, national or international levels. Projects are developed and implemented by youth organizations and primarily for the benefit of youth (aged 18 to mid-30s). They are selected in consideration of the transformational change they can generate. All projects present potential for a multiplier effect and sustainability. In Somalia, for instance, one project centers around organized workshops on peace and human rights education for young people involved in armed conflicts. Many former participants are now trainers and incite armed fighters to join the training. In the first two editions of the program: 24 projects (4% of the applications) were implemented in 22 countries, countries, costing a total of 570,000 USD; over 150,000 individuals benefited from the project activities; most projects included several of the following: awareness-raising, training, dialogue with policy-makers, creation of support networks, interventions with community leaders and media campaigns; strong points including reaching marginalized youth, bridging the intergenerational gap and crossing cultural or religious borders in unprecedented ways.

The Fellowship Program

The fellowship program is a joint initiative, developed with the support of the German government, the Hermes Foundation for Peace and in partnership with the League of Arab States, ISESCO, the governments of Qatar and Jordan, the Organization of Islamic Cooperation, the British Council and the Institute of International Education. Its current objective is to contribute to a better mutual knowledge and understanding between peoples and societies from Muslim-majority countries around the Arab world from Europe and North America. So far, two pilot programs have been implemented, one in 2010 and one in 2011, for groups of roughly 15 participants from the Arab world, as well as from Europe and North America. They included well-known journalists, diplomats and several leaders from Arab states in transition. Fellows met with CEOs of successful companies and leaders of organizations and foundations working on development issues, international and regional news networks and political

42

groups. Back home, working in their respective fields of political, media, business and/or development, many of the fellows will be able to apply what they learned to their daily lives and work, as well as to the groups and constituencies with which they collaborate.

The Education Program

UNAOC believes youth is a driving force for change. Thus, educating youth is a core mission of the Alliance. The week-long boarding Summer School's design is based on a process of mutual learning, using the participants' varied experiences as a starting point for the training and learning process. Participants compare their approaches to work and participation as young leaders in increasingly diverse societies, preparing them to become agents of change when they return to their own communities. The pedagogical team works pro-bono and includes members from dynamic professional backgrounds and diverse regions of the world. They include scholars, experts, politicians, facilitators and trainers. Summer Schools gather close to 100 youth aged between 18 and 35, ensuring geographical, cultural, and gender balance. Summer Schools can be held wherever a host university offers to partner with the UNAOC and EMUNI (Euro-Mediterranean University) in implementing this project. In 2010 and 2011 they were held in Portugal, in Aveiro and Lisbon respectively. In 2012, two summer schools were held one in Coimbra, Portugal and the other one in Amman, Jordan. Two additional Winter Schools took place in Latin America and Asia respectively. In 2013, three Summer Schools are planned: two in the Euro-Mediterranean region and one in Africa. Three Winter Schools are also planned in Asia, Latin America and the Middle East.

Online education of religion and culture is also included, as well as the research network of the Alliance. There are information exchange center and certain media providing education to reduce the illiteracy rate of citizens. What's more, there is a project called UNITWIN, which is joint-organized by UNAOC and UNESCO. Eight universities participate in the project and study how to reduce bias and obstacles during dialogue among civilizations.

The Mobilizing Citizens' Initiative and Creativity Programs

There are mainly three programs in this section.

First, in 2011, the UNAOC and the BMW Group launched the BMW group Award for Intercultural Innovation in support of the Alliance of Civilizations, under the auspices of the United Nations (also known as the Intercultural Innovation Award). This activity is designed to encourage intercultural dialogue and cooperation around the world. In 2011, the top ten projects were invited to present their achievements at the Forth Annual Forum of the UNAOC in Doha, Qatar. The UNAOC and the BMW Group are helping winners to become more efficient, to expand and, wherever relevant, to enable a transfer of innovative ideas and best practices to other contexts or settings.

Second, campaign called "Do one thing for diversity and inclusion" was launched in May 2011 by a group of public and private organizations. This campaign succeeded in mobilizing thousands of people around world. In 2012, it suggested "10 little things you can do to celebrate the World Day for Dialogue among Civilizations", including visiting a museum of the civilization one is not familiar with.

Third, PLURAL+, a youth video festival on migration, diversity and inclusion is another attempt at engaging young citizens and using art to build bridges across civilizations. UNAOC works in cooperation with the IOM and partners worldwide in this program to encourage and award young people for producing videos in which they express their feelings and visions with respect to issues linked to diversity, migration and social inclusion. From 2009 to 2010, 450 videos from 72 countries were submitted to PLURAL+. The selected videos have been screened in multi-media platforms.

The Migration Program

An online Community on Migration and Integration Building Inclusive Societies (IBIS) was created in 2010 in partnership with the IOM. It provides information on promising practices and successful models of integration for migrant populations. It promotes further involvement of all stakeholders in integration by supporting coordinated efforts and cooperation. This program aims to feature positive experiences and success stories. It initiated a video project showcasing examples of successful integration of migrants in cities. The first video project was completed in Italy with the support of the Italian government. New projects are being launched in various other countries.

The Network of Dialogue Café

Dialogue Café is a non-profit initiative, which uses cutting-edge video-conferencing technology to enable face-to-face conversations between diverse groups of people from around the world. It allows them to create a global community for sharing experiences, learning from each other and working together to make the world a better place. Dialogue Café are already open in Paris, Lisbon, Amsterdam, Rio de Janeiro, Cleveland and Ramallah, London, Beirut, Wroclaw and Sao Paulo. New Dialogue Café in Tunisia, Belgrade, Lagos, and Brisbane are in the pipeline and will be operational by mid 2013. The feedback of the project is remarkable: young people in Belgrade, Ramallah and Barcelona sharing stories about their heritage while Women from Cairo, Rio de Janeiro, Doha and Amsterdam discussing the role of education and employment in empowering women. What's more, Multi-city conferences and events on topics such as climate change, creativity and innovation, ageing and social exclusion connecting Beijing, San Francisco, Tokyo and Melbourne.

New Projects

UNAOC continues to introduce new projects with creativity. Right after Doha forum 2011, there are many new projects added to the Alliance's agenda. Firstly, there are projects preventing intercultural tensions and crises-combating stereotypes, misperceptions, discrimination and xenophobia, including creating a network of museums and centers for tolerance and launching an online youth campaign, calling on political leaders, decision-makers and citizens to speak out against fear, intolerance and xenophobia. Secondly, there are projects raising awareness towards valuing cultural diversity as an asset rather than a liability, including a new initiative which further explores the role of creative industries to empower women and an educational program named "Generation 2030", which is joint-organized by the Alliance and the International Foundation for Survival and Development of Humanity and Russian Ministry of Foreign Affairs, UNESCO, UNICEF and NGOs. Thirdly, UNAOC encourage people to live together with our differences with greater ease in an age of diversity, communicating across cultures and peoples, and building inclusive and tolerant societies. Authorities, civil society actors and media to address the topical issue of "reconciling diversity and cohesion" aiming at producing some policy recommendations. In 2012–2013, UNAOC launches a UNAOC Youth Cultural Festival on the basis of a proposal made by a group of independent experts supporting the Organizing Committee of the Doha Forum. Fourthly, UNAOC will promote actions and policies for addressing cross-cutting issues and developing new tools, for instance, building an online platform for a future UNAOC Diversity Observatory aimed at gathering knowledge and exchanging expertise.

The Dialogue among Civilization: the UN Mission and China's Role

After entering the new century, international community continues to go through changes and adjustments: first, the uncertainty and complexity of international relations are highlighted. International relations, especially relations between major powers are still in adjustment instead of merging into a new pattern. Non-state actors start to play more and more important roles in international relations while transnational and interregional activities are accelerated. In the meantime, global issues get more public attention. Second, the interdependency and vulnerability of the world are increasing. High-speed developing technologies reduce the dependency among human beings and nature while increase it among countries. Advanced technology accelerates the flow of people, goods and information. However, the vulnerability of human is also magnified. Third, the transformation of the international system is entering a critical period. After twenty years of adjustment, major powers are having more stable relations while raising powers expand their interests overseas, transforming their economic power into political forces. The theme of international relations in this new era becomes clear. Reforms and changes are being made in International system from International Monetary Fund to the United Nations Security Council. Fourth, the trend of international community getting organized and legalized continues to be strengthened. Regulating countries' foreign policy and relations by organized and legitimate methods becomes the consensus of international community and receives support from most of the countries. For developed countries, advantages of capital, technology, institutional and diplomatic will help them obtain favorable position in international system while for developing countries; the legalization of international relations will help to protect their basic interests and allow them to influence international system through collective actions. Fifth, raising powers are bringing new changes in international system. Countries in Asia, Africa and Latin-America have already become regional power and call for new order in international relations. Their power and interests are expanding and demanding more voices and rights in participation and decision-making in global issues.

Given the fact of these adjustments and changes, on the one hand, the United Nations will still be a universal, representative and authoritative intergovernmental organization which is unique and irreplaceable, on the other hand, the United Nations are meeting various internal and external challenges. For instance, internal challenges are the questions and doubts about the effectiveness of the United Nations General Assembly, representative of the UN Security Council, and a number of United Nations agencies' role, for example, the Trusteeship Council's; the external challenges are the existence of G20 and NATO making UN face the danger of being marginalized, especially when NATO played a dominant role in Libya issue. How to relocate itself and play a more important role in the new international system is a fresh task for the United Nations. Encouraging dialogue among civilizations can be an important starting point for the United Nations in the process of promoting the maintenance of peace, development and human rights.

Dialogue of civilization can bring mutual understanding. History told us that in the process of exchange of human civilization, not only natural barriers and isolation, but also ideological barriers and misunderstandings needed to be overcome. Through dialogue, mutual understanding of each other's interests and needs, ideas and thoughts will be achieved. Through this, communication, exchange, consultation, negotiation and seeking common ground while reserving differences among all parties become possible. Mutual understanding and trust are built in this way. Dialogue among civilizations plays the role of bridge in the following three aspects: Firstly, it can promote cooperation between governments, international organizations, civil society and non-governmental organizations and encourage dialogue and exchange between different cultures in the communities. Secondly, it enables governments in different countries to take joint action to treat culture diversity properly and eliminate conflicts. Thirdly, it also contributes to strengthening the United Nations when it conducts other tasks, such as preventing wars and peace-keeping.

Mutual understanding promotes joint cooperation among countries. Understanding and trust is the key to achieve cooperation. Differences of Ideology, social system and development model should not become obstacles to cooperation, especially not excuses for mutual confrontation. Cultural diversity should be the driving force and starting point of exchanges and cooperation instead of conflicts. Culture exchange is the basic way to achieve mutual understanding. However, building understanding and trusts among cultures is a long run which calls for the spirit of tolerance, humility and respect. Only by doing this, cooperation among countries to promote common interests and resolve conflicts can be possible to realize. Interests are the basis of cooperation as well as the root of conflicts in international relations. Only by trusting each other based on comprehensive understanding, can countries join hands in a lasting and effective way.

Cooperation brings peace and development. As former UN Secretary-General Kofi Annan said in a report regarding to United Nations Year of Dialogue among civilizations, "the establishment of the United Nations was intended to provide a paradigm of international relations based on inclusion rather than exclusion." He suggested that dialogue among civilizations is the way to achieve that. He believed that through understanding and mutual respect, we can reduce misunderstanding and mistrust, laying the foundation for using non-violent means to resolve conflict. Current UN Secretary General Ban Ki-moon also said that the Alliance of Civilizations is a useful complement to the Counter-Terrorism Strategy adopted by the UN General Assembly in 2006, as well as a strong support of the United Nations' actions in carrying out preventive diplomacy and promoting sustainable peace. With globalization and cultural diversity as background, dialogue between different civilizations seems to be the best choice to resolve national, ethnic, racial, religious and civilization conflicts effectively. Another mission of the United Nations is to promote the development, in which dialogue can also play a significant role. Through the exchange of experiences and cooperation to seek for proper solutions, we can solve our current and future economic and social problems together.

China has unique advantages and great potential in participating in UN's activities of dialogue among civilizations.

First of all, China has always recognized United Nations' central role in international affairs and multilateral diplomacy. She is also actively involved in the civilization dialogue led by the United Nations. In September 2001, in response to the call of "Dialogue among Civilizations" made by the United Nations, Foreign Affairs Committee of CPPCC (Chinese People's Political Consultative Committee) held a seminar called "Twenty-first. Century Forum-Symposium on Dialogue Among Civilizations" in Beijing, which invited celebrities and experts as well as scholars at home and abroad to have discussions and exchange ideas on the issue of Dialogue among Civilizations. Song Jian, Vice Chairman of CPPCC was invited by Kofi Annan to become one of the 19 members of the UN special panel of prestigious public figures for dialogue among civilizations. China advocates dialogue and exchanges among cultures and civilizations in the framework of ASEM, and hosted the first session of the conference on cultures and civilizations in the ASEM process. In 2007, the ASEM conference of dialogue among different belief was held in Nanjing, China.

Secondly, promoting dialogue among civilizations fits China's future development strategy. The seventh session of the Sixth Plenary Session of the Party passed the resolution "CPC Central Committee's decision on deepening reform of cultural system to promote socialist cultural development and prosperity of a number of major issues", which mentions that there are more urgent requirements calling for enhancing soft power and international influence of China currently. To solve this, it's important to raise the level of opening up and promote Chinese culture to the whole world. Hence, we must carry out cultural exchanges in multiple forms, increase participation in world civilization dialogue, and learn from each other to enhance the appeal and influence of Chinese culture in the world.

Thirdly, Confucianism, as an important representative of the Chinese culture, is an important force in world civilization dialogue. The concept of harmony derived from Confucianism as a unique Chinese cultural spirit and wisdom of life has great value and provides reasonable ideological source of the contemporary world peace, development

49

and cooperation. It provides wisdom for pursuing harmony relations not only between people, different social classes, human beings and nature, but also between nations and states.

Fourthly, Nishan Forum on world civilization is organized by China and has great impact. Nishan Forum is held to promote fine traditions of Chinese culture, demonstrate openness, diversity, inclusiveness and pursuit of harmony of Chinese culture, promote exchange and dialogue between Chinese civilization and the western one, and enhance mutual understanding and respect among people of different countries to build a harmonious world. The first Nishan forum is held in Nishan, the birth place of Confucius in September 2010. The theme of this forum is "harmony with diversity and the harmonious world". In April 2011, UNESCO and the Paris branch of the Confucius Institute of the People's Republic of China held a future‑oriented meeting on "Confucianism and New Humanism in a Globalized World" at UNESCO Headquarters. In November 2012, at the United Nations Headquarters in New York, New York Forum on World Civilizations, with the theme, "Harmony based on shared values‑beyond national identities and beliefs: dialogue between Confucianism and Christianity" was held and achieved great success.

Last but not the least, the United Nations Alliance of Civilizations starts to value the East as an important area for dialogue among civilizations. The Alliance's early activities are mainly focus on promoting dialogue and reconciliation between the Muslim and Western societies. Currently, the Alliance is committed to expanding activities into the Asia‑Pacific region, and promoting cultural understanding and cooperation there. China is expected to play a key role. As an initiative of UN, UNAOC decided to launch more projects in Asia mainly according to the following considerations: First, most societies in the Asia‑Pacific region have diversified cultural, language, religion, political conditions. The Alliances can provide relatively low‑key, non‑interventionist yet practical policy tools to help this region to turn diversity into unique advantage. Second, domestic diversity often embodies at the district level in the Asia‑Pacific where Confucianism, Muslim, Christian, Buddhist, Taoist, Hindu and secular society had to negotiate a series of questions on the differences with each other. Third, religion and culture could provide great help in promoting higher level of cooperation among countries and building more effective regional institutions in

Asia Pacific region. Fourth, even though Eastern civilization still has limited voice in the world, but according to the Alliance of Civilizations, the oriental civilization could make a more important contribution to the global dialogue on cultural understanding. On November 29 and 30, 2012 UNAOC Asia and Pacific regional consultation was held in Shanghai which was co-organized by UNAOC and UN Association of China. The theme of the consultation was "Harmony through Dialogue and Diversity". During the conference, participants take active part in discussions around topics such as, "Combining Cultural Traditions and Modern Social Life", "Secularism vs. Resurgence of Religion", "Dialogue of Cultures and Civilizations as an Emerging Paradigm in International Relations", "Increasing Knowledge and Understanding of Asian Cultures in the United Nations System", "How Can Chinese Traditional Culture Contribute to the Spirit 'Many Cultures, One Humanity'?", "Possibilities for Dialogue in Situations of Conflict and Tension", "How Can the Younger Generation Contribute to Cross-cultural Harmony?", "Adapting Educational Institutions and Policies to the needs of 'Intercultural Dialogue and Harmony'?". About 150 leaders from Governments, academic, corporate sector, media, youth, civil society from China and almost all countries in the region have attended the consultation.

It can be forecasted that the Oriental civilization with Confucian culture as the main body will play an important role in the United Nations Dialogue among civilizations. Hence, China will surely make new contributions to the dialogue among civilizations.

References:

The First Alliance of Civilizations Forum Report, http://www.unaoc.org/images/aoc%20forum%20report%20madrid%20complete.pdf.

The Second Alliance of Civilizations Forum Report, http://www.unaoc.org/docs/AoC_Istanbul-09web.pdf.

The Third Alliance of Civilizations Forum Summary of Outcomes, http://www.unaoc.org/rioforum/wp-content/uploads/2010/06/100614-outcomes-final.pdf.

The Forth Global UN Alliance of Civilizations Forum Report, http://unaoc.org/docs/UANOC%20Doha%20Forum%20Report.pdf.

UNAOC Project Description, http://unaoc.org/docs/UNAOC%20Project%20

Descriptions.pdf.

Rio Forum Website, http://rioforum.unaoc.org/.

Doha Forum Website, http://www.qatar4unaoc.org/.

The Dialogue among Civilizations, http://www.un.org/documents/dialogue.htm.

The United Nations Alliance of Civilizations Website, http://www.unaoc.org/.

Zhang Guihong is Professor of International Relation Studies; and Executive Director at Center for UN Studies, Fudan University, Shanghai, China. He is member of the executive board of the United Nations Association of China, China's Association of South Asian Studies as well as Shanghai Association of International Studies; council member of China-India Friendship Association; also serves as Vice President of Association of Asian Scholars (AAS) as well as Convener of AAS in China. He published many books, such as *Beyond Balance of Power: US Security Strategy toward South Asia after the End of Cold War, A Study of China-US-India Relations* (co-author), *UN Secretary-General* (editor), *Fudan UN Studies* (editor), *UN and Dialogue among Civilizations* (editor), and *UN Development Report* (annual book, editor). His expertise is in the UN-related issues, Sino-U.S.-Indian relations, International Organizations, and Asia-Pacific security.

Yang Rujia is Assistant at Center for UN Studies of Fudan University, and her current research focuses on United Nations and Dialogue among civilizations.

World Public Forum
"Dialogue of Civilizations" (Rhodes)

Ni Peimin

I.Dialogue of Civilization as a Historical Phenomenon

Ten years ago (2002), the United Nations declared May 21st to be the "World Day for Cultural Diversity for Dialogue and Development." To reflect the path of dialogue among civilizations in the past ten years, it is necessary to first have a brief clarification of the concept of dialogue of civilizations and the main ways through which it can take place, with which the reflection maybe done with a broader context of human history.

The word "dialogue" usually brings to mind the Platonic kind of inquiry conducted through rational conversations or debates for the sake of clarifying concepts and reaching agreements. Indeed, in its Greek origin the word came from $\delta\iota\acute{\alpha}$ (diá), which means through or in between, and $\lambda\acute{o}\gamma o\varsigma$ (logos), which means word, speech, and reason. Though the term is originally associated with the use of reason and language, it can also be understood more broadly as "flowing through of meaning". Based on this broader understanding of the term, dialogue of civilizations may take many forms of cultural encounters, exchanges, crashes, and mutual transformations. Not only can the debates between different schools of Greek philosophy and the competition between the schools of thought in ancient China during the Spring and Autumn and Warring States periods be considered as dialogues of civilizations, Princess Wencheng's marriage to the Tibetan King Songtsän Gampo, Zheng He's voyage to the south across the ocean, the Crusades' expedition to the east, and Columbus' "discovery" of America can all be considered activities of dialogue of civilizations under this broader sense of the term.

We may roughly classify the ways through which such broadly understood dialogue of civilizations can take place into four categories: cultural, militant, commercial, and political. By "cultural" I mean those exchange activities that are cultural in content and, more importantly, conducted with civility. Activities belong to this kind include peaceful missionary undertakings, translation and publication of literatures, academic discussions, sports and art events, etc. By "militant", I mean those spread of civilization or ideology through militant or other forms of compulsory assimilation, such as the early colonization of other countries and regions by the Europeans. "Commercial" is meant to stand for dissemination of cultures through trading, investment, and immigrations for material conditions of living. Finally, "political" covers encounters between civilizations through diplomacy, political cooperation, or negotiation between governments, etc. Further distinctions can be made within each of these four categories. For example, the "cultural" category can be further divided into verbal (academic research, translation, etc.) and nonverbal (music, dance, sports, etc.) exchanges; exchanges that happen unintentionally and brought about intentionally; one-directional spread of culture and multi-directional, mutual exchanges; and exchanges within one civilization or exchanges between different civilizations, etc.

The kind of dialogue that the United Nations' "World Day for Cultural Diversity for Dialogue and Development" promotes is certainly not any other forms of dialogue understood in the broader sense of the term. It means a specific form of dialogue within the parameter of the "cultural" kind. That is, it is intentionally organized, multi-directional dialogue conducted through verbal communication between different civilizations. This specific kind of dialogue is not only different from militant intervention and forceful assimilation of cultures; it is diametrically opposed to it. It is also very different from the commercial and political forms of cultural exchanges, although they may have certain levels of overlap (e.g. people may engage in civilized verbal dialogues in business or political negotiation). Strictly speaking, it does not even include many forms of cultural exchanges, such as non-verbal cultural exchanges in sports and arts, cultural exchanges inside of one civilization or between civilizations

54

but not conducted purposefully for the sake of dialogue. In other words, what it promotes is dialogues via verbal exchanges that are purposefully organized through bringing representatives of different civilizations together for the purpose of increasing mutual understanding and reaching consensus.

Historically speaking, this kind of dialogue of civilization did not happen until the end of the 19th century. [1] The most famous landmark event was "the World Parliament of Religions" held in Chicago in 1893. The Conference is widely regarded as the mark of the beginning of modern dialogue of civilizations. Although the entire 17-day meeting was overwhelmingly dominated by Christianity from the English-speaking world, [2] commendable was the fact that all the speakers in the general assembly were treated as equal in status. Unfortunately, the subsequent meetings of the Parliament were interrupted for many years. Exchanges between civilizations in the ensuing years were largely carried out through the use of military force and power in the midst of two World Wars, Communist revolutions, and national independence movements. But these militant conflicts and dominance of power also spurred a deeper realization of the need for dialogue of civilizations. Consequently during the latter part of World War II and the post-war era, activities of dialogue among civilizations increased. In 1939, the University of Hawaii started to organize "East-West Philosophers Conferences", trying to promote exchanges and mutual understanding between the East and the West from their respective philosophical roots. [3] Shortly after the WWII, the United Nations passed the famous "Universal Declaration of Human Rights." The Declaration was both a product of painful reflections on the cruel reality emerged from Western

---

[1] Before that, there were only sporadically dialogues between individual persons, such as the dialogue between some Song Dynasty Confucians and Buddhists, and, in the late Ming, between the Jesuit missionaries and Confucians.

[2] Among the 194 presentations in the entire conference, 152 were by Christians. The ratio of presentations by representatives of other religions is: Buddhism 12, Judaism 11, Hinduism 8, Islam 2, Parsi 2, Shintoism 2, Confucianism 2, Daoism 1, Jainism 1 (RH Seager: *The World's Parliament of Religions, Chicago, Illinois, 1893: America's Religious Coming of Age*, Ph.D. Diss., Harvard University, 1986, p.87).

[3] The conference was held once every 10 years, and later became once every 5 years. The latest one was the tenth conference held in 2011.

civilizations and a fruit of dialogue of civilizations. [1] Ever since, activities of dialogue of civilizations became increasingly frequent and widespread. In 1958, Zhang Junmai, Tang Junyi, Mou Zongsan, and Xu Fuguan jointly published *A Declaration of Chinese Culture to the Scholars of the World*. In 1967, The Society for Asian and Comparative Philosophy was established in the US. In 1978, Temple University established its Institute for interreligious, Intercultural Dialogue (IIID). [2] In 1988, the Council for a Parliament of the World's Religions was formed and, in 1993, the 100th anniversary of the "World Parliament of Religions", it convened an unprecedented conference in Chicago, which gathered together over eight thousand participants from all over the world. The meeting passed a very famous document, titled "Towards a Global Ethic: An Initial Declaration", expressing the basic moral consensus endorsed by all the world's major religions and spiritual traditions. In the same year (1993), Oxford University established "The International Interfaith Centre". Afterwards, the World Parliament of Religions held three consecutive conferences, once in every five years: 1999 in Cape Town, South Africa, 2004 in Barcelona, Spain, 2009 in Melbourne, Australia. The number of participants increased from 7000 in 1999 to over 10000 in 2009. In November, 1998, the United Nations General Assembly passed a resolution proposed by the President of Iran Mohammad Khatami, which declared 2001 as the Year of Dialogue among Civilizations. In 1999, "The Foundation for Interreligious and Intercultural Research and Dialogue" (FIIRD) was established in Geneva, Switzerland. In August, 2000, two thousand preeminent religious and spiritual leaders of the world representing various faith traditions gathered together at the Headquarters of the United Nations for a Millennium World Peace Summit of Religious and Spiritual Leaders.

During the United Nations' Year of Dialogue among Civilizations, 2001,

---

[1] Among the members of the United Nations Commission on Human Rights who contributed to the creation of the document were outstanding Confucian scholars P. C. Chang 张彭春 , representative of the Republic of China, and Wu Teh Yao 吴德耀 . The clause that all men "should act towards one another in a spirit of brotherhood" in the *Universal Declaration* was added to it upon the recommendation of P.C. Chang, after the famous statement in the Confucian Analects that "all within the four seas are brothers" (12.5).

[2] It was renamed as Global Dialogue Institute in 2008.

the tragic events of 911 shocked the world. This coincidence is symbolic to the era in which we live - On the one hand is the acceleration of violent conflicts and destructions, and on the other hand is the upheave of dialogue of civilizations and the awareness of its urgency. On November 2, 2001, UNESCO passed the "Universal Declaration on Cultural Diversity", which propelled a new wave of dialogues among civilizations. Countless research and education institutes, foundations, organizations, and publications on dialogue of civilizations emerged. [1] It was also during the United Nations Year of Dialogue among Civilizations China became actively engaged in the global movement. [2]

The history of the moment is very rich in content. Its origin and evolution and the attitudes of different countries, religions, and civilizations toward this movement are all worthy of careful study, adequate to form a large array of research topics.

---

[1] Such as World Public Forum "Dialogue of Civilizations" established in 2001, World Council of Religious Leaders established in Thailand in 2002, United Nations Alliance of Civilizations established in 2005, The Centre for Dialogue established in Melbourne and the International Center for Dialogue among Civilizations established under the leadership of the former President of Iran Mohammad Khatami in 2006, the Centre for Inter-religious and Intercultural Dialogue established in Dhaka University, Bangladesh, in 2008.

[2] Discussions about culture and civilization began in China shortly after the "Cultural Revolution". The influential TV series "River Eulogy" in the late 1980s was an example of reflection and comparison of Chinese and Western civilizations. At that time, however, not only the concept of dialogue of civilizations was not known in China, the country was mainly facing the task of moving out of the shadow of the "Cultural Revolution", opening its doors to the outside world, and learning from the West about modernization. It was not ready to start organized dialogues with other civilizations yet. The situation changed after the turn of the millennium. In 2003, China hosted the first Cultural and Civilization meeting within the parameter of Asia Europe Meeting (ASEM). Since 2005, China hosted biennial Symposium on China-Arab Relations & Dialogue between China-Arab Civilizations. The annual Beijing Forum started in 2004 is another important platform for dialogue of civilizations, which has so far hosted more than 2700 participants from 70+ countries. Also started in 2004, the biennial Shanghai World Forum on China Studies (co-sponsored by China's State Council Information Office and the Shanghai Municipal Government) is yet another venue where dialogue of civilizations takes place. In 2007, ASEM Interfaith Dialogue meeting was held in Nanjing, China. In June 2011, the first international Forum of Dialogue between Islam and Confucian Civilizations (co-sponsored by Yunnan University and Almustafa Open University of Iran) was held in Yunnan, China. A most important landmark event was that, under the leadership of the former vice president of the People's Congress of China Xu Jialu, the first Nishan Forum on World Civilizations was held at Confucius birthplace in 2010.

On the whole, we can see that what happened in the past ten years in dialogue of civilizations are not incidental events. They are the results of rational reflections on the deep crisis of the modern era that have brought the entire human race and the entire planet Earth into abyss. They are the natural extension of the countless practices of dialogue of civilizations in the latter half of the last century. If we say that the maturity of a person cannot be measured by how strong his muscles are or how vigorous his physical body is, but rather by his intellect and his moral development, then the dialogue of civilizations in the past ten years can be said to be a sign of maturity of the entire human race reached through the experience of crisis and suffering.

2. A Case Study: World Public Forum "Dialogue of Civilizations"

In the past ten years, one of the most important platforms of dialogue of civilizations in the world is World Public Forum (WPF) "Dialogue of Civilizations". It was established in 2002, the year in which the United Nations declared the World Day for Cultural Diversity for Dialogue and Development. With two headquarters, one in Moscow and one in Vienna, WPF has formed close connections with many international organizations, such as United Nations Educational, Scientific, and Cultural Organization (UNESCO), Arab League Educational, Cultural and Scientific Organization (ALECSO), the Asia-Europe Foundation (ASEF), and International Association for Intercultural Education (IAIE). The main goals of WPF are to unite the efforts of the global community to protect the spiritual and cultural values of humankind, to create a space for constructive dialogue among major civilizations of the modern world, and to introduce the spirit of cooperation and understanding into everyday life and the various crisis and challenges that the entire human race are facing. Since 2003, WPF has hosted annual conferences at Rhodes Island, Greece, the birthplace of Western civilization with an average of 500–600 participants each time. Among the participants are distinguished scholars, religious leaders, representatives of international organizations, government officials (occasionally heads of nations), and news reporters. [①] In addition to the annual conference at Rhodes, WPF also periodically holds dialogue meetings on special topics in various places around the globe, [②] including a conference in Beijing which the WPF convened together with the Chinese Foundation of International Research, on "Dialogue of Civilizations and a Harmonious World" (July, 2010), and a "Russia–China Economic Cooperation in World Economic System Transformations", organized by the Russian Public Foundation "Dialogue of Civilizations" and Shanghai Institute for International Studies in Shanghai (July, 2010). Starting from 2010, WPF sponsored a Rhodes Youth Forum. The first one convened 150 young representatives from 34 countries to discuss the common future that the young generation is facing and their mission in the world today. So far the Youth Forum has held three annual conferences at Rhodes, one special conference in New Delhi, India, launched an international movement called "Youth

---

① Based on the name lists of the "International Coordination Committee" and "Experts and Participants" provided by the official web page of WPF, the rough proportion is: Scholars and experts from various areas of study 73%, religious leaders 4%, politicians and representatives of international organizations 14%, media 9%. Among the scholars, the fields most represented are economics (17%), political science (11%), law (11%), and sociology (10%). Among the politicians, the countries most represented are Russia (21%), India (9%), and Austria (9%).

② For example, WPF held two conferences at Jawaharlal Nehru University (New Delhi), on the themes of "Dialogue in the Context of Globalization" (2004) and "Development Model and Global Integration" (2007). In Latin America, WPF held an international conference in Cuba entitled "Latin America in the 21st century: Universalism and Originality" (2005). In Europe, WPF held three international conferences in Prague, the capital of the Czech Republic, entitled "Europe in the 21st Century: the Crossroads of Civilizations" (2004), "East-West: Integration and Development" (2006), and "Prague Dialogue on Europe in the 21st Century" (2009); an international seminar in the UNESCO Headquarters in Paris, France, entitled "Dialogue of Cultures and Civilizations: A Bridge Between Human Rights and Moral Values", and a follow up meeting on "Ancient Civilizations, New Beginnings: a Dialogue of Change" (2007); and an international Regional Conference "European Civilization Space: Baltic Dialogue" in Tampere, Finland (2007). In the Middle East, WPF held a special round-table on Christian-Muslim dialogue in Jordan (2006) and an international conference in Manama city, Kingdom of Bahrain, entitled "Bahrain Dialogue of Civilizations" (2008). In Canada, WPF held an international conference in Ottawa on "Education as a Dialogue Model of Social Development" (2008). In CIS countries (Commonwealth of Independent States) WPF held an International Conference "Role of Historical and Cultural Heritage in the Dialogue of Civilizations" in Almaty, Republic of Kazakhstan (2009). In addition, WPF held a WPF Summit meeting (high-level experts) in Vienna to discuss the most pressing socio-cultural problems facing the world today (2008).

Time", organized summer camps, created a web site, and inaugurated a magazine. In addition to all these, WPF has also organized some recreational cultural events to promote cultural exchange and understanding. [1]

WPF is a public forum. Its participants are individuals, who represent different civilizations rather than political groups or governments. As the Co-chair of WPF Fred Dallmayr puts it, WPF is not a government institution or inter-governmental organization (such as UN, UNESCO, or WHO), although it maintains friendly relations with many governments. It is not a political party or a business pursuing its special interest, although it welcomes participation from people of all parties. It is not an academic organization, although it has academics in its midst. It is not a religious organization or religious sect, although it concerns the question: To which extent do religions or religious beliefs further or obstruct a viable public life in the world? Finally it is not a social club existing simply for the enjoyment of members, although it hopes that participants also enjoy its conferences as well as each other's company. WPF is, as its name indicates, a global public forum committed to the dialogue of civilizations. It has its own commitment, a moral or ethical commitment: a commitment to a world where public affairs are settled not by the clash of civilizations through militant might but by dialogues or reasoned discourse of participants in a public arena. [2]

WPF's Founding President is Vladimir Yakunin. He is the president of the state-run Russian Railways company, a close ally of Russian President Vladimir Putin, and a candidate for Russian President in 2006. Being a high rank government official and a CEO of a huge corporation, his main interest, however, is in promoting dialogue of civilizations. He personally attended and chaired most of the WPF's events, from their beginning to end. Because of Yakunin, the dialogue of civilizations organized by WPF has a strong Russian presence. Participants from Russia have invariably been more than others at all the annual meetings of WPF. A rough estimate of the participants

---

[1] For example, upon the invitation from WPF, over 2500 people attended the "Cultures Invite to Table" event held in Freud Park in Vienna on May 19, 2011, enjoying the rich varieties of music, dance, and food from different parts of the world.

[2] Dallmayr, Fred (2011): *Who are We? What is WPF-Dialogue of Civilizations?*, http://www.wpfdc.org/en/328-who-are-we-what-is-wpf-dialogue-of-civilizations .

shows that about 23% were from Russia, 7% from India, and 2.5% from China. [1] The percentage of Russian Participants is almost 10 times of China. This is certainly due to the fact that WPF is a platform built largely by Russians, but it also shows that the post-cold-war Russia takes dialogue of civilization seriously, and that they are trying hard to find the identity of their culture in the map of world civilizations and even become a leader in dialogue of civilizations. The strong presence of India in WPF is also noticeable. This is similarly associated with the fact that a co-founder of WPF was a well-known public intellectual and entrepreneur, Jagdish Chandra Kapur. But likewise there is a deeper background behind. Kapur once said to the author of this article in person that, "if Russia, India, and China can work together to lead the dialogue of civilizations, it would be powerful enough to counter the dominance of the West."

Indeed, even though the percentage of American and West European participants in WPF is not low, they are almost without exception critical of Western hegemony and the enlightenment rationality. This fact shows that, like many other platforms of dialogue of civilizations, WPF is not entirely neutral in its position. Its basic principle and orientation is to advocate peaceful dialogue and to oppose clash of civilizations. Of the four forms of dialogue of civilizations defined broadly, the governments of the United States and other major Western countries have the upper hand in three of them, namely the militant, commercial, and political forms. This is especially the case with the United States, which has a military expense equal to the total military expenses of all the other countries in the world put together. Yet in the cultural form, not only is the US not in the leading position, it is often viewed as a source of conflicts among civilizations, a force that the global movement of dialogue of civilizations intends to restrain, to criticize, and even to oppose.

---

[1] Proportions of participants from other parts of the world are: North America 12%, Europe 41%, Middle East 8.5%, South America 3%, Africa 2%, Australia 0.5% (based on the name lists of the "International Coordination Committee" and "Experts and Participants" provided by the official web page of WPF).

3. Some Reflection on the Model of Dialogue
of Civilizations

How should we understand dialogue of civilizations more accurately and more constructively? According to Samuel Huntington, once civilizations in the world start to encounter one another, their mutual clash will be inevitable. This "clash of civilizations" may be called the "Jungle Model". In order to survive, different civilizations have to either overcome others or be overcomed, with no third alternative. Based on this kind of understanding, the best choice would certainly be using militant, economic, and political forms of expansion to allow one's own civilization to become a dominant force, and eventually replace all other civilizations. These ways would be more straightforward than trying to persuade others to give up their own civilizations. [①] The lack of interest in following the United Nations' call for dialogue of civilizations on the side of the governments of the US and other major Western countries has close connection with this line of thinking.

Of course it would be unfair to conceive the US and other major Western countries simply as jungle beasts. These countries have made significant achievements in protecting minorities and cultural diversities. But it does not take much effort to notice that they have never allowed other cultures to influence their mainstream culture. Their multiculturalism may be called the "Zoo Model" - though there are all varieties

---

[①] Even though Huntington's curse about the clash of civilization has been repeatedly denounced as entirely opposite of what dialogue of civilizations tries to achieve, clash of civilizations could happen in platforms of dialogue of civilizations as well. There is a danger of conceiving and practicing dialogue as if it were nothing but verbal combat, aiming at winning the argument and defeating alternative views. This is the jungle model applied to the narrowly defined dialogue of civilizations. There is actually a fine line between the jungle model and having healthy disagreements and debates. To be fair, those who have this jungle model tendency may even have very good intentions. They may conceive themselves to be doing others a great favor, liberating us from wrong views and wrong values. The difference between a genuine dialogue and a verbal combat is not in whether we shy away from our differences and disagreements, or whether we may have heated debates, but in the way we deal with them and in our final purpose. What we try to do is to increase mutual understanding and reflections through civilized rational discussion, rather than using rhetoric eloquence to silence others.

of animals in a zoo, they are kept in separate cages for display, with no real encounters and exchanges between them. Their mainstream culture is like the zoo keeper who will protect the animals and provide necessary conditions for their survival. The zoo keeper would even organize activities to increase public awareness about animals, especially endangered species, such as having a "monkey week", or "panda month". Dialogue of civilizations done in such a model is certainly better than nothing, but its significance is no more than getting limited tolerance of difference and adding some decorations of plurality to cover up the fact that the society is still dominated by a monolithic culture.

Still another alternative is a "Stage Model". We often use "platform" to describe forums of dialogue of civilizations on which people from different civilizations can present their own perspectives and values. The stage model is obviously better than both the jungle model and the zoo model in some important ways, as long as we make the stage public, meaning that everyone can have access to participate. Unlike the jungle model, it celebrates differences, and unlike the zoo model, it not only brings different "actors" and "actresses" to the same place, on the same stage, in the same "show", but also allows them to have real encounters to each other. Taking different platforms of dialogue of civilizations as stages will also highlight the importance of gaining the right of language and the need for different civilizations to build their own platforms. ①

However, using the stage model to characterize dialogue of civilizations is still inadequate. Even when the stage model is used to promote fair representation of different voices, the right to be on the stage itself does not entail the need to listen

---

① Of course stages for dialogue of civilizations cannot be set up for solo performances of one's own culture. For instance, Nishan Forum cannot be a place where only Confucian scholars exchange their ideas about Confucianism, even if these ideas are about global issues; it must invite representatives of other civilizations to participate in discussions. Otherwise it would not be dialogue of civilizations. This is somewhat like the Olympics. Indeed, the host country of Olympics would have some advantages. Not only would their team be the first to march into the stadium during the opening ceremony, it has been shown that the team of the host country will always have better performances in the games than it is in a different country. But if there is no global participation and the team of the host country is the only one there to make the show, it would certainly not be Olympics. The host should also not to make representatives from other countries mere spectators. The success of dialogue of civilizations is fundamentally dependent on whether there is true dialogue. This is something that both WPF and Nishan Forum need to work on.

to other voices. It makes dialogue of civilizations sounds like mere performances, allowing each actor or actress to have a moment of glory on the stage, or even like nothing but a field of competition for the right of language.

Probably it is more appropriate to use a "Healthcare Model", i.e., to take dialogue of civilizations as healthcare for the troubled world, to supplement the stage model. Healthcare model has at least the following four advantages: First, dialogue of civilizations movement has a strong practical orientation. It is not a coincidence that the modern upheave of dialogues of civilizations happened at the same time when the tragic events of 911 took place. The rise of the movement and its development corresponds precisely to the rise of deep global crises. It is like having doctors from the world's different civilizations to come together to diagnose the problems for the world. Using the healthcare model can increase people's consciousness to the practical problems and their awareness of the significance and urgency for having dialogue of civilizations.

Second, dialogue of civilizations is not merely giving diagnosis of problems; it is more importantly a treatment itself, a treatment that resembles what Traditional Chinese Medicine (TCM) does for human body! It signifies that people are increasingly on guard against the dominance of materialistic way of life and the use of material force to suppress symptoms of our problems; it signifies that people are using a holistic way of thinking to view the world as a dynamic and interrelated system; and it signifies that people are mobilizing and revitalizing the energies of the resources of all civilizations to treat our problems at the more fundamental level, namely the level of our cultures and basic values. Seeing from the healthcare model, we find that the choice of Rhodes Island, the birthplace of Socratic dialogue, and Nishan, the birthplace of Confucius, is like choosing two key acupuncture points on the body of the globe, from which the energy of these respective civilizations can be utilized and other acupuncture points in the world can be connected and mutually resonated. Comparing different platforms of dialogue of civilizations to acupuncture points cannot only make us aware of their uniqueness but also understand the necessity to have collaborations between them.

Third, just like the purpose of TCM is for health and not merely for gaining knowledge, dialogue of civilizations is not merely for gaining mutual understandings and reaching some consensus. Even though verbal discourse is a major form of dialogue of civilizations, the consensus it is able to obtain is limited to abstract principles. After all, dialogue of civilizations cannot be merely based on verbal discourses, and the harmony of the world cannot merely rely on abstract consensus. Using healthcare model is helpful for us to see the connections between verbal dialogue and other forms of cultural exchange.

Last but not least is the characterization that TCM works slowly but, through restoring a patient's own immune system rather than suppressing symptoms, it is good for removing the root of the problems. Similarly, in resolving global crises, dialogue of civilization works much more slowly than other methods such as military intervention, economic sanction, and political pressure. These other methods are still necessary in some situations, like in medication TCM and Western medicine are both indispensable. But these other methods do not remove the root of the problems; moreover, they are often the causes of deeper problems. The obsession to see quick results in addressing global crises is as strong as modern people's resistance to TCM, if not more. [1]

In Chinese we have a saying: "When a disease hits you, it is like an avalanche; when a disease is recovering, it is like removing single fibers from a piece of cloth, one at a time." In the past ten years, dialogue of civilizations has obviously become a

---

[1] For example, the US House of Representatives passed a resolution on Oct. 28, 2009 to honor the 2560th anniversary of the birth of Confucius, recognizing his invaluable contributions to philosophy and social and political thought. But the proposal met some objections. Republican Representative of Arizona Jeff Flake used a mocking tone, imitating Confucius, "He who spends time passing trivial legislation may find himself out of time to read healthcare bill." Republican Representative from Utah Jason Chaffetz said, "We love Confucius, but what a joke to vote" (http://politicalticker.blogs.cnn.com/2009/10/29/gop-rep-house-vote-on-confucius-birthday-a-joke/ accessed Nov. 15, 2012). Comments on the Internet show that a significant amount of American people share the view of these two politicians. Many said that the House of Representatives were putting aside all of America's problems and wasting their time on honoring an ancient Chinese. The current upsurge of interest in learning Chinese in the West is actually motivated mainly by their intent to do business with China. Those who are really interested in traditional Chinese culture, want to engage in dialogue with Chinese civilization, and treat Chinese traditional culture as a resource are still very few. This kind of situation is also quite serious in China. Many Chinese still dream that political, economic, and military power is everything the country needs and wholesale acceptance of Western enlightenment values is the direction for China. Although everywhere in China you can see projects of restoring traditional Chinese cultural heritage, most of them are motivated by using it as a source for making economic gains.

global trend, and it is beyond any doubt the hope of the human race. It might be hard for us to present impressive numerical indications of the achievements of dialogue of civilizations in the past ten years. What we can be sure about is that this is a long and difficult path, on which we need to have the determination of "though knowing that it cannot be done, yet keep doing it anyway"! [1]

Ni Peimin earned his B.A. and M.A. from Fudan University in China and his Ph.D. from the University of Connecticut in the US He is currently a tenured philosophy professor at Grand Valley State University in Michigan and Editor-in-chief of the ACPA book series on *Chinese and Comparative Philosophy* (New York: Global Scholarly Publications). Ni served as a visiting professor at the University of Hawaii at Manoa and at the University of Hong Kong. He was President of the Association of Chinese Philosophers in North America and the Society for Asian and Comparative Philosophy. His works include six books, such as *Confucius-Making the Way Great* (English version 2010, and Chinese translation 2012), *On Confucius* (2002), and over sixty scholarly essays in Chinese and English. Ni's scholarly work concentrates on philosophical dialogue between China and the West.

---

[1]　Confucius was described as a man "who knows that it cannot be done and yet keeps doing it anyway" (*The Analects*, 14.38).

Challenges Imposed by Chinese Civilization

Tan Mingran

As China's influence increases around the world, it catches more and more attention among Euro-American scholars and politicians. For the first time in American history, China's rise became an independent debating topic in the 2012 presidential election. In fact, since 2007, American universities have started to increase their budgets on Chinese research. They have changed index of Chinese books in libraries from Wade-Giles to pinyin, and sent more students to study in China. They have also opened more positions on teaching Chinese language and history. At the same time, Chinese people and "Made in China" flood every corner of the globe. As a result, some Western scholars start reevaluating Chinese culture, and believe that it can supplement the insufficiency of Western civilization. As Karl Heinz Pohl says, "An encounter with Confucianism could, at least, makes us aware of some blind spots in the Western model. It might even give us the vision of an alternative modernity, one that is possibly less built on self-interest and the notion of conflict... and last not least a (re-) discovery of the way of the Mean as a means to achieve social harmony." [1] However, some scholars insist that China's rise is shrinking the West (Halper 2010: preface), and will lead to the conflict of civilization (Huntington 1993). Either Chinese civilization is seen as a supplement or as a threat; there is no doubt that it is viewed as a challenge to the dominance of Western civilization. In the following, I will analyze how Chinese

---

[1] Pohl, Karl Heinz: *Ethics for the 21st Centrury—The Confucian Tradition*, in http://www.uni-trier. de/fileadmin/fb2/SIN/Pohl_Publikation/ethics_for_the_21st_century.pdf.

civilization can challenge the West, and whether this challenge can last.

Before discussing the topic, let's first define the meaning of civilization in our context. Despite various definitions, civilization is regarded as a cultural entity, and refers to the overall way of life of a people. It involves the values, norms, institutions, and modes of thinking to which successive generations in a given society have attached primary importance. (Huntington 1996: 41) It is a "cultural area"… ranging from the form of its houses the material of which they are built, their roofing, to skills like featuring arrows, to a dialect or group of dialects to tastes in cooking, to a particular technology, a structure of beliefs, a way of making love, and even to the compass, paper, the printing press. (Ferguson 2010: preface) In short, civilization includes both spiritual and material existence of a people as well as its technical know-how. Based on this definition, I will explore the challenge of Chinese civilization to the West from economic, political and cultural aspects.

1. China's Challenge on Economy

After a glimpse of Western scholars' views, Chinese challenge on economy mainly can be summarized as two points: (1) China's unique development model competes with the Washington Consensus, and (2) China's support of developing countries with its huge US dollar reserve dwarfs the World Bank and IMF and affects the effectiveness of their policy in promoting democracy.

It is well-known that China's unique development model has avoided shock therapy, pursuing instead a more gradual pace of reform. "Contrary to neoliberal prescriptions, the state has actively intervened in the Chinese economy and played a key role in setting economic policy, establishing functional government institutions, regulating foreign investment, and mitigating the adverse effects of globalization on domestic constituencies." (Peerenboom 2007: 5) This model has been termed as Beijing Consensus, Yellow River Capitalism, Walled World, state-managed capitalism, etc. However, their essences are same, i.e., China is following a market-authoritarian model instead of a market-democracy model, a pragmatic approach to reforms and support for a larger role for the state in guiding the economy and ensuring equitable growth, and an emphasis on self-determination to prevent powerful international actors from unduly influencing China's development choices, and—more problematically, a wholesale rejection of the WC. (Peerenboom 2007: 6)

WC or Washington Consensus is a term invented in 1989 by John Williamson. It advocates that democratic political reform is the prerequisite of economic development. Being bundled with the loans provided by World Bank and IMF, it has coerced some developing countries to adopt democratic polity on a low level of wealth. As a result, Indonesia, Cambodia and Bangladesh have become poorer and more chaotic after being democratized; and Latin Americans have lost confidence in democracy because of the lack of economic growth, the deterioration of public services, the rise of crime, and the persistence of widespread corruption. A 2003 survey found that more than 50 percent of respondents of Latin Americans agreed with the statement, "I wouldn't mind if a non-democratic government came to power if it could solve economic problems."(Halper 2010: 133)

Just as these developing countries are struggling in the economic mire generated by democratization, China has accomplished its economic take-off through postponing democratization. China's success, in Joshua Cooper Ramo's words, "marks a path for other nations around the world who are trying to figure out not simply how to develop their countries, but also how to fit into the international order in a way that allows them to be truly independent, to protect their way of life and political choices in a world with a single massively powerful centre of gravity." (Halper2010: 214) For governments in Africa, Central Asia, Latin America, and even the Middle East, China's rise means that there is no longer a binary choice between assimilation to the West and isolation. Peerenboom goes on to comment, The Beijing Consensus replaces the discredited Washington Consensus, an economic theory made famous in the 1990s for its prescriptive, Washington-knows-best approach to telling other nations how to run themselves. (Peerenboom 2007: 7)

The allure of the Chinese model extends beyond China's border quickly. In their quest to mimic Chinese success, countries as diverse as Brazil, Russia and Vietnam are copying Beijing's activist industrial policy that uses public money and foreign investment to build capital-intensive industries. (Leonard 2008:121) Many African countries directly invite China to establish special economic zones. The reason is that

Chinese model provides rapid growth, stability and the promise of a better life for its citizens, which are what many developing countries are striving for. Undoubtedly, the popularity of this model will inevitably shrink the influence of Washington Consensus, challenging the dominant Western value.

Historically speaking, Washington Consensus may have been proven to be effective only in America's taking-off. With its constitutional democracy and immigrant population, the United States has maintained its market-democracy model for more than 200 years. However, for West European countries, all of which experienced taking-off without democracy. In fact the most common form of governance during Europe's industrial revolutions was the monarchical state, absolutist or constitutional. In Martin Jacques' view, there is an inherent authoritarianism involved in the process of take-off and modernization-the need to concentrate society's resources on a single objective-which, judging by history, people are prepared to tolerate because their own lives are dominated by the exigencies of economic survival and the desire to escape from poverty. (Jacques 2009: 212–214) Obviously, market-democracy model is not suitable for other countries universally, and even before the appearance of the Chinese model, the United States' promotion of it has already met setbacks in Cambodia, Bangladesh and Indonesia. For this reason, with regard to US's relentless promotion of its market-democracy model, Peerenboom criticizes, "Paradoxically, the US, the leader of the free world, decides for others what is in their best interests and imposes the costs of its decisions on them in the name of democracy." (Peerenboom 2007: 180)

If Beijing Consensus challenges Washington Consensus by providing an alternative model of development, China's loans to the developing world further financially undermines the leverage of IMF and World Bank which have been used as tools to promote free market and democracy. With China's loans without restrictions, the developing countries do not need to risk the disintegration of their governments in order to get IMF or World Bank's aid with added clauses. For example, the IMF spent years negotiating a transparency agreement with the Angolan government only to be told hours before the deal was due to be signed that the authorities in Luanda were no longer interested in the money: they had secured a $2 billion soft loan from China. This tale has been repeated across the continent-from Algeria to Chad, Ethiopia to Nigeria, Sudan to Uganda, and Zambia to Zimbabwe. (Leonard 2008: 120) As a result,

"The most serious human rights abusers in the world have a new sugar daddy, as do the proliferators, the 'genociders', and just about every other category of state malcontent." (Halper 2010: 212) It goes without saying that Washington Consensus is further shrank during the process, and the promotion of democracy is put aside by many governments.

To make many Westerners annoyed, China demands more voices in global forums that the West founded and presumed to dominate, such as the United Nations, the IMF, the World Bank, and the WHO. On a trip to Moscow in November 2008, Chinese Prime Minister Wen Jiabao spoke of the importance of building a new international financial order by attaining new levels of financial and industrial cooperation among China, Russia, and other groups, like the Shanghai Cooperation Organization. Wen also stressed the need to give developing nations more to say in global institutions such as the International Monetary Fund so that these nations could play a bigger role in international regulatory mechanisms and supervision over financial institutions in countries whose currencies are held as reserves around the world - namely the United states. (Halper 2010: 5) Undoubtedly, all these behaviors are seen as China's challenges to the West and seeking for a novel world order.

2. China's Challenges on World Politics

Pertaining to China's rise in economy, its influence on world politics is increasing, too. Its success in economic reform has helped it win a lot of followers and expand its political room in global arenas. Its financial resources also facilitate its establishment of various forums through which its interests are secured and its voices are heard. Using a sentence from Sunzi's Art of War, China is seeking its political room through "global strategy and diplomacy" instead of showing military muscle. It seldom confronts the United States directly, but secures its own interests with an indirect way.

Chinese diplomats know very well that most developing countries do not like the infringement of sovereignty and the interference of domestic affairs by Western countries, so they use this kind of feeling to fight against America's universalism and exceptionalism. They never claim that American universalism is not popular, but let President Yoweri Kaguta Museveni of Uganda deliver the message in 2006: "The

Western ruling groups are conceited, full of themselves, ignorant of our conditions, and they make other people's business their business, while the Chinese just deal with you as one who represents your country, and for them they represent their own interests and you just do business."(Halper 2010: 100) With regard to many moves proposed by Western countries, China seldom exercises its veto power in the United Nations, but solves the problems through other means. For example, Beijing has been willing to allow the Organization of Islamic States to take the lead in weakening the new Human Rights Council in 2006. Beijing also appointed an envoy to Darfur in 2007, supporting the idea of a UN peacekeeping mission, pressurizing the Sudanese government to negotiate with rebel forces, but, at the same time, it has stuck to a line of influence, not intervention, refusing to accept sanctions against the regime, and insisting that forces should only be deployed with the Sudanese government's consent. (Leonard 2008: 129)

This subtle diplomacy has been devastatingly effective - contributing to a massive fall in US influence: in 1995 the USA won 50.6 per cent of the votes in the United Nations general assembly; by 2006, the figure had fallen to just 23.6 per cent. On human rights, the results are even more dramatic: China's win-rate has rocketed from 43 per cent to 82 per cent, while the USA's has tumbled from 57 per cent to 22 per cent. The New York Times' UN correspondent James Traub has detected a paradigm shift in the United Nations' operations, and said, "It's a truism that the Security Council can function only insofar as the United States lets it. The adage may soon be applied to China as well." For this, Mark Leonard concludes, the United Nations is becoming a powerful amplifier of the Chinese world-view. (Leonard 2008: 129–130)

In addition, China is expanding its influence upon such international organizations as World Bank, WHO, WTO and IMF. In Halper's view, (China) and other newcomers in these institutions are increasingly forming clubs and other associations that outnumber the old-timers in a process that threatens to leave Western governments feeling like strangers in their own houses. Merely the size of the meeting table at the London G20 meeting in early 2009 highlighted an important new reality: that the answers to the world's problems no longer lie primarily in Washington and Brussels. They also lie increasingly in new centers of economic power and new forms of global cooperation beyond the member list of NATO. (Halper 2010: 212)

At the same time, China is making its voices being heard widely through establishing such forums as Shanghai Cooperation Organization, China-African Cooperation Forum, East Asia Summits, etc. China plays a dominant role in these organizations and the United Stated is not invited. For example, BRICK Summit 2009: the principle aim of the meeting was to discuss how to conduct trade and provide aid in ways that excluded the United States. Russian President Dmitry Medvedev described the meeting as an opportunity for these countries to "build an increasingly multi polar world order", and to move beyond an "artificially maintained uni-polar system" with "one big centre of consumption, financed by a growing deficit, and thus growing debts, one formerly strong reserve currency, and one dominant system of assessing assets and risks". When they asked to attend the meeting as observers, officials of the newly installed Obama administration received a simple nyet. (Halper 2010: 28–29)

There is no doubt that economic power plays a great role in China's challenge toward the West in global political arenas. But we should not neglect the appeal of the Five Principles of Peaceful Coexistence, especially the respect of sovereignty and non-interference of other countries' internal affairs. To some degree, these five principles express the common desires of most developing countries which got independent from their colonizers. As we know, "The world of 1900 was an imperial world 'of territorial empires spreading across much of the globe; and of informal empires of trade, unequal treaties and extraterritorial privilege (for Europeans)–and garrisons and gunboats to enforce it–over most of the rest. Concepts of international law (invented in Europe) dismissed claims to sovereignty (and justified foreign intervention) unless the state concerned met a 'standard of civilization' that was approved in Europe." (Darwin 2008: 298–299) Although the United Nations claims that all countries are equal and enjoy same respect for their sovereignty and culture, regardless of size and population, nevertheless, American exceptionalism and universalism remind the developing countries of their colonial past. On the one hand, the United States is unwilling to be bound by rules made for others. As Mahbubani observes, "When American interests were aligned with global interests, there would be no problems. ...However, when American interests diverge from global interests, its dominance of the UNSC could create serious distortions... The US effectively used its power to go against the clear wishes of the international community." (Mahbubani 2008: 113) On the other hand, the Americans believe what was good for America was good for the world. Democratic institutions on the American model, America's version of the market economy, and a commercial culture made for mass consumption were the best guarantees of wealth and stability. (Darwin 2008: 482) As a result, although most countries dare not to challenge America's hegemony, in order to survive and protect their own interests, they do not endorse America's positions either. As China's insistence on the respect of sovereignty meets most countries' desire, China naturally becomes the representative of the developing countries, and wins their support.

In short, through smile and non-confrontation diplomacy, China is winning more and more friends on the globe. Instead of promoting democracy and human rights, China puts more importance on the development of economy and the improvement of people's living standard. Rather than coercing other countries to accept its value, China respects their sovereignty and cultures, providing them non-attached loans. From a short and medium perspective, more and more countries will accept China's model in order to develop their economy. In current world situation, as most countries are still in poor condition, they will prefer economic development to American democracy and human rights. However, from a long-term perspective, as people's living standard increasing, they will demand more voices in governmental decisions, and democracy and human rights will become more appealing. Therefore, currently, it is important for the United States to help the rest of the world to become rich. Only after people liberate themselves from the struggle for survival, will they have mind and time to consider democracy and human rights.

3. China's Challenge in Culture

Wealth and economic strength are preconditions for the exercise of soft power and cultural influence. With huge wealth accumulated in industrial revolution, since 1800, Euro-American culture has played a dominant role in the process of globalization. Western dress and living style have been popular around the world. Everywhere you go in the region you feel the presence of the West. Skyscrapers, Hollywood Film, MacDonald, basketball and iPad 3 are still the symbols of modernity. People in the developing world are still fond and proud of studying in Euro-American universities, and pay high respect and admiration to Western-educated persons. To some degree, it can be said that Euro-American culture is changing the global culture, and people are becoming more westernized. The historian J. M. Roberts wrote, in a somewhat triumphalist vein: "What seems to be clear is that the story of Western civilization is now the story of mankind, its influence so diffused that old oppositions and antitheses are now meaningless. "(Jacques 2009: 45)

However, no matter how influential Western culture is, it cannot uproot other indigenous cultures, such as Confucianism, Islam and Hinduism. On the contrary, with the economic development of these cultural areas, these cultures will become more popular. For example, in 1990s, with the fast development of Guangdong area, speaking Cantonese once became a fad. Now, with the economic prosperity in China and India, Confucianism and Hinduism is exerting and will exert more influence around the world, at least temporarily. An indicator of this is that a rising number of Americans are learning Mandarin and Marshal Arts.

According to some Western scholars, the first cultural challenge China poses on the West should be Confucian value. Different from American democracy which promotes individualism, Confucian value advocates collectivism, mutual responsibility and benefit among family and social members. It puts individuals into the web of social relations and emphasizes family and social harmony. In March 2007, the Prime Minister Wen Jiabao remarked: "From Confucius to Sun Yat-sen, the traditional culture of the Chinese nation has numerous precious elements, many positive aspects regarding the nature of the people and democracy. For example, it stresses love and humanity, community, harmony among different viewpoints, and sharing the world in common." (Jacques 2009: 217) In other words, if China truly develops a kind of democracy, its new version will be imbued with heavy Chinese characteristics, different from American democracy based on individualism. Bergsten has a bolder prediction, saying, "There is the strong possibility that China is trying to develop a new model of politics that it will call democratic but that will not include the elements of pluralism, contestation and direct elections that the U.S. regards as essential part of democracy." (Bergsten 2008: 11)

The second cultural challenge should be Chinese version of modernity and the approaches to achieve it. Chinese scholars seem to have separated modernity from

Western culture as early as China's Self-strengthening Movement in 1860s. Their philosophy, "Chinese learning as essence, while Western learning as practical use", demonstrated that their conception of modernity focused mainly on technological dimension. Although China's Self-strengthening Movement ended in failure, its counterpart, Japanese Meiji Restoration offered the world a different version of modernity, a graft of Western technology onto Japanese Confucian culture. Later, many scholars clearly indicate that modernity is not identical with westernization. (Darwin 2008: 14; Huntington 1996: 69; Cohen 1984: 72) Fareed Zakaria rightly states, "Becoming a modern society is about industrialization, urbanization, and rising levels of literacy, education, and wealth. The qualities that make a society Western, in contrast, are special." (Zakaria 2011: 87)

Undoubtedly, this separation of modernity from Westernization forms a new obstacle for the spread of American values. It overthrows American universalism that what is good for Americans will be good for the rest, and Westernization is the prerequisite of modernity. As a result, people will modernize their nations on the basis of their own culture, and will not rely too much on American or Western prescription any more. The Western dominance of the globe is further shrunk. At this point, it is not surprising that Western scholars and politicians react so strong to Beijing Consensus or Yellow-River Capitalism which provides a new approach for modernity.

The third challenge will be Chinese active promotion of their culture on the globe. As early as 1993, Cui Zhiyuan already asked Chinese intellectuals to step out of their uncritical worship of Western capitalism. (Leonard 2008: 14) Meng Peiyuan also rejected to interpret Chinese culture with Western thought as a frame of reference. In his view, Chinese should plan their own modernity based on Chinese history and experience, instead copy Western versions.[1] With a growing sense of self-belief among Chinese scholars, the idea that China must learn from the West is being joined by the proposition that the West needs to learn from the East. (Jacques 2009: 380)

Chinese government responds to its scholars' demand promptly. In 2004, Li Changchun started China's Overseas Propaganda (Waixuan Gongzuo). With a budget of

---

[1] Meng Peiyuan: *My Exploration in Chinese Philosophy*《我的中国哲学研究之路》, http://www.confuchina.com/xuezhe%20wenji/meng%20peiyuan.htm.

720 million US dollars, China aims to establish media offices and Confucius Institutes around the world, introducing Chinese culture and economic model and teaching Chinese Mandarin.(Halper 2010: 9–10) China also increases its offer of scholarships to foreign students, expecting foreign students to help spread Chinese values. It goes without saying that China still cannot compete with America on global influence, but it will join the process of reshaping the world order, providing an alternative for Euro - American value.

4. The Sustainability of China's Challenge

China's advantages to challenge the West can be enumerated as follows. China has 1.8 trillion US dollar reserves, and has become the center of global manufacturing. "Made in China" has become synonymous with a host of mass - produced consumer products throughout the world. China's double - digit growth rate has driven up the prices for raw material and benefited countries with resources. At the same time, the developed world is also enjoying the low - cost manufacturing base and extremely cheap imports from China. In addition, China has inexhaustible cheap labors. However, according to Martin Jacques' analysis, China also has three disadvantages: technology bottleneck, scarce resources and export - driven economy. These three disadvantages will make it impossible for China to follow the resource - intensive American model of progress; and that will happen long before China gets anywhere near the US's present living standard. (Jacques 2009:170)

First, history has proven more than once that technology plays a critical role in sustaining an economy. In 1800s, it was spinning machines that made Britain subdue its Indian and Chinese competitors and became the global manufacturing center. At the end of the 1980s, it was a range of new industries and technologies, most notably in computing and the internet that the United States found a new lease of economic life, leaving Japan far behind. (Jacques 2009: 63) Now, despite China being the global manufacturing center, China does not have much advanced technology of its time to power its economy. Instead, it mainly depends on low - end manufacturing, and exploits the huge supply of cheap unskilled labor and thereby produces at rock - bottom prices. As the proportion represented by manufacturing is very small - around 15 per cent of the final price - with the bulk of costs being creamed off by design, marketing, branding and so forth, tasks which are still overwhelmingly carried out in Western and Japanese multinationals, (Jacques 2009: 174) China's status as a manufacturing center will be easily shattered once China challenges the interests of the developed world. In fact, as Huntington proposes, non - Western civilizations will continue to attempt to acquire the wealth, technology, skills, machines and weapons that are part of being modern... This will require the West to maintain the economic and military power necessary to protect its interests in relation to these civilizations.(Huntington 1993) Implicitly, Western countries will continue their technology blockade to China in order to thwart China's challenge.

Second, China's growth has been extremely resource - intensive, demanding of land, forest, water, oil and more or less everything else. Of course, such a level of demand would be unsustainable in terms of the world's available resources. In addition, China's competition for resources will cause conflicts with the developed world and makes it more difficult for further development. At present, China has disputes with Japan and South East Asia on oceanic resources, and its oil suppliers such as Libya and Iran, are also overthrown or harassed by the United States. Hence, it becomes necessary for China to upgrade its technology to make full use of present resources and cut down its import.

If these two disadvantages can be lessened by technology upgrade, China's heavy reliance upon export will submit its fate to the hands of the developed world. By the 2008 global crisis, the European Union accounted for around 22 percent of Chinese exports and the United States 18 percent. (Jacques 2009: 164) If Japan was taken into account, the percentage for the developed countries would be higher. After the crisis, in response to the decline of export, Chinese government called for expanding internal consumption. It invested a lot of money on infrastructure, public welfare, and education and lowered interest rates. However, the annual growth rate of the first three quarters was still below the expected 8%. It will be very like below 7% as the developed world continue struggling in the crisis, which will lead the West to adopt stricter protectionist measures. Once China's growth rate were below 7%, social unrest ignited by unemployment and corruption would get rid of any opportunity for China to challenge the West.

Then, whether can China find a solution through technological upgrade? In the near future, the answer seems negative. The reason is that most Chinese are seeking near-sighted interest and few can sit down to do research with a care-free mind. Chinese society is a power-oriented one, and people pay more respect to officials than Nobel Laureate because the former can bring benefit immediately. As a result, the day a scientist becomes famous is also the day he becomes a technocrat in China. This kind of ethos makes everyone spend time and energy on how to get promotion, and no one will care much about the upgrade of technology. Therefore, China's challenge to the West is only temporary.

5. The Response of the West

Despite the fact that China's challenge is only temporary, the West, especially the United States, still become very sensitive. As Martin Jacques describes, "We are so used to the world being Western, even American, that we have little idea what it would be like if it was not. The West, moreover, has a strong vested interest in the world being cast in its image, because this brings multifarious benefits... For reasons of both mindset and interest, therefore, the United States, and the West more generally, finds it difficult to visualize, or accept, a world that involves a major and continuing diminution in its influence." (Jacques 2009: 45)

Of course, the dissolution of Western hegemony incurs not only the change of power center, but also the loss of superiority, wealth and attention. Take ancient China as an example, before its defeat by the West, China dominated its tribute states, and Chinese enjoyed a superior sense toward the people around its empire. After being defeated, Chinese lost not only territories and wealth, but also respect from its neighboring people. Hence, it is understandable that the West are preparing to defend their dominance even when China shows any sign of challenge.

Huntington suggests maintaining the superiority of the West in technology, machines and weaponry in order to limit the expansion of the military strength of Confucian and Islamic states. At the same time, through exploiting differences and conflicts among Confucian and Islamic states, the West should dissolve the Confucian-Islamic military connection. Through creating allies with Judo-Christian countries and Japan, limit and contain Confucian and Islamic states. Through supporting other civilizations groups sympathetic to the West, and strengthening international institutions that reflect and legitimate Western interests and values, maintain Western predominance, protect Western interests and promote Western political and economic values. (Huntington: 1993)

Bergsten's proposition can be viewed as a detailed miniature of Huntington's exploitation of differences and conflicts among Confucian and Islamic states. He asks the United States to establish interest allies in Chinese inland, both top and low level governments. He insists that American officials, politicians and merchants go to local places and learn about their policy, culture and way of thinking. (Bergsten 2008: 85)

Halper's prescription is more detailed. Like Huntington, he proposes to prevent an Asian economic union through worsening the disputes between China, Japan, Pakistan and India. He calls for the use of China's internal problems, especially ethnic separatist trends, to disintegrate China. As for the United States, he recommends energy saving and independence, and investment incentive. Most importantly, he proposes more funding and larger development programs for domestic infrastructure, R&D, skilled workforces, and the education of students in key areas of high-tech and engineering sectors. In his view, the United States could kill two birds with one stone and transfer some of the money used to subsidize agriculture into subsidizing education. (Halper 2010: 240) Halper's proposal reminds us of how America succeeded in leaving Japan behind in the 1980s through computing and internet technological revolution.

In addition, Halper asks the United States to learn from China on how to interact with African countries. He suggests that the States loosens its requirements on loans and support to African countries, helps construct their infrastructures, and acknowledges their special circumstances. He recommends establishing America-African Summit, and opening American market to African countries to compete with China for influence and resources. He also calls for American leaders to treat leaders from small countries with enough respect and increase American popularity around the world. (Halper 2010: 233–235)

Besides the aforesaid proposals, other scholars make bold predictions to enhance the threat from China. Naill predicts that within the decade (from December 2010), China will overtake the United States in terms of gross domestic product just as (in 1963) Japan overtook the United Kingdom. (Ferguson 2010: Preface) Halper observes, unless China and India suffer outbreaks of serious military conflagration or a calamitous domestic crisis, they will become the world's largest economies in the middle of this century. (Halper 2010: 41) Martin Jacques and others believe that China will reshape the world order with its Confucian tradition. (Jacques 2009: 318; Bergsten 2008: 12; Leonard 2008: 115)In response to scholars' proposals, American government loses no time to shift its military focus to East Asia, strengthening its containment of China, for Americans try to dissuade any potential adversary (now China) from pursuing a military build-up in hopes of surpassing, or equaling, the power of the United States. It fears that China will rapidly modernize its military along with its economic success, challenges American hegemony and affects American interests around the globe.

Facing American containment, China's response will be unpredictable. However, whether a war breaks out will depend on the patience and reasonable judgment of the two sides. On the one hand, if China's economic prosperity causes America's economic downturn or becomes an obstacle of the development of American economy, then the United States may act like Great Britain in 1800s who destroyed China's economy with coercive opium-selling. On the other hand, if China cannot tolerate American containment just as Germany could not tolerate British containment in 1909, a war may happen, too. Anyway, China should prepare for the worst measures that America may take in terms of the French thinker de Tocqueville's word. After a visit to America, the French thinker once said in 1835, "If we reason from what passes in the world, we should almost say that the European is to the other races of mankind what man himself is to the lower animals: he makes them subservient to his use, and when he cannot subdue he destroys them." (Darwin2008: 24) Then the American white colonizers soon put into practice of his words in the liquidation of American Indians. In fact, after the United States becomes the superpower, it has been doing its best to wipe out any challenger to its hegemony and global interest. Japan is America's loyal and subservient ally, but America destroyed its economy through an appreciation of yen when Japanese economy showed the sign to surpass America's in 1980s. When Saddam Hussein and

Muammar Gaddafi challenged America's hegemony, they were annihilated without the authorization of the United Nations. All these events demonstrate that the United States will waste no time when an opportunity comes to defeat its opponent.

However, America seems to show extremely tolerant to China's rise. The reasons may be: (1) China and America have formed "Chimerica", coined by Moritz Schularick and Naill Ferguson, a relationship between parsimonious China and profligate America. (Ferguson 2010: preface) If Chinese start selling US Treasury bonds, or cease buying them, the dollar will plummet and so will the value of their dollar assets. (Jacques 2009: 360) If the United States attacks China and China do sell US Treasury bonds, the global dollar system will collapse and the US hegemony will end soon. To some degree, the two countries now enter into a symbiotic relationship. (2) China has done its best to accommodate the United States around the world. On the issues on North Korea and Iran, China actively cooperated with the US; on Darfur and Myanmar, China also listened to the West's will. China also gradually appreciates RMB and lessens the pressure of US dollar. (3) China has adequate defensive force and can resist the US's attack. Moreover, China also has global strategic weapons to deter and take avenge of America's nuclear attack. All these factors may lead the two countries to sit down and negotiate plans for the future.

6. The Possibility of a Peaceful Dialogue

The "Chimerica" or symbiotic relationship makes a peaceful dialogue possible between China and the United States. However, to keep the dialogue peaceful, both sides should recognize the other's culture and value with a fair mind, too.

First, the West or American should give up their domineering manners developed since the colonial period, especially, the United States should respect its interlocutors, and adopt a cooperative manner instead of the argument, "only we can do this, and you cannot do this."(Leonard 2008: 93) As the West are so used to the world being Western, even American, as Martin Jacques observes, it will be very difficult for the West to condescend in their dialogue with other people. But difficulty does not mean impossibility. Just as the 1900s White Americans could not accept to be equal with black people, their descendants changed their mind and elected a black man their president in 2008. Also, from Qianlong Emperor's letter to King George III, the 1700s Chinese did not acknowledged any valuable things from barbarians, but after being defeated, their descendants completely accept Western science and technology. Even for Euro-Americans, their mindset of dominance is a recent phenomenon, too. During the Renaissance, many great Western thinkers, such as Kant, Leibniz and Voltaire, highly acknowledged the good points of Chinese culture and hoped to complement the Western tradition with it. Therefore, Euro-Americans should truly accept "the other" and acknowledge the existence of alternatives for human development. Otherwise, it will bring about conflicts and harms to all human beings if, as Mahbubani says, some people believe that Western civilization represents the apex of human civilization, and that any alternative would portend a new dark age. (Mahbubani 2008: 125)

Along with giving up their domineering manners, the West or Americans should abandon their double standard when dealing with problems of human rights in the developing countries. As Ron Wheeler critically points out, Western states are seldom targeted in the United Nations Commission resolutions and that none has been targeted for domestic human rights violations of any kind. In fact, the West or Americans have turned the Commission into a "court" where they put developing countries on trial. (Wheeler: 1999) In the case of China, the US and other Western powers should correct their partiality to gross violations of human rights occurring in their allies, such as Burundi, Colombia, Nigeria, Uganda, India, Saudi Arabia, and countless other countries, and yet are quick to criticize China even though most Chinese enjoy more extensive freedoms and a better standard of living than ever before. (Peerenboom2007: 164) In Peerenboom's view, both sides will need to be more self-critical about their own shortcomings with respect to human rights. (Peerenboom 2007: 277)

Second, Chinese people should step out of their sense of "being humiliated" or sense of inferiority. Since the defeat of Opium War, Chinese people, from top to low, lost their orientation. Gradually, they not only accepted the superiority of Western science and technology, but also started doubting the values of their own culture, especially Confucianism. To some degree, since the time of Self-Strengthening Movement, all Chinese leaders have taken learning and importing Western technology as their first concern. Among common Chinese, Western society represents order, wealth and superiority. This has been demonstrated by the never-fading wave of studying abroad among Chinese students, especially in Western Europe and North America. If Chinese starts a dialogue with Euro-Americans with such a mindset of worshipping the West, the tone and character of the talk will be tilted to the West, and the outcome will not be constructive.

However, despite Chinese worship of Western technology and wealth, Chinese as a nation never loses its confidence in its own culture. To some degree, from the time of Self-Strengthening Movement, Chinese people always followed the road of "Chinese values as the substance, while western learning as the practical use" (Marxism also becomes sinicized through Mao Zedong and Liu Shaoqi's interpretations). After China becomes more successful in its economic and diplomatic policies, Chinese people's openness to Western culture becomes a valuable asset from its period of humiliation. Just as Paul A. Cohen observes, "Western people stepped in the 1700s Chinese' old way, when the representatives of all other great cultures have been compelled to take fundamental stock of our own culture, deliberately dismantle large portions of it, and put it back together again in order to survive. Never have Westerners had to take other peoples' views of us really seriously." (Jacques 2009: 100) Therefore, it is predictable that the future of Chinese culture will be a hybrid of Chinese and Western culture, just as Neo-Confucianism is a mix of Confucianism and Buddhism. Chinese people will have the wisdom and confidence to manage a peaceful dialogue with the Americans.

In addition, other factors also force America to concede more room and power to the rest of the world. Euro-Americans get dominance through the technology and wealth generated from Industrial Revolution. However, by the 21st century, wealth is shifting to the rest of the world. Shanghai, Mumbai, Dubai and others become new centers of wealth, and the monopoly of wealth by the West has been further weakened by the 2008 financial crisis. At the same time, science and technology are viewed to be separated from Western culture and are believed to be able to grow prosperously in other cultures, and most countries provide scientists and engineers great academic freedom and facilities. The blockade of technology diffusion becomes less and less efficient. Although the United States is spending billions on military upgrade, its new technology can be soon copied or easily cracked. To maintain a dominant and unchallengeable force will become more and more unsustainable. Therefore, a practical option for the United States will be no better than peaceful negotiation.

References:

Bergsten, C. Fred (et al.)(2008): *China's Rise: Challenges and Opportunities*, Washington, DC: Peterson Institute for International Economics: Center for Strategic and International Studies, p. 269.

Cohen, Paul (1984): *Discovering History in China: American Historical Writing on the Recent Chinese Past*, New York: Columbia University Press, p. 296.

Darwin, John (2008): *After Tamerlane: The Global History of Empire since 1405*, New York: Bloomsbury Press: Distributed to the trade by Macmillan, 1st, p. 574.

Ferguson, Niall (2010): *Civilization: The West and Rest*, New York: the Penguin Press, p. 402.

Halper, Stefan (2010): *The Beijing Consensus: How China's Authoritarian Model Will Dominate the Twenty-first Century*, New York: Basic Books, p. 296.

Huntington, Samuel P. (1993): The Clash of Civilizations?, *Foreign Affairs,* 72.3, pp. 22+.

Hungtington, Samuel P. (1996): *The Clash of Civilizations and the Remaking of World Order*, New York: Simon and Schuster Paperbacks.

Jacques, Martin (2009): *When China Rules the World: The Rise of The Middle Kingdom and the End of the Western World,* London: Allen Lane, p. 550.

Kristof, Nicholas D. (1993): "The Rise of China", *Foreign Affairs,* 72.5, pp. 59+.

Leonard, Mark (2008): *What does China think?*, London: Fourth Estate, p. 164.

Mahbubani, Kishore (2008): *The New Asian Hemisphere: the Irresistible Shift of Global Power to the East*, New York: Public Affairs, p. 314.

Meng, Peiyuan: *My Exploration in Chinese Philosophy*《我的中国哲学研究之路》, http://www.confuchina.com/xuezhe%20wenji/meng%20peiyuan.htm.

Peerenboom, Randall (2007): China Modernizes: Threat to the West or Model for the Rest? Oxford, New York: Oxford University Press, p. 406.

Pohl, Karl Heinz: *Ethics for the 21st Century—The Confucian Tradition*, http://www.uni-trier.de/fileadmin/fb2/SIN/Pohl_Publikation/ethics_for_the_21st_century.pdf.

Wheeler, Ron (1999): The United Nations Commission on Human Rights, 1982–

1997: A Study of 'Targeted' Resolutions, *Canadian Journal of Political Science,* 32:75.

Zakaria, Fareed (2011): *The Post-American World: Release 2.0*, New York: W. W. Norton & Co., Updated and expanded ed., p. 314.

Tan Mingran earned his Ph.D. degrees from Peking University and University of Toronto, and currently is Associate Professor of Philosophy at Shandong University; his recent research areas include Chinese philosophy and comparative philosophy.

The Eastern World's Endeavor: Nishan Forum on World Civilizations

Gao Shuqun

Nishan Forum on World Civilizations ("Nishan Forum" for short) was initiated in 2008 by Xu Jialu, Vice Chairman of the 9th and 10th NPC Standing Committee. Its purpose is to fulfill the spirit of the resolutions of the United Nations on dialogue among civilizations, make efforts to carry out the world's civilization dialogue in the hometown of Confucius, maintain the world's cultural diversity, and promote the building of a harmonious world. According to Xu Jialu, the establishment of a forum on world civilizations in Nishan aims to inherit the spirit of Confucius such as "Harmony is the most precious", "Harmony without uniformity" and "If three of us are walking together, at least one of the other two is good enough to be my teacher", and enhance mutual respect, understanding, tolerance and harmony among civilizations by promoting civilization dialogues. As the birthplace of Confucius, Nishan was originally named Niqiu Mountain and later was renamed Nishan to avoid offending Confucius' personal name - Qiu. As recorded in the *Records of the Grand Historian*, "Confucius' parents went to pray at Nishan and gave birth to Confucius afterwards." Located in Tai - Yi Mountain region in southeast of Mount Tai, Nishan is a remaining branch in the westward extension of Tai - Yi Mountains. The open Qufu Plain lies to the west of Nishan. Before the age of three, Confucius lived with his parents in Luyuan Village, a village at the southern foot of Nishan. Luyuan Village was regarded by later Confucianists as the original hometown of Confucius. When Confucius was three, his father died and his mother took him to leave Luyuan Village and move to Queli. Queli is the world - famous hometown of Confucius. After his death, Confucius was buried on the south bank of Sihe River in north of Lu State, which is the present Confucius Cemetery. His old house in Queli was the earliest place for worshipping Confucius, and on this basis, was expanded to the Confucius Temple. In order to worship Confucius in Nishan, later generations named the small cave where Confucius was born as Confucius Cave to be protected. In addition, Confucius Temple and Nishan Academy were built at the eastern slope of Nishan as dedicated venues for people to worship Confucius and inherit his doctrines. For thousands of years, Nishan, Qufu Confucius Temple and Qufu Confucius Cemetery have been called the three holy lands of Confucianism, attracting numerous people to come here to pay homage to Confucius every year. In 2007, 100 Confucian masters jointly established an ancient-style academy in the woods at the eastern foot of Nishan, i.e. Nishan Shengyuan College, with Mou Zhongjian as the first president, Tu Weiming as the first honorary president and Xu Jialu as the first senior adviser. This College is the permanent venue of Nishan Forum on World Civilizations.

1. Organizational Structure and Preliminary Work of Nishan Forum

Nishan Forum is a non-governmental platform. Under the leadership of Xu Jialu, Nishan Forum was jointly initiated by its permanent host organizations, namely Nishan Forum Organizing Committee, Chinese People's Institute of Foreign Affairs, United Nations Association of China, China Association for International Friendly Contact, China Religious Culture Communication Association, Confucius Institute Headquarters, Shandong University, Renmin University of China, Beijing Normal University, and Institute of Chinese Culture. Xu Jialu acts as the president of Nishan Form Organizing Committee. Vice presidents include Xing Bensi, Li Zhaoxing, Zhao Qizheng, Ye Xiaowen, Ru Xin, Wu Jianmin, Chen Jian, Hu Zhanfan, Liu Changle, Yang Wenchang, Xu Lin, Master Xue Cheng (Buddhism), Zhang Jiyu (Taoism), Ji Baocheng, Liu Chuansheng, Zhong Binglin, Zhu Zhengchang, Xu Xianming and Chen Qiutu. Xu Xianghong serves as secretary-general, and Xing Bensi and Pang Pu as directors of the Academic Committee. Academic research bases are the Advanced Institute for Confucian Studies and the Center for Judaic and Inter-Religious Studies of Shandong University, Institute for Advanced Study of the Humanities and Religion of Beijing Normal University, and Institute of Religious Studies of Renmin University of China. Chinese National Commission for UNESCO is the forum's guiding organization, and Phoenix TV, China News Service, Guangming Daily and Shandong Satellite TV are strategic cooperative organizations. From the above-mentioned organizational structure, Nishan Forum is actually a free association for dialogue among civilizations, and such dialogue is exactly a bond linking all people.

Nishan Forum is distinctly academic, non-governmental and open. More strictly speaking, it is a forum on ideology, philosophy and art. By more focusing on ideological, academic or even artistic perspectives, Nishan Forum provides a family-like harmonious dialogue scenario for the communication and understanding among different civilizations: Sitting in the courtyard at the hometown of Confucius, people can enjoy wonderful music, exchange their respective knowledge of classics, understanding of the world, perceptions of life and imagination of the future. The reason that Nishan Forum has been set in Nishan Valley, an open field far away modern urban communities, rather than in those bustling cities, is the pursuit of the spirit of returning to human's original nature. President Xu Jialu said this may help different civilizations jointly reflect on and solve the common problems faced by the human beings. Nishan Forum has been designed to be held in Nishan every two years, which is called forums in even-numbered years. Between two forums, Nishan Forum organizes a variety of activities in different parts of the world, which is called activities in odd-numbered years. The purpose is to shorten the distance between Nishan Forum and the world, and promote friendly exchanges among different civilizations. The ethical rule of Nishan Forum is "Harmony without uniformity" and "What you do not wish for yourself, do not do to others".

In order to help Nishan Forum run well, President Xu Jialu made some preliminary attempts in organizing dialogues. He also took the opportunity of visiting abroad and meeting with foreign guests, and asked for advices from people around the world so as to find out how to organize Nishan Forum smoothly. Later, all these activities were collected into *For World Peace,* a book published by Hua Yi Publishing House in September 2010. The title of the book reflects his inner voice to promote civilization dialogues, which can be regarded as his popular expression of the purpose of Nishan Forum. In January 2009, he went to Los Angeles to have a sincere and friendly conversation with Robert H. Schuller, the founder of Crystal Cathedral. They felt like old friends at their first meeting, and became sincere friends. Invited by Xu Jialu to attend the first Nishan Forum, Dr. Schuller accepted the invitation and fulfilled his promise. In September 2010, although his physical condition was very bad and doctors advised him not to come to China, Dr. Schuller insisted on coming to Nishan, and a chair was specially prepared for him during his speech. When speaking in Los Angeles, Xu Jialu said: "Standing on the rostrum of this transparent Crystal Cathedral, I feel I have no restraint and depression as if I am in the embrace of nature. The warm sunshine sprinkles on each corner and on each person's body and mind, purifying everyone's minds." He further stated, "Chinese and Western cultures have differences. I believe that these differences should not constitute a barrier to the harmony between us. On the contrary, such differences should be a driving force for us to promote communication and exchange. China and the United States are just on the opposite sides of the earth. If we would not communicate, it is hard for us to understand each other." [1] His speech received prolonged applause. Through his speech, we can understand why President Xu Jialu initiated Nishan Forum.

The team of Nishan Forum Organizing Committee includes avant-garde figures involving in dialogue among civilizations. For example, Ru Xin, Former Vice President of Chinese Academy of Social Sciences, is one of the earliest Chinese scholars who participated in the world's dialogue among civilizations. Before the US 911 events, Ru Xin was invited to attend a number of important international conferences on dialogue among civilizations. However, according to his introduction, Chinese scholars have very weak voice in the international academic field. Another example is Zhao Qizheng, Former Director of the State Council Information Office. He once had the famous "Riverside Talks" with Dr. Luis Palau, an American religious leader. Ye Xiaowen, who previously served as the director-general of State Administration for Religious Affairs for 14 years, is a scholar-oriented official. In addition, Former Foreign Minister Li Zhao Xing, Chen Jian, Former Under-Secretary-General of the United Nations, and Former Chinese Ambassador to France Wu Jianmin have rich experience

---

①   Xu Jialu: *For World Peace*, Hua Yi Publishing House, September 2010, Edition 1, pp. 9–11.

in international exchanges and have better understandings of Western culture and the situation of different civilizations. Master Xue Cheng, Vice President of the Buddhist Association of China, and Zhang Jiyu, Vice President of Chinese Taoist Association, are representatives of China's religious communities. Known as "Justice of the Peace", Phoenix TV's President Liu Changle has been active on the media and cultural stage around the world. Xu Lin is a cultural ambassador engaged in communicating with the world through Chinese language. Nishan Forum Organizing Committee is an expert team with rich experience in international exchange and civilization dialogue. They work together to promote the dialogue and exchange among world civilizations, demonstrating the wish of Chinese people to get peace and resolve human crises.

2. Nishan Forum Creates a New Situation of Dialogue among Civilizations

In 2010, Xu Jialu began to lead the team of Nishan Forum to officially get on the stage of civilization dialogue. To this end, he made a profound decision. On May 17, just before the United Nations' World Day for Cultural Diversity for Dialogue and Development (referred to as the World Day for Dialogue among Civilizations) on May 21, a senior academic symposium, celebrating the World Day for Dialogue among Civilizations, was held by Nishan Forum Organizing Committee in Beijing.[①] His idea is to first organize an enlightenment activity to help Chinese people learn more about this global festival. 12 cultural masters were invited to attend the meeting and deliver their speeches. Nishan Forum Organizing Committee also invited Guangming Daily to co-host the symposium. At the meeting, Xu Jialu made an important speech titled "A Long-Term Game and A Great Task", unequivocally elaborating

---

① In 2002, the United Nations General Assembly passed a resolution that declared every May 21 to be the "World Day for Cultural Diversity for Dialogue and Development", which was also referred to as the "World Day for Dialogue among Civilizations" or the "World Day for Cultural Development". Since then, UNESCO holds activities every year for celebrating the festival, but activities organized by non-governmental organizations are very rare. In China, this international festival even has not fully entered the view of the public.

the perception and proposition of civilization dialogue. He said, "Dialogue among civilizations is a product of the game between two kinds of propositions and trends, namely the unification and diversification of the world's civilizations." After in-depth explanation, he said: "Today, civilization dialogue is a reflection of human conscience and kindness, while arrogance, obstinacy, superiority and intolerance are in essence an embodiment of human evil. The duty for dialogue among civilizations is to awaken the ancient aspiration and wisdom of mankind, analyze the situation at present, try to make use of the necessary conditions for human happiness and peace so as to effectively curb or even eliminate evil, and prepare the sufficient conditions for human happiness and peace."[1] Xu Jialu also expounded on the active participation of Chinese civilization in dialogue among world civilizations. His speech, together with the lectures of other scholars, was published by Guangming Daily and specially titled "The World Day for Dialogue among Civilizations - Voices from China" by Liang Shu, Chief Editor of the Chinese Classic Culture section of Guangming Daily. This was the beginning for Nishan Forum to send out its voice. On August 26, a press conference of the first Nishan Forum was held by Nishan Forum Organizing Committee at the News Conference Hall of the State Council Information Office. Vice presidents Zhao Qizheng, Ye Xiaowen and Wu Jianmin as well as Executive Director Huang Xingyuan and Secretary–General Xu Xianghong were invited to attend the conference. It was the first appearance of Nishan Forum to domestic and foreign media, attracting their great attention.

At 9:00 am, September 26, 2010, the opening ceremony of the first Nishan Forum was grandly held in sunny Nishan Valley. Thinkers, politicians, religionists, educators, artists, media reporters and other people from 13 countries and regions of Asia, Europe and America came together, presenting a spectacular gathering for dialogue among civilizations. Before the opening ceremony, the organizer invited the participants to visit Confucius Temple, Nishan Academy and Confucius Cave. Many participants had not visited Nishan before, and even a few of them did not know the existence of Nishan. So through the visit, they had more intuitive understandings of

---

[1] Secretariat of Nishan Forum: *The World Day for Dialogue among Civilizations - Voices from China*, China International Press, August 2010, Edition 1, pp. 10–12.

Nishan and Confucius. Before the opening ceremony, an inauguration ceremony of the Monument of Nishan Forum on World Civilizations was held in the square of Nishan Shengyuan College, which was presided over by Xu Lin and unveiled by Xu Jialu and Chinese famous calligrapher-Ouyang Zhongshi.[①] The opening ceremony of the first Nishan Forum began with Chinese folk music performance.[②] The brilliant performances by Shangdong Song and Dance Ensemble and Shandong Elderly Chorus made the participants forget their fatigue after journey and the differences between each other. They were all immersed in the world of music. After the music performance, Wu Jianmin presided over the opening ceremony. At the beginning, Chen Jian, Former Under-Secretary-General of the United Nations, read the congratulatory messages from Former French President Jacques Chirac and Sha Zukang, Under-Secretary-General of the United Nations. Mr. Chirac expressed in his congratulatory letter, "Current world faces the rising nationalism and the weakening characteristics of various countries. I am very glad to see China host a forum for dialogue among civilizations." "Current world is suffering from much unrest. Under this situation, China's wisdom and pursuit of harmony are beneficial. The Nishan Forum draws inspiration from Confucius. Confucius told us: without respect for diversity, we cannot pursue harmony. This thought points out the way to go for us." Then, Ms. Qin Lan, Official of UNESCO, read the congratulatory message from Director-General of UNESCO Irina Bokova. Ms. Bokova said in her letter, "As we all know, about 500 years after the death of the great Chinese thinker Confucius, Confucianism deeply

---

① *The Monument of Nishan Forum on World Civilizations* was composed by Xu Jialu, handwritten by Ouyang Zhongshi, produced by the craftsmen of Sishui County, and supervised by Chen Hongfu, standing behind the front gate of Nishan Shengyuan College. This reflects an idea of Nishan Forum Organizing Committee, i.e. from the first one, each Nishan Forum would leave some tangible cultural heritage at the forum venue, recording every major event about "dialogue among civilizations" which takes place at the site.

② Chinese folk musician Liu Wenjin was invited by Nishan Forum Organizing Committee to create "Nishan Carol" and "Ode to Confucius". At the performance, he personally acted as a conductor. The show participated by nearly 100 performers made the audience get completely immersed, and thus achieved great success. American Scholar John Berthrong said he was so honored to hear such wonderful music in Nishan. When someone mentioned that Confucius was also a famous musician, many people expressed their praise sincerely.

influenced the emergence of Christianity. In fact, both Confucianism and Christianity advocate the doctrine of the mean and mutually beneficial ethics. Meanwhile, both of them advocate harmonious coexistence of people in the world. The idea of 'Harmony without uniformity' is completely consistent with the main task of UNESCO, i.e. ensuring the protection and dissemination of different cultures. I sincerely hope this forum will achieve fruitful results. Meanwhile, I also hope this forum will exert far more extensive and profound influence than Confucius' birthplace Qufu." Afterwards, Former Indonesian President Megawati Sukarnoputri, Former Hungarian Prime Minister Megyessy Peter, and famous Confucian scholar Tu Weiming delivered their speeches. Finally, Xu Jialu addressed the participants on behalf of Nishan Forum Organizing Committee. After the opening ceremony, the first dialogue between Xu Jialu and Robert H. Schuller was presided over by Zhao Qizheng, and was sincere and enthusiastic. This is a historical dialogue between Confucianism and Christianity, thus creating a precedent.

The theme of the first Nishan Forum was "Harmony without uniformity and the Harmonious World-Dialogue between Confucian Civilization and Christian Civilization". Within two days, a total of 18 dialogues were held, some of which were demanded by the scholars themselves. The dialogues were conducted in various forms, such as academic symposiums, one-to-one or two-to-two dialogue, and a TV forum by Phoenix TV. On the evening of September 26, a freestyle dialogue with the theme of "Confucius and Jesus Christ" was particularly held. American pastor Henry Holley said, "I have great respect for Confucius, but I do not believe in Confucianism, because my religion is Christianity. We discussed love, tolerance, friendship and courtesy together and I am very pleased to have the opportunity to participate in these discussions." Scholars enjoyed such dialogues. Another favorite scenario for scholars was that a dialogue was held on the lawn in front of the quaint Nishan Academy, with two chairs for two persons to sit and open talks. At this site, Tu Weiming discussed with Iain Torrance, an American theologian, for up to 2.5 hours. Mr. Torrance said, "China is a civilization of tolerance and also a civilization of dialogue. I think that by learning from Confucianism, I can become a better Christ-follower." The first Forum was concluded on September 27, passing the world's first "Declaration of Human Harmony". Xu Jialu addressed the closing ceremony, "The participants highly valued the slogan of this forum: Charity, Integrity, Tolerance and Harmony. Confucian and Christian civilizations are the two most influential civilizations in the world. Holding dialogues and exchanges between the two major civilizations is both meaningful and pressing. In future, further communication and understanding should be pursued to establish a new relationship, in which the two civilizations will respect, admire and accommodate each other on a new basis." Finally, he emphasized, "I hope the voice in favor of dialogues and against conflicts can become the strongest one in our time! I hope the light of human wisdom will penetrate through the mist of material and greed of humanity itself and allow humanity see the blue sky!"

The First Nishan Forum was just followed by the National Day holiday, during which the number of tourists to Nishan rose by five times than the same period of the previous year.

Held in Nishan on May 21–23, 2012, [①] the Second Nishan Forum continued the "Dialogue between Confucian Civilization and Christian Civilization" and set its theme as "Belief, Morality, Respect, Solidarity". Compared to the First Nishan Forum, the second one presented some new ideas:

(1) Grandly celebrating the World Day for Dialogue among Civilizations. Its 10th anniversary (2002–2012) was on May 21, 2012. Therefore, Nishan Forum Organizing Committee made a careful preparation. Firstly, the Organizing Committee invited UNESCO and the United Nations Alliance of Civilizations to co-host the event and got their enthusiastic response. Director-General of UNESCO originally planned to attend, but due to other business later, appointed Assistant Director-General Hans d'Orvile to attend. The United Nations Alliance of Civilizations sent Senior Advisor Jean-Christophe Bas, together with two of its ambassadors-Candido Mendes and Pan Guang, to participate in. Secondly, Nishan Forum Organizing Committee and Shandong Province specially produced a "Quadrate Ding Engraved with Dialogues

---

① This is an arrangement specially made for the World Day for Dialogue among Civilizations. From the second forum, Nishan Forum has been and will be held at this fixed time. President Xu Jialu said that this is not only the best response to the United Nations' advocacy of inter-civilization dialogue but also the best way to celebrate the World Day for Dialogue among Civilizations, the purpose of which is to let everyone remember the date.

among Civilizations" [①] for commemorating the 10th anniversary of the United Nations' World Day for Dialogue among Civilizations. The Ding was installed on the same day of the opening ceremony. Domestic and foreign guests attending the grand installation ceremony included President Xu Jialu; Li Xiaojie, Vice Minister of the Ministry of Culture and Director General of State Administration of Cultural Heritage; Shandong Governor Jiang Daming; Vicente Fox Quesada, Former Mexican President; Hans d'Orville, Assistant Director-General of UNESCO; and Jean-Christophe Bas, Senior Advisor of the United Nations Alliance of Civilizations. At the ceremony, the activity "Do One Thing for Diversity and Inclusion" was launched. [②] Thirdly, a series of academic activities were organized, including the international seminar for the group writing this report. All participants jointly reviewed and summarized the practices and experience in the past decade of the world's dialogue among civilizations, and looked forward to the development trends for the next ten years of such dialogue. This made Nishan and Nishan Forum more closely connect to the United Nations and the world's civilization dialogue, and enhanced the sense of responsibility of various civilizations that participate in dialogue. During the forum, Nishan Forum Organizing Committee organized working talks with UNESCO and the United Nations Alliance of Civilizations respectively, making in-depth discussions on future cooperation and reaching consensus in many aspects.

(2) Holding the "International Doctoral Candidate Forum" for the first time. This

---

① "Quadrate Ding Engraved with Dialogues among World Civilizations" was designed and produced by Lou Jiaben, Professor of China Central Academy of Fine Arts. The Ding takes the shape of ancient Chinese square bronze ware. Its pattern fully embodies the spirit of the world's cultural diversity and expresses the harmony between man and nature. The two doves of peace on the Ding's ears symbolize the spirit of peace and harmony of inter-civilization dialogue. The text on the front of the Ding is "Celebrating the 10th Anniversary of the United Nations' World Day for Cultural Diversity for Dialogue and Development", and that on the back is the abstract of "Declaration on Human Harmony". Shangdong young artist Yin Ming participated in the design work. Sishui County and Nishan Shengyuan College provided full support for the design, production and placement of the Ding.

② "Do One Thing for Diversity and Inclusion" is a global campaign initiated by the United Nations Alliance of Civilizations. Nishan Forum Organizing Committee actively responded and participated in. For this purpose, the organizing committee conducted campus interviews in some of Shandong universities, and sent interview images directly to the website designated by the United Nations Alliance of Civilizations for global browsing.

was a pioneering work of the Second Nishan Forum. President Xu Jialu highly valued the participation of youths in dialogue among civilizations. Earlier, the United Nations Secretary-General Ban Ki-moon specially made a statement to point out that it was the time for young people to move towards the stage of civilization dialogue. Nishan Forum took the lead in response, commissioning the Advanced Institute for Confucian Studies of Shandong University and the Institute for Advanced Study of the Humanities and Religion of Beijing Normal University to be responsible for this work. Students from various places were encouraged to apply. More than 20 American students came at their own expense to attend. After being informed of this event, John Chiang Hsiao-yen, Vice Chairman of the Kuomingtong Party, specially came from Taiwan to attend this International Doctoral Candidate Sub-Forum. Those young doctoral candidates submitted high-quality articles and conducted active discussions, which became a major highlight of the forum. At the closing ceremony, two young representatives read on the rostrum the declaration drafted by them and passed based on democracy-"Proposal for Youth Marching to the Front Stage of Dialogue among World Civilizations". It was the first proposal in the world representing the participation of young people in civilization dialogue, which was of milestone significance in the history of civilization dialogue.

(3) Holding the "International Seminar on Protecting Cultural Heritage and Promoting Civilization dialogue for Ancient Civilizations of the World" for the first time. It is an activity co-hosted by Nishan Forum Organizing Committee, State Administration of Cultural Heritage, and Shandong Provincial Bureau of Cultural Heritage. Civilization dialogue is closely related to ancient civilizations. Ancient civilizations were significant places for creating and feeding human civilization, and were the origins of major civilizations in the modern world. Ancient civilizations have not only non-renewable ancient cultural heritages but also rich historical experience in the development of civilization, accumulating historical wisdom for civilizations to experience and resolve tribulations. Ancient civilizations have an important say in today's civilization dialogue. In many aspects, the development of modern civilizations has been achieved at the cost of ancient cultural heritages. In many countries and regions, numerous tangible and intangible cultural heritages have been ruined because of wars, conflicts or even hunger, and this kind of tragedy still happens around the

world almost every day. Most of ancient civilizations are developing countries. They are the weaker in the family of the world's civilizations, and thus need more protection and more international solidarity and cooperation. As an attempt, this seminar on ancient civilizations seemed hurried and imperfect in many aspects due to late preparation. Nevertheless, the activity received positive response from the experts and scholars of most ancient civilized countries. In particular, the embassies of these countries in China gave strong support. In order to compensate for the unavailability to invite relevant organizations and personnel because of insufficient time, the activity "Foreign Ambassadors and Envoys to Cultural Heritage Site of Confucius and Mencius" was organized with the support of embassies of these countries, making this event more meaningful. The seminar on ancient civilizations was held as scheduled. Moreover, with the support of CCTV, a TV forum was produced by Shandong Satellite TV and presided over by a CCTV's leading presenter. To be particularly important, this event received positive affirmation from UNESCO. Assistant Director-General Hans d'Orville specially attended and addressed the seminar. Many top experts in the heritage sector of the world participated in the seminar and made their speeches. After the seminar, the "Nishan Consensus: Protecting Cultural Heritage and Promoting Civilization dialogue for Ancient Civilizations of the World" was announced. In addition, the commencement ceremony for 88 key heritage protection projects of Shandong Province was held. This is the first time for the world's ancient civilizations to come together due to inter-cultural dialogue.

In terms of scale, level and representativeness, the Second Nishan Forum was far more beyond the first one: the whole event lasted three days; participants came from 22 countries and regions in five continents; dialogue-based activities numbered 52; participants were from various sectors and fields; and 11,600 person-times of participants attended as nonvoting delegates and listeners. Participating foreign scholars included: Martin Palmer, Senior Adviser on Belief and Environment to the United Nations Secretary-General Ban Ki-moon; Candido Mendes, President of International Social Science Committee; Fred Dallmayr, Executive Chairman of World Public Forum; Yersu Kim, Deputy Chairman of International Federation of Philosophical Societies; Henry Holley, Vice President of the Billy Graham Evangelistic Association; Valérie Terranova, Former Cultural Adviser of Former French President

Jacques Chirac; Darrol Bryant, Director of the Center for Dialogue and Spirituality in the World's Religions; Michael Kahn-Ackerman, Former Director of the Goethe-Institut in China; Olga Orive, President of the National Committee of ICOMOS Mexico; Francesco Caruso, Special Adviser of UNESCO; and Stewart J. Brown, Head of the School of Divinity at the University of Edinburgh. Former Mexican President Vicente Fox Quesada said, "The reason I traveled to China from far is that I hope to feel the thoughts of Confucius while sitting next to this wise man and in this beautiful environment at Nishan." "My greatest hope is that Nishan Forum will cross mountains and rivers and spread to every part of the world, helping people better understand each other through this forum." Fred Dallmayr, Executive Chairman of World Public Forum, stated, "I am very pleased to see that the concept of cross-cultural dialogue has taken roots in China, especially at Nishan Forum." "What makes me much happier is that the venue of Nishan Forum is adjacent to the birthplace of Confucius. It is the best site to hold a forum on world civilizations, because, in my mind, Confucius perfectly interprets what a civilization means." Famous American evangelical pastor Henry Holley said, "I am very honored, especially in my age of 85, to get an opportunity to speak again on Nishan Forum. The theme of this Forum is of great significance, which is related to the future of China and all the peoples in the world including the United States. I hope Nishan Forum will use its unique influence to bring peace and harmony to human society."

Another important experience of the Second Nishan Forum is to absorb the participation of local universities. The open organization of the forum allows all communities to get involved as much as possible. Shandong University, Qufu Normal University, Jining University and Nishan Shengyuan College have played a key role. Teachers and students actively took part and formed a large team of volunteers, including the beautiful scenery consisting of young students. Local farmers, workers and civil servants gathered around for watching. The forum organizing committee specially organized specific academic lectures, inviting renowned scholars to make reports for them. Shanghai Symphony Orchestra gave a free performance for participants. Shandong Friendship Publishing House held a special book exhibition and set up "Nishan Library" at the venue of Nishan Forum. The Second Nishan Forum demonstrated that, for dialogue among civilizations, what have been said is not so important. Only close emotional communication among people is most significant. On May 23, President Xu Jialu addressed the closing ceremony:

As the president, I cannot make a comprehensive, detailed and thorough summary of this forum. I can only use concise language to outline the basic situation of the past two days. The contents of this forum are richer and more diversified than the last one. Belief, religion, classics, cultural heritage protection, media, economy, enterprises, environmental protection, and healthcare became the topics of our speeches and dialogues, which involve various disciplines. However, we never digressed from the general theme - "Harmony without uniformity and the Harmonious World" and the subject of this forum - "Belief, Morality, Respect, Solidarity". This fact reminds us that any kind of culture is rich, complex, and the space for the dialogue among different people is infinitely vast. Therefore, the dialogue should be comprehensive and continuous.

The popularity of this forum is beyond my expectation. Old friends meet again and feel exceptionally happy, and new friends even wish they had known each other earlier. What can connect distant people together? I believe it is the love for humanity, the thinking of reality, and the confidence in rationality.

Over the past decade, wise men around the world, including many friends here, have made many efforts to appeal for cultural diversity and civilization dialogue. The result of continuous appealing is that the proposal of cultural uni-polarization in academia and university classrooms is getting weaker and weaker. However, we cannot stay in the stage to argue about what the dialogue among different civilizations "should" or "may" do. It seems that we should focus on "how" to go forward. That is to say, we should think about how different civilizations get well along with each other. In fact, this problem has been talked of in submitted articles and the dialogues during the forum. I recommend that our dialogues should be gradually deepened... For example, during the forum, Chinese and foreign scholars have put forward many suggestions on what problems should be discussed and how to discuss these problems. Here, I would like to present the following questions for your reference.

How to promote the dialogue among educational institutions and/or religious organizations in each country? At present, there have been discussions about such problems, but they seem to be more limited to information exchange among educational and religious organizations. Such dialogues have not gone deep into the levels on how countries provide the students and believers with whole-person education, the cultural motivation behind respective education and religion, and how education and religion deal with the world's current crises.

How to promote people-to-people dialogue? Travel and studying abroad are opportunities for extensive people-to-people contact. However, travel usually becomes a sightseeing tour, or including shopping. Students studying abroad mainly focus on the knowledge and skills in science, technology, economy and finance. The situation will be quite different if more and more tourists and students abroad pay attention to the culture, history, religions and relevant cultural phenomena of other countries, and more and more students abroad want to become scholars studying the culture of other countries. In such cases, public diplomacy will really become a reality. In an open country, everyone is a diplomat.

How to promote the dialogue among media? The dialogue in this field in particular needs to go beyond the scope of business and technology, calling a spade. Issues like press freedom and journalistic ethics can be the topic of dialogue.

How to promote barrier-free communication among different languages? The languages used in the field of technology are the easiest to translate. Once involving belief and morality, the degrees of difficulty are hard to imagine for ordinary people. Communication with barriers, which seems to be achieved, is in fact unsuccessful communication, because you may feel blocked when trying to understand the other's inner thoughts. This work needs the help of the scholars of all countries in philosophy, sociology, religious studies, literature and history etc. It is very important to promote the cooperation among relevant scholars in the research of this issue.

Finally, how to promote inter-governmental dialogue? As we all know, since ancient times, inter-governmental communication has been only limited to ongoing matters. Specific issues are discussed, but the culture behind them is always ignored. As a result, such issues easily get entangled and become hard to deal with. History has entered the 21st century, why can't we break through the convention and call on heads of all governments to become members of civilization dialogue?

What I have said might be seen as a "Utopian Fantasy" by some friends. I admit I am an idealist, but the human beings have exactly always been living in imagination and ideas. The "world of universal harmony" imagined by Chinese ancients and the "Utopian world" experimented by Fourier and Owen are still inspiring Chinese people. In Marinaleda Village in the Spanish autonomous region Andalusia, more than 3,000 villagers still happily live in a society constructed by the village head Juan Manuel Sánchez Gordillo according to Utopia. Compared to the imagination of future society by predecessors, the ideas about how different civilizations can achieve harmonious coexistence seem like a little thing and an example. I cite these examples just for explanation. I firmly believe that only if people make face-to-face communication, talking about issues and their inner thoughts, a real communication in the strict sense can be achieved, and therefore people can completely understand and get well along with each other. This is applicable to the relationship within a family, among ethnic groups or among countries.

After the Second Nishan Forum, the World Public Forum invited Nishan Forum Organizing Committee to attend the Rhodes Forum held in Greece on October 3–7, 2012. Vice President Liu Changle attended and delivered a speech on behalf of Nishan Forum. The United Nations Alliance of Civilizations also invited the organizing committee to attend the Asia-South Pacific Consultations convened in Shanghai on November 29–30, 2012. Gao Shuqun attended on behalf of Nishan Forum and made a speech on behalf of the Chinese mainland, putting forward specific suggestions on the civilization dialogue in Nishan by Nishan Forum Organizing Committee and the United Nations Alliance of Civilizations.

3. Nishan Forum Enters the United Nations Headquarters

At the invitation of UNESCO, Paris-Nishan Forum on World Civilizations was held at UNESCO Headquarters in Paris, France on April 16, 2012. [①] The event was co-hosted by Confucius Institute Headquarters and UNESCO, with the theme of "Confucianism and New Humanism in a Globalized World". More than 200 guests attending the Forum included senior officials, experts and scholars from France, Germany, Britain, the US, Spain, Bulgaria, Hungary, Tunisia, Sri Lanka, Mali and other countries, diplomats and officials of all countries to UNESCO, as well as personnel from French academic and educational circles. Irina Bokova, Director-General of UNESCO, stressed in her opening speech, "Globalization makes human relations closer than ever before. Globalization is not only economic integration but also cultural fusion, and cultural fusion requires the support of new humanism. Reconsidering the relations between countries or between man and nature by using the thoughts of Confucius should be one of the important connotations of new humanism. Today, it is of great significance to discuss Confucianism and new humanism in UNESCO Headquarters. A new world needs new humanism, which will promote the progress of the world." Former French Prime Minister Jean-Pierre Raffarin said, "The relation of Confuciansim and new humanism is not just a philosophical proposition but also a political issue. Only mutual respect between people can achieve balance and harmony. The thoughts of Confucius are of modernity, which can constitute the core of new humanism. And human beings need a kind of new humanism with a broader sense."

---

① As Former Chinese Ambassador to France, Wu Jianmin enjoys a high reputation in France and Europe. The convening of Paris-Nishan Forum was first of all due to his promotion. Meanwhile, Xu Bo, who was once an assistant of Wu Jianmin and now works for UNESCO as an assistant of Assistant Director-General Hans d'Orville, also made great efforts. Ms. Valérie Terranova, an old friend of Wu Jianmin in France and the Former Cultural Adviser of Former French President Jacques Chirac, played an important part in this event. It was her who first advised Nishan Forum Organizing Committee to hold an inter-civilization dialogue at UNESCO Headquarters. After Paris-Nishan Forum, Ms. Terranova was invited to attend the Second Nishan Forum and participated in the first dialogue together with Wu Jianmin. In the dialogue, she sincerely expressed that China has grown into an "elephant", and thus should not and cannot hide behind big trees any longer. Her vivid metaphor left a deep impression on other participants.

When delivering his speech, President Xu Jialu said, "As a concept promoting the emergence of industrialization and modern society, humanism has made a significant contribution to the progress of mankind. However, in recent 300 years of historical course, humanism has undergone metamorphosis or alienation. Freedom, equality and universal love have become quite different from what enlightenment thinkers expected in the past. The present facts prove that we need to think about the new humanism on the basis of historical experience, which may be necessary for human to heal mental trauma and may be the hope of the earth in future." Vice Presidents Wu Jianmin, Xu Lin and Secretary-General Xu Xianghong of Nishan Forum Organizing Committee, Zhou Hong, Director of the Institute of European Studies of Chinese Academy of Social Sciences, Cao Weidong, Vice President of Beijing Normal University, attended the forum and made speeches.Paris-Nisahn Forum was a huge success, presenting an unprecedentedly spectacular event. During the forum, permanent ambassadors and officials of more than 50 countries to UNESCO participated in the whole course. They showed their great interest and asked questions actively. The conference venue was full of audiences, some of whom had to stand. After the event concluded in the evening, many people still discussed with each other and would not leave. Confucius, Confucianism, "Harmony without uniformity" and "new humanism" became popular words for participants. After the forum, diplomatic envoys of Egypt, Hungary, Sri Lanka, Afghanistan, Benin, Pakistan, Iraq, Gabon, Denmark, Slovakia, Bulgaria, Portugal, Brazil, India and Honduras expressed their congratulations to the forum for its success. Vatican's permanent observer to UNESCO sent a letter to China's permanent mission, stating that "the forum gives an opportunity to listen to different viewpoints of countries from around the world on Confucianism and new humanism" and asking for the drafts of all speakers. Hans d'Orville, Assistant Director-General of UNESCO, said, "UNESCO Headquarters organizes many similar activities. But the activities that can attract such great concern are really rare. The theme of this forum advocates the world's cultural diversity, and integrates human history and reality. Chinese and foreign speakers have profound academic attainments and broad international vision. Their speeches were based on the combination of theory and practice, inspiring to the deep thinking of the problems and challenges faced by the world at present." Mr. Olabiyi Babalola Joseph Yai, Former Chairman of the Executive Board of UNESCO and Permanent Delegate of Benin to UNESCO, believed that, "What UNESCO needs most now is this kind of thought experiment. You may agree or disagree with speakers' points of view, but their questions and the resulting inspiration to people to think about these issues are extremely important." China's Permanent Delegate to UNESCO You Shaozhong said, "The successful convening of Paris-Nishan Forum fully demonstrates that, in today's complex, volatile and turbulent world, the international community pays more attention to the voices of emerging countries, especially that of China."

Paris-Nishan Forum opened a door for Nishan Forum to spread to Europe, America and the United Nations.

Invited by the United Nations Department of Economic and Social Affairs, New York-Nishan Forum on World Civilizations, with the theme of "Harmony Based on Shared Values-beyond National Identities and Beliefs: Dialogue between Confucianism and Christianity", was held at the United Nations Headquarters in New York on November 10–11, 2012. It was co-hosted by China Energy Fund Committee and the United Nations Department of Economic and Social Affairs, and presided over by Dr. Patrick Ho Chi-ping, Deputy Chairman and Secretary-General of China Energy Fund Committee.[①] During the two days, 5 academic dialogues and exchanges were organized, discussing issues like philosophy, religion and harmony and exploring the ways for dialogue and harmony among different civilizations. More than 100 guests attended the forum, including President Xu Jialu; Wu Hongbo, Under-Secretary-General of the United Nations; Vuk Jeremić, President of the United Nations General Assembly; Wang Min, Deputy Permanent Representative of China to the United Nations; Sun Guoxiang, Chinese Consulate General in New York; Theodore McCarrick, Former Chairman of the United Nations NGO Committee on Freedom of Religion or Belief and Archbishop Emeritus of Washington, D.C.; Leonard Swidler,

---

① China Energy Fund Committee (Hong Kong) was the main sponsor and organizer of New York-Nishan Forum. Its President Chan Chauto was later elected Vice President of Nishan Forum Organizing Committee, and its American Branch President Zhang Wu and all his colleagues took on the whole organization and reception. Dr. Patrick Ho Chi-ping, who had studied and worked in the United States for 16 years, presided over all the dialogues within the two days. He said that, Confucian and Christian civilizations are the world's two most important civilizations and their relations are discussed at the United Nations Headquarters, which is crucial for building a harmonious world and will open up a new path for the dialogue between the two civilizations.

President of the Dialogue Institute - Interreligious, Intercultural, International; Douglas Johnston, President of the International Center for Religion & Diplomacy, Washington; James Hackett, Former Chairman of the US Federal Reserve Bank of Dallas; John Borelli, Former Consultant to the Vatican's Pontifical Council for Interreligious Dialogue; Marie Dennis, Co-President of Pax Christi International; American Futurist Mark Stahlman; Liu Changle, Chairman of Phoenix Satellite Television Holdings Limited; Xue Cheng, Vice President of the Buddhist Association of China; Zhang Jiyu, Vice President of the China Taoist Association; Zhang Ping, Vice President of Chinese People's Institute of Foreign Affairs; Xie Zhixiu, Executive Director of Nishan Forum Organizing Committee; Gao Shuqun, Executive Deputy Secretary-General of Nishan Forum Organizing Committee; as well as scholars and research students of relevant United Nations agencies, famous Chinese and American universities and research institutions. At New York-Nishan Forum, President Xu Jialu delivered a keynote speech titled "Reexamining the Source of Civilization and Constructing Human Ethics". He said:

Today, it's symbolically significant for us to have a dialogue between Confucius and Jesus Christ at the United Nations Headquarters. Established after the cruelest war in human history, the United Nations is committed to safeguarding human rights, maintaining and promoting the world peace. Over the last half century, numerous politicians and experts have stood here to call for reconciliation and peace, which influences the whole world. Today, international scholars and religionists are having a dialogue here with a view to narrowing cultural misunderstanding, promoting a harmonious world and building long-lasting peace never before in human history. Politicians talk about politics, while we discuss cultures. However, we all share the same goal. As an old Chinese saying goes, different approaches yield the same result. Although our opinions may not influence government decision-making immediately, yet our voice will exert a much more profound influence than the statements or declarations made here by politicians. A harmonious or conflicting relationship between countries or races depends on whether we can understand culture and inherited ideologies of our counterparts. Even so, culture still serves as the best means and channel to facilitate communications across different countries, ethnic groups and religions. Representing the soul of a nation, culture acts as a base and land for a nation to choose its future at a certain period of time. Increasing understanding of each other's cultures plays an important role in fostering friendship, broadening dialogues and deepening mutual trust. As a part of culture, politics is only a cultural form dominated by the core of culture-world views and values.

As recent human history has taught us, different civilizations shall increase communications rather than fighting with each other. Since the United Nations unanimously passed the resolution that declared every May 21 to be the World Day for Cultural Diversity for Dialogue and Development in 2002, many countries have held all kinds of dialogue activities to increase the understanding of different civilizations by scholars and the general public, which fosters friendship between people of different countries. The Second Nishan Forum on World Civilizations, held in the hometown of Confucius-Nishan, Shandong Province-on May 21, 2012, is an event to celebrate the 10th anniversary that the United Nations passed the resolution. This activity is well received by the society, which encourages us to carry forward. In my opinion, after ten years of efforts, dialogues among different civilizations shall further enrich their connotations by surpassing the current stage of "we need dialogues" and "we can have dialogues". After facing crisis, what should we do and what responsibilities shall different civilizations shoulder? Many scholars have examined those questions and we should also yearn for finding viable answers to them.

Today, I would like to deliver my opinions from a different angle which is shown from my speech title "Reexamining the Source of Civilization and Constructing Human Ethics".

"Reexamining the source of civilization" is to review fundamental cultural ideologies at the beginning of civilizations, which, to religion, is to revisit the original religious meaning the prophets created. The reason I think in that way is that if we only look at the cruel reality and the painful and bitter human development journey, we are often filled with despair and confusion, because we still fail to find solutions to all kinds of disastrous consequences caused by ourselves. Due to cultural diversity and current prevailing cultural conflicts, the future of human destiny faces many uncertainties. However, if we interpret the original points of human religions with radical historicism, we can find some common anticipation shared by different cultures. And this is a start point for finding solutions. Bearing that in mind, through reflection, debate and exploration, we can go back to the original intention of sages in Axial Age - an aspiration to having the universal commonwealth and a harmonious world.

First, I would like to talk about Chinese culture. Until today, many people still believe that the Chinese have no religious beliefs and that misunderstanding even has a negative impact on the way the world looks at China. A man without religion is like a horse without a bridle, so does a nation. Chinese do have religions. Chinese culture is rooted in Confucianism, Buddhism and Taoism. Among them, the influence of Confucianism has been the most profound. As we all know, Buddhists believe Buddha, while Taoists worship different gods. Then, what about Confucianism? Confucianists worship Confucius - the founder of Confucianism, and value "Ren" (Benevolence) and "Li" (Ritual) virtues advocated by Confucius. "Ren" values universal fraternity as the highest standard. "A man should overflow in love to all, and cultivate the friendship of the good". Based on "Ren" as an outward expression, "Li" shapes and coordinates interpersonal relations and the relationship between man and nature. Chinese see Confucius as a holy teacher, not a god. Although most Chinese do not worship a universally - accepted personal god who creates everything including human beings, Chinese people do worship Lao Tse, Goddess Matsu and all sorts of other gods, while holding their respect for morality and Confucius. As Confucius proposed that "Respect the ghosts and spirits, but keep them at a distance", therefore Chinese, including atheists, tolerate all religions with a respectful, inclusive and equal attitude. Rulers in all ages also made policies based on such attitude held by the public.

Second, I want to brief you on some ancient Chinese histories. Foreign religions introduced to China include Nestorianism (a Christological doctrine advanced by Nestorius and known as Oriental Assyrian Orthodox, which was considered a heresy until recognized by Martin Luther in the 17th century), Indian Buddhism, Judaism, Islamism, Catholicism and Christianity. Since the Han Dynasty (206 BC—220), or more accurately, since the first century BC to now, the

Chinese government has granted foreign religionists the same rights and freedom as local Chinese, such as the rights to live, travel, conduct business, study, preach and build churches in China. With a long history hard to keep track of, we cannot describe how foreign religions were introduced to China in ancient times in details although we can find some clues from the remained historical and cultural relics. Among them, a small Jewish community in Kaifeng, the capital city of the Song Dynasty (960 – 1279), attracts attention of historians and missionaries in the world. In 1163, the first Jewish church was established in downtown, Kaifeng City. Judaism was called "Yicileye" (Chinese transliteration of "Israel") at that time. Relying on their excellent management skills, Jews entered the upper-middle-class in the society back then; sometimes they even assumed government positions through examination. According to the research by Chinese scholars, there once was a Jew named Issac acting as senior official in the Yuan Dynasty (1271 – 1386) (refer to *Jews and China* by Pan Guang and Wang Jian).

Due to time limit, I won't elaborate on the relationship between China and foreign religions. I would like to highlight one point. Since ancient times, there have been many theoretical arguments among Confucianism, Buddhism and Taoism. Actually, the internal fractional strife has never ceased within all these three religions. However, China has never had a religious war. A Chinese saying - "A gentleman uses his tongue, not his fists" - best describes the relationships among them. Thanks to arguments, these three religions have complemented their own weaknesses by learning from each other's advantageous doctrines and ritual procedures. Thus, all of them have made unprecedented strides. For example, Buddhism accelerated its localization process; Confucianism strengthened its research on metaphysics and virtue internalization; and Taoism formed its own theoretical system by learning from Confucianism and Buddhism. These three religions reached their peak in the Tang (618 – 907), Song and Yuan dynasties particularly. Among them, the achievements of Confucian philosophy were the most distinctive, which is still a hot topic in today's sinology and Chinese philosophy research.

Since ancient times, Chinese people have tolerated different foreign religions as they find common ethical values in different religions. On a basis of seeking common ground while reserving differences, we obtain a win-win situation.

As I said previously, Chinese tolerated, accepted and absorbed foreign religions in history. Inheriting this tradition, the Chinese wholeheartedly stand for settling the disputes in this chaotic world through dialogues and firmly object to use of force.

Now, let's return to the title of my speech *Reexamining the Source of Civilization and Constructing Human Ethics*. Today, ethical values advocated by civilizations are unprecedentedly suffering from unprecedented damages. Actually, misunderstanding among different civilizations is worsening to varying degrees. One of the key reasons is that people only focus on the surface layer of civilization, such as different religious objects, life attitudes and artistic presentations, while the fundamentals lying in different civilizations are ignored. Such core values were completely accumulated at the original development stage of all civilizations.

Life and death, this life and afterlife are always central themes for all civilizations. For example, the concept of Sanskrit had emerged in Indian civilization before the establishment of Brahmanism (e.g. *Aitareya Upanishad*, Chapter I), and "Sanskrit" refers to self, namely god, spirit, truth, intelligence and happiness (e.g. *Vajrasacika Upanishad*). These concepts had been absorbed by Brahmanism and Buddhism. The god belief in Hebrew civilization was from *Bible & Old Testament*. Moses met God and received the commandments from God. God created man after his own image. God represents a spirit of infinite power and goodness. Confucian values virtues on a basis of "Ren" (Benevolence), which is the highest spiritual level. Sage is the highest spiritual pursuit that no ordinary man can reach it. Confucius said, "At seventy, I could follow my heart's desire without overstepping the line." This actually is a reflection of that spirit. "Goodness" and "Love" are ultimate goals of all religions. Either in awe of god or in fear of going to hell after death, people abided by the rule of law and controlled their desires with self-discipline. So, it's either simple or complex for people to solve the confusion on life and death, this life and afterlife when all religions were created.

Compared to ancient people, more and more modern people only care for material comfort. Compared to spiritual pursuit, material comfort is more comfortable and easier to obtain, but it is also more superficial. In the name of god's will, self-discipline and the rule of law are discarded. People become fearless and pursue for material benefits by all means. This is the root cause of all kinds of social issues, environmental problems and country conflicts in the world today. If each nation could rationally review its national history, ideological history or religious history and look for the truth of life and the universe promoted by its original belief, people will truly find happiness. More and more people will be inspired to pursue goodness, and give up their current lifestyle featured as nervous, tired, empty and dangerous. This is an inevitable journey for returning the nature of human beings.

In current world, ethics is classified by wealth rather than nationality or religion. The rich have rich ethics, while the poor have poor ethics; the stronger have stronger ethics, while the weak have weak ethics. When different ethics meet together, civilization conflict put forward by Prof. Huntington will inevitably occurred. Therefore, it's time for intellectuals working together to discuss how to construct common ethics for all humans. Ethics is an issue cared by all countries and all peoples while without any dispute. So, I believe that constructing human ethics will be positively responded in the world.

Although both ancient and modern scholars interpret the meaning of goodness differently, goodness is a shared content for all beliefs regardless of nationality. Hence, it should become a content of common ethics for the future human beings. 10 days ago, Mr. Tu Weiming, Former Professor of Harvard University, launched the World Ethics Institute at Peking University. I was lucky enough to be invited to the opening ceremony. Scholars from different countries present at the ceremony praised this establishment by Peking University. I believe that some friends here today may be interested in this news. The establishment of this institute reflects a trend of the world's ideology circle. Intellectuals from different countries shall fulfill their duties of studying and constructing universally-accepted ethics. In this regard, I believe, the experience of Chinese people over the last thousands of years will provide a reference for the world. Spinoza, Kant and other great philosophers devoted their life to investigating human ethics and moral reasoning. In the 21st century, we are looking forward to establishing universally-accepted ethics and contributing to human peace and happiness.

There is no doubt that the construction of human ethics begins with communication. In ancient agrarian and pastoral ages, our ancestors explored a communication channel in Asian countries and across Asian and European lands with their feet and horseshoes. At that time, the relationship between Europe and Asia and among Asian countries was defined as friendly and harmonious. Now, we have advanced transport and telecommunication facilities. Such convenient transport and telecommunication facilities at present are far beyond our ancestor's imagination and fairy tales. People's communication shall pay more attention to its connotation and quality. Although time is changing, the essence of communication is unchanged at all. I believe that constructing human ethics will become a highlight of scholar communications in the future.

One day, people will eventually detest such ethics and politics that drive the whole nation into an antagonizing, dangerous and fighting situation. A new world dreamed by Jesus Christ, Shakyamuni and Confucius will finally come true.

The success of New York-Nishan Forum led to great response in the United Nations and the United States. Vuk Jeremić, President of the United Nations General Assembly, attended the closing reception and delivered important remarks. He pointed out that the successful convening of New York-Nishan Forum at the United Nations Headquarters demonstrated the strong support of Nishan Forum Organizing Committee to the dialogue among civilizations advocated by the United Nations, representing the development trend of civilization in this era. He praised that such dialogues help eliminate barriers and promote world peace. Wang Min, Deputy Permanent Representative of China to the United Nations, said that such a success made the following things come true for the first time: it was the first time for Chinese people to have a dialogue on Confucian and Christian civilizations in New York; it was the first time for an NGO to organize an civilization dialogue at the United Nations Headquarters; and it was a Chinese NGO that made such a breakthrough in the history of the United Nations. Relevant people of New York generally considered it to be "a miracle" that China's Nishan Forum carries out a dialogue between Confucian and Christian civilizations in New York and the United Nations Headquarters.

New York-Nishan Forum showed that direct face-to-face dialogue can help eliminate prejudice, misunderstanding and misjudgment, and develop new friendships. Although he was more than 80 years old, Cardinal Theodore McCarrick, Archbishop Emeritus of Washington, D.C., addressed the forum and got immediate response from Xu Jialu, which produced an unexpected effect. Cardinal McCarrick started with a proposition that the world is a big family and all people are brothers and sisters. Xu Jialu responded that this proposition is consistent with a Confucian thought-"Unity of man and nature" and "People are my brothers and all things are my kinds". When Cardinal McCarrick mentioned that, when preaching, he mainly gives three kinds of talks-love, cooperation and forgiveness. Xu Jialu said that this happens to coincide with "The benevolent loves others", "Harmony without uniformity", "Principle of loyalty and forgiveness" and other Confucian doctrines. Cardinal McCarrick finally concluded that a dialogue usually should proceed in five steps-talk, discussion, understanding, appreciation and cooperation. Xu Jialu was surprised at such a historical coincidence and providential arrangement, since he once addressed the closing ceremony of the Second Nishan Forum in May that, when different civilizations or peoples with different faiths have a dialogue, they should know, understand, appreciate, learn from each other and work together to make mutual progress. They shook hands several times in the dialogue to salute each other. During New York-Nishan Forum, Hurricane Sandy struck the United States and New York was heavily hit by the hurricane, Xu Jialu and other Chinese scholars reached New York on time to attend the forum in spite of danger, which left a good impression on American people.

4. Confucian Civilization Returns to the Center Stage of World Civilizations

The establishment of a forum on world civilizations in Nishan, as well as the organization of dialogues between Confucian and Christian civilizations around the world including the United Nations Headquarters, mark the strong returning of

Confucian Civilization to the center stage of world civilizations after staying in silence for a century, the starting point of which is to participate in dialogue among world civilizations. As repeatedly stressed by President Xu Jialu, being the only strong civilization in the world, Western civilization (mainly refers to Christian civilization) has brought deep crises for current world and mankind's future development after experiencing hundreds of years of expansion. In the new book: *Elegy for Sea?— Revelation of European Civilization*, Wang Yiwei pointed out that a distinctive characteristic of European civilization is "overexpansion" and its unique "original sin", "open without tolerance, double standard i.e. diversification internally and universality externally, coexistence of development and destruction".[1] This judgment is rather accurate. Looking at the world, almost all of the world's deep-seated crises can be traced back to Western civilization, which verifies that "either success or failure boils down to the same roots". Moreover, other civilizations except Western civilization can hardly have equal dialogue with Western civilization. Only Western civilization tells its own stories. Confucian civilization has almost been suppressed into a hopeless situation. However, 100 years later, Confucian civilization miraculously survived and stood up. China's accession to the WTO in 2000 was a turning point, and Beijing Olympic Games in 2008 was an uplifting point. Year 2010 witnessed another significant point that China surpassed Japan in GDP and became the world's second largest economy after the US. All these have demonstrated the historical strength of Confucian civilization. Early in the 1970s, British historian Arnold Toynbee made predictions on this. Once again in the 1990s, when American scholar Samuel Huntington put forward the "Clash of Civilizations" he talked of Confucian, Islamic and Christian civilizations and believed that it is possible for the first two civilizations to challenge the last one and thus cause a clash of civilizations. The view of worries extended globally and aroused resonance. After that, with the outbreak of the US 911 Event and the rapid rise of China, the view of worries further spread throughout the world. This was actually the Western thinking of civilization but very popular around the world, because Confucian civilization, or the Chinese civilization, began to lose

---

[1] Quoted from Transform Our Views on European Civilization by Chen Xin, *Wen Wei Po* newspaper, May 6, 2013.

the right to speak as early in 1840. Confucian civilization has been alienated from the world for long time, even in Chinese mainland. However, wise men around the world are still optimistic about Confucian civilization, because it is a civilization with the longest history and thus has rich historical experience in dealing with complex, multiple issues and crises. When Western civilization is not capable of handling with the world's current crises, the world would turn to look at the East, Confucius and Confucian civilization. "Unity of Man and Nature", "Harmony without uniformity" and "What you do not wish for yourself, do not do to others" and other philosophies are exactly the civilization and wisdom needed most urgently by the world. These ideas were raised by Confucius 2,500 years ago and have been practiced by Chinese people for 2,500 years. President Xu Jialu observantly captured the demand of the world and decided to come to Nishan, a remote place far from big cities. Based on this forum on world civilizations, he initiated and organized many dialogues between Confucian and Christian civilizations. Of course, such dialogues will be long-term and sustained. The accession of Confucian civilization to the center stage of world civilizations does not mean that it tries to overwhelm Western civilization or other civilizations in the world. Instead, it just brings the ways of Confucius civilization for thinking and solving problems to the world, trying to tell the world that the common future of humanity will probably not be so bad if we may choose another way to get along with each other and solve crises and problems.

The purpose of the returning of Confucian civilization to the center stage of world civilizations is to face and step into the future, rather than going back to the past. Xu Jialu said, "In recent decades, Western academia continues to question, criticize and reconstruct its own culture, and this ideological trend has gradually become the mainstream in Western ideology circle. Meanwhile, many people began to pay attention to Eastern culture, especially the spectacular wisdom in Chinese culture. Thereafter, China also started a process of re-understanding itself. The so-called 'Craze for Traditional Chinese Culture' or 'Craze for Confuciansim' is an academic demonstration of this process. The reflection of Western ideology circle, their concern for Eastern culture, and China's rumination of its own spiritual heritage will be, or have been, or are being integrated, which becomes the most active current in the ideology circles of China and the world. It is essential for the world's future, and for human to get rid of artificial myths and the resulting nightmares that entangle mankind and to pursue eternal peace and happiness, which is a historical inevitability in line with the way of human growth and cultural development." [①] These remarks clearly point out the direction for the development of our civilization. The mankind is a big family, and the crises faced by human beings are the common crises for all civilizations. As the world's oldest civilization, Confucian civilization returns to the center stage of world civilizations, which aims to join forces with other civilizations, make efforts to ease the extreme tension between man and man, between man and society or between man and nature, further explore a new kind of civilization‑based relations between man and nature and between civilizations, and eventually build a harmonious world on the basis of "Harmony without uniformity".

Gao Shuqun is an economics professor with an engineering degree from Tsinghua University. He has engaged in the research and promotion of Confucian civilization in the home town of Confucius for many years. Now, he serves as Deputy Bureau Director of Cultural Heritage Bureau of Shandong Province, Deputy-Director of Shandong Provincial Office for Planning and Construction of Chinese Cultural Symbolic City, Deputy Director of the Shandong University Cross-Civilizations Dialogue Research Center. From 2008 to currently, he acts as Executive Deputy Secretary-General of the Secretariat of Nishan Forum on World Civilizations and a key drafter of the Declaration of Human Harmony.

[①] Quoted from Xu Jialu's speech at the establishment ceremony of Advanced Institute for Confucian Studies of Shandong University on April 21, 2010. The original text was included in *For World Peace*, Hua Yi Publishing House, September 2010, Edition 1, pp. 190–195. At that time, Xu Jialu was employed as President of the Institute.

The Momentum and Trends of Civilization Dialogues

Gao Shuqun

Originated by the end of the 20th century and developed in the early 21st century, civilization dialogue is in essence a universal awakening of mankind's civilization-consciousness. Put succinctly, civilization dialogue is a manifestation and extension of civilization-self-consciousness. The higher the level of civilization-consciousness is, the more thorough and effective the "dialogue" will be. In this sense, the flourishing civilization dialogue in the 21st century is practically heralding the advent of a globally civilization-conscious era. In other words, the 21st century will be a civilization-self-awakening century, when civilization-self-awareness or civilization-self-consciousness will become more and more normal and universal.

Civilization dialogue and civilization-self-consciousness further reveal another important fact: a profound paradigm shift is taking place in the evolution of human civilizations. The emergence of civilization dialogue has literally announced that the era when "strong" civilizations domineer over the other civilizations is about to end. As "dialogue only takes place between equals" [1], the term clearly suggests that all civilizations are equal, and no civilization shall seek to prevail or domineer over the other; secondly, it also acknowledges the existence of mutual respect among civilizations, with no such differences to be perceived between them as one being more noble, bigger or stronger than the other; and thirdly, "dialogue" is a two-way communication process, not one-sided exchange, nor lecturing. For these reasons,

---

[1] Words by Dr. Tu Weiming in a CCTV interview.

the burgeoning of the civilization dialogue will undoubtedly terminate the hegemonic status the western civilization has been enjoying for hundreds of years, ushering in a new era when a multiplicity of civilizations perceive, engage and interact with one another on an equal footing.

The proliferation of the Internet, the rapid inter-continental flow of people, and the rise of an increasingly diverse pattern of world power have enabled civilization dialogue and civilization-self-consciousness to gradually defuse the risk of inter-civilization confrontations, and also allowed civilization dialogue to get more life-oriented and less academic: it is now not a "game" of reasoning anymore, but rather, a mutual accommodation of life experiences— it is exactly because of their differences that various civilizations tolerate each other, appreciate each other, and ultimately embrace each other. A new trend has emerged among the world civilizations: they are now learning how to live in harmony.

The decade-old anti-terrorism campaign has shown that wars and terrorist acts can't solve the fundamental problems simmering between civilizations. The world now has a growing need to reshape the relations between different nations and racial groups by balancing the relations between civilizations. Inter-civilization relations have been steadily evolving into important bilateral or multilateral relations, with civilization dialogue fast becoming an emerging paradigm of international relations. We simply can't afford to turn a blind eye to inter-civilization problems anymore. In response to the new trend, the United Nations is currently shifting its focus from addressing inter-national relations to dealing with inter-civilization relations.

The decade-old civilization dialogue is a highly organized and orderly dialogue among civilizations, a salient characteristic attributable to the United Nations established in the previous century. The operating procedure of the United Nations effectively ensures that superpowers can no longer do whatever they want. For instance, the United States once announced its withdrawal from the UNESCO before rejoining the organization later, which showed the superpower's deference, however reluctant, to the United Nations authority. Under the direction of the United Nations, three important trends are now steadily emerging in worldwide civilization dialogue:

The first trend is that the UNESCO has begun to commit itself to promoting civilization dialogue through the promotion of the new humanism. During the first stage of the UNESCO-led civilization dialogue, i.e. the ten years(1999–2009) during which Kōichirō Matsuura served as Director-General of UNESCO, the organization urged the United Nations to take a series of important measures to facilitate civilization dialogue; during the second stage, i.e. the period from November, 2009 when Irina Bokova took over the position of Director-General [1] till now, the organization has been actively deepening civilization dialogue and striving to promote civilization dialogue by further enhancing the new humanism.

The second trend is that the United Nations Alliance of Civilizations (UNAOC) has begun to shift its strategic focus to Asia. The organization held Regional Consultations for Asia-South Pacific in cooperation with United Nations Association of China in Shanghai on November 29–30, 2012, officially announcing that the UNAOC has come to Asia. Mr. Cui Tiankai, then Chinese Vice-Minister of Foreign Affairs, delivered the opening speech, warmly welcoming the organization into the region. The United Nations Alliance of Civilization (UNAOC) was established at the initiative of the Governments of Spain and Turkey, with a particular focus on improving relations within and between Western and Muslim societies and addressing persistent tensions and divides. However, in 2007, the UNAOC initiated proceedings to shift its strategic focus to Asia.

The third trend is that the Confucian civilization has begun to move from the sidelines to the center stage. Civilization dialogue was originally intended to address the tension between the western Christian civilization and the Islamic civilization. When former President Mohammad Khatami of Iran first proposed the idea of civilization dialogue in 1998, he was aiming to promote communication between the two clashing civilizations of Iran, only to see the most important civilization dialogues in the 21st century having gradually pushed the Confucian civilization to the center, making it one of the major participants in the world civilization dialogue. [2]

The three aforementioned trends are pointing in one direction: since promoted

---

[1] Irina Bokova will serve for 4 years, and may be re-elected for a second term.

[2] After 911, anti-terrorist campaigns consumed a lot of the "energy" of the US and the western world, making it difficult for the Christian-Islamic dialogue to continue and deepen. In the meantime, China's rapid economic rise also compelled the US and the western world to treat China increasingly as a major competitor, ushering in a new chapter of inter-civilization competition.

by the UNESCO, the new humanism has become more and more aligned with the Confucianism; and the development of the new humanism also needs a boost from the Confucianism [①]. UNAOC's shift of focus to Asia is actually a strategic advance into the very heartland of the Confucian civilization. The recovery of the Confucian civilization echoes two of the aforementioned trends, which in turn will further boost the rapid revival of the Confucian civilization. Therefore, the overall trend is very clear: toward Asia and the diverse Asian civilizations. Although other parts of the civilized world, such as Northern Europe, South America and Africa, have all showed keen interest in the civilization dialogue over the past decade, in the foreseeable future, the world civilization dialogue will take place mainly between Asian civilizations and different Asian civilizations, with China and the Confucian civilization yet to face more opportunities and still greater challenges.

Facing the future, the Confucian civilization will undoubtedly enjoy a vital position. But so far, no country in the world, including China itself, has conducted any serious assessment of what kind of role the Confucian civilization will play in the 21st century. The US, Japan and other western countries have shown more interest in China's economy and military power than in its Confucian civilization, which is actually the very force that can truly change the world. The Confucian civilization redux is bound to exert a profound, fundamental impact on the development of the world's civilizations.

Historically, the Confucian civilization has long distanced itself from the "world affairs", almost absolutely oblivious to the centuries-old conflict between the western Christian civilization and the Middle East Islamic civilization, with the third pole of the earth, the Tibetan Plateau, effectively blocking its view of the West-Islam confrontations. Such geographic barriers as plateaus, oceans and expansive deserts "help" isolate the Confucian civilization from the outside world, making it a relatively "closed" civilization. The unique attributes of the Confucian civilization determined that this civilization had to fight for its survival for much of its history, with major wars mainly occurring between

---

①   The new humanism might be richly rooted in Confucianism, as to a certain extent the European humanism owed its formation to Confucianism.

nomadic and agricultural populations (interspersed with enduring harassment of coastal areas by Japanese pirates). The main factors that influence the birth and development of civilizations include drought, floods, earthquakes, diseases and foreign invasions. In the years without the occurrence of these natural or man-made disasters, the Confucian society enjoyed a generally peaceful, harmonious and prosperous existence. However, the natural and geographic environment in which the Confucian civilization is located determined that this civilization must learn to live in constant "anxiety and fear". "Flooding hazard" is an important factor that builds the attributes of the Confucian civilization. In a sense, the Confucian civilization is actually a "water-controlling" civilization. China's early scientific, philosophic and religious developments were all related to the activity of "controlling water". For the Confucians, the war was always the very last resort. Throughout China's long history, the feeble political and diplomatic policy of "marriage alliance" had been adopted for over 1,000 years instead of military campaigns. Two of the most prosperous dynasties in China, the Han and the Tang, actually saw the most instances of "marriage alliances" of all dynasties. The legendary Silk Road leading from China's Western Regions to the Middle East and then the Europe has always been a "route of peace", not a "route of war". The reserved nature of the Confucian civilization remained largely unknown to the outside world for much of the world history. However, when the influence of the western civilization swept the world, things had undergone a fundamental change. For the "weak" civilizations, the spread of the European Christian civilization around the world was fraught with disaster and misery, causing the extinction of quite many civilizations. Just when the Western powers were about to put an end to China of the Confucian civilization, hundreds of millions of Chinese people at the bottom of the Chinese society promptly formed a tidal wave of patriotic fervor and momentum to "fight for survival and save the country". Upholding the Confucian precept of to "sacrifice one's life for the cause of justice", over 30 million people committed their lives to the preservation of an ancient civilization. Even women and children joined the glorious cause, the success of which was another testament to the tenacity and resilience of the Confucian civilization. In reviewing this period in history, some western scholars went so far as to call Mao Zedong the "New Moses" and liken the "Long March" to a "journey to the Promised

121

Land" [1], which is a western way of re-interpreting and applauding China's march into a new chapter of its civilized history under the leadership of the Communist Party of China. The Chinese people also received heartfelt thanks from the Jews who suffered a lot during the WWII, who hailed those Chinese who rescued Jews during the war as the "Chinese Schindlers". As a son of former Jewish residents in China, former Israeli Prime Minister Ehud Olmert once remarked that "we are lucky to be able to grow up under the influences of two cultures—the Jewish culture and the Chinese culture. The former tells us how to choose life, while the latter teaches us how to persist in our lives." [2] So now you can see the Confucian civilization is radically different from the western civilization in that it is full of love, humility, civility, tolerance and enterprise. Therefore, if we borrow insights and approaches from the Confucian civilization, to solve the problems related to the world's civilizations, it will become much easier. As one of the Confucius' teachings goes, "in the usages of ritual it is harmony that is prized; the Way of the Former Kings from this got its beauty. What exactly is the Way of the Former Kings? It actually refers to the spirit of comity, harmony and respect". Mutual respect, understanding and tolerance are sometimes all we need to solve most of the problems plaguing the world right now. As we know, the Confucian "worldview" in ancient times was actually very limited; but after it makes its grand comeback, this oriental civilization's outlook on the world will be very much a global one.

In the course of the decade-old civilization dialogue, there are three major forces promoting the rapid recovery and revival of the Confucian civilization. The first force is the Chinese government. In addition to drawing upon the Confucian civilization to respond to the "civilization dialogues" and using Confucian ideas to elucidate to the world the essence of state civilization, Chinese leaders have also taken various measures to incorporate such Confucian concepts as "Min Ben" (literally "people as the root") and "Harmony" into their political platforms and foreign policies. In his speech at Harvard University on December 11, 2003, former Chinese Premier Wen Jiabao observed that "Peace-loving has been a time-honored quality of the Chinese

---

[1]   Yang Huilin: "Sinology and Identity Wavering in 'Ism'", *Dushu Magazine*, Issue 2, p.3

[2]   Zhang Yinghui: "The China Complex of a Distinguished Jewish Family – In Tribute to the 20th Anniversary of Establishment of Diplomatic Relations between China and Israel", *World Affairs*, April 1, 2012, issue 1578.

nation. The Chinese nation has rich and profound cultural reserves. 'Harmony without uniformity' is a great idea put forth by ancient Chinese thinkers. It means harmony without sameness, and difference without conflict. Harmony entails co-existence and co-prosperity, while difference conduces to mutual complementation and mutual support. To approach and address issues from such a perspective will not only help enhance relations with friendly countries, but also serve to resolve contradictions in the international community." On September 16, 2005, in his speech at the roundtable meeting of the summit marking the 60th anniversary of the United Nations, the then Chinese President Hu Jintao proposed in clear terms to "uphold the spirit of inclusiveness to build a harmonious world together". On February 27, 2010, the then Premier Wen Jiabao engaged in an Internet chat with Chinese netizens, during which he dwelled upon the Confucian morality. He said, "What exactly is morality? There are two most important moral qualities: the first one is the capacity to love people. Confucius once said, 'benevolence means to love people'. Every entrepreneur, indeed every member of the society shall know to love the people and love the nation; and the second one is compassion. Again, just as Confucius once so brilliantly pointed out, 'What you do not wish for yourself, do not do to others'. Or as the Confucian philosophy advocates, compassion serves as the very foundation of morality. Mencius also said, 'whoever is devoid of the heart of compassion is not human', literally treating the heart of compassion as the basis of human being. Those enterprises that only care about their own interests, or worse yet, act in an unscrupulous manner to seek profits at the expense of others, are deplorable, and also punishable by law". On April 15, 2011, in his speech at the Boao Forum for Asia, former Chinese President Hu Jintao proposed to "respect diversity of civilizations" and build a "new order of world civilizations", further explaining that "there exist diverse civilizations in the world, just like there are diverse species in the nature. The world today is home to over 200 countries and regions, more than 2,500 ethnic groups and 6,000-plus languages. As different musical notes make a beautiful melody, people of different ethnicities, colors and historical and cultural backgrounds have jointly made our world a splendid and colorful place. Dialogue, exchanges and integration among different civilizations form the powerful current of human civilizations, surging ahead ceaselessly. The diversity of civilizations is not only an objective reality, but also a fact conducive to the growth of the world's civilizations. Therefore, people around the world shall respect the diversity of civilizations, and strive to pursue common ground amid diversity, seek harmony in differences, and achieve development through exchanges. Only in a world like this can a long-term peace and development be achieved and assured". On June 27 of the same year, in his speech at the Royal Society of Britain, former Chinese Premier Wen Jiabao quoted some famous remarks by the late Mr. Fei Xiaotong, a well-known Chinese sociologist, which go: "The world will be a harmonious place if people appreciate their own beauty and that of others, and work together to create beauty in the world," and further observed that "these thoughts best illustrate the open and inclusive mindset of China today." The second force hails from overseas. Such prominent intellectuals as Mr. Tu Weiming have played a key role in these efforts. During the period of the decade-old civilization dialogue, Mr. Tu traveled extensively around the world with the aim of introducing to the world the Confucian civilization and spreading the Confucian thoughts and the Chinese culture to every corner of the globe, having helped restore the dignity and prestige of the Confucian civilization as a worthy counterpart to the Christian civilization and the Islamic civilization in civilization dialogues. And the third force originates from the Chinese civil society, including that of Mainland, Hong Kong, Macao and Taiwan. All relevant parties actively participate in the cause, nurturing an atmosphere of academic diversity and prosperity, and paving the way for the grand comeback of the Confucian civilization. During this period, the dialogue between Confucianism and other civilizations as spearheaded by Mr. Xu Jialu in Nishan held a deeply symbolic significance. The welcoming attitude adopted by the various United Nations agencies toward the Nishan Forum actually reflects the world's rising consciousness for welcoming the Confucianism back to the center stage of the world's civilizations.

The civilization dialogue in the next decade obviously will take place in Asia as the central arena. In the region, the UNESCO is poised to enhance its promotion of the new humanism, and the development of the UNAOC in Asia will also further strengthen the interconnectedness between various Asian civilizations, during which the Confucianism is bound to play a pivotal role. The other civilized parts of the world, including Africa, Latin America and Northern Europe, will also get involved to varying degrees, with the various world's ancient civilizations further accelerating their convergence in Asia, finally culminating in the formation of a "Harmony without uniformity" alliance of civilizations, during which the "new order of world civilizations" as proposed by former president Hu Jintao might be realized. And the Confucianism has a vital role to play in determining the success of this grand cause. The Confucian civilization enjoys a rich historical heritage for playing a constructive role in Asia. In China, a unique blending of Confucianism, Buddhism and Taoism has been embraced for centuries, while a historical "Confucian cultural sphere" spans in such other Asian countries as South Korea, Singapore, Thailand and Viet Nam. With Confucius, Qufu and Confucianism as the "bonding agents", the Confucian civilization might collaborate with various international organizations including the United Nations in its campaign to cross great oceans to build closer ties with civilizations in America and Europe, and soar over the Tibetan Plateau to further its friendship with the Indian and Islamic civilizations, while also seeking to build the whole new relationships with such other civilizations as the African civilization. New dialogues might be conducted first with non-Asian civilizations, and after relevant achievements are made and relevant experience accumulated, efforts will be made to promote the formation of consensus among various Asian civilizations and further their development. Nevertheless, the main dialogue arenas will undoubtedly concentrate in Asia and its surrounding areas.

Postscript

Xu Xianghong

When the organizing committee of the Nishan Forum, cooperated with the headquarter of Confucius Institute, meet to arrange the Nishan Forum in Paris, located in the headquarter of UNESCO in France (spring, 2012), the idea to compile a report was hanging around the committee members' minds. A decades ago, proposed and promoted by UNESCO, organized dialogues between different civilizations emerged and soon have developed into a huge movement globally. We have to document this movement. The chair of the Nishan Forum and other organizers expressed their full support and high expectation for this idea. It proves later that this was a complicate and difficult academic task. Meanwhile, the Institute of Advanced Study for Confucianism in Shandong University offered a financial help to the project. Later, Dr. Tu Weiming, Vincent Shen, and Hans Kung joined in the advisory board. All of these supports were the important and positive forces for the completion of this book. In addition, we want to express our deep appreciation to the respectable Xu Jialu, who wrote a preface to the book in this hottest season.

In conducting the project, Dr. Xie Wenyu from Shandong University and Prof. Gao Shuqun from Qufu Normal University had played a major role. With Dr. Xie's supervision, the writing team was formed by Profs. Liu Tiewa, Zhang Guihong, Ni Peimin, Tan Mingran, and Gao Shuqun, who contributed chapters respectively. Besides, graduate students Xu Huan, Li Jiangyu, and Xie Yipin from Shandong University participated in the project. The project was completed over one year.

Yet, it is just a beginning; as the Chair of the Nishan Forum, the Respectable Xu Jialu, pointed out: "The study on civilization dialogue is a brand new subject." Now, the report is going to be published. To follow the step, we are working on establishing the Center for Cross-civilization Dialogue, affiliating with Shandong University, Jinan, Shandong, which will function as the academic think tank for the Nishan Forum. We will trace up closely the activities of cross-civilization dialogues around the world. We truly believe that these activities will open a new chapter of human civilization development.

With the limitations here and there, this report may not be sufficient, and is open for discussion. We welcome criticism and correction from the reader.

6th August, 2013

In the office of the Nishan Forum Secretary

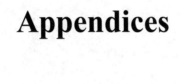

Appendices

Appendices

Appendix 1:

UNESCO Universal Declaration on Cultural Diversity

November 2, 2001

The General Conference

Committed to the full implementation of the human rights and fundamental freedoms proclaimed in the Universal Declaration of Human Rights and other universally recognized legal instruments, such as the two International Covenants of 1966 relating respectively to civil and political rights and to economic, social and cultural rights,

Recalling that the Preamble to the Constitution of UNESCO affirms "that the wide diffusion of culture, and the education of humanity for justice and liberty and peace are indispensable to the dignity of man and constitute a sacred duty which all the nations must fulfil in a spirit of mutual assistance and concern",

Further recalling Article I of the Constitution, which assigns to UNESCO among other purposes that of recommending "such international agreements as may be necessary to promote the free flow of ideas by word and image",

Referring to the provisions relating to cultural diversity and the exercise of cultural rights in the international instruments enacted by UNESCO,

Reaffirming that culture should be regarded as the set of distinctive spiritual, material, intellectual and emotional features of society or a social group, and that it encompasses, in addition to art and literature, lifestyles, ways of living together, value systems, traditions and beliefs,

Noting that culture is at the heart of contemporary debates about identity, social cohesion, and the development of a knowledge-based economy,

Affirming that respect for the diversity of cultures, tolerance, dialogue and cooperation, in a climate of mutual trust and understanding are among the best guarantees of international peace and security,

Aspiring to greater solidarity on the basis of recognition of cultural diversity, of awareness of the unity of humankind, and of the development of intercultural exchanges,

Considering that the process of globalization, facilitated by the rapid development of new information and communication technologies, though representing a challenge for cultural diversity, creates the conditions for renewed dialogue among cultures and civilizations,

Aware of the specific mandate which has been entrusted to UNESCO, within the United Nations system, to ensure the preservation and promotion of the fruitful diversity of cultures,

Proclaims the following principles and adopts the present Declaration:

Identity, Diversity and Pluralism

Article 1 – Cultural diversity: the common heritage of humanity

Culture takes diverse forms across time and space. This diversity is embodied in the uniqueness and plurality of the identities of the groups and societies making up humankind. As a source of exchange, innovation and creativity, cultural diversity is as necessary for humankind as biodiversity is for nature. In this sense, it is the common heritage of humanity and should be recognized and affirmed for the benefit of present and future generations.

Article 2 – From cultural diversity to cultural pluralism

In our increasingly diverse societies, it is essential to ensure harmonious interaction among people and groups with plural, varied and dynamic cultural identities as well as their willingness to live together. Policies for the inclusion and participation of all citizens are guarantees of social cohesion, the vitality of civil society and peace. Thus defined, cultural pluralism gives policy expression to the reality of cultural diversity. Indissociable from a democratic framework, cultural pluralism is conducive to cultural exchange and to the flourishing of creative capacities that sustain public life.

Article 3 – Cultural diversity as a factor in development

Cultural diversity widens the range of options open to everyone; it is one of the roots of development, understood not simply in terms of economic growth, but also as a means to achieve a more satisfactory intellectual, emotional, moral and spiritual existence.

Cultural Diversity and Human Rights

Article 4 – Human rights as guarantees of cultural diversity

The defence of cultural diversity is an ethical imperative, inseparable from respect for human dignity. It implies a commitment to human rights and fundamental freedoms, in particular the rights of persons belonging to minorities and those of indigenous peoples. No one may invoke cultural diversity to infringe upon human rights guaranteed by international law, nor to limit their scope.

Article 5 – Cultural rights as an enabling environment for cultural diversity

Cultural rights are an integral part of human rights, which are universal, indivisible and interdependent. The flourishing of creative diversity requires the full implementation of cultural rights as defined in Article 27 of the Universal Declaration of Human Rights and in Articles 13 and 15 of the International Covenant on Economic, Social and Cultural Rights. All persons have therefore the right to express themselves and to create and disseminate their work in the language of their choice, and particularly in their mother tongue; all persons are entitled to quality education and training that fully respect their cultural identity; and all persons have the right to participate in the cultural life of their choice and conduct their own cultural practices, subject to respect for human rights and fundamental freedoms.

Article 6 – Towards access for all to cultural diversity

While ensuring the free flow of ideas by word and image care should be exercised that all cultures can express themselves and make themselves known. Freedom of expression, media pluralism, multilingualism, equal access to art and to scientific and technological knowledge, including in digital form, and the possibility for all cultures to have access to the means of expression and dissemination are the guarantees of cultural diversity.

Cultural Diversity and Creativity

Article 7 – Cultural heritage as the wellspring of creativity

Creation draws on the roots of cultural tradition, but flourishes in contact with other cultures. For this reason, heritage in all its forms must be preserved, enhanced and handed on to future generations as a record of human experience and aspirations, so as to foster creativity in all its diversity and to inspire genuine dialogue among cultures.

Article 8–Cultural goods and services: commodities of a unique kind

In the face of present-day economic and technological change, opening up vast prospects for creation and innovation, particular attention must be paid to the diversity of the supply of creative work, to due recognition of the rights of authors and artists and to the specificity of cultural goods and services which, as vectors of identity, values and meaning, must not be treated as mere commodities or consumer goods.

Article 9–Cultural policies as catalysts of creativity

While ensuring the free circulation of ideas and works, cultural policies must create conditions conducive to the production and dissemination of diversified cultural goods through cultural industries that have the means to assert themselves at the local and global level. It is for each State, with due regard to its international obligations, to define its cultural policy and to implement it through the means it considers fit, whether by operational support or appropriate regulations.

Cultural Diversity and International Solidarity

Article 10–Strengthening capacities for creation and dissemination worldwide

In the face of current imbalances in flows and exchanges of cultural goods and services at the global level, it is necessary to reinforce international cooperation and solidarity aimed at enabling all countries, especially developing countries and countries in transition, to establish cultural industries that are viable and competitive at national and international level.

Article 11–Building partnerships between the public sector, the private sector and civil society

Market forces alone cannot guarantee the preservation and promotion of cultural diversity, which is the key to sustainable human development. From this perspective, the pre-eminence of public policy, in partnership with the private sector and civil society, must be reaffirmed.

Article 12–The role of UNESCO

UNESCO, by virtue of its mandate and functions, has the responsibility to:

(a) Promote the incorporation of the principles set out in the present Declaration into the development strategies drawn up within the various intergovernmental bodies;

(b) Serve as a reference point and a forum where States, international governmental and non-governmental organizations, civil society and the private sector may join together in elaborating concepts, objectives and policies in favour of cultural diversity;

(c) Pursue its activities in standard-setting, awareness-raising and capacity-building in the areas related to the present Declaration within its fields of competence;

(d) Facilitate the implementation of the Action Plan, the main lines of which are appended to the present Declaration.

Annex II Main lines of an action plan for the implementation of the UNESCO Universal Declaration on Cultural Diversity

The Member States commit themselves to taking appropriate steps to disseminate widely the "UNESCO Universal Declaration on Cultural Diversity" and to encourage its effective application, in particular by cooperating with a view to achieving the following objectives:

1. Deepening the international debate on questions relating to cultural diversity, particularly in respect of its links with development and its impact on policy-making, at both national and international level; taking forward notably consideration of the advisability of an international legal instrument on cultural diversity.

2. Advancing in the definition of principles, standards and practices, on both the national and the international levels, as well as of awareness-raising modalities and patterns of cooperation, that are most conducive to the safeguarding and promotion of cultural diversity.

3. Fostering the exchange of knowledge and best practices in regard to cultural pluralism with a view to facilitating, in diversified societies, the inclusion and participation of persons and groups from varied cultural backgrounds.

4. Making further headway in understanding and clarifying the content of cultural rights as an integral part of human rights.

5. Safeguarding the linguistic heritage of humanity and giving support to expression, creation and dissemination in the greatest possible number of languages.

6. Encouraging linguistic diversity-while respecting the mother tongue-at all

135

levels of education, wherever possible, and fostering the learning of several languages from the earliest age.

7. Promoting through education an awareness of the positive value of cultural diversity and improving to this end both curriculum design and teacher education.

8. Incorporating, where appropriate, traditional pedagogies into the education process with a view to preserving and making full use of culturally appropriate methods of communication and transmission of knowledge.

9. Encouraging "digital literacy" and ensuring greater mastery of the new information and communication technologies, which should be seen both as educational disciplines and as pedagogical tools capable of enhancing the effectiveness of educational services.

10. Promoting linguistic diversity in cyberspace and encouraging universal access through the global network to all information in the public domain.

11. Countering the digital divide, in close cooperation in relevant United Nations system organizations, by fostering access by the developing countries to the new technologies, by helping them to master information technologies and by facilitating the digital dissemination of endogenous cultural products and access by those countries to the educational, cultural and scientific digital resources available worldwide.

12. Encouraging the production, safeguarding and dissemination of diversified contents in the media and global information networks and, to that end, promoting the role of public radio and television services in the development of audiovisual productions of good quality, in particular by fostering the establishment of cooperative mechanisms to facilitate their distribution.

13. Formulating policies and strategies for the preservation and enhancement of the cultural and natural heritage, notably the oral and intangible cultural heritage, and combating illicit traffic in cultural goods and services.

14. Respecting and protecting traditional knowledge, in particular that of indigenous peoples; recognizing the contribution of traditional knowledge, particularly with regard to environmental protection and the management of natural resources, and fostering synergies between modern science and local knowledge.

15. Fostering the mobility of creators, artists, researchers, scientists and intellectuals and the development of international research programmes and

partnerships, while striving to preserve and enhance the creative capacity of developing countries and countries in transition.

16. Ensuring protection of copyright and related rights in the interest of the development of contemporary creativity and fair remuneration for creative work, whileat the same time upholding a public right of access to culture, in accordance with Article 27 of the Universal Declaration of Human Rights.

17. Assisting in the emergence or consolidation of cultural industries in the developing countries and countries in transition and, to this end, cooperating in the development of the necessary infrastructures and skills, fostering the emergence of viable local markets, and facilitating access for the cultural products of those countries to the global market and international distribution networks.

18. Developing cultural policies, including operational support arrangements and/or appropriate regulatory frameworks, designed to promote the principles enshrined in this Declaration, in accordance with the international obligations incumbent upon each State.

19. Involving all sectors of civil society closely in the framing of public policies aimed at safeguarding and promoting cultural diversity.

20. Recognizing and encouraging the contribution that the private sector can make to enhancing cultural diversity and facilitating, to that end, the establishment of forums for dialogue between the public sector and the private sector.

The Member States recommend that the Director-General take the objectives set forth in this Action Plan into account in the implementation of UNESCO's programmes and communicate it to institutions of the United Nations system and to other intergovernmental and non-governmental organizations concerned with a view to enhancing the synergy of actions in favour of cultural diversity.

Appendix 2:

Convention on the Protection and Promotion
of the Diversity of Cultural Expressions

Paris, 20 October 2005

The General Conference of the United Nations Educational, Scientific and Cultural Organization, meeting in Paris from 3 to 21 October 2005 at its 33rd session,

Affirming that cultural diversity is a defining characteristic of humanity,

Conscious that cultural diversity forms a common heritage of humanity and should be cherished and preserved for the benefit of all,

Being aware that cultural diversity creates a rich and varied world, which increases the range of choices and nurtures human capacities and values, and therefore is a mainspring for sustainable development for communities, peoples and nations,

Recalling that cultural diversity, flourishing within a framework of democracy, tolerance, social justice and mutual respect between peoples and cultures, is indispensable for peace and security at the local, national and international levels,

Celebrating the importance of cultural diversity for the full realization of human rights and fundamental freedoms proclaimed in the Universal Declaration of Human Rights and other universally recognized instruments,

Emphasizing the need to incorporate culture as a strategic element in national and international development policies, as well as in international development cooperation, taking into account also the United Nations Millennium Declaration (2000) with its special emphasis on poverty eradication,

Taking into account that culture takes diverse forms across time and space and that this diversity is embodied in the uniqueness and plurality of the identities and cultural expressions of the peoples and societies making up humanity,

Recognizing the importance of traditional knowledge as a source of intangible and material wealth, and in particular the knowledge systems of indigenous peoples, and its positive contribution to sustainable development, as well as the need for its adequate protection and promotion,

Recognizing the need to take measures to protect the diversity of cultural expressions, including their contents, especially in situations where cultural expressions may be threatened by the possibility of extinction or serious impairment,

Emphasizing the importance of culture for social cohesion in general, and in particular its potential for the enhancement of the status and role of women in society,

Being aware that cultural diversity is strengthened by the free flow of ideas, and that it is nurtured by constant exchanges and interaction between cultures,

Reaffirming that freedom of thought, expression and information, as well as diversity of the media, enable cultural expressions to flourish within societies,

Recognizing that the diversity of cultural expressions, including traditional cultural expressions, is an important factor that allows individuals and peoples to express and to share with others their ideas and values,

Recalling that linguistic diversity is a fundamental element of cultural diversity, and **reaffirming** the fundamental role that education plays in the protection and promotion of cultural expressions,

Taking into account the importance of the vitality of cultures, including for persons belonging to minorities and indigenous peoples, as manifested in their freedom to create, disseminate and distribute their traditional cultural expressions and to have access thereto, so as to benefit them for their own development,

Emphasizing the vital role of cultural interaction and creativity, which nurture and renew cultural expressions and enhance the role played by those involved in the development of culture for the progress of society at large,

Recognizing the importance of intellectual property rights in sustaining those involved in cultural creativity,

Being convinced that cultural activities, goods and services have both an economic and a cultural nature, because they convey identities, values and meanings, and must therefore not be treated as solely having commercial value,

Noting that while the processes of globalization, which have been facilitated by the rapid development of information and communication technologies, afford unprecedented conditions for enhanced interaction between cultures, they also represent a challenge for cultural diversity, namely in view of risks of imbalances between rich and poor countries,

Being aware of UNESCO's specific mandate to ensure respect for the diversity of cultures and to recommend such international agreements as may be necessary to promote the free flow of ideas by word and image,

Referring to the provisions of the international instruments adopted by UNESCO relating to cultural diversity and the exercise of cultural rights, and in particular the Universal Declaration on Cultural Diversity of 2001,

Adopts this Convention on 20 October 2005.

I. Objectives and Guiding Principles

Article 1 – Objectives

The objectives of this Convention are:

(a) to protect and promote the diversity of cultural expressions;

(b) to create the conditions for cultures to flourish and to freely interact in a mutually beneficial manner;

(c) to encourage dialogue among cultures with a view to ensuring wider and balanced cultural exchanges in the world in favour of intercultural respect and a culture of peace;

(d) to foster interculturality in order to develop cultural interaction in the spirit of building bridges among peoples;

(e) to promote respect for the diversity of cultural expressions and raise awareness of its value at the local, national and international levels;

(f) to reaffirm the importance of the link between culture and development for all countries, particularly for developing countries, and to support actions undertaken nationally and internationally to secure recognition of the true value of this link;

(g) to give recognition to the distinctive nature of cultural activities, goods and services as vehicles of identity, values and meaning;

(h) to reaffirm the sovereign rights of States to maintain, adopt and implement policies and measures that they deem appropriate for the protection and promotion of the diversity of cultural expressions on their territory;

(i) to strengthen international cooperation and solidarity in a spirit of partnership with a view, in particular, to enhancing the capacities of developing countries in order to protect and promote the diversity of cultural expressions.

Article 2 – Guiding principles

1. Principle of respect for human rights and fundamental freedoms

Cultural diversity can be protected and promoted only if human rights and fundamental freedoms, such as freedom of expression, information and communication, as well as the ability of individuals to choose cultural expressions, are guaranteed. No one may invoke the provisions of this Convention in order to infringe human rights and fundamental freedoms as enshrined in the Universal Declaration of Human Rights or guaranteed by international law, or to limit the scope thereof.

2. Principle of sovereignty

States have, in accordance with the Charter of the United Nations and the principles of international law, the sovereign right to adopt measures and policies to protect and promote the diversity of cultural expressions within their territory.

3. Principle of equal dignity of and respect for all cultures

The protection and promotion of the diversity of cultural expressions presuppose the recognition of equal dignity of and respect for all cultures, including the cultures of persons belonging to minorities and indigenous peoples.

4. Principle of international solidarity and cooperation

International cooperation and solidarity should be aimed at enabling countries, especially developing countries, to create and strengthen their means of cultural expression, including their cultural industries, whether nascent or established, at the local, national and international levels.

5. Principle of the complementarity of economic and cultural aspects of development

Since culture is one of the mainsprings of development, the cultural aspects of development are as important as its economic aspects, which individuals and peoples have the fundamental right to participate in and enjoy.

6. Principle of sustainable development

Cultural diversity is a rich asset for individuals and societies. The protection, promotion and maintenance of cultural diversity are an essential requirement for sustainable development for the benefit of present and future generations.

7. Principle of equitable access

Equitable access to a rich and diversified range of cultural expressions from all over the world and access of cultures to the means of expressions and dissemination constitute important elements for enhancing cultural diversity and encouraging mutual understanding.

8. Principle of openness and balance

When States adopt measures to support the diversity of cultural expressions, they should seek to promote, in an appropriate manner, openness to other cultures of the world and to ensure that these measures are geared to the objectives pursued under the present Convention.

II. Scope of application

Article 3 – Scope of application

This Convention shall apply to the policies and measures adopted by the Parties related to the protection and promotion of the diversity of cultural expressions.

III. Definitions

Article 4 – Definitions

For the purposes of this Convention, it is understood that:

1. Cultural diversity

"Cultural diversity" refers to the manifold ways in which the cultures of groups and societies find expression. These expressions are passed on within and among groups and societies.

Cultural diversity is made manifest not only through the varied ways in which the cultural heritage of humanity is expressed, augmented and transmitted through the variety of cultural expressions, but also through diverse modes of artistic creation, production, dissemination, distribution and enjoyment, whatever the means and technologies used.

2. Cultural content

"Cultural content" refers to the symbolic meaning, artistic dimension and cultural values that originate from or express cultural identities.

3. Cultural expressions

"Cultural expressions" are those expressions that result from the creativity of individuals, groups and societies, and that have cultural content.

4. Cultural activities, goods and services

"Cultural activities, goods and services" refers to those activities, goods and services, which at the time they are considered as a specific attribute, use or purpose, embody or convey cultural expressions, irrespective of the commercial value they may have. Cultural activities may be an end in themselves, or they may contribute to the production of cultural goods and services.

5. Cultural industries

"Cultural industries" refers to industries producing and distributing cultural goods or services as defined in paragraph 4 above.

6. Cultural policies and measures

"Cultural policies and measures" refers to those policies and measures relating to culture, whether at the local, national, regional or international level that are either focused on culture as such or are designed to have a direct effect on cultural expressions of individuals, groups or societies, including on the creation, production, dissemination, distribution of and access to cultural activities, goods and services.

7. Protection

"Protection" means the adoption of measures aimed at the preservation, safeguarding and enhancement of the diversity of cultural expressions.

"Protect" means to adopt such measures.

8. Interculturality

"Interculturality" refers to the existence and equitable interaction of diverse cultures and the possibility of generating shared cultural expressions through dialogue and mutual respect.

IV. Rights and obligations of Parties

Article 5 – General rule regarding rights and obligations

1. The Parties, in conformity with the Charter of the United Nations, the principles of international law and universally recognized human rights instruments, reaffirm their sovereign right to formulate and implement their cultural policies and to adopt measures to protect and promote the diversity of cultural expressions and to strengthen international cooperation to achieve the purposes of this Convention.

2. When a Party implements policies and takes measures to protect and promote the diversity of cultural expressions within its territory, its policies and measures shall be consistent with the provisions of this Convention.

Article 6 – Rights of parties at the national level

1. Within the framework of its cultural policies and measures as defined in Article 4.6 and taking into account its own particular circumstances and needs, each Party may adopt measures aimed at protecting and promoting the diversity of cultural expressions within its territory.

2. Such measures may include the following:

(a) regulatory measures aimed at protecting and promoting diversity of cultural expressions;

(b) measures that, in an appropriate manner, provide opportunities for domestic cultural activities, goods and services among all those available within the national territory for the creation, production, dissemination, distribution and enjoyment of such domestic cultural activities, goods and services, including provisions relating to the language used for such activities, goods and services;

(c) measures aimed at providing domestic independent cultural industries and activities in the informal sector effective access to the means of production, dissemination and distribution of cultural activities, goods and services;

(d) measures aimed at providing public financial assistance;

(e) measures aimed at encouraging non-profit organizations, as well as public and private institutions and artists and other cultural professionals, to develop and promote the free exchange and circulation of ideas, cultural expressions and cultural activities, goods and services, and to stimulate both the creative and entrepreneurial spirit in their activities;

(f) measures aimed at establishing and supporting public institutions, as appropriate;

(g) measures aimed at nurturing and supporting artists and others involved in the creation of cultural expressions;

(h) measures aimed at enhancing diversity of the media, including through public service broadcasting.

144

Article 7 – Measures to promote cultural expressions

1. Parties shall endeavour to create in their territory an environment which encourages individuals and social groups:

(a) to create, produce, disseminate, distribute and have access to their own cultural expressions, paying due attention to the special circumstances and needs of women as well as various social groups, including persons belonging to minorities and indigenous peoples;

(b) to have access to diverse cultural expressions from within their territory as well as from other countries of the world.

2. Parties shall also endeavour to recognize the important contribution of artists, others involved in the creative process, cultural communities, and organizations that support their work, and their central role in nurturing the diversity of cultural expressions.

Article 8 – Measures to protect cultural expressions

1. Without prejudice to the provisions of Articles 5 and 6, a Party may determine the existence of special situations where cultural expressions on its territory are at risk of extinction, under serious threat, or otherwise in need of urgent safeguarding.

2. Parties may take all appropriate measures to protect and preserve cultural expressions in situations referred to in paragraph 1 in a manner consistent with the provisions of this Convention.

3. Parties shall report to the Intergovernmental Committee referred to in Article 23 all measures taken to meet the exigencies of the situation, and the Committee may make appropriate recommendations.

Article 9 – Information sharing and transparency

Parties shall:

(a) provide appropriate information in their reports to UNESCO every four years on measures taken to protect and promote the diversity of cultural expressions within their territory and at the international level;

(b) designate a point of contact responsible for information sharing in relation to this Convention;

(c) share and exchange information relating to the protection and promotion of the diversity of cultural expressions.

Article 10 – Education and public awareness

Parties shall:

(a) encourage and promote understanding of the importance of the protection and promotion of the diversity of cultural expressions, *inter alia*, through educational and greater public awareness programmes;

(b) cooperate with other Parties and international and regional organizations in achieving the purpose of this article;

(c) endeavour to encourage creativity and strengthen production capacities by setting up educational, training and exchange programmes in the field of cultural industries. These measures should be implemented in a manner which does not have a negative impact on traditional forms of production.

Article 11 – Participation of civil society

Parties acknowledge the fundamental role of civil society in protecting and promoting the diversity of cultural expressions. Parties shall encourage the active participation of civil society in their efforts to achieve the objectives of this Convention.

Article 12 – Promotion of international cooperation

Parties shall endeavour to strengthen their bilateral, regional and international cooperation for the creation of conditions conducive to the promotion of the diversity of cultural expressions, taking particular account of the situations referred to in Articles 8 and 17, notably in order to:

(a) facilitate dialogue among Parties on cultural policy;

(b) enhance public sector strategic and management capacities in cultural public sector institutions, through professional and international cultural exchanges and sharing of best practices;

(c) reinforce partnerships with and among civil society, non-governmental organizations and the private sector in fostering and promoting the diversity of cultural expressions;

(d) promote the use of new technologies, encourage partnerships to enhance information sharing and cultural understanding, and foster the diversity of cultural expressions;

(e) encourage the conclusion of co-production and co-distribution agreements.

Article 13 – Integration of culture in sustainable development

Parties shall endeavour to integrate culture in their development policies at all levels for the creation of conditions conducive to sustainable development and, within this framework, foster aspects relating to the protection and promotion of the diversity of cultural expressions.

Article 14 – Cooperation for development

Parties shall endeavour to support cooperation for sustainable development and poverty reduction, especially in relation to the specific needs of developing countries, in order to foster the emergence of a dynamic cultural sector by, *inter alia*, the following means:

(a) the strengthening of the cultural industries in developing countries through:

(i) creating and strengthening cultural production and distribution capacities in developing countries;

(ii) facilitating wider access to the global market and international distribution networks for their cultural activities, goods and services;

(iii) enabling the emergence of viable local and regional markets;

(iv) adopting, where possible, appropriate measures in developed countries with a view to facilitating access to their territory for the cultural activities, goods and services of developing countries;

(v) providing support for creative work and facilitating the mobility, to the extent possible, of artists from the developing world;

(vi) encouraging appropriate collaboration between developed and developing countries in the areas, *inter alia*, of music and film;

(b) capacity-building through the exchange of information, experience and expertise, as well as the training of human resources in developing countries, in the public and private sector relating to, *inter alia*, strategic and management capacities, policy development and implementation, promotion and distribution of cultural expressions, small-, medium- and micro-enterprise development, the use of technology, and skills development and transfer;

(c) technology transfer through the introduction of appropriate incentive measures for the transfer of technology and know-how, especially in the areas of cultural industries and enterprises;

(d) financial support through:

(i) the establishment of an International Fund for Cultural Diversity as provided in Article 18;

(ii) the provision of official development assistance, as appropriate, including technical assistance, to stimulate and support creativity;

(iii) other forms of financial assistance such as low interest loans, grants and other funding mechanisms.

Article 15 – Collaborative arrangements

Parties shall encourage the development of partnerships, between and within the public and private sectors and non-profit organizations, in order to cooperate with developing countries in the enhancement of their capacities in the protection and promotion of the diversity of cultural expressions. These innovative partnerships shall, according to the practical needs of developing countries, emphasize the further development of infrastructure, human resources and policies, as well as the exchange of cultural activities, goods and services.

Article 16 – Preferential treatment for developing countries

Developed countries shall facilitate cultural exchanges with developing countries by granting, through the appropriate institutional and legal frameworks, preferential treatment to artists and other cultural professionals and practitioners, as well as cultural goods and services from developing countries.

Article 17 – International cooperation in situations of serious threat to cultural expressions

Parties shall cooperate in providing assistance to each other, and, in particular to developing countries, in situations referred to under Article 8.

Article 18 – International Fund for Cultural Diversity

1. An International Fund for Cultural Diversity, hereinafter referred to as "the Fund", is hereby established.

2. The Fund shall consist of funds-in-trust established in accordance with the Financial Regulations of UNESCO.

3. The resources of the Fund shall consist of:

(a) voluntary contributions made by Parties;

(b) funds appropriated for this purpose by the General Conference of UNESCO;

(c) contributions, gifts or bequests by other States; organizations and programmes of the United Nations system, other regional or international organizations; and public or private bodies or individuals;

(d) any interest due on resources of the Fund;

(e) funds raised through collections and receipts from events organized for the benefit of the Fund;

(f) any other resources authorized by the Fund's regulations.

4. The use of resources of the Fund shall be decided by the Intergovernmental Committee on the basis of guidelines determined by the Conference of Parties referred to in Article 22.

5. The Intergovernmental Committee may accept contributions and other forms of assistance for general and specific purposes relating to specific projects, provided that those projects have been approved by it.

6. No political, economic or other conditions that are incompatible with the objectives of this Convention may be attached to contributions made to the Fund.

7. Parties shall endeavour to provide voluntary contributions on a regular basis towards the implementation of this Convention.

Article 19 – Exchange, analysis and dissemination of information

1. Parties agree to exchange information and share expertise concerning data collection and statistics on the diversity of cultural expressions as well as on best practices for its protection and promotion.

2. UNESCO shall facilitate, through the use of existing mechanisms within the Secretariat, the collection, analysis and dissemination of all relevant information, statistics and best practices.

3. UNESCO shall also establish and update a data bank on different sectors and governmental, private and non-profit organizations involved in the area of cultural expressions.

4. To facilitate the collection of data, UNESCO shall pay particular attention to capacity-building and the strengthening of expertise for Parties that submit a request for such assistance.

5. The collection of information identified in this Article shall complement the information collected under the provisions of Article 9.

V. Relationship to other instruments

Article 20 – Relationship to other treaties: mutual supportiveness, complementarity and non-subordination

1. Parties recognize that they shall perform in good faith their obligations under this Convention and all other treaties to which they are parties. Accordingly, without subordinating this Convention to any other treaty,

(a) they shall foster mutual supportiveness between this Convention and the other treaties to which they are parties; and

(b) when interpreting and applying the other treaties to which they are parties or when entering into other international obligations, Parties shall take into account the relevant provisions of this Convention.

2. Nothing in this Convention shall be interpreted as modifying rights and obligations of the Parties under any other treaties to which they are parties.

Article 21 – International consultation and coordination

Parties undertake to promote the objectives and principles of this Convention in other international forums. For this purpose, Parties shall consult each other, as appropriate, bearing in mind these objectives and principles.

VI. Organs of the Convention

Article 22 – Conference of Parties

1. A Conference of Parties shall be established. The Conference of Parties shall be the plenary and supreme body of this Convention.

2. The Conference of Parties shall meet in ordinary session every two years, as far as possible, in conjunction with the General Conference of UNESCO. It may meet in extraordinary session if it so decides or if the Intergovernmental Committee receives a request to that effect from at least one-third of the Parties.

3. The Conference of Parties shall adopt its own rules of procedure.

4. The functions of the Conference of Parties shall be, *inter alia*:

(a) to elect the Members of the Intergovernmental Committee;

(b) to receive and examine reports of the Parties to this Convention transmitted by the Intergovernmental Committee;

(c) to approve the operational guidelines prepared upon its request by the Intergovernmental Committee;

(d) to take whatever other measures it may consider necessary to further the objectives of this Convention.

Article 23 – Intergovernmental Committee

1. An Intergovernmental Committee for the Protection and Promotion of the Diversity of Cultural Expressions, hereinafter referred to as "the Intergovernmental Committee", shall be established within UNESCO. It shall be composed of representatives of 18 States Parties to the Convention, elected for a term of four years by the Conference of Parties upon entry into force of this Convention pursuant to Article 29.

2. The Intergovernmental Committee shall meet annually.

3. The Intergovernmental Committee shall function under the authority and guidance of and be accountable to the Conference of Parties.

4. The Members of the Intergovernmental Committee shall be increased to 24 once the number of Parties to the Convention reaches 50.

5. The election of Members of the Intergovernmental Committee shall be based on the principles of equitable geographical representation as well as rotation.

6. Without prejudice to the other responsibilities conferred upon it by this Convention, the functions of the Intergovernmental Committee shall be:

(a) to promote the objectives of this Convention and to encourage and monitor the implementation thereof;

(b) to prepare and submit for approval by the Conference of Parties, upon its request, the operational guidelines for the implementation and application of the provisions of the Convention;

(c) to transmit to the Conference of Parties reports from Parties to the Convention, together with its comments and a summary of their contents;

(d) to make appropriate recommendations to be taken in situations brought to its attention by Parties to the Convention in accordance with relevant provisions of the Convention, in particular Article 8;

(e) to establish procedures and other mechanisms for consultation aimed at promoting the objectives and principles of this Convention in other international

151

forums;

(f) to perform any other tasks as may be requested by the Conference of Parties.

7. The Intergovernmental Committee, in accordance with its Rules of Procedure, may invite at any time public or private organizations or individuals to participate in its meetings for consultation on specific issues.

8. The Intergovernmental Committee shall prepare and submit to the Conference of Parties, for approval, its own Rules of Procedure.

Article 24 – UNESCO Secretariat

1. The organs of the Convention shall be assisted by the UNESCO Secretariat.

2. The Secretariat shall prepare the documentation of the Conference of Parties and the Intergovernmental Committee as well as the agenda of their meetings and shall assist in and report on the implementation of their decisions.

VII. Final Clauses

Article 25 – Settlement of disputes

1. In the event of a dispute between Parties to this Convention concerning the interpretation or the application of the Convention, the Parties shall seek a solution by negotiation.

2. If the Parties concerned cannot reach agreement by negotiation, they may jointly seek the good offices of, or request mediation by, a third party.

3. If good offices or mediation are not undertaken or if there is no settlement by negotiation, good offices or mediation, a Party may have recourse to conciliation in accordance with the procedure laid down in the Annex of this Convention. The Parties shall consider in good faith the proposal made by the Conciliation Commission for the resolution of the dispute.

4. Each Party may, at the time of ratification, acceptance, approval or accession, declare that it does not recognize the conciliation procedure provided for above. Any Party having made such a declaration may, at any time, withdraw this declaration by notification to the Director-General of UNESCO.

Article 26 – Ratification, acceptance, approval or accession by Member States

1. This Convention shall be subject to ratification, acceptance, approval or accession by Member States of UNESCO in accordance with their respective

constitutional procedures.

2. The instruments of ratification, acceptance, approval or accession shall be deposited with the Director-General of UNESCO.

Article 27 – Accession

1. This Convention shall be open to accession by all States not Members of UNESCO but members of the United Nations, or of any of its specialized agencies, that are invited by the General Conference of UNESCO to accede to it.

2. This Convention shall also be open to accession by territories which enjoy full internal self-government recognized as such by the United Nations, but which have not attained full independence in accordance with General Assembly resolution 1514 (XV), and which have competence over the matters governed by this Convention, including the competence to enter into treaties in respect of such matters.

3. The following provisions apply to regional economic integration organizations:

(a) This Convention shall also be open to accession by any regional economic integration organization, which shall, except as provided below, be fully bound by the provisions of the Convention in the same manner as States Parties;

(b) In the event that one or more Member States of such an organization is also Party to this Convention, the organization and such Member State or States shall decide on their responsibility for the performance of their obligations under this Convention. Such distribution of responsibility shall take effect following completion of the notification procedure described in subparagraph (c). The organization and the Member States shall not be entitled to exercise rights under this Convention concurrently. In addition, regional economic integration organizations, in matters within their competence, shall exercise their rights to vote with a number of votes equal to the number of their Member States that are Parties to this Convention. Such an organization shall not exercise its right to vote if any of its Member States exercises its right, and vice-versa;

(c) A regional economic integration organization and its Member State or States which have agreed on a distribution of responsibilities as provided in subparagraph (b) shall inform the Parties of any such proposed distribution of responsibilities in the following manner:

(i) in their instrument of accession, such organization shall declare with

153

specificity, the distribution of their responsibilities with respect to matters governed by the Convention;

(ii) in the event of any later modification of their respective responsibilities, the regional economic integration organization shall inform the depositary of any such proposed modification of their respective responsibilities; the depositary shall in turn inform the Parties of such modification;

(d) Member States of a regional economic integration organization which become Parties to this Convention shall be presumed to retain competence over all matters in respect of which transfers of competence to the organization have not been specifically declared or informed to the depositary;

(e) "Regional economic integration organization" means an organization constituted by sovereign States, members of the United Nations or of any of its specialized agencies, to which those States have transferred competence in respect of matters governed by this Convention and which has been duly authorized, in accordance with its internal procedures, to become a Party to it.

4. The instrument of accession shall be deposited with the Director-General of UNESCO.

Article 28 – Point of contact

Upon becoming Parties to this Convention, each Party shall designate a point of contact as referred to in Article 9.

Article 29 – Entry into force

1. This Convention shall enter into force three months after the date of deposit of the thirtieth instrument of ratification, acceptance, approval or accession, but only with respect to those States or regional economic integration organizations that have deposited their respective instruments of ratification, acceptance, approval, or accession on or before that date. It shall enter into force with respect to any other Party three months after the deposit of its instrument of ratification, acceptance, approval or accession.

2. For the purposes of this Article, any instrument deposited by a regional economic integration organization shall not be counted as additional to those deposited by Member States of the organization.

Article 30 – Federal or non-unitary constitutional systems

Recognizing that international agreements are equally binding on Parties regardless of their constitutional systems, the following provisions shall apply to Parties which have a federal or non-unitary constitutional system:

(a) with regard to the provisions of this Convention, the implementation of which comes under the legal jurisdiction of the federal or central legislative power, the obligations of the federal or central government shall be the same as for those Parties which are not federal States;

(b) with regard to the provisions of the Convention, the implementation of which comes under the jurisdiction of individual constituent units such as States, counties, provinces, or cantons which are not obliged by the constitutional system of the federation to take legislative measures, the federal government shall inform, as necessary, the competent authorities of constituent units such as States, counties, provinces or cantons of the said provisions, with its recommendation for their adoption.

Article 31 – Denunciation

1. Any Party to this Convention may denounce this Convention.

2. The denunciation shall be notified by an instrument in writing deposited with the Director-General of UNESCO.

3. The denunciation shall take effect 12 months after the receipt of the instrument of denunciation. It shall in no way affect the financial obligations of the Party denouncing the Convention until the date on which the withdrawal takes effect.

Article 32 – Depositary functions

The Director-General of UNESCO, as the depositary of this Convention, shall inform the Member States of the Organization, the States not members of the Organization and regional economic integration organizations referred to in Article 27, as well as the United Nations, of the deposit of all the instruments of ratification, acceptance, approval or accession provided for in Articles 26 and 27, and of the denunciations provided for in Article 31.

Article 33 – Amendments

1. A Party to this Convention may, by written communication addressed to the Director-General, propose amendments to this Convention. The Director-General shall circulate such communication to all Parties. If, within six months

155

from the date of dispatch of the communication, no less than one half of the Parties reply favourably to the request, the Director-General shall present such proposal to the next session of the Conference of Parties for discussion and possible adoption.

2. Amendments shall be adopted by a two-thirds majority of Parties present and voting.

3. Once adopted, amendments to this Convention shall be submitted to the Parties for ratification, acceptance, approval or accession.

4. For Parties which have ratified, accepted, approved or acceded to them, amendments to this Convention shall enter into force three months after the deposit of the instruments referred to in paragraph 3 of this Article by two-thirds of the Parties. Thereafter, for each Party that ratifies, accepts, approves or accedes to an amendment, the said amendment shall enter into force three months after the date of deposit by that Party of its instrument of ratification, acceptance, approval or accession.

5. The procedure set out in paragraphs 3 and 4 shall not apply to amendments to Article 23 concerning the number of Members of the Intergovernmental Committee. These amendments shall enter into force at the time they are adopted.

6. A State or a regional economic integration organization referred to in Article 27 which becomes a Party to this Convention after the entry into force of amendments in conformity with paragraph 4 of this Article shall, failing an expression of different intention, be considered to be:

(a) Party to this Convention as so amended; and

(b) a Party to the unamended Convention in relation to any Party not bound by the amendments.

Article 34 – Authoritative texts

This Convention has been drawn up in Arabic, Chinese, English, French, Russian and Spanish, all six texts being equally authoritative.

Article 35 – Registration

In conformity with Article 102 of the Charter of the United Nations, this Convention shall be registered with the Secretariat of the United Nations at the request of the Director-General of UNESCO.

Annex Conciliation Procedure

Article 1 – Conciliation Commission

A Conciliation Commission shall be created upon the request of one of the Parties to the dispute. The Commission shall, unless the Parties otherwise agree, be composed of five members, two appointed by each Party concerned and a President chosen jointly by those members.

Article 2 – Members of the Commission

In disputes between more than two Parties, Parties in the same interest shall appoint their members of the Commission jointly by agreement. Where two or more Parties have separate interests or there is a disagreement as to whether they are of the same interest, they shall appoint their members separately.

Article 3 – Appointments

If any appointments by the Parties are not made within two months of the date of the request to create a Conciliation Commission, the Director-General of UNESCO shall, if asked to do so by the Party that made the request, make those appointments within a further two-month period.

Article 4 – President of the Commission

If a President of the Conciliation Commission has not been chosen within two months of the last of the members of the Commission being appointed, the Director-General of UNESCO shall, if asked to do so by a Party, designate a President within a further two-month period.

Article 5 – Decisions

The Conciliation Commission shall take its decisions by majority vote of its members. It shall, unless the Parties to the dispute otherwise agree, determine its own procedure. It shall render a proposal for resolution of the dispute, which the Parties shall consider in good faith.

Article 6 – Disagreement

A disagreement as to whether the Conciliation Commission has competence shall be decided by the Commission.

Appendix 3:

Alliance of Civilizations (Part I)
Report of High Level Group

November 13, 2006

I. Bridging the World's Divides

1.1 Our world is alarmingly out of balance. For many, the last century brought unprecedented progress, prosperity, and freedom. For others, it marked an era of subjugation, humiliation and dispossession. Ours is a world of great inequalities and paradoxes: a world where the income of the planet's three richest people is greater than the combined income of the world's least developed countries; where modern medicine performs daily miracles and yet 3 million people die every year of preventable diseases; where we know more about distant universes than ever before, yet 130 million children have no access to education; where despite the existence of multilateral covenants and institutions, the international community often seems helpless in the face of conflict and genocide. For most of humanity, freedom from want and freedom from fear appear as elusive as ever.

1.2 We also live in an increasingly complex world, where polarized perceptions, fueled by injustice and inequality, often lead to violence and conflict, threatening international stability. Over the past few years, wars, occupation and acts of terror have exacerbated mutual suspicion and fear within and among societies. Some political leaders and sectors of the media, as well as radical groups have exploited this environment, painting mirror images of a world made up of mutually exclusive cultures, religions, or civilizations, historically distinct and destined for confrontation.

1.3 The anxiety and confusion caused by the "clash of civilizations" theory regrettably has distorted the terms of the discourse on the real nature of the predicament the world is facing. The history of relations between cultures is not only one of wars and confrontation. It is also based on centuries of constructive exchanges, cross-fertilization, and peaceful co-existence. Moreover, classifying internally fluid and diverse societies along hard-and-fast lines of civilizations interferes with more illuminating ways of understanding questions of identity, motivation and behavior. Rifts between the powerful and the powerless or the rich and the poor or between different political groups, classes, occupations and nationalities have greater explanatory power than such cultural categories. Indeed, the latter stereotypes only serve to entrench already polarized opinions. Worse, by promoting the misguided view that cultures are set on an unavoidable collision course, they help turn negotiable disputes into seemingly intractable identity-based conflicts that take hold of the popular imagination. It is essential, therefore, to counter the stereotypes and misconceptions that deepen patterns of hostility and mistrust among societies.

1.4 In this context, the need to build bridges between societies, to promote dialogue and understanding and to forge the collective political will to address the world's imbalances has never been greater. This urgent task constitutes the *raison d'être* of the Alliance of Civilizations. Launched by the Secretary-General of the United Nations in 2005 on the co-sponsorship of the Prime Ministers of Spain and Turkey, the Alliance of Civilizations affirms a broad consensus across nations, cultures and religions that all societies are bound together in their humanity and interdependent in their quest for stability, prosperity and peaceful co-existence.

1.5 The Alliance seeks to address widening rifts between societies by reaffirming a paradigm of mutual respect among peoples of different cultural and religious traditions and by helping to mobilize concerted action toward this end. This effort reflects the will of the vast majority of peoples to reject extremism in any society and support respect for religious and cultural diversity. To guide this initiative, the Secretary-General has established a High-level Group of eminent persons. This is their report. [1] On the basis of its analysis, it evaluates relations between diverse societies and examines the emergence of the contemporary trend toward extremism with special attention to relations between Western and Muslim societies, bearing in mind that such characterizations do not reflect the vast diversity within each. It recommends

---

[1] This report reflects the consensus view of the members of the High-level Group; it does not imply universal agreement on all points.

a practicable program of action for states (at national, regional, and local levels), international organizations, and civil society, which it hopes will assist in diminishing hostility and in promoting harmony among the nations and cultures of the world.

II. Guiding Principles

2.1 An Alliance of Civilizations must by nature be based on a multi-polar perspective. As such, the High-level Group has been guided in its deliberations by principles which set out the framework for promoting a culture of dialogue and respect among all nations and cultures. The Charter of the United Nations, the Universal Declaration of Human Rights of 1948 which seeks to free humanity of fear and misery, as well as the other fundamental documents on cultural and religious rights [1] are the basic reference for these principles as listed below.

2.2 An increasingly interdependent and globalized world can be regulated only through the rule of law and an effective multilateral system, with the United Nations system at its core. This requires adherence to international law and covenants including all rights and responsibilities governing the conduct of war as articulated in International Humanitarian Law (particularly the Geneva Conventions), respect for the institutions that establish them, and support for mechanisms that adjudicate violations of these norms.

2.3 A full and consistent adherence to human rights standards forms the foundation for stable societies and peaceful international relations. These rights include the prohibition against physical and mental torture; the right to freedom of religion; and the right to freedom of expression and association. The integrity of these rights rests on their universal and unconditional nature. These rights should therefore be considered inviolable and all states, international organizations, non-state actors, and individuals, under all circumstances, must abide by them.

2.4 Diversity of civilizations and cultures is a basic feature of human society and a driving force of human progress. Civilizations and cultures reflect the great wealth and heritage of humankind; their nature is to overlap, interact and evolve in relation to one

---

[1] See reference documents featured on the Alliance of Civilizations website, http://www.unaoc.org.

another. There is no hierarchy among cultures, as each has contributed to the evolution of humanity. The history of civilizations is in fact a history of mutual borrowing and constant cross-fertilization.

2.5 Poverty leads to despair, a sense of injustice, and alienation that, when combined with political grievances, can foster extremism. Eradication of poverty would diminish those factors linked to economic marginalization and alienation and must therefore be aggressively pursued, as called for in the Millennium Development Goals.

2.6 Terrorism can never be justified. In order to succeed in enabling international institutions and governments to stop terrorism, we need to address all the conditions conducive to it, recognising the links between peace, security, social and economic development, and human rights. In this regard, the recently approved UN Global Counter-Terrorism Strategy represents an important landmark.

2.7 Democratic governance that is representative of citizens and responsive to their needs and aspirations provides the most effective means for individuals to achieve their full potential. To be successful, democratic systems must emerge organically from within each society's culture, reflecting its shared values and adapted to the needs and interests of its citizens. This is only possible when people are free and feel in control of their destiny.

2.8 Religion is an increasingly important dimension of many societies and a significant source of values for individuals. It can play a critical role in promoting an appreciation of other cultures, religions, and ways of life to help build harmony among them.

III. The Global Context

Overview

3.1 Political and technological developments during the twentieth century raised the hope and possibility for an unprecedented period of harmony between nations and a vast improvement in global well-being. Indeed, much has been achieved. Multilateral cooperation and civil society activism paved the way to a number of positive developments in international relations, including a ban on the use of landmines, the establishment of international criminal tribunals, and the initiation of a wide range of cooperative initiatives aimed at eradicating diseases or fighting poverty. Despite these achievements, however, a general malaise continues to be felt in many quarters regarding the state of the world. There is a widespread perception that the multilateral institutions established to advance universal principles and to improve general well-being are ineffective mainly due to the lack of support of the most powerful countries and a real fear that the prospect of a more peaceful, stable, and prosperous future for today's youth is at risk. In some cases, this pessimism is the result of particular local, national, or regional dynamics, but there is also a broader global context that must be considered.

3.2 In social, political and economic terms, the West is both driving globalization and yet seemingly threatened by some of its trends. Western powers maintain overwhelming political, economic, and military power in the world, including disproportionate influence in multilateral political and economic bodies. Porous borders, mounting population flows from poor to rich countries, un-integrated immigrant communities and cross-border spillovers of economic, environmental, health and even physical security factors have highlighted both the interdependence of societies and the widening gaps between them.

3.3 In terms of economic well-being, income inequality has continued to rise in recent decades and current studies indicate that increased integration into the world economy has actually exacerbated the divergence in the economic growth of countries. Thus over half of humanity still leads a life of deprivation, and the gap between poor and rich, both among and within nations, seems inexorably on the rise. Health and education systems in developing countries remain inadequate. Destruction of the environment is intensifying, proliferation of nuclear, biological, and chemical weapons seems to escape effective control, and global arms sales-both official and illegal-evade monitoring.

3.4 In terms of political well-being, there is a growing perception that universal principles of human rights and democratic governance are only vigorously defended in those cases where they are viewed by some states to be in their own interests-a selective approach that undercuts the legitimacy of the multilateral institutions mandated to articulate, advance, and advocate for those principles. Eloquent statements in support of democracy lose their relevance when democratically elected governments

162

are shunned and sometimes subverted by powerful countries.

3.5 The mechanisms and technologies by which communities interact with one another appear to have developed faster than our collective political will to use them for the benefit of all. This environment offers a fertile ground for the emergence of identity-based politics, which can, in turn, lead to violent tensions among communities and fuel hostile relations among them.

Identities and Perceptions

3.6 Diverse cultural identities are an integral part of the richness of human experience and as such must be respected and promoted. In particular, traditions and customs play a key role in the development and transmission of modern identity. But the inexorable push toward a "globalized" world has challenged group identities in many parts of the world, including Latin America, Africa and Asia. The advances of the latter half of the twentieth century opened up the possibility that diverse nations and cultures would communicate more easily, negotiate their interests on a more level playing field, and pursue common goals while maintaining their distinctive identities and belief systems. What many feel has emerged instead is an international system that offers the prospect of economic well-being for some in exchange for greater conformity and homogenization of cultures, complete with the dislocation of families and communities brought about by urbanization, the negation or appropriation of traditional lifestyles, and environmental degradation. Where communities feel they are faced with marginalization, foreclosed options for the future or even oppression and eradication, some inevitably respond by asserting their primary identities more forcefully.

3.7 In democratic societies, when groups sharing a history of discrimination or victimization make claims for equal rights and political participation, they may be addressed peacefully through, for example, affirmative action. In political systems which offer no channel for grievances to be heard, political and militant groups often emerge, advocating the use of violence to achieve redress. Perceived as liberation movements by some, they are considered as threats to national security by others. At the extreme end of the spectrum, radicals vying for economic or political gain can exploit feelings of humiliation or deprivation to attract recruits for political parties or militant groups formed along religious or ethnic lines. Slanted projections in the media,

163

sometimes with substantive analysis but more often in superficial and simplistic terms, aggravate mutually negative perceptions.

Emergence of Extremism

3.8 The exploitation of religion by ideologues intent on swaying people to their causes has led to the misguided perception that religion itself is a root cause of intercultural conflict. It is therefore essential to dispel misapprehensions and to give an objective and informed appraisal of the role of religion in modern day politics. Indeed, a symbiotic relationship may be emerging between religion and politics in our time, each influencing the other. As an example from the past, the seemingly secular colonial enterprise of the 'civilizing mission' or the nineteenth century conviction of 'manifest destiny' in reality had deep religious roots. Conversely, the overtly religious platforms of some contemporary movements conceal political ambitions that appropriate religion for ideological ends.

3.9 From the mid-nineteenth century to the middle of the twentieth century, many intellectual and political elites assumed that modernization would extinguish religion's vitality. As people became wealthier, enjoyed greater political freedom, and attained higher levels of education, the argument went, secularization and secularism as a legal and political principle would also advance, relegating religion to a much less significant role in world events. But in recent decades almost every major world religion has challenged this assumption, and has established a role in politics. There is increasing support in some societies for a greater role for religion in public life. Most express this desire in peaceable ways, persisting in a world that many view to be increasingly hostile to faith. But a tiny proportion of religiously motivated groups worldwide take part in acts of violence.

3.10 At this juncture, it is important to clarify our understanding of certain commonly used terms. "Fundamentalism" is a Western term coined by Protestant Christians which is not readily applicable to other communities. It is frequently used to describe movements which are disturbed by the marginalization of religion in secular society and seek to reinstate its central role. Even though all these movements are in fact highly innovative and even unorthodox, they often call for a return to the roots of religious tradition and a literal adherence to basic texts and principles irrespective of historical factors. Notwithstanding the imprecision with which the term

164

is used, what is important to note here is that such movements exist across most faith traditions. Moreover, they are not inherently violent. What is common to them is a deep disappointment with and fear of secular modernity, which many of them have experienced as invasive, amoral, and devoid of deeper meaning. Extremism, on the other hand, advocates radical measures in pursuit of political goals. It is not, by nature, religious, and can also be found in secular movements. In some cases, fundamentalist and extremist ideologies can be used to justify acts of violence and even terrorist attacks on civilians.

3.11 It is imperative to recognize that none of the world religions condones or approves the killing of innocents. All promote the ideals of compassion, justice and respect for the dignity of life. However, in a wide range of recent conflicts in many parts of the world religion has been exploited to justify intolerance, violence and even the taking of life. Recently, a considerable number of acts of violence and terrorism have been committed by radical groups on the fringes of Muslim societies. Because of these actions, Islam is being perceived by some as an inherently violent religion. Assertions to this effect are at best manifestly incorrect and at worst maliciously motivated. They deepen divides and reinforce the dangerous mutual animosity among societies.

3.12 Extremism and terrorism are not motivated solely by exclusivist interpretations of religion, nor are non-state actors alone in employing them. Indeed, secular political motives were responsible for some of the most horrifying reigns of terror in living memory, such as the Holocaust, the Stalinist repressions in the Soviet Union, and more recent genocides in Cambodia, the Balkans, and Rwanda, all perpetrated by state powers. In sum, a cursory look at the twentieth century indicates that no single group, culture, geographic region, or political orientation has a monopoly on extremism and terrorist acts.

3.13 Wherever communities believe they face persistent discrimination, humiliation, or marginalization based on ethnic, religious, or other identity markers, they are likely to assert their identity more aggressively. As long as the source of resentment persists, and particularly when it is aggravated by increased humiliation or by despair in the normal political process, moderate leaders will always struggle to match the allure of those who stoke feelings of collective anger and offer fellowship and redress through exclusivist ideologies, adversarial politics and violence. Effective counter-measures cannot rely solely on attacking adherents of such ideologies - in fact such tactics are likely to inflame the very sentiments they seek to eradicate. The only durable solution lies in addressing the roots of the resentment and anger that make exclusivist and violent ideologies attractive in the first place. Nowhere have exclusivist ideologies, adversarial perceptions, cultural arrogance, and media stereotypes combined more dangerously with conflicts bred of perceived and real injustices than in relations between Western and Muslim societies.

IV. The Political Dimension

Historical Narratives

4.1 Building on the efforts of the Dialogue Among Civilizations [1] and other related initiatives [2], the Alliance of Civilizations must examine - within a multi-polar and comprehensive approach - the state of relations between diverse contemporary societies, their world-views and the reciprocal perceptions that shape these relations. The analysis here focuses on relations between Western and Muslim societies though the approach taken by the High-level Group to this issue may serve as a reference for the bridging of other divides in the interest of establishing peace and harmony.

4.2 Notwithstanding historical periods of tension and confrontation between adherents of the three major monotheistic religions - conflicts which themselves were often more political than religious in nature - it is important to note that peaceful co-existence, beneficial trade and reciprocal learning have been hallmarks of relations between Christianity, Islam and Judaism from their earliest period until today. During medieval times, Islamic civilization was a major source of innovation, knowledge acquisition, and scientific advancement that contributed to the emergence of the Renaissance and the Enlightenment in Europe. Historically, under Muslim rule, Jews and Christians were largely free to practice their faiths. Many rose to high political positions and Jews in particular took refuge in Muslim empires at different times

---

[1] See the Global Agenda for the Dialogue Among Civilizations (A/60/259).

[2] In particular, the Declaration and Program of Action for a Culture of Peace referred to, together with the Dialogue Among Civilizations and the Alliance of Civilizations, in paragraph 144 of the 2005 World Summit Outcome of the UN General Assembly.

in history to escape discrimination and persecution. Similarly, in recent centuries, political, scientific, cultural, and technological developments in the West have influenced many aspects of life in Muslim societies and many Muslims have sought to immigrate to Western nations in part for the political freedoms and economic opportunities found there.

Relations Between Societies of Western and Muslim Countries

4.3 Selective accounts of ancient history are used by radical movements to paint an ominous portrait of historically distinct and mutually exclusive faith communities destined for confrontation. Such distorted historical narratives must be countered. More important for the purposes of this report is the fact that this history does not offer explanations for current conflicts or for the rise in hostility between Western and Muslim societies. On the contrary, the roots of these phenomena lie in developments that took place in the nineteenth and twentieth centuries, beginning with European imperialism, the resulting emergence of anti-colonial movements, and the legacy of the confrontations between them.

4.4 The partition of Palestine by the United Nations in 1947, envisaging the establishment of two states - Palestine and Israel - with a special status for Jerusalem, led to the establishment of the state of Israel in 1948, beginning a chain of events that continues to be one of the most tortuous in relations between Western and Muslim societies. Israel's continuing occupation of Palestinian and other Arab territories and the unresolved status of Jerusalem - a holy city for Muslims and Christians as well as Jews - have persisted with the perceived acquiescence of Western governments and thus are primary causes of resentment and anger in the Muslim world toward Western nations. This occupation has been perceived in the Muslim world as a form of colonialism and has led many to believe, rightly or wrongly, that Israel is in collusion with "the West". These resentments and perceptions were further exacerbated by Israel's recent disproportionate retaliatory actions in Gaza and Lebanon.

4.5 In another critical context, the Middle East emerged as a vital source of energy crucial for prosperity and power. Cold War powers vied for influence in the strategic and resource rich countries of the region, often in the form of military and political interventions that contributed to stunting those countries' development and eventually backfired on the powerful countries with repercussions that continue to be felt today.

One of these events was the 1953 coup in Iran, the aftermath of which demonstrated both the limitations and the dangers of foreign interference in a country's political development.

4.6 The Soviet invasion and occupation of Afghanistan in 1979 opened another line of confrontation. As part of the Western policy of supporting religious opposition to contain Communism, the US and its allies, including some Muslim governments in the region, bolstered the Afghan resistance-the "mujahedin"-eventually forcing the Soviet retreat in 1989. After a period of instability, the Taliban regime seized control of the country and supported Al Qaeda, fomenting deep hostility against the West and setting in motion a chain of events which were to scar the start of the new Millennium.

4.7 The terrorist attacks perpetrated by Al Qaeda on the United States in September 2001 drew near universal condemnation irrespective of religion or politics and demonstrated the depth of this extremist group's hostility. They provoked a forceful retaliation against the Taliban regime in Afghanistan. Later, these attacks were presented as one of the justifications for the invasion of Iraq, whose link with them has never been established, feeding a perception among Muslim societies of unjust aggression stemming from the West.

4.8 In the context of relations between Muslim and Western societies, the perception of double standards in the application of international law and the protection of human rights is particularly acute. Reports of collective punishment, targeted killings, torture, arbitrary detention, renditions, and the support of autocratic regimes contribute to an increased sense of vulnerability around the globe, particularly in Muslim countries, and to a perception of Western double standards. Assertions that Islam is inherently violent and related statements by some political and religious leaders in the West-including the use of terms such as "Islamic terrorism" and "Islamic fascism"-have contributed to an alarming increase in Islamophobia which further exacerbates Muslim fears of the West.

4.9 Conversely, violent attacks targeting civilian populations in the West, including suicide bombings, kidnappings, and torture, have led to an atmosphere of suspicion, insecurity and fear in the West. Many in the West also perceive double standards on the part of Muslim leaders. Indeed, while Western military operations are widely condemned by Muslims, this is not the case with intra-Muslim conflicts.

Sectarian violence between Shias and Sunnis in certain Muslim countries and the atrocities committed against civilians in Darfur, for instance, have not led to widespread condemnation in the Muslim world.

4.10 These reciprocal perceptions of double standards contribute to the climate of suspicion and mistrust that undermines relations between Muslim and Western societies.

Trends in Muslim Societies

4.11 Late in the colonial age, many Muslim thinkers urged their communities to adapt to changing times. Following independence, several Muslim leaders embarked on programs of modernization to bring development to their populations. These policies were often viewed by religious parties as driven by a secularization agenda. More recent decades have witnessed the growth of a diverse array of religio-political movements-loosely termed "Islamist"-that have gained credibility and popular support in part by providing sorely needed social services, especially in health and primary education, to deprived sectors of society. They stand in contrast to many of the ruling regimes which are widely viewed as having failed to provide sufficiently for the economic and social welfare of their populations.

4.12 In evaluating the relations between Western and Muslim societies it is important to note that Islamist activism does not necessarily produce Islamist militancy within societies and the latter does not automatically lead to violent confrontation with the West. It is the invasion of certain Muslim countries by Western military forces and their continued presence in these countries, combined with the suppression of political movements in the Muslim world, that are among the reasons for violent manifestations. As evidenced throughout history and across many countries, political repression as well as the prolongation of occupation help entrench violent resistance. This raises the issue of the dynamics at play within the Muslim world that are affecting relations between Muslim societies and the rest of the world.

4.13 The current predicament from which much of the Muslim world suffers cannot be attributed solely to foreign interference. An internal debate between progressive and regressive forces is playing out on a range of social and political issues throughout the Muslim world as well as on interpretations of Islamic law and traditions. In simplified yet evident terms, resistance to change in several Muslim societies is at the root of their disadvantaged position relative to other societies that are advancing rapidly in the contemporary age. There appears to be a growing realization among Muslims that the authoritarianism and conformity that have marked many of their societies in past centuries are severe detriments to them in an increasingly integrated and interdependent world. It seems apparent that all Muslim societies would benefit from increased dialogue and debate to identify those factors internal to their own societies which have inhibited their development and full integration into global political, economic, and intellectual communities, and to generate ideas on how to overcome these barriers.

4.14 In some cases, self-proclaimed religious figures have capitalized on a popular desire for religious guidance to advocate narrow, distorted interpretations of Islamic teachings. Such figures misportray certain practices, such as honor killings, corporal punishment, and oppression of women as religious requirements. These practices are not only in contravention of internationally-agreed human rights standards, but, in the eyes of respected Muslim scholars, have no religious foundation. Such scholars have demonstrated that a sound reading of Islamic scriptures and history would lead to the eradication and not the perpetuation of these practices.

4.15 Many of these practices relate directly to the status of women. In some Muslim societies, ill-informed religious figures, in some cases allied with unenlightened conservative political regimes, have succeeded in greatly restricting women's access to public and professional life, thereby hampering their prospects and potential for self-fulfillment. The effect on those women, on society at large, and on future generations, has been to inhibit economic and social development as well as democratic pluralism. This problem can only be overcome through laws that ensure full gender equality in accordance with internationally-agreed human rights standards. Such measures are most likely to succeed if supported by religious education that is based upon a sound interpretation of religious teachings. It must be noted, however, that in many parts of the world, including Western countries, much progress is still needed with regard to the status of women.

4.16 Who prevails in these intra-Muslim struggles is central not only to the future of Muslim societies, but also to their future relations with the rest of the world, which is why we take up this matter here. Clearly these tensions can only be settled by Muslim

170

societies themselves. While there is no obvious role for non-Muslims to play, Western activists and governments in particular should avoid certain actions that have negative repercussions on debates taking place in Muslim societies. Propagation by Western media and official authorities of over-simplified explanations that either blame Islam as a religion or that falsely pit secularists against religious activists has a detrimental effect. This includes media coverage that gives time and space only to the most extreme of the religious voices in the Muslim world and to the most anti-Muslim ideologues in the West to counter them. Similarly, some media products generated in Muslim countries that presents mostly or entirely negative portrayals of other communities feeds polarization. The use of expressions such as "Islamic terrorism" in the West and "modern Crusaders" in the Muslim world exacerbates the mutual hostility.

4.17 Among the intra-Muslim debates that most directly affect relations with Western societies is that over the concept of "jihad". The notion of jihad is a rich one with many shades of meaning, ranging from the struggle between good and evil that is internal to every individual (often referred to as the "greater" jihad in Islam) to the taking up of arms in defense of one's community (the "lesser" jihad). Increasingly, this term is used by extremists to justify violence with little consideration for the historical context and the related religious exigencies that most Muslim scholars agree should inform its application. When such exhortations to violence by radical factions are picked up and amplified by media and Western political leaders, the notion of "jihad" loses the multiple meanings and positive connotations it has for Muslims and becomes only associated with violent and negative meanings which have been wrongly attributed to the term.

4.18 For many Muslims, the only perceived successes in shaking off occupation or political domination by Western countries over the past thirty years have been those led by religio-political-military movements and non-state actors. The ability of such groups, which are perceived to be militarily, economically, and politically overwhelmed by Western nations, to succeed through asymmetric warfare in resisting invasion and occupation, generates feelings of solidarity and support. Fear of Western domination is so acute and widespread that support for resistance movements exists even among some who do not share the broader political or religious ideologies of these groups, or who are concerned about what the long-term effect of their ascendance might be on political and social liberties. It is therefore not surprising that among the most alienated and frustrated segments of Muslim societies where feelings of powerlessness and victimization are most acute, the revolutionary rhetoric of the most radical religio-military movements find some traction and support.

4.19 Moreover the actions of such groups, all of which emerged in the context of political opposition, stand in stark contrast to the perceived failures of official regimes in many Muslim countries. Indeed, many of these regimes are viewed as unable to resist foreign interference or as being closely allied with certain Western nations that are perceived to support the occupation of Muslim countries or the repression of fellow-Muslims.

4.20 In this context, there is a growing perception within and beyond the Muslim world that distinctions need to be made between, on the one hand, national movements which resist foreign occupation and, on the other hand, terrorist groups with global ambitions. This view is not shared by all in the international community. Resistance groups should be encouraged to pursue their goals through non-violent participation in political processes and democratic representation. For global terrorist groups, a "clash of civilizations" is a welcome and potent slogan to attract and motivate a loosely knit network of operatives and supporters. We must make it clear that, in our view, no political end, whether arising from historical injustice or contemporary provocation, and whether committed by resistance organizations, global militant groups, or by states, can justify the targeting of civilians and non-combatants. Such actions must be condemned unequivocally.

V. Towards an Alliance of Civilizations:
General Policy Recommendations

The Middle East

5.1 With regard to relations between Muslim and Western societies, we must acknowledge the contemporary realities that shape the views of millions of Muslims: the prolonged Israeli-Palestinian conflict, the violence in Afghanistan, and the increasingly violent conflict in Iraq.

5.2 We must stress the growing urgency of the Palestinian issue, which is a major factor in the widening rift between Muslim and Western societies. In this regard, it is

172

our duty to express our collective opinion that without a just, dignified, and democratic solution based on the will of all peoples involved in this conflict, all efforts - including recommendations contained in this report - to bridge this gap and counter the hostilities among societies are likely to meet with only limited success.

5.3 Our emphasis on the Israeli - Palestinian conflict is not meant to imply that it is the overt cause of all tensions between Muslim and Western societies. Other factors also create resentment and mistrust, including the spiraling crisis in Iraq, the continued instability in Afghanistan, issues internal to Muslim societies, as well as terrorist attacks on civilian populations in many countries. Nevertheless, it is our view that the Israeli - Palestinian issue has taken on a symbolic value that colors cross - cultural and political relations among adherents of all three major monotheistic faiths well beyond its limited geographic scope.

5.4 Achieving a just and sustainable solution to this conflict requires courage and a bold vision of the future on the part of Israelis, Palestinians and all countries capable of influencing the situation. We firmly believe that progress on this front rests on the recognition of both the Palestinian and Jewish national aspirations and on the establishment of two fully sovereign and independent states living side by side in peace and security.

5.5 Reaching this objective will require Israel not only to accept but to facilitate the establishment of a viable Palestinian state. The peace accords involving Israel, Egypt and Jordan demonstrate that such constructive steps taken in line with international law are workable. Moreover, the terms of reference agreed to by all parties at the Madrid Conference in 1991, the peace initiative by President Clinton in 2000, and the peace proposal by the Arab League at its meeting in Beirut, Lebanon in 2002, make it clear that the framework for a broad - based accord does exist and the political will can be generated.

5.6 Of primary importance in this regard is the mutual recognition of the competing narratives that emerged following the establishment of the state of Israel. In the eyes of most Jews and Israelis this event was the result of a long - standing aspiration to build a Jewish homeland and was immediately followed by an attack from neighboring Arab countries. For Palestinians and a majority of people in the Muslim world, however, the establishment of Israel was experienced as an act of aggression that led to the expulsion of hundreds of thousands of Palestinians and to the occupation of their lands. It is worth noting that these competing narratives are mirrored in divergent interpretations of recent history: different ways of describing conflicts, occupation, and peace negotiation efforts.

5.7 A White Paper on the Israeli-Palestinian conflict. The competing narratives of Palestinians and Israelis cannot be fully reconciled, but they must be mutually acknowledged in order to establish the foundations of a durable settlement. To this end, we recommend the development of a White Paper analyzing the Israeli-Palestinian conflict dispassionately and objectively, giving voice to the competing narratives on both sides, reviewing and diagnosing the successes and failures of past peace initiatives, and establishing clearly the conditions that must be met to find a way out of this crisis. Such a document could provide a firm foundation for the work of key decision-makers involved in efforts to resolve this conflict. A level-headed and rational analysis would make it clear to the Palestinian people that the price of decades of occupation, misunderstanding and stigmatization is being fully acknowledged, while at the same time contributing to exorcize the fears of Israelis. This effort would strengthen the hand of those who seek a just solution to this conflict while weakening extremists on all sides, as they would no longer be the champions of a cause they have been able to appropriate because its story had been left untold or deliberately ignored by the community of nations.

5.8 A re-invigorated multilateral peace process. As a further step in a renewed effort to solve the problems that lie at the heart of the Middle East crisis, the High-level Group calls for the resumption of the political process, including the convening, as soon as possible, of an international conference on the Middle East Peace Process, to be attended by all relevant actors, with the aim of reaching a comprehensive peace agreement.

5.9 International compacts with Iraq and Afghanistan. [1] The international

---

① The *International Compact with Iraq* sponsored by the Government of Iraq, the United Nations, and the World Bank was initiated at the Abu Dhabi Preparatory Meeting on 10 September 2006.

See www.iraqcompact.org. The *Afghanistan Compact,* resulting from consultations between the government of Afghanistan, the United Nations, and the international community, was launched at the London Conference on Afghanistan from 31 January to 1 February, 2006. See www.fco.gov.uk.

community should respond with a sense of responsibility to the political and humanitarian crisis in Iraq. The High-level Group expresses its full support for the efforts of the Arab League to build domestic political consensus in Iraq and for the full implementation of the International Compact with Iraq. Similarly, though in a different regional context, the High-level Group expresses its full support for the recently initiated International Compact with Afghanistan.

5.10 Political pluralism in Muslim countries. One of the factors contributing to the polarization between Muslim and Western societies and to the rise in extremism in these relations is the repression of political movements in the Muslim world. Therefore, it is in the interest of Muslim and Western societies alike that ruling parties in the Muslim world provide the space for the full participation of non-violent political parties, whether religious or secular in nature. To this end, foreign governments should be consistent in their support for democratic processes and not interfere when the results do not fit their political agenda. This call for expanded political pluralism applies not only to countries in the Middle East or in the larger Muslim world, but to all nations.

Other General Policy Recommendations

5.11 A renewed commitment to multilateralism. As noted throughout this report, many of the problems facing the international community can only be addressed effectively within a multilateral framework. It is therefore incumbent upon states to reinforce multilateral institutions-particularly the United Nations-and to support reform efforts that will strengthen the capacity and performance of these institutions.

5.12 A full and consistent respect for international law and human rights. Polarization between communities grows when universal human rights are defended-or perceived to be defended-selectively. Therefore, establishing genuine dialogue among nations requires a common understanding of international human rights principles and a universal commitment to their full and consistent application. In particular, this dialogue must be founded on respect for human rights (including freedom of conscience, freedom of expression and protection from torture and other inhuman or degrading treatment), as defined in the Universal Declaration of Human Rights, the Geneva Conventions, and other basic documents, as well as on a recognition of the authority of international criminal courts.

5.13 Coordinated migration policies consistent with human rights standards. Migration is most effectively managed when policies are coordinated between countries of origin, transit and destination for migrants and when they are consistent with international human rights law, international humanitarian law, and international agreements which guide the protection of refugees and internally displaced persons.

5.14 Combating poverty and economic inequities. An Alliance of Civilizations can only be fully realized within an international framework that includes the commitment of all countries to work toward the achievement of the Millennium Development Goals. The urgency of this matter can hardly be overstated. Global inequalities are growing at a staggering rate. In Africa, half the population lives under a dollar a day. Although the continent accounts for nearly a sixth of world population, it represents less than 3% of global trade and lags behind in other areas, including investment, education and health. [1] These problems must be tackled urgently, as the increasing gap between rich and poor plays an important role in fueling resentment and eroding global solidarity.

5.15 Protection of the freedom of worship. Freedom of religion and freedom of worship are fundamental rights to be guaranteed by all countries and faith communities. Therefore, particular attention must be paid to the respect for religious monuments and holy sites, as they have a significance that goes to the core of individual and collective religious identity. The violation and desecration of places of worship can grievously damage relations between communities and raise the risk of triggering widespread violence. In line with the resolution adopted by the UN General Assembly in 2001, [2] therefore, we believe that governments should take a strong stand against the desecration of holy sites and places of worship and take responsibility for their protection. We also call upon civil society and international organizations to help promote a culture of tolerance and respect for all religions and religious sites.

5.16 Exercising responsible leadership. Many of the issues feeding tensions

---

① According to the 2005 Human Development Report, produced by the United Nations Development Programme, in 2003, Africa received US$13 billion in foreign direct investment, compared to US$216 billion for the EU, US$147 for Asia and US$95 for North America. Moreover, 18 of the continent's 53 countries experienced a decline in standards of living between 1990 and 2003.

② See UN Resolution on "Protection of Religious Sites" (A/RES/55/254) adopted by the General Assembly on 31 May 2001.

between communities arise at the crossroads of politics and religion. One of these issues is the impact of inflammatory language sometimes used by political and religious leaders and the destructive effect such language can have when disseminated by the media. Such language fuels the spread of hatred and mistrust resulting in Islamophobia, xenophobia, and anti-Semitism. In the current climate of fear and suspicion that grips communities throughout the world, leaders and shapers of public opinion have a special responsibility to promote understanding among cultures and mutual respect of religious belief and traditions. Given the influence and the respect they command, it is their duty to avoid using violent or provocative language about other people's beliefs or sacred symbols.

5.17 The central importance of civil society activism. While political steps are necessary in order to advance each of the policy recommendations noted above, political action taken without the support of civil society often falls short of effecting lasting change. The High-level Group therefore calls for a greater role and involvement of civil society in the mechanisms for the advancement of its recommendations and, in particular, for the peaceful resolution of conflicts.

5.18 Establishing partnerships to advance an Alliance of Civilizations. The High-level Group recommends the development of partnerships in the framework of the Alliance of Civilizations with international organizations that share its goals, and the reinforcement of their interaction and coordination with the UN system. Special attention should be given to those international organizations that are part of the UN family and those organizations that have already been cooperating with the High-level Group of the Alliance of Civilizations, namely: the United Nations Educational Scientific and Cultural Organization (UNESCO), the European Union, the Organization for Security and Cooperation in Europe (OSCE), the Organization of the Islamic Conference (OIC), the League of Arab States, the Islamic Educational Scientific and Cultural Organization (ISESCO), United Cities and Local Governments (UCLG), and the World Tourism Organization (UNWTO), as well as other international and national organizations, public or private.

5.19 The primary purpose of the analysis in Part I of this report-both at the global level and at the level specific to relations between Muslim and Western societies-is to lay the basis and assert the moral grounds for concerted action at institutional and civil society levels to foster cross-cultural harmony and to enhance global stability. The remainder of this report (Part II-Main Fields of Action and Thematic Recommendations) explores the primary means by which such action could be taken-analyzing the key roles that education, youth, migration and media are currently playing in relations between societies and proposing actions that could be taken in each of these sectors to improve relations.

Members of the High-level Group

Co-Sponsors

1. Prof. Mehmet Aydin (Turkey) Co-chair — Minister of State of Turkey and Professor of Philosophy

2. Prof. Federico Mayor (Spain) Co-chair — President, Culture of Peace Foundation and Former Director-General, UNESCO

Middle East

3. Seyed Mohamed Khatami (Iran) — Former President of Iran

4. Her Highness Sheikha Mozah bint Nasser al Missned (Qatar) — Consort of the Emir, State of Qatar and Chairperson, Qatar Foundation for Education, Science and Community Development

5. Dr. Ismail Serageldin (Egypt) — President, Bibliotheca Alexandria

North Africa

6. Dr. Mohamed Charfi (Tunisia) — Former Education Minister of Tunisia

7. Mr. André Azoulay (Morocco) — Adviser to His Majesty King Mohammed VI of Morocco

West Africa

8. Mr. Moustapha Niasse (Senegal) — Former Prime Minister of Senegal

Southern Africa

9. Archbishop Desmond Tutu (S. Africa) — The Rt. Hon. Archbishop of Cape Town

West Europe

10. Mr. Hubert Védrine (France) — Former Minister of Foreign Affairs, France

11. Ms. Karen Armstrong (UK) — Historian of Religion

East Europe

12. Prof. Vitaly Naumkin (Russia)   President of the International Center for Strategic and Political Studies and Chair, Moscow State University

North America

13. Prof. John Esposito (US)   Founding Director, Prince Al-Waleed bin-Talal Center for Muslim-Christian Understanding (Georgetown University) and Editor-in-Chief of the Oxford Encyclopedia of the Islamic World

14. Rabbi Arthur Schneier (US)   President, Appeal of Conscience Foundation and Senior Rabbi, East Park Synagogue

Latin America

15. Mr. Enrique Iglesias (Uruguay)   Ibero-American organization, Secretary-General organization and Former President, Inter-American Development bank

16. Prof. Candido Mendes (Brazil)   Secretary-General, Académie de la Latinité

South Asia

17. Dr. Nafis Sadik (Pakistan)   Special Adviser to the UN Secretary-General

18. Ms. Shobhana Bhartia (India)   Member of Parliament, India; Vice Chairperson and Editorial Director, The Hindustan Times, New Delhi

South East Asia

19. Mr. Ali Alatas (Indonesia)   Former Foreign Minister of Indonesia

East Asia

20. Prof. Pan Guang (China)   Director and Professor, Shanghai Academy of Social Sciences

Appendix 4:

The Nishan Declaration of Human Harmony (2010)

The Declaration of Human Harmony

On September 27, 2010, the Chinese and foreign experts and scholars attending the First Nishan Forum jointly issued the Nishan Declaration – The Declaration of Human Harmony. It is the first theme declaration on human harmony in the world and an important achievement of the First Nishan Forum, which will exert important influence on dialogue and exchange between different civilizations and the building of a harmonious world.

The full text:

On September 27, 2010, one day before the 2,561st anniversary of the birth of the great ancient Chinese thinker and educator Confucius, we review the human wisdom of that age when wise people were needed and emerged more than 2,500 years ago and jointly issue the following a declaration of harmony at the First Nishan Forum on World Civilizations:

Troubled over the present state of world affairs;

Anxious about our common human future;

Distressed by the brutal reality of war, slaughter, and conflict;

And confronted with a deteriorating global environment,

Human beings everywhere are perplexed and confused. Having solemnly pondered and acknowledged the wisdom of our predecessors,

We advocate harmony;

We advocate loving-kindness;

We advocate tolerance;

We advocate decorum and civility;

We advocate faithfulness and reliability;

We advocate"never doing to others what you would not have done to yourself";

We advocate "loving all creatures as we would love ourselves" and "the unity of Heaven and humanity";

We advocate the principle that "while we enjoy the beauty of our own culture, we also appreciate the beauty of other civilizations";

We advocate the belief that within the four seas, all people are brothers and sisters;

We advocate for a harmonious world and for the principle of "harmony with diversity".

For the purpose of building a harmonious world,

And for the purpose of conserving our common globe,

We appeal for mutual understanding and respect by which to resolve grievances;

We appeal for dialogue and communication as a means to avoiding conflicts;

We appeal for frugality and low-carbon emissions in order to sustain our home earth;

We appeal for solidarity and collaboration to build our future together.

We hope and pray that—

Our advocacies and appeals will be echoed and embraced by the entire world.

We hope and pray that—

Our advocacies and appeals will be transformed into common practices for all human beings.

A Proposal for Young People to Take an Active Part in Dialogues among World Civilizations (2012)

A philosopher once said, "the Youth is the king of life". Young people are energetic, active, and ambitiously exploring. They are today's masters, tomorrow's leaders, and are entrusted with the hope of mankind. Today, my fellows and I want to read this letter to the youth of the world to call for the youth to do as follows:

We advocate:

Despite different races, different genders, different ethnicities, different value systems, we youth should unite together, shoulder the mission for the sustainable development, and actively step towards the front stage of the cross-civilization dialogues.

We advocate:

The youth of the world should respect and understand human civilizations of all kinds, and include different cultures and beliefs, in virtue of objective perspectives with embracing hearts. We have the responsibility to protect the diversity of human civilizations, just as we have responsibilities to protect the planet's biodiversity.

We advocate:

The youth of the world who hold different religious beliefs and are cultivated out of various spiritual forms should have mutual respect, understanding, and empathy. We should fight against various racial and cultural discriminations and oppose all forms of ethnocentrism.

We advocate:

Young people with different nationalities and different religious beliefs have the responsibility and duty to embrace their own culture with great depth and sophistication, and share the task with future generations and throughout the world.

We advocate:

All young people should have an open mind and a learning attitude to listen to the voices of different civilizations and to learn from the merits of others, in order to promote the development of their own cultural traditions and the common prosperity of human civilizations.

Our aim is to reinforce the dialogues among different civilizations, promote the harmonious development of mankind, to resolve their conflicts and thus achieving the peaceful coexistence of world civilizations. The diversity of cultural and religious beliefs should not be the root cause of clashes among civilizations. Rather they should be the starting point of cultural exchanges and cooperation. The blossom of one flower alone can not create a spring; only the flourishing of hundreds of flowers can do it. The dominance of one single civilization is not a blessing of mankind; it is the mutually reinforced development of various civilizations that is the great fortune of mankind! The Greek philosopher Heraclitus once said: "The different tones produce the most beautiful harmony." Confucius also advocated the ideal of "harmony but not sameness". We do not ignore the differences of human civilizations; yet it is precisely these differences that become the unending dynamic of civilizations.

Dear friends, let us put aside the differences of our race, gender, ethnicity, and beliefs, and march courageously, hand in hand, to the front stage of world culture dialogues. Let youth shine, to create a fresh civilization; let youth shine, to keep human civilization forever young. With a melody of youthful dialogues, we shall orchestrate a harmonious symphony amongst different civilizations.

Issued at the Second Nishan Forum on World Civilizations, May, 2012.

Appendix 6:

Nishan Consensus (2012)

—— On the Protection of Ancient Civilizations' Cultural Heritage
and the Promotion of Dialogues among Civilizations

On May 21, 2012, the second Nishan Forum on World Civilizations was held at Nishan. May 21 this year is the 10th anniversary of the United Nations "World Day for Cultural Diversity for Dialogue and Development". Experts and scholars from home and abroad like India, Mexico, Italy and America gathered at Qufu - the birth place of Confucius. Dialogues and exchanges were conducted on the theme: Cooperation and Responsibility of Ancient Civilizations. The following consensus has been reached:

First, respecting each other. Cultural heritage is the common wealth of human kind. In the long historical process, nations of the world have created brilliant and colorful culture with their intelligence and ingenuity. These valuable cultural heritages, which embody the joint wisdom of humanity, witness the history of human development.

What belongs to a nation belongs to the human kind as a whole. Diversity is an essential feature of the world civilization. Respecting each other's historical and cultural traditions is the basic principle to maintain cultural diversity. In the origination and development of human civilization, ancient civilizations have made tremendous contributions. In the new period, we are expected to assume the historical mission to constantly enrich and advance the cause of global heritage.

Second, enhancing cooperation. The development of the world brings unprecedented opportunities for cultural heritage protection. However, globalization brings much severer pressure and challenges at the same time. Thus, to realize the sustainable development of cultural heritage has already become an imperative task for the international community.

International cooperation is the fundamental way to protect heritage and sustain the development of human civilization. The development of human history is the process of continuous communication, integration and innovation. The practices of strengthening dialogue among various civilizations and enthusiastically participating in international multilateral exchanges and cooperation for cultural heritage protection play a significant role in cultural heritage protection, passing down national spirit, building human cultural ecology of respect, tolerance, harmony and development among nations as well as promoting world peace and development.

Third, facing the future. Cultural heritage belongs to both the past and future. As the masterpiece jointly created by man and nature, cultural heritage is the lasting historical memory and spiritual home for mankind. It is also the cultural source for the contemporary to inherit history and forge ahead into the future.

Cultural heritage protection is supposed to be incorporated into the development of mankind, to guide the progress of civilization and to bring new life to the people. For today and future, we should put the long history of various nations and the cultural foundation on which we rely for survival and development under a better protection. All what we have done today is for the aim of passing on the spiritual and emotional carrier of all nations.

Ancient civilizations appeal to all nations to promote the sustainable development of cultural heritage with a joint effort, so as to achieve sustainable development of human civilization!

Appendix 7:

Chronicle of Civilization Dialogue

(2002–2012)

1. On 21 September 1998 at the 53rd session of the UN General Assembly, Iranian President Seyed Mohammad Khatami called for institutionalizing dialogue and "replacing hostility and confrontation with discourse and understanding." In particular, Khatami invited the international community to broaden and encourage dialogue among civilizations on the environment, peace and security. The thrust of the initiative was an appeal to human understanding that genuine dialogue on a global scale, involving all stakeholders, offers the only practical way to ensure meaningful and effective international cooperation. On 4 November 1998, the General Assembly adopted Resolution 53/22, proclaiming 2001 as the UN Year of Dialogue among Civilizations. It called on governments and the UN to plan and implement cultural, educational and social programmes to promote the concept of dialogue among civilizations, including through conferences and seminars and disseminating information.

2. The United Nations Educational, Scientific and Cultural Organization (UNESCO) convened the Second Round Tables for Ministers of Culture "2000–2010: 'Cultural diversity: Challenges of the Marketplace'" in Paris, 11–12 December 2000. This Second Round Table analyzed both the challenges posed by globalization and the role to be played by UNESCO in this context. It concluded that, the development of cultural industries in every country should not only adapt to the market economy and make use of global broad market space, but also particularly protect the cultural diversity and avoid that chasing economic interests erode the cultural diversity.

3. Organized by the Republic of Lithuania, the Republic of Poland and the United Nations Educational, Scientific and Cultural Organization, the International Conference on Dialogue among Civilizations was held in Vilnius, Lithuania, 23–26 April 2001. It was a major event in the celebration of the United Nations Year of Dialogue among Civilizations. Bringing together leaders, decision-makers, distinguished scholars and

artists from different parts of the world, the Conference offered a "polyphony" of voices in a debate on the complex issues affecting relations between different cultures and civilizations. At the conclusion of the event, the Vilnius Declaration was adopted.

4. Organized by the I.R. Iran and with the active collaboration of the United Nations (UN) and the United Nations Environment Programme (UNEP), the International Seminar on Environment, Religion and Culture was held in Tehran from 18–20 June 2001. The seminar adopted the Tehran Declaration on Environment, Religion and Culture, committing participants, among other things, to promote education on the environmental content of religion and to promote environmentally responsible behavior.

5. The International Conference on the Dialogue of Civilizations was held from 31 July to 3 August 2001 in Tokyo and Kyoto. Experts from academia, politics and other walks of life came together to jointly tackle the questions at the core of the UNU Project on the Dialogue of Civilizations: What are the prerequisites of a meaningful dialogue? And how can we best facilitate it? With over 40 speakers from 23 different countries, the conference gave a clear picture of the many aspects that are involved in a meaningful dialogue of civilizations. It showed that even for those who have been much involved in issues of dialogue, discussions are not always easy, in particular when they touch upon specific values and norms. It also very clearly proved, however, that as long as there is agreement among all parties involved that it is better to talk than to fight each other, dialogue is possible and actually leads to new and creative solutions to the common problems facing mankind.

6. The Foreign Affairs Committee of the Chinese People's Political Consultative Conference (CPPCC) hosted "21st Century Forum—Seminar on Dialogue among Civilizations" in Beijing, on September 11, 2001. The seminar invited Celebrities, experts and scholars from home and abroad, and carried out multifaceted exchanges and discussions. Song jian, Vice Chairman of the CPPCC, Chinese Academy of Engineering, gave the opening speech at the seminar. The seminar lasted for two days. The issues including three major aspects such as the role of exchange among civilizations in promoting the development of human history, the impact of dialogue among civilizations on the development of international relations, and the role of the united nations in promoting dialogue among civilizations. Representatives from China,

Egypt, Greece, the United States and other countries respectively expressed their point of view at the seminar.

7. The Universal Declaration on Cultural Diversity was adopted by the 31th UNESCO General Conference at UNESCO headquarters in Paris, on November 2, 2001. The declaration advocated protecting the cultural diversity as a fortune which was full of life and thus can continue to develop. In this sense, it was the common heritage of humanity and should be recognized and affirmed for the benefit of present and future generations.

8. The 7th symposium on Chinese Christianity and other Religious Scholars in North America, which was jointly sponsored by Chinese Christian Scholars Association in North America and Westminster Theological Seminary, was held successfully at Westminster Theological Seminary, Philadelphia, June 7–10, 2002. More than 70 Chinese scholars participated in the symposium. They were from the United States, Canada, mainland China, Hong Kong, Taiwan and the United Kingdom. The symposium received 45 papers, the theme of which was "Dialogue between Christianity and Chinese Culture". The content of these papers covered many aspects such as "dialogue between Christianity and Chinese culture", "history of Chinese Christianity" and "the current situation of Christianity in China".

9. The Symposium on the Dialogue between Civilizations sponsored by Nanjing University and Harvard-Yenching Institute, Harvard University, was held in Nanjing August 8–10, 2002. More than 50 representatives from home and abroad universities and research institutions attended the meeting. From the perspectives of history and reality, the Representatives had an insightful dialogue regarding such issues as the dialogue and conflict, assimilation and opposition between civilizations, especially the communication between the Hui Muslim and Confucianists in China. They had achieved promising result on various levels.

10. The World Summit on Sustainable Development (WSSD) was held from 26 August to 4 September 2002 in Johannesburg, South Africa. The WSSD adopted two main documents: the Johannesburg Declaration on Sustainable Development and the Johannesburg Plan of Implementation (JPOI). The JPOI noted that peace, security, stability and respect for human rights and fundamental freedoms, including the right to development, as well as respect for cultural diversity, are essential for

achieving sustainable development. The JPOI contained time-bound targets for the implementation of sustainable development in the following areas: basic sanitation; chemicals; integrated water resources management; oceans and fish stocks; alternatives to ozone-depleting substances; reduction in the current rate of loss of biological diversity; small island developing states; food security in Africa; and energy access in Africa.

11. The 1st Youth Dialogue of the Asia-Europe Meeting (ASEM), entitled "A World Without Borders? Asia-Europe Youth Responses to Globalization" in Copenhagen, Denmark, September 19–22, 2002. It created new friendships, a common vision, and a wish to continue the dialogue. This was the common views expressed by 63 participants and observers from 24 ASEM countries. According to the theme of the dialogue, it was a joint collaboration between the Asia-Europe Foundation (ASEF) and the Danish Youth Council (DUF). During the three-day gathering, participants were engaged in intensive discussions on four key issues related to globalization, namely, Migration; Youth Participation for Good Governance; Global Images and Identities; and Youth Employment, Education and Lifelong Learning. The meeting succeeded in bringing forth an ASEM Youth Statement on Globalization, which captured points of convergence and noted recommendations by the participants on possible responses to the challenges of globalization.

12. The 9th Francophonie Summit, which lasted for three days and passed the Beirut Declaration, closed in Beirut, the capital of Lebanon, October 20, 2002. The summit stressed that the peaceful settlement of the question of Palestine and Iraq should be in accordance with the frame of U.N. Resolution, that is, commitment to the principles of dialogue among civilizations, which call for "dialogue" but not "confrontation", "peace" but not "war", "democracy" but not "autocracy" and "multipole" but not "monopole".

13. The International Ministerial Conference on the Dialogue among Civilizations "Quest for New Perspectives" was held in New Delhi, India, 9 & 10 July 2003. The Conference was conceived to become a major contribution to defining global interaction of the 21st century through the lenses of intercultural dialogue and mutual interaction between cultures and civilizations. It focused on issues at the heart of UNESCO's mandate: (1) education as an instrument of dialogue; (2) science

and technology (*incl.* IT) as the new frontiers for global unity and connectivity; (3) preservation of cultural diversities and spiritual values in an era of globalization. New Delhi Declaration was adopted at the Conference. Representatives at the Conference requested "all governments and civil society to support actively a dialogue within and among civilizations and cultures so that it will become an effective instrument of transformation, a yardstick for peace and tolerance, and a vehicle for diversity and pluralism".

14. The 21st World Congress of Philosophy, the theme of which was "Philosophy Facing World Problems", was held at Conference and Exhibition Center, Istanbul, Turkey, August 10–17, 2003. This congress attracted thousands of scholars from all over the world, including more than 2000 delegates. Habermas, Contemporary famous German philosopher, was happy to attend the congress and made a keynote speech. The aim of the congress was to emphasize that we need to use philosophy to deal with major global issues in the beginning of the new century, and let philosophy play a role in the creating of a world without fear and poverty.

15. The First Annual Session of the World Public Forum "Dialogue of Civilizations" took place between 3–6 September 2003 on the Greek island of Rhodes. It was held amid a complicated international situation and thus confirmed the necessity for a broad international discussion devoted to reaching mutual understanding among representatives of different civilizations. In 2003 the Rhodes Forum became the most representative among public forums, and since then it is held annually. At the first session of the Forum the delegates accepted the Rhodes declaration "Dialogue of civilizations for a humane order." The Declaration called for continued discussion on the destiny of mankind and declared the goal to make the Forum a dynamic force in the international arena.

16. The First Congress on World Religions was held in Astana, capital of Kazakhstan, September 22–24, 2003. Over 150 representatives from 18 countries and international religious organizations attended the congress. The theme of the congress was "Peace, Tolerance and Dialogue", which advocated the harmonious coexistence of different religions, in order to eliminate the violence and hatred. In a certain sense, this theme can be seen as a concrete reflection of today's world trend of religious dialogue.

17. The First Symposium of the International Forum on World Civilizations, which

was jointly sponsored by Center for Research and Comparison of World Civilizations, Chinese Academy of Social Sciences, School of Foreign Languages at Nanjing Normal University and Macao Foundation, took place in Nanjing, November 6 – 8, 2003. The issues of the symposium to discuss included theory of civilization, dialogue and communication among civilizations through cultural diversity, the role of culture in the international relations and international politic, and so on. Representatives from over 20 countries and from some universities and institutes in China attended this Symposium, and they submitted more than 30 papers.

18. The two - day Asia - Europe Meeting on Culture and Civilization took place in the morning in Beijing, on December 3, 2003. Nearly 200 representatives from 26 members of the Asia - Europe Meeting and all social circles attended the meeting. They took cultural diversity and cultural unity as the theme, carried out dialogue on Asia - Europe's common value which existed in the cultural, ethnic and socio - economic diversity.

19. The International Symposium on Global Justice and Dialogue between Civilizations was held in East China Normal University January 8 – 12, 2004. Participants came from China, America, Australia, Singapore, Norway and other countries. Chen Qun, Vice - Chancellor of East China Normal University, Skirbekk, academician of Norwegian Academy of Science and Karrer, Project Leader of Carnegie Commission, attended the opening ceremony and made a congratulatory speech. Tong Shijun, Assistant to the President, presided over the symposium.

20. The United Nations Educational, Scientific and Cultural Organization (UNESCO) convened the International Symposium on Dialogue among Cultures and Civilizations, in Sana'a, Yemen, on 10 – 11 February 2004. The starting point of the Symposium was that the contribution of Arab - Muslim culture to other world civilizations deserves to be carefully and accurately assessed on the basis of scientifically grounded approaches. At the symposium, the The notion of a dialogue among cultures and civilizations was mainly approached from five different angles: globalization and dialogue; the contribution of education to the dialogue; the contribution of Arab culture to other cultures; the role of dialogue in curbing terrorism; and dialogue between East and West.

21. The First Annual Meeting of Beijing Forum hosted by Peking University was

held in Beijing August 23–25, 2004. The theme of the forum was "The Harmony of Civilizations and Prosperity for All". Coming from 32 countries of the five continents of the world, over 200 well-known scholars attended the forum. There were also 225 famous scholars from Mainland China, Hong Kong, Macao and Taiwan. Beijing Forum aimed at promoting the study of humanities and social sciences around the world. It endeavored to promote academic development and social progress across the world in order to contribute to the development and prosperity of humankind. Beijing Forum believed in promoting and safeguarding the progress of the human society through the peaceful integration of civilizations. Beijing Forum is held annually since then.

22. The 2nd International Symposium on New century's Civilizations among China, Japan and Korea was held in Lanzhou September 7–8, 2004. It was jointly hosted by the Institute of Japanese Studies, Chinese Academy of Social Sciences, Gansu Provincial People's Government Foreign Affairs Office, Japanese Research Institute of Future Engineering and South Korea Sejong Institute. The symposium focused on the theme of "Creating A Harmonious Civilization, Promoting Development in East Asia" and had a in-depth discussion on major issues such as future world civilizations, the diversity of civilization, the role of peaceful Asia, etc. About 70 politicians and scholars from the above three countries had a discussion about how to create harmonious civilizations in the new century.

23. The China-Japan Conference on Modern Civilizations and Religious Dialogue, which was jointly host by the Institute of World Religions, Chinese Academy of Social Science, and the Institute of Oriental Philosophy (IOP), Japan, was held at Academic Hall at Chinese Academy of Social Sciences, October 12–13, 2004. About 100 experts and scholars from colleges and universities in Beijing, various research institutes and related organizations attended the conference. This was the first time that China and Japan jointly hosted a conference on Religious Dialogue. At the meeting, scholars of the two countries started religious dialogue from different ways, enriched and deepen the understanding of religious dialogue.

24. The International Conference on Interaction, Rise and Fall of Chinese and Western Civilizations, which was jointly organized by the Institute of History, Chinese Academy of Social Science, and School of Society and History, Fujian Normal University, was held at Wuyishan, November 12–14, 2004. The conference received

51 papers and outlines. In the three-day meeting, 50 representatives from domestic and overseas colleges and universities, research institutes had a multi-faceted and multi-level discussion and analysis on Interaction, Rise and Fall of Eastern and Western Civilizations, and gained fruitful academic achievements.

25. The International Conference on The Spread and Development of Confucianism in the World was held at the Renmin University of China, December 3–5, 2004. The conference was jointly sponsored by Renmin University of China and The Korea Foundation for Advanced Studies, in collaboration with the Confucius Institute and Centre for Asian Studies, Renmin University of China. About 130 experts and scholars from more than 10 countries attended the conference, the conference received more than 70 papers. The aim of the conference, on the one hand, was to communicate Chinese and Western culture, to promote the spread and development of Confucianism, on the other hand, to understand the situation of overseas Confucianism and provide advices and proposals for the contemporary China digging out the cultural resource of Confucianism.

26. The Asia-Pacific Regional Conference on "Dialogue among Cultures and Civilizations for Peace and Sustainable Development", jointly organized by the Socialist Republic of Vietnam and UNESCO, took place in Hanoi, Vietnam, December 20–22, 2004. This regional conference sought to provide a forum for direct and open dialogue among institutions and individuals dedicated to dialogue among cultures and civilizations to discuss orientations, strategies and measures for political action at different levels and cross-cutting sectors. Participants were requested to highlight exemplary approaches and innovative strategies for promoting the dialogue among cultures and civilizations, especially those relating to education and culture. Ideas and recommendations for consolidating, advancing and networking the regional joint approaches were identified with a view to adopting a final policy-oriented conclusion for future action in this domain.

27. The International Conference on Peace Research sponsored by Department of History, Nanjing University, in partnership with Forgiveness and reconciliation Research Center, Coventry University, UK, Macao Foundation and The Amity Foundation, ceremoniously opened at International Conference Center, Nanjing, on March 4, 2005. Over 50 experts and scholars from Mainland China, Macao and foreign

countries attended the conference, and they had a three days' discussion around the theme of "Confrontation, Conflict and Solution in the History of Mankind".

28. In March 27–30, 2005, Cuba hosted the WPF "Dialogue of Civilizations" international conference entitled "Latin America in the 21st century: Universalism and Originality". The subject of this meeting was the current situation in Latin America, a region that is undergoing a process of civilizational self-determination. One of the main achievements of the conference was situating the most important Latin American issues within the international context. Participants of the conference declared their intention to defend freedom of social choice and multipolarity within the world community.

29. The International Conference on the Dialogue among Civilizations, Cultures and Peoples convened at UNESCO headquarters in Paris on 5 April 2005. At this meeting, Mohammad Khatami, President of Iran, urged open dialogue among civilizations as a necessary condition to improve international relations and development and called for the establishment of a Global Forum for the Promotion of Dialogue among Civilizations and Cultures.

30. The International Conference on Environment, Peace, and the Dialogue among Civilizations and Cultures, which was organized by the Dept. of Environment, Islamic Republic of Iran, and the United Nations Environment Programme (UNEP) in co-operation with United Nations University and UNESCO, took place in Tehran, Iran, May 9–10, 2005. More than 20 ministers from various countries, international organizations, religious groups and NGOs attended the conference. Meanwhile, more than 100 officials, scholars and researchers presented, too. The aim of the conference was to investigate the interaction of environment, peace and security, in the context of multilateral dialogue among civilizations, and also to discuss the necessity and meaningfulness of multilateral dialogue.

31. Center For Judaic and Inter-Religious Studies of Shandong University hosted the International conference on Inter-Religious Dialogue among Confucianism, Judaism and Christianity in the East Campus of Shandong University, May 30–31, 2005. About 40 experts on Jewish culture and inter-religious Studies from domestic and overseas universities and research institutes gathered at Shandong University and discussed about the subject.

32. The China-Europe Conference on Human Rights' Dialogue was jointly

organized by Chinese Foreign Ministry and European Commission. Its two Panels: on Freedom of Expression and on Death Penalty were held simultaneously in Jianguo Garden Hotel, Beijing, June 20–21, 2005. This was the 13th conference of the China-Europe Conference on Human Rights' Dialogue.

33. The International Conference on Zheng He's travel to the West and Dialogue among Civilizations was held in Yinchuan, June 30—July 3, 2005. The conference was sponsored by Ningxia Academy of Social Sciences, in partnership with the Cultural Office of the Embassy in Beijing, The Islamic Republic of Iran. The topics of the conference were "Zheng He's Travel to the West and the Spread of Civilizations", "The Relation between Persian-Arab Islamic Civilization and Chinese Islamic Civilization", "Revive the Silk Road, Advance the Development of the Trading Tie between China and Islamic countries" and "Dialogue among Civilizations". More than 130 experts and scholars from China, Iran, Pakistan, Japan and Bulgaria attended this conference, and they submitted 78 paper in Chinese or in English to the conference. The conference received high attention by some relevant organizations in Chinese and Iranian governments and media.

34. On July 14, 2005, Secretary-General Kofi Annan announced the launch of the Alliance of Civilizations initiative in a statement at the United Nations Headquarters, New York. The initiative s intended to respond to the need for a committed effort by the international community—both at the institutional and civil society levels—to bridge divides and overcome prejudice, misconceptions, and polarization which potentially threaten world peace. The Alliance will aim to address emerging threats emanating from hostile perceptions that foment violence, and to bring about cooperation among various efforts to heal such divisions. The call for an alliance was initiated by Prime Minister José Luis Rodriguez Zapatero of Spain, and co-sponsored by Prime Minister Recep Tayyip Erdogan of Turkey. Both Governments will continue, as co-sponsors, to provide support.

35. The First Asia-Europe Meeting (ASEM) Inter-Faith Dialogue was held in Bali, Indonesia, July 21–22, 2005. 174 representatives from Indonesia, UK, Thailand and 25 other Asian and European countries attended the meeting. The representatives brought forth the Bali Declaration on Building Interfaith Harmony within the International Community, calling upon the mutual understanding, respect and

195

harmonious coexistence between different religions and beliefs within the international community.

36. The 7th International Conference on Contemporary New Confucianism was held in Wuhan University, September 9–12, 2005. The conference was sponsored by Wuhan University, Taipei Asian Humanities Academic Research Foundation, Taipei *Swan Lake Magazine* and the Institute of Philosophy, Central University of Taiwan. About 150 scholars from home and aboard attended the conference, and they submitted more than 120 papers. The theme of the conference was "Confucianism, Contemporary New Confucianism and the Contemporary World". Scholars made a hot discussion on the topics such as "The Thoughts of Modern and Contemporary New Confucianism of Three Generations", "The Role and Significance of Confucianism in the Contemporary Era" and "The Further Development of Contemporary New Confucianism".

37. The 2nd International Forum on World Civilizations was sponsored by Research Center for World Civilizations' Comparison, Chinese Academy of Social Sciences, in collaboration with Shenzhen University, Zhongshan Institute, University of Electronic Science and Technology of China, Macao Foundation and Macao Polytechnic Institute. The 2nd forum elaborately planned three different symposiums, September 19–20, 2005, and their themes respectively were "World Civilizations and Theory of Civil Society", "Asia and World Civilizations" and "Contemporary World and World Civilizations". This was the next forum following the first forum held in 2003. The three symposiums were held respectively in Shenzhen, Zhongshan and Macao.

38. The International Conference on Dialogue among Civilizations jointly host by Nanjing University, Harvard-Yenching Institute, Harvard University, and Ningxia Academy of Social Sciences, was held in Ningxia, November 18–21, 2005. Over 100 experts, scholars and religious leaders from domestic and overseas universities and research institutes attended the conference. Weiming Tu, Director of Harvard-Yenching Institute gave a key-note speech. And the theme of the conference was "Cultural Dialogue and Cultural Awareness". During the four days' conference, the participating experts explored in depth the world-wide significance and philosophical meaning of the dialogue between Islam and Confucianism, and explained the epochal significance of the leaning, understanding and dialogue among different cultures at many levels.

39. The Conference on Christianity and Cross-Cultural Dialogue host by Christian Research Center, Chinese Academy of Social Sciences, was held in Paragon Hotel, Beijing, December 7–10, 2005. More than 100 experts and scholars from all over the country attended or audited the conference, and About 50 of them submitted and presented their papers. The topics were "The Basic Theory on Christianity and Cross-Cultural Dialogue", "Compare and Dialogue between Religions", "Cultural View and Thoughts", "Reflections on the History of Ideas", "Christianity and Confucianism", "Social Politics and Social Research", "Christianity and the Chinese situation". The conference had a extensive communication and in-depth discussion on these topics.

40. The International Symposium on Confucianism and Asian Humanistic Value was held in Renmin University of China, December 3–5, 2005. The symposium was jointly sponsored by Renmin University of China and The Korea Foundation for Advanced Studies, in partnership with Confucius Institute and Centre for Asian Studies, Renmin University of China. Over 150 experts and scholars from about 10 countries attended the symposium, and they submitted about 100 papers to the symposium. The topics of the symposium were "Confucianism and Its Tradition", "The Humanistic Value of Confucianism", "Confucianism and Dialogue among Civilizations", "Confucianism and East Asian Culture", "Confucianism and Harmonious Society", "The Modern Transformation of Confucianism". The symposium had a enthusiastic discussion on these topics.

41. The Two-Day Special Summit of Islamic States closed in Mekka, Islamic shrine, on December 10, 2005. All 57 member states of the Organization of Islamic Conference were represented at the summit; most of the representatives are the heads of state or government. The summit published a final statement and brought forth the Mekka Declaration and Programme of Action for the Next 10 Years. For this reason, the participants discussed about the issues about religion, politics, economy and society, obtained a lot of agreements and promising results. They claimed, extremism and terrorism were not elements of Islam. They were against any extremist ideas and actions in the name of religion, maintained that equal dialogue among civilizations should be done based on the mutual understanding and let the world know better of Islam.

42. The East Asian Religious Leaders' Forum was held in Jakarta, capital of

Indonesia, January 12–13, 2006. More than 200 representative of religion from East Asian attended the forum. The topics of the forum were "Poverty, Illiteracy, Unemployment"; "the Role of Religion in Building Safety and Preventing Terrorism and Extremism"; "Commemorate the Chinese Great Navigator, Messenger of Peace, Zheng He".

43. The African Regional Conference on the Dialogue among Civilizations, Cultures and Peoples was held in Abuja, Nigeria, June 20–21, 2006. The conference was jointly organized by UNESCO and the Federal Government of Nigeria and co-hosted by the Chief Olusegun Obasanjo, President of Nigeria and Mr Koïchiro Matsuura, Director-General of UNESCO who also participated in this conference. The special focus of the conference was on the potential of education and science to foster dialogue, better understanding and mutual knowledge of each other.

44. The International Symposium on Aesthetics and Multicultural Dialogue jointly hosted by Chinese Society of Aesthetics, the Institute of Philosophy, Chinese Academy of Social Sciences, and Sichuan Normal University, was held in Chengdu, June 26–28, 2006. About 20 council members of International Association of Aesthetics and 40 scholars from domestic attended the symposium. The participants had a sufficient discussion and communication on the theme of the symposium, and reached a consensus: today's global aesthetics was facing the problem of "intercultural" change.

45. The Symposium on Silk Road and Dialogue among Civilizations was held in Kashi, Xinjiang, August 1–3, 2006. It was jointly sponsored by Chinese Foreign Relations History Society, Xinjiang Academy of Social Sciences, College of Liberal Arts, Jinan University, School of History and Culture, Northwest University for Nationalities, Xinjiang Normal University, and Kashi Teachers College, and it was organized by Xinjiang Academy of Social Sciences and Kashi Teachers College. More than 100 representatives took part in the symposium, and many of them are experts from domestic famous for the studies of Silk Road. The symposium received 79 papers and these papers covered a very broad field of study, and the symposium focused on the union of the history and reality of the Silk Road, and had a important meaning to promote the studies of the Silk Road in the new century.

46. The 8th Congress of the World Conference on Religion and Peace was held in Kyoto, Japan, August 26–29, 2006. Over 1500 delegates from nearly 100 countries

and regions attended the conference, including more than 500 religious people. The theme of the congress was "Resist Violence, Share Safety", with its three sub-topics: resolving conflicts; building peace; and promoting the sustainable development. Participants made speeches general and group discussions on these topics. Finally, the congress brought forth the Kyoto Declaration, to call on dialogue and cooperation among religions, resisting violence together, preserving peace, promoting development and protecting the earth, the common home of human beings.

47. The 6th Harvard-Yenching International Symposium was held in Industrial park, Suzhong, September 22–25, 2006, sponsored jointly by Nanjing University, Harvard-Yenching Institute and Suzhou Industrial Park Administrative Committee. More than 80 Harvard-Yenching alumni from home and abroad attended the conference. The theme of the Symposium was "Cultural Awareness and Cultural Identity: in the View of East Asian" , and it followed the last three symposiums on dialogue among civilizations. The last three symposiums were also held in Suzhou, and the themes of them were respectively "The Global Significance of Indigenous Knowledge", "The Meaning of East Asia Modernization" and "Globalization and Cultural Diversity".

48. To commemorate the 125th anniversary of the birth of Lu Xun, the 70th anniversary of the death of Lu Xun, the International Symposium on "Lu Xun: Cross-cultural Dialogue" was held in Shaoxing, Lu Xun's hometown, October 17–18, 2006. The Symposium is sponsored by Modern Chinese Literature Research Society, Beijing Lu Xun Museum and Shaoxing Municipal People's Government, and organized by Shaoxing Municipal CPC Committee Propaganda Department, Shaoxing University and Shanghai Lu Xun Memorial Hall. More than 120 experts and scholars from home and abroad attended the symposium.

49. The International Conference on Cultural Diversity and the Contemporary World was held in Sun Yat-sen University, on November 24, 2006. The conference was organized by Department of Anthropology, Sun Yat-sen University, and it attracted more than 500 experts, scholars and officers from more than 20 countries and regions. The representatives of the conference came from different disciplines and fields, such as anthropology, ethnology, sociology, folklore, archaeology, museology, government branch and NGO. They discussed about a wide variety of subjects.

50. The 1st Civilization Forum and the 5th Anniversary of Civilization Magazine was held in Academic Hall, Chinese Academy of Social Sciences, December 24, 2006. The theme of the forum was "Propagation of Civilization, Harmony of China". The forum issued the BingXu Civilization Declaration, clarified the understanding of the relationship among culture, civilizations and propagation, and expressed the good will that human civilization needs harmonious propagation, dialogue and exchange.

51. On March 13–14, 2007, World Public Forum "Dialogue of Civilizations" organized an international seminar under the aegis of UNESCO. The event took place in UNESCO Headquarters in Paris, France. The subject of the seminar was "Dialogue of Cultures and Civilizations: A Bridge between Human Rights and Moral Values". Participants from more than 30 countries took part in the event.

52. The International Sinology Conference on Dialogue among Civilizations and Harmonious World was held in Beijing, March 26–28, 2007. The conference was jointly sponsored by the Office of Chinese Language Council International (Hanban) and Renmin University of China, and organized by Institute of Chinese Language Council International, School of Liberal Arts and School of Chinese Classics, Renmin University of China. The aim of the conference was to advance the communication and collaboration in the field of contemporary international sinology studies, through the in-depth dialogue and discussion of the leading scholars, in order to highlight the value of Chinese traditional culture in building a harmonious world. The conference invited over 200 experts and scholars to attend, including some very top experts in world sinology, and the 5 topics of it were "Sinology Studies as a Dialogue between Civilizations", " 'The Image of China' Changes in the Process of Sinology Research", "Chinese Traditional Culture: Interpretation and Influence", "Sinologist and the History of Sinology" and "The Promotion of Mandarin around the World and the Cross-Cultural Communication". The participants presented and discussed these topics in assembly and in group. The conference received more than 100 papers.

53. The International Seminar on "Multiculturalism and International Law", which was organized by the Silk Road Institute of International Law and the College of Humanities and Social Sciences at Xi'an Jiaotong University, took place in Jianguo Hotel, Xi'an, April 13–14, 2007. Nearly 20 well-known experts in international laws attended the seminar from China mainland, Hong Kong, Canada, USA, France,

Germany, Japan, Uruguay, Austria, Romania, Nigeria and other countries and regions.

54. The International Forum on the Harmony and Innovation of Civilizations, host by Zhejiang University, was held in Hangzhou, April 17–19, 2007. More than 50 scholars, from 15 countries and regions including China, the United States, the United Kingdom, Germany, France, Switzerland, Italy, Egypt, Turkey, Spain and Japan, attended the forum. And these participants stood for nowadays the world's major civilizations and cultural system. The topics of the forum were "the harmony, collaboration and development of multiculturalism in the world", "historical relation and vision of the future among world civilizations" and "the modern value and independent innovation of Chinese civilization". The scholars had a extensive communication and deep discussion on these topics and acquired some important results.

55. The International Symposium on Dialogue among Civilizations was held at Southwest Jiaotong University, April 20–22, 2007. The theme of symposium was "Fusion of Horizons and Cultural Interaction". This symposium was sponsored by Comparative Literature and Contemporary Culture Research Center, College of Arts and Communication, Southwest Jiaotong University. More than 100 famous experts from home and abroad attended the symposium, including Mr. Fokkema, Honorary Chairman of International Comparative Literature Association. The symposium made a hot discussion on dialogue among civilizations.

56. On 24–25 of May, 2007 in Tbilisi, Georgia, the Second International Forum was held on "Globalization and Dialogue between Civilizations". The organizes of the II International Forum were: the Ministry of Foreign Affairs of Georgia, the Ministry of Education and Science of Georgia, the Ministry of Culture, Monuments Protection and Sport of Georgia, International Foundation for the Support of Education and Solidarity in Business Life, and International Foundation "Dialogue Eurasia Platform". Around 30 participants, renowned public and religious figures, political scientists, scholars and representatives of culture, analyzed the contribution of Dialogue to Peace.

57. On 30th of May to 2nd of June, 2007, the international Symposium of the "Dialogue between Confucians and Christians in the Contemporary Context: Thought and Practice" was held at the campus of Hong Kong Baptist University. The symposium attracted more than 40 scholars with the traditions of Confucianism,

Marxism, and Christianity, who were from mainland China, Hong Kong, Taiwan, and North America. The theme of the symposium focused on "what is the common concern?" The symposium was sponsored by Shandong University (Jinan) and Hong Kong Baptist University.

58. On June 4–5, 2007, World Public Forum "Dialogue of Civilizations" organized the International Regional Conference "European Civilization Space: Baltic Dialogue" in Tampere, Finland. More than two hundred participants took part in the conference. Participants of the conference focused on the prospects of cooperation in the field of innovations, energy and transport.

59. The 1st Symposium on Religious Dialogue and Harmonious Society was held in Lanzhou, June 4–6, 2007. This symposium was sponsored by College of Philosophy and Social Sciences, Christian Culture Research Center, the Institute of Islamic Culture, Lanzhou University. Nearly 50 experts and scholars from 30 academic institutions of Religious Studies attended this symposium. They mainly focused on 4 topics of discussion : (1) religious dialogue and harmonious society; (2) religious pluralism and harmonious society; (3) religious dialogue; (4) the past and present of Christianity and Islam in northwest China. This symposium was co-sponsored by the Culture Regeneration Research Society (CRRS).

60. The Third Asia-Europe Meeting (ASEM) Inter-Faith Dialogue was held in Nanjing, China, June 19–21, 2007. Nearly 200 representatives from 37 members and 4 observers of the ASEM gathered together. Focused on "Deepen Inter-Faith Dialogue, Achieve Peace, Development and Harmony", the meeting discussed such issues as how inter-faith dialogue played a role in responding to Globalization, maintaining peace, promoting social integration and development, promoting cultural and educational cooperation, etc. The meeting urged the ASEM members to respect for diversity of social system, development path and culture; emphasized the importance of timely and full realization of the Millennium Development Goals for eradicating poverty, promoting development, and achieving common prosperity; urged the ASEM members to strengthen cooperation in the field of cultural exchange and educational cooperation.

61. The 15th International Conference on Chinese Philosophy was held grandly at Wuhan University, June 25–27, 2007. This conference was sponsored jointly by International Society for Chinese Philosophy (ISCP), Society of Chinese Philosophy,

Chinese Confucian Academy, the Institute of Philosophy, Chinese Traditional Culture Research Center, Confucius and Confucianism Research Center of Wuhan University. Over 200 scholars were invited to the conference from 14 countries and regions, including China, the United States, Canada, Germany, the United Kingdom, Denmark, Spain, Taiwan and Hong Kong. Guo Qiyong, Current President of the International Society for Chinese Philosophy, served as the chairman of this symposium. And the symposium was carried out according to the theme on "Dialogue between Chinese Philosophy and Global Civilizations in the 21st Century".

62. The Symposium on Dialogue among Civilizations and the Development of Middle East was held in Shanghai successfully, August 25–26, 2007. This symposium was sponsored jointly by Chinese Society of Middle East, the Institute of Eurasian Studies, Shanghai World History Society, Center for International Studies, Shanghai Academy of Social Sciences. As an important academic activities of 50 anniversary of the establishment of Chinese Society of Middle East and Shanghai Association for International Studies, this symposium invited about 60 experts and scholars to attend and discuss about the problem of Middle East, and they came from 20 universities and research institutes, including Ministry of Foreign Affairs, Chinese Academy of Social Sciences, Northwest University, Yunnan University, Southwest University, Henan Normal University, Shanghai Institute for International Studies and so on.

63. The International Symposium on Mutual Understanding of Three East Asian Countries in The Process of Modernization was held at Nankai University, September 9–10, 2007. This symposium was sponsored by Nankai University and Daito Bunka University, in partnership with Japan Foundation, and it was organized by Modern World History Research Center, the Institute of Japanese Studies, Nankai University. More than 70 scholars and experts took part in the symposium. The successful symposium advanced the academic exchanges among East Asian Countries, and promoted the understanding of the modernization of each country.

64. The Conference on World Religions and Dialogue among Civilizations was held in Ohria, famous cultural city of Macedonia, October 26–28, 2007. More than 200 scholars and delegates of religion from more than 20 countries participated in the conference. This conference was jointly sponsored by Ministry of Culture of the Republic of Macedonia and United Nations Educational, Scientific and Cultural

Organization. The theme of the conference was "The Contribution of Religion and Culture to Peace, Mutual Respect and Coexist" this was the first meeting of the Conference on World Religions and Dialogue among Civilizations , it would be held every three years in the future. The conference brought forth the declaration, which called on advancing dialogue among civilizations and religions, giving up prejudices, respecting for the diversity of religions and civilizations, condemning the violence of religion, Strengthening religious education and respecting for woman's rights.

65. Hosted by the Government of Spain on January 15 – 16 in Madrid, the First Alliance of Civilizations Global Forum convened political leaders, representatives of international and regional bodies, religious leaders, youth, corporate executives, civil society groups, and foundations for open dialogue on reducing polarization between nations and launching joint initiatives to promote cross-cultural understanding globally. The presence of over 900 participants and 89 official delegations in Madrid is testament to the interest that the Alliance is generating throughout the world. The Global Forum was organized around 3 plenary sessions and 8 working sessions over the course of two days. Participants from 78 countries discussed issues as diverse as the role of the media in intercultural dialogue, the challenges and demands facing religious leaders as advocates for peace, and the opportunities that multiculturalism can provide to the business world. Taking a practical approach, the Global Forum offered a unique international platform to governmental agencies, international organizations and representatives of civil society to forge partnerships and develop concrete initiatives in the sphere of intercultural and inter-religious dialogue, particularly in the Alliance's priority areas of education, youth, migration and the media.

66. The 1ˢᵗ Forum on Dialogue among Civilizations was held in Macao, April 18 – 21, 2008. It was sponsored jointly by Ye Shengtao Research Society, China Religious Culture Communication Association, Yan-Huang Culture Research Association and China Cultural Communication Association (Macao). Over 100 experts and religious figures attended the forum from Mainland, Hong Kong, Macao and Taiwan. The theme of this forum was "Chinese Civilization and Social Harmony", hoping that the forum can lead the society to think more deeply over the Chinese culture, through the high-level dialogue among participation of famous experts. And the aim of the forum was also to survey the positive influence and reformation of Chinese Culture in the process

of inheritance and development, think about the relation between Chinese culture and the development of contemporary social modernization, in order to make a contribution to the further inheritance and longer influence of Chinese culture in the Chinese community.

67. The International Symposium on Religion, which was organized by Muslim World League (MWL), was held in Madrid, the capital of Spain, on July 16, 2008. About 300 religious leaders from various countries took part in the three-day symposium. And they came from the world's major religious groups, such as Islam, Judaism, Christianity, Hinduism and Buddhism. The symposium sought for common values of different religions and the spirit of creating world peace, so as to investigate the ways to live together peacefully, understand and cooperate with each other.

68. The 22nd World Congress of Philosophy was held in Seoul, South Korea from July 30 to August 5, 2008, at the Seoul National University. The theme of this congress was "Rethinking Philosophy Today". This was the first time World Congress of Philosophy held in Asia.

69. The International Conference on Dengzhou and Marine Silk Road was held in Penglai, October 11 – 13, 2008. And this conference was sponsored jointly by Ludong University, UN Organizing Committee of the Series Activities of Pan Silk Road, Chinese Society for Historians of China's Foreign Relations, Qilu Culture Research Center, Shandong Normal University, and Penglai Municipal People's Government and it was organized by Ludong University and Penglai Municipal People's Government. More than 60 famous experts and journalists from home and abroad attended the conference, including correspondents from Modern Korea, and Guangming Daily. The topics of the conference were "Ancient Dengzhou and the Marine Silk Road", "Shandong Peninsula and the Marine Silk Road", "The Role and Statue of Shandong Peninsula in the History of China, Korea and Japan's Relations" and so on, the participants had a deep and extensive talk and communication on these topics.

70. The World Public Forum "Dialogue of Civilizations", under the patronage of UNESCO, convened a meeting of high-level experts to discuss the most pressing socio-cultural problems facing the world today in the Hofburg Palace in Vienna on November 10, 2008. The meeting, which brought together about 40 experts, high-ranking politicians and public dignitaries from around the world, focused on the most

current problems that have been prompted by globalization and aggravated by the current financial-economic situation facing the world.

71. The China-Kingdom of Saudi Arabia Scholars Forum, which was jointly sponsored by the Institute of Middle Eastern Studies, Northwest University, and King Saudi University, Saudi Arabia, in collaboration with the Department of Arabic, Xi'an International Studies University, was held at Northwest University, November 10-12, 2008. More than 30 representatives from home and abroad participated in the forum, including four Saudi scholars from King Saudi University and Gasim University. The opening ceremony of the forum was presided by Tiezheng Wang, Director of the Institute of Middle Eastern Studies, Northwest University. Professor Zongzhe Ren, Vice-Chancellor of Northwestern University, and Saudi Dr. Mohammad A. A. Aleshaikh, respectively made a speech at the opening ceremony. The forum had a productive discussion on the trend of "Islam Al-wasatiyah (golden mean or moderatism)".

72. On 6-7 April 2009, the Second Global Forum of the United Nations Alliance of Civilizations (UNAOC) was held in Istanbul, Turkey. The UNAOC Global Forum is the world's premier event aimed at advancing intercultural understanding. Over 1,000 participants—among them some Heads of Government, over 50 Ministers, as well as policy-makers, foundations, the media and grassroots leaders from around the world—convened in Istanbul, to forge new partnerships and generate ideas aimed at building trust and cooperation among diverse communities. The Forum also served as an opportunity to take stock of initiatives developed by the Alliance of Civilizations and to launch practical projects in collaboration with civil society and corporate partners.

73. The International Symposium on Conflict, Dialogue and Civilization Construction was held in Macao, on May 18, 2009. It was jointly sponsored by School of Social Sciences and Humanities, University of Macau, and Tertiary Education Services Office, Government of the Macao Special Administrative Region. More than 40 experts and scholars attended the symposium from Mainland China, Taiwan, Hong Kong, Macao and Japan.

74. The 6th Annual Meeting of Beijing Forum—Beijing Forum (2009), jointly organized by Peking University, Beijing Municipal Commission of Education, and Korea Foundation for Advanced Studies, took place in Beijing grandly, on November

6, 2009. This forum lasted for 3 days and took "The Harmony of Civilizations and Prosperity for All—Looking Beyond the Crisis to a Harmonious Future" as the theme. Mr. Ban Ki-moon, Secretary-General of UN, issued a video statement specially for the convening of this forum. From more than 40 countries and regions, Above 300 world-renowned experts and scholars attended the meeting. They explored from both theoretical and practical aspects, researched for the policies to prevent the crisis and approaches to go through the crisis, and contributed their wisdom and strength to the harmonious development of the world.

75. The 3rd International Symposium on Dialogue among Civilizations and Conversation with Civilizations was held in Lingfeng Hotel, Hangzhou, October 16–18, 2009. The symposium was sponsored by Zhejiang University and The Chinese University of Hong Kong, the theme of which was "Buddha Meets Jesus in the 21st Century". And it was organized by Christianity and Cross-Cultural Research Center, Zhejiang University. There were 43 representatives attended the symposium from domestic and overseas universities and research institutes. The last two symposiums were held respectively in Shaanxi Normal University and The Chinese University of Hong Kong.

76. The 1st Conference on the Cultural Dialogue between China and Canada was held in Beijing, November 12–13, 2009. This conference was sponsored jointly by Chinese People's Association for Friendship with Foreign Countries and Canadian International Cultural Foundation, in order to promote further the cultural communication between China and Canada and advance the mutual understanding between Chinese people and Canadian people. The representatives had a deep discussion and communication on traditional and contemporary culture, according to the topics of the conference, such as changes, diversity, partnership, communication, cultural diplomacy, creative city, and leading the next generation.

77. The International Symposium on Tradition and Contemporary World was held in Beijing, December 12–13, 2009. The symposium was jointly sponsored by Value and Cultural Studies Center, School of Philosophy and Sociology, Beijing Normal University, and the Editorial of Journal of World Philosophy of the Institute of Philosophy, Chinese Academy of Social Sciences, the theme of which was "Towards a Multicultural, Multi-ideological and Multi-value Dialogue". The participants had an

in-depth discussion and communication on these hot issues: "Cultural Diversity and Contemporary World", "Modern Life in the Perspective of Philosophy and Ethics", "The Interpretation of Confucianism and Its Contemporary Value", "Contemporary Social Order and Political Philosophy" and so on.

78. The 4th International Symposium of the International Forum on World Civilization, which was sponsored jointly by Research Center for World Civilizations' Comparison, Chinese Academy of Social Sciences, Ideological and cultural research center, Shanghai Academy of Social Sciences, School of Foreign Languages, Nanjing Normal University and Macao Foundation, took place at Chinese Academy of Social Sciences in Beijing, April 16–17, 2010. The theme of the symposium was "New Process of Contemporary World Civilization and New Development of the Studies of Civilization". More than 70 experts and scholars participated in the symposium from home and aboard, including Germany, Canada, Russia, Japan and Korea. The topics of the symposium focused on the important issues which contemporary world civilizations were facing.

79. The Fourth International Symposium on the Condition of Religious Life in Vietnam and China, which was sponsored by the Institute of Comparative Religion, Sun Yat-Sen University, Southwest Frontier Ethnic Studies Center of Yunnan University, and the Institute of Religious Studies, Vietnam Academy of Social Sciences, took place in Hanoi, Vietnam, April 27–28, 2010. The Chinese and Vietnam scholars in depth exchanged views with each other based on the cooperative Research of last three symposiums, faced with new religious issues in China and Vietnam.

80. "A Dialogue between Chinese & Arabic Civilizations-International Language and Culture Seminar" was held in Cairo, May 6–7, 2010. This seminar is jointly organized by Confucius Institute, and Department of Chinese Studies of Cairo University. The participants had a in depth discussion and exchange on the ideas and concepts of teaching Chinese and Arabic; the difference and fusion of eastern and western cultures; comparison of Chinese and Arabic; and the translation of Chinese and Arabic.

81. The China Folklore Photographic Association, which has an operational relations with UNESCO, assisted in launching the "UNESCO week and International Year of Cultural Rapprochement into China" on May 21, 2010. The activity was

attended by cultural officials from more than 10 provinces of China. A series of national and international cultural activities were organized in many provinces in China under the International Year of Cultural Rapprochement, including a National Photo Contest in Gansu province.

82. The International Conference on the Fusion of Confucianism and Christianity was held at Wuhan University, May 24, 2010, which is sponsored by the Institute of Euro-American Religions and Cultures, School of Philosophy and Confucius and Confucianism Research Center, Wuhan University. Three American experts and other experts from domestic universities attended the conference.

83. The 3rd Forum of the United Nations Alliance of Civilizations was held in Rio de Janeiro from 27 to 29 May 2010. With several thousand registered participants including political and business leaders, mayors, civil society, youth, journalists, foundations, international organizations, and religious leaders from all around the world, the Rio Forum showed that the UN Alliance of Civilizations has been firmly consolidated as the United Nations' main platform for global dialogue, aimed at improving understanding and cooperative relations among nations and peoples across cultures and religions. Focused on "Bridging Cultures, Building Peace", the 3rd Forum of the UN Alliance of Civilizations was an exceptional place for relationship building, for gaining insights into the world's most pressing cross-cultural challenges and for turning ideas into action.

84. The 4th International Conference on Dialogue among Civilizations was held in Nanjing, June 11–14, 2010, which is sponsored by Nanjing University and Harvard-Yenching Institute. The theme of the conference was "The Centennial Process of the Cultural Understanding and Cultural Dialogue". There were 84 delegates attending the conference. They were from the the United States, Japan, Italy and China's domestic universities and research institutes. The core issue of the meeting to discuss was "dialogue between Hui Muslim and Confucianism", which was dialogue between Islam and Chinese traditional Confucianism. The conference received 43 papers.

85. The First International Symposium on Zheng He, which was jointly sponsored by International Zheng He Society, Malacca State Government, Malacca Museum Administration and Zheng He Cultural Museum, took place in Malacca, famous tourist city of Malaysia, July 5, 2010, under the theme of "Zheng He and Afro-Asian World".

Nearly 100 experts and scholars attended the symposium from China, Singapore, Malaysia, the United States, Australia , New Zealand and other countries and regions.

86. The 2010 Cross-Strait Symposium of China Central Asian Culture was held at Tarim University, August 10–12, 2010. More than 130 experts attended the symposium, and 90 of them from 50 units in Hong Kong, Macao, Taiwan and Mainland China submitted high-quality papers. The Ever-changing of Silk Road and Systematical Exposition of Central Asian Culture was the theme of the symposium. The Comprehensive studies highlighted the aim of the symposium.

87. The one-day International Conference on Friendly Dialogue between Islam and Christianity was held in Damascus, capital of Syria, October 15, 2010. The participants appealed to the peaceful coexistence, friendly dialogue between Islam and Christianity, opposed all forms of terrorism. The delegations from more than 30 countries attended the conference, which discussed about the importance of advancing solidarity and cooperation between Islam and Christianity, in order to cope with a variety of challenges and threats.

88. The 2nd Symposium on the Fusion of Civilizations: Dialogue between Islam and Christianity took place in Beijing, October 21–23, 2010. It was was jointly sponsored by the Institute of World Religions, Chinese Academy of Social Sciences, the Institute of Hui Islam, Ningxia Academy of Social Sciences, and Christianity and Chinese Culture Research Center, Alliance Bible Seminary. More than 100 delegates and honored guests participated in the symposium, including both experts from some universities and research institutes and delegates from political circles and religious society. The symposium last for two days, and more than 40 experts and scholars made a speech according to the theme of the symposium.

89. The 6th International Symposium on the Dialogue between Chinese Civilization and Arabic Civilization, which was sponsored by the Department of Arabic, Beijing Foreign Studies University, took place at the International Conference Center, Foreign Language Teaching and Research Press, December 4–5, 2010. More than 80 experts and scholars from China and Arab countries had a productive and extensive discussion on the Dialogue between Chinese Civilization and Arabic Civilization. This international symposium was held once a year since 2005.

90. The 21st Century World Forum on Chinese Culture, which was jointly

sponsored by Singapore Global Chinese Arts & Culture Society, Association for Yan Huang Culture of China, and Department of Chinese language and literature, National University of Singapore, took place in Singapore, December 7, 2010. The theme of the forum was "Cultural Symbiosis: Exchange, Fusion, and Development between Chinese Culture and Southeast Asian Culture". The forum was divided into three sessions and more than 20 panels, including "Pluralistic Co-existence of Chinese Culture and World Civilizations", "Evolution and Meaning of Chinese Culture and Southeast Asia Ethnic Groups", "the Relationship between Culture and Society", and "Chinese Culture and Social Development of Singapore and Malaysia". The forum was founded in 1998 on the initiative of Association for Yan Huang Culture of China, aimed at promoting dialogue and exchange between Chinese culture and world culture.

91. On April 7–9, 2011, the 1ˢᵗ World Forum on Cross-cultural Dialogue, which was jointly sponsored by United Nations Alliance of Civilizations and Government of Azerbaijan, opened in Baku, Azerbaijan. 500 representatives from 102 countries from all continents, many international organization, NGOs, media representatives, scholars, experts and etc. participated in the Forum. The forum was organized under the motto- "United by Common Values, Enriched by Cultural Diversity".

92. In co-operation with Turkish foundations and research institutions, the International Progress Organization (I.P.O.) organized from 6 to 13 May 2011 a series of lectures and seminars in Turkey on the role of religion in contemporary society. A group of researchers and students from Austria, France, Germany, Greece, Italy, Pakistan and the United States, representing the disciplines of Philosophy, Religious Studies, Political Science, International Law, and International Relations, discussed issues of multiculturalism, inter-religious dialogue and Muslim-Western relations with scholars and students from Turkish Universities and cultural foundations.

93. The First Annual Meeting of the Taihu Lake Cultural Forum, which was jointly sponsored by Taihu Culture Forum, China Federation of Literary Art and Art Circles, Jiangsu Provincial People's Government and Chinese People's Institute of Foreign Affairs, took place in Suzhou, Jiangsu Province, May 18–19, 2011. Liu Yandong, State Councilor, attended the opening ceremony and made a speech. About 500 State leaders, officials, scholars and experts took part in the forum, the theme of which was "Advancing the Cooperation and Dialogue among Civilizations, Promoting

the Harmony and Development of the World". The aim of the forum was to gather politicians and famous scholars from various countries to communicate and discuss about the most urgent issues which contemporary international society was facing in the development of human civilization and cultural exchanges, so as to find out a mechanism for global cooperation to solve the problems. During the period of the forum, there were four sub-forums respectively on "Historical Revelation and Real Value of Different Civilizations", "Chinese Civilization and World Civilizations", "The Cultural Diversity and the Progress of Human Civilization" and "Building the Harmonious World: the Function of Government and Folk Force".

94. The 1st International Symposium on Dialogue between Hui Muslim Civilization and Confucian Civilization, which was jointly sponsored by Yunnan University and Mustafa International University, Iran, organized by Iranian Research Center of Yunnan University, took place at Yunnan University, June 25, 2011. The aim of the symposium was to promote the communication of the two civilizations, promote the traditional friendship of people in the two countries, help the comprehensive and healthy development of the political, economical and cultural relation between China and Iran, and help the construction of the harmonious world. The symposium focused on "Peace", "Harmony", "Justice" and other topics both in the Islamic Civilization and Confucian Civilization.

95. The International Symposium on Sanxingdui and Silk Road in South: Southwest China and Eurasian Ancient Civilizations, which was jointly sponsored by the Pre-Qin History Society of China, Chinese Foreign Relations History Society, the Center for Bashu Cultural Studies and the College of Historical Culture and Tourism of Sichuan Normal University and Sanxingdui Museum, took place in Sanxingdui Museum, Guanghan, July 28-29, 2011. More than 70 experts and scholars attended the symposium from more than 30 domestic and overseas universities and research institutes. And the symposium received nearly 40 papers.

96. The 9th annual session of the World Public Forum "Dialogue of Civilizations" took place on the Greek island of Rhodes, October 5-13, 2011. More than 600 representatives from 70 countries attended the forum. Delegates from international organizations, government departments of various countries, non-governmental organizations, research institutions, and religious organizations, engaged in a frank

dialogue and exchanges on these issues: future prospects of civilization, policies to deal with the future challenges, new social response to the uneven development of current world, dialogue model of the international community interaction, cross-cultural international institutions and laws, the challenges to current economic development and social development, the meaning of religion and traditional civilization for peace, the media's impact on globalization, etc. And they issued a number of valuable insights and constructive suggestions, which formed the Rhodes Declaration of the forum's 9th annual session, and enhanced mutual understanding and communication among civilizations.

97. During the period October 10–20, 2011, the Confucius Culture Tour and the China-Europe Civilization Conversation Activity Series both sponsored by the Chinese People's Association for Friendship with Foreign Countries, the Frey Exhibition Group, the Business Confucius Institute in Athens, Confucius institute at the University of Rome La Sapienza, and Switzerland-China Cultural Communication Association was held in Zurich, Switzerland, Rome, Italy, and Athens, Greece. Shandong Cultural Delegation attended the above activities and started a content-rich cultural communication. On October 18, China-Europe Cultural Communication Symposium was held in Athens. Its theme was "Transmission of Confucius and Socrates' Thoughts and Their Practical Significance". More than 100 representatives from China, Greece, Italy, and the United Kingdom attended the conference. Participants have a lively discussion about the thoughts of Confucius and Socrates, especially about their ideas of "Benevolence", "Virtue", "Trust", "Justice" and "Heaven".

98. The 19th International Conference on China, Chinese Civilization and the World, which was sponsored by Far East Branch of Russian Academic of Sciences, opened ceremoniously at Russian Academy of Sciences, October 19, 2011. In order to commemorate the 100th anniversary of Revolution of 1911, the sponsor took "The course of 100 years of China towards Progress and Modernity" as the theme of this year's conference. Nearly 200 Russian, Chinese and European scholars attended the conference. They discussed the course of 100 Years of China towards progress and modernization from perspectives of history, philosophy, economy and the path of Chinese development.

99. The United Nations Alliance of Civilizations convened its Fourth Global

Forum in Doha, Qatar from December 11 – 13, 2011. Over 2,000 participants, including political and corporate leaders, civil society activists, youth groups, faith communities, research centers, foundations and journalists, came together to achieve an agreement for joint actions to improve relations across cultures, combat prejudice and build lasting peace. The Doha Forum convened a diverse network of actors that are working on this issue to share ideas, learn from each other, and listen to the needs of the grassroots in different communities around the world.

100. The Symposium on Ecological wisdom: Dialogue between Prairie Civilization and Mountain civilization was held in Hohhot, August 1 – 2, 2011. More than 80 experts and scholars from State Nationalities Affairs Commission and 35 universities and research institutes participated in the symposium. The symposium made a discussion and communication in three aspects, which are "Ecology Theory and Ecology Philosophy", "Local Knowledge and Survival Wisdom" and "Ecological Practice and Ecological Strategy".

101. The International Symposium on Marine and Land transportation, and World Civilization, which was sponsored by Research Center of Canton Port, Sun Yat-Sen University, was held at Sun Yat-Sen University, December 3 – 6, 2011. 28 scholars from China, the United States, Russia and Iran submitted their excellent research results. And they had a productive discussion in accordance with the following five topics, which were Medieval Manichaeism; The History of Sino-Russian Relations; Medieval China and Western Regions Civilization; Medieval China and the South China Sea Civilization; and Canton in the Qing Dynasty and Western Civilization. These topics covered the history of Sino-foreign relations happened through the Marine and Land transportation, and reflected the theme of the symposium. Since 2006, Sun Yat-Sen University continuously had hosted several international symposiums on the world contact of Canton Port.

102. The Paris-Nishan Forum was held in the headquarters of the United Nations Educational, Scientific and Cultural Organization (UNESCO) on April 16, 2012, under the theme of "Confucianism and New Humanism in a Globalized World". The event was featured by the participation of over 200 people, including envoys of respective countries in the UNESCO, and representatives from the political, educational and cultural communities of France. This Paris-Nishan Forum was divided

into three sessions, including "Harmony with Diversity and Urgent Demands of the Globalized World", "Harmony with Diversity and Cultural Dialogue" and "Harmony with Diversity and New Humanism" which invited over 20 officials of international organizations, sociologists and historians from 9 countries to launch high-level talks, including China, France, the United Kingdom, the United States, Spain, Tunisia, Hungary, Sri Lanka and Mali.

103. The 2nd Nishan Forum on World Civilizations, which was named after Great ancient Chinese thinker and educator Confucius' birthplace, was held with ceremony at Shengyuan College, Nishan, May 21-23, 2012. Honored guests, thinkers, educators and People from more than 20 countries and regions gathered in the foot of Nishan Mountain, and started a high-level communication and dialogue. In the 3-day forum, there were more than 40 keynote speeches, branch meetings, doctoral forums and high-level dialogues among Confucian scholars and Christian scholars. The 2nd Nishan Forum received about 100 papers, and attracted more than 10 thousand person-time to attend or audit. The forum produced a consensus on protecting cultural heritage and promoting dialogue among civilizations. The forum took "Belief, Morality, Respect and Friendship" as the theme, in order to make the voice of "dialogue instead of confrontation" to the world.

104. The First Partners Forum for the United Nations Alliance of Civilizations took place in Istanbul on May 31 and June 1, at the invitation of Prime Minister Erdoğan of Turkey. This major event brought together governments, intergovernmental organizations as well as businesses, foundations and individuals who have shown a strong commitment to realizing the vision of a world free from intercultural conflicts and divides, where cultural diversity is an asset and not a liability. The Forum was co-chaired by UNSG Ban Ki-moon.

105. The Symposium on China and Islamic Civilization, which was jointly sponsored by Chinese Academy of Social Sciences and Research Centre for Islamic History, Art and Culture (IRCICA), Organization of the Islamic Conference (OIC), took place at Chinese Academy of Social Sciences, June 28-29, 2012. Participants came from home and aboard including Turkey, Saudi Arabia, Egypt, Qatar, the United States, the United Kingdom, Malaysia, Pakistan. They had a hot discussion on 6 topics: historical relation between China and Muslim world; art communication and interaction

between China and Muslim world; literatures and languages; science, religion and thought; the relation between contemporary world and Muslim world; and China and Muslim world in the process of globalization.

106. The 5th World Confucian Conference and 2012 Confucius Cultural Award Ceremony, which was sponsored jointly by Ministry of Culture of PRC and Shandong Provincial People's Government, took place at the Confucius Institute, Qufu, Confucius's hometown, on October 5, 2012. Over 100 experts and scholars participated in this international conference, from more than 10 countries and regions. They together discussed about "Contemporary Significance of Confucianism", which was the theme of conference, hoping to promote the harmonious development of human society through equal dialogue among different civilizations. And they also had a extensive dialogue about the real issues, such as "Confucian ethics and market ethics", "Chinese Meta-Classics and Modern Civilizations" and "Confucianism and National Education".

107. The 3rd World Conference on Sinology was held in Beijing, November 3–5, 2012. "World Conference on Sinology" was sponsored jointly by the Office of Chinese Language Council International (Hanban) and Renmin University of China, and it was organized by Institute of Chinese Language Council International, School of Liberal Arts, Renmin University of China. The theme of the conference was "Sinology and the World Today" for the purpose of promoting the communication between Chinese mainstream academic and overseas sinology and investigating other global villagers' understanding of China and the meaning of "China's Road" to the rest of the world, so as to intensify the theme of "Dialogue among Civilizations" and "Cultural Exchanges". Meanwhile, The conference had two thematic forums, one was for Confucius Institutes and the Communication of World Cultures, the other was for the Recipients of Literary Awards in China and Other Countries. More than 100 experts and scholars took part in this conference.

108. To commemorate the twentieth anniversary of Korea-China diplomatic relations, the Fourth International Forum on Chinese Character Culture in Korea, China and Japan took place at Cheju University, Korea, August 25, 2012. It was jointly sponsored by China Writing Research and Application Center, East China Normal University, Korean Korean Chinese Character Research Institute, Kyungsung

University, and School of humanities, Cheju University. The theme of the forum was "Building and Sharing of Digital Archives of Ancient Chinese Literature Data Collection in Chinese Cultural Circle and New discussion on Chinese Character Culture in the East and West". About 90 experts and scholars attended the forum from South Korea, China, Japan, USA, Germany, France, Norway, China Taiwan and other countries and regions. And they submitted more than 60 papers to the forum.

109. The 10th Annual Meeting of The World Public Forum "Dialogue of Civilizations" was held at Rhodic Island, Southeastern Greece, October 4, 2012. The five-day forum gathered over 500 experts, scholars and representatives from nearly 80 countries. The participants had a in depth discussion on extensive issues, such as "World Political Changes", "International Economic Order", "Ecological Protection", "Dialogue of Civilizations" and "Future Development of Education". The World Public Forum "Dialogue of Civilizations" was founded in 2003, promoting constructive dialogue among civilizations in order to jointly respond to global challenges. Now the forum had been a unofficial dialogue mechanism with international influences.

110. The New York Forum on World Civilizations, which was organized by China Energy Fund Committee (CEFC), took place at United Nations Headquarters, New York, November 10–11, 2012. The theme of the forum was "Harmony Based on Shared Values–beyond National Identities and Beliefs: Dialogue between Confucianism and Christianity", for the purpose of providing a good opportunity to enhance understanding between civilizations such as Confucianism and Christianity.

111. The Asia-Pacific Consultation Meeting of United Nations Alliance of Civilizations convened at the International Convention Center, Shanghai, November 29–30, 2012. The meeting was jointly sponsored by United Nations Alliance of Civilizations and United Nations Association of China. About 150 Representatives were invited to the meeting from China, India, Australia, New Zealand, Malaysia, Thailand, Philippines, Indonesia, Japan, Korea, China Taiwan, and other dozens of countries and regions, including representatives of international and regional organizations, leaders of private agency and NGO, media representatives etc. The theme of the meeting was "Harmony through Dialogue and Diversity".

112. The two-day 7th International Symposium of the World Forum on Chinese Culture in the 21st Century closed in Melbourne, Australia, on December 2, 2012. Mr.

Xu Jialu made a speech on the opening ceremony. The theme of the symposium was "Dialogue among Civilizations and the Spirit of Chinese Culture". Over 120 Chinese and foreign scholars from Australia, Europe, and America spoke at the Forum, and called for greater dialogue and interaction between Chinese and Western culture.

Compiler: Xu Huan

Appendix 8:

Who is Who in Civilization Dialogue

(2002–2012)

Abe, Masao (1915–2006) was a Japanese Buddhist and professor in religious studies. He became well known for his work in Buddhist-Christian interfaith dialogue. He transformed the Christian idea of God into the Buddhist "emptiness", this caused widely discussed among the western Christian scholars. It was seen as the classical case of Buddhist-Christian dialogue. Abe also wrote on the experience of Zen.

Al-Afghani, Jamal ad-Din (1838–1897) was an Islamic philosopher, political activist and the founder of Pan-Islamism. He was also the pioneer of modern renaissance movement of Arab countries. He devoted his life to social and religious reform. He called out that Islamic countries stay solidarity under the jurisdiction of a unified Caliphate, to resist together the aggression of European imperialism and engage in national rejuvenation. He took advantage of assembly and the press to actively promote his ideas, to inspire religious feeling and patriotic enthusiasm of Muslim in Eastern countries.

Al-Banna, Hassan (1906–1949) was an Egyptian scholar of Sufism, representative of fundamentalism and founder of Muslim Brotherhood. Al-Banna was a schoolteacher, social activist and Sunni imam, devoting himself to promoting Egypt's social reform and political reform movement in the Islamic world. He was best known for founding and leading the Muslim Brotherhood in the 1930s. It is one of the largest and most influential 20th century Muslim revivalist organizations, still active in the Islamic world until today.

Lee, Chi Chung Archie (1950–) is a professor of CUHK's Department of Cultural and Religious Studies. He is one of the major advocators of Scriptural Reasoning in China. His representative works are *Discourse and Identity: A Study of the Megilloth and Textual Practice and Identity Making: A Study of Chinese Christian Writings*.

Athenagoras I (1886–1972) was the 268th Ecumenical Patriarch of Constantinople from 1948 to 1972. His meeting with Pope Paul VI in 1964 in Jerusalem led to rescinding the excommunications of 1054 which historically mark the Great Schism. This was the turning point in the changes of relationship between the Catholic and Orthodox.

Bartolomeos, Patrik I. (1940–) is the Archbishop of Constantinople (Ecumenical Patriarch), since 2 November 1991. He is nominally the highest clergy for the Orthodox Church. He began to promote the cross-religious dialogue between the Orthodox Church and Jewish groups since 1977, the cross-religious dialogue between the Orthodox Church and Islamist groups since 1986. He organized a series of international conferences to deepen the dialogue among Jews, Christians and Muslims, since 1994.

Benedict, Ruth (1887–1948) was an American anthropologist and folklorist. She studied under Franz Boas, who has been called the father of American anthropology, and his teachings and point of view are clearly evident in Benedict's work. Most of Benedict' studies were about the origin of American Indian culture. She was aware that any kind of culture is a mixture of elements of many other cultures. In addition to the study of small society without writing language, she also studied Japanese culture, in order to help western understand the culture of Japanese society. Benedict's main works were *Patterns of Culture* (1934), *The Chrysanthemum and the Sword* (1946) , etc.

Berthrong, John (1946–) was a associate professor of comparative theology at Boston University since 1989. Dr. Berthrong committed himself to projects and activities about interfaith dialogue. His teaching and research interests are on inter-religious dialogue, Chinese religion and philosophy, Comparative philosophy, and theology. His representative works include: *All Under Heaven: Transforming Paradigms in Confucian-Christian Dialogue, Transformations of the Confucian Way*, etc.

Buber, Martin (1878–1965) was an Austrian-born Israeli Jewish philosopher, Translator and educator. His research work focused on theistic religion, relationships and groups. Martin Buber was a cultural Zionist, he was active in the German and Israeli Jewish organizations and educational organizations. He was also a steadfast supporter of implementation of a Palestinian state solution (in opposition to the two-state solution). Buber was best known for his philosophy of dialogue. *I and Thou* was his most important book, Buber presented a humanistic philosophy in it.

Cai Yuanpei (1868–1940) was a Chinese educator, revolutionist, politician, and Republic of China's first minister of education. He served as president of Peking University from 1916 to 1927. He innovated Peking University and set a trend of "knowledge" and "freedom". In 1928 he helped to found and became the first president of the Academia Sinica.

T. C. Chao (Zhao Zichen, 1888–1979) was a Chinese Christian theologian and scholar. He was one of the most influential theologians in the twentieth century. He was the early founder of Chinese contextual theology and he was also the earliest advocator of "Chinese systematic theology". He enjoyed a high reputation in the Western Christian world, known as "the chief scholar of interpreting the Christian faith for Eastern mind".

de Chardin, Pierre Teilhard (1881–1955) was a French philosopher, paleontologist, geologist and Jesuit priest. He had lived in China for more than 20 years. All his writings have been collected into *Complete Works of Teilhard de Chardin*, the representatives of which were *The Phenomenon of Man, The Future of Man* and *The Divine Milieu.*

Chen Ming (1962–) is a secretary-general of institute of world religions, CASS, and dean of XINFU School of Chinese Classics. In 1992, he completed his Ph.D. at the Department of Religion, Chinese Academy of Social Sciences. He published Historical and Cultural Functions of Confucianism. He founded scholarly journals *Original Dao* and had been serving as editor in chief. He has been pursuing to establish Confucianism in the context of modern time.

Chung-ying Cheng (1930–) is a Chinese-American scholar and professor of philosophy at the University of Hawaii. He is regarded as one of the representatives of "the third generation of Neo-Confucianism". He is a famous philosopher of management, honorary president of International Society for Chinese Philosophy ("ISCP"), president of International Association of I-Ching Studies and president of International Qualification Assessment Committee for World Iching Hierophants. As a representative of Confucian studies abroad, professor Cheng has been long engaged in introducing Chinese philosophy to the Western world.

Cheng Yen (Wang Jinyun, 1937–) is a Chinese Buddhist nun and philanthropist. She built the first Tzu Chi Hospital in Hualien City and extended Tzu Chi undertaking to the world. For over 30 years, she totally has collected more than 10 billion new Taiwan dollars. Nearly one fifth of Taiwan's population, that is, more than 400 million people participate in her charity event more or less. She has over ten million volunteers in the world. People call her "Oriental Mother Teresa", "Kwan-yin Bodhisattva of the human world".

Clooney, Francis X. (1950–) is a professor of Harvard Divinity School and serves as director of the Center for the Study of World Religions, contemporary representative of comparative theology. His major works are *Theology after Vedanta: An Exercise in Comparative Theology, Seeing through Texts, Hindu God, Christian God* and *Divine Mother, Blessed Mother*. In July 2010, he was elected a Fellow of the British Academy.

Cobb, John B. (1925–) is an American United process theologian and process philosopher, who played a crucial role in the development of process theology. Cobb has published dozens of important works. His masterpieces are *Christ in a Pluralistic Age, Transforming Christianity and the World: A Way Beyond Absolutism and Relativism, Process Theology* and *Sustainability: Economics, Ecology, and Justice.*

Cone, James H. (1938–) is a Union Theological Seminary professor, representatives of the Black theology . He writes *A Black Theology of Liberation* and *Black Theology and Black Power.* He advocates looking for identity of blacks within the scope of the theological meaning. He points out that black power is not only consistent with the Gospel of Jesus Christ, indeed it is the Gospel of Jesus Christ itself, and it is not hostile to Christianity.

Cupitt, Don (1934–) is an eminent English philosopher of religion and scholar of Christian theology. He has been a professor of the University of Cambridge and an Anglican priest. He was noted for his ideas about "non-realist" philosophy of religion. He has published 36 works, Among his most famous works are *Taking Leave of God, The Sea of Faith, After God: The Future Of Religion, Mysticism After Modernity, Is Nothing Sacred?: The Non-Realist Philosophy of Religion: Selected Essays.* He presented "non-realistic God" to seek for the meaning of regarding religion as a masterpiece of human. He advocated this view of religion meanwhile, and then he affirmed the continuing validity of religious thought as well as the continuing validity of religious activities, which praise spiritual and social values.

Daisaku, Ikeda (1928–) is president of Sōka Gakkai International (SGI), a Buddhist association of more than 12 million members in 192 countries and territories, and founder of several educational, cultural and peace research institutions. Until now, Ikeda is said to be world-famous Buddhist thinker, philosopher, educator, social activist, poet laureate and International humanitarian. He won United Nations Peace Award in 1983, Humanitarian Award by the UN Refugee Agency in 1989, and Albert Einstein Peace Award in 1999.

Dallmayr, Fred R. (1928–) is Packey J. Dee Professor in the departments of philosophy and political science at the University of Notre Dame. He has been a visiting professor at Hamburg University in Germany and at the New School for Social Research in New York, and a Fellow at Nuffield College in Oxford. He has been teaching at Notre Dame University since 1978. Among his recent publications are: Achieving Our World: Toward a Global and Plural Democracy (2001); Dialogue Among Civilizations: Some Exemplary Voices (2002); Integral Pluralism: Beyond Culture Wars (2010). He is a past president of the Society for Asian and Comparative Philosophy (SACP). He is currently the Executive Co-Chair of "World Public Forum - Dialogue of Civilizations".

Das, Bhagwan (1869–1958) was an Indian philosopher, a reformer of Vedanta philosophy. He served as professor at the Central Hindu College. he rejected Adi Shankara's statement that "the world is unreal". And from the standpoint of idealism, he linked the psychological theory of ancient Indian yoga school with Western positivist psychology, attempted to build a new system of psychology. He wrote *The science of peace, an attempt at an exposition of the first principles of the science of the self, The Science Of Social Organization*, etc.

Dawson, Christopher (1889–1970) was a British cultural philosopher and historian. Dawson has been called "the greatest English-speaking Catholic historian of the twentieth century". But his main interest was cultural philosophy, especially the relationship between faith and cultural changes. His main works included *The Age of the Gods* (1928), *Progress and Religion: An Historical Inquiry* (1929), *Christianity and the New Age* (1931), *Medieval Religion and Other Essays* (1934), *Religion* *and the Modern State* (1936), *Religion and the Rise of Western Culture* (1950) and *Understanding Europe* (1952).

Fei Xiaotong (1910–2005) was a pioneering Chinese researcher and professor of sociology and anthropology; he was also noted for his studies in the study of China's ethnic groups. He was the founder of Chinese sociology and anthropology. He served as vice chairman of Standing Committee of the Seventh and Eighth National People's Congress, of the sixth National Committee of the Chinese People's Political Consultative Conference (CPPCC).

Ford, David Frank (1948–) is born in Dublin, he is an academic and public theologian. He has been the Regius Professor of Divinity at the University of Cambridge since 1991. His research interests include political theology, ecumenical theology, Christian theologians and theologies, theology and poetry, the shaping of universities and of the field of theology and religious studies within universities, hermeneutics, and inter-faith theology and relations. He is the founding director of the Cambridge Inter-Faith Programme and a co-founder of the Society for Scriptural Reasoning.

Fredericks, James L. (1951–) is a American professor of Loyola-Marymount University, He has long been engaged in Buddhist Studies as well as in dialogue practice and theoretical research between Buddhism and Christianity. He is one of the representatives of contemporary comparative theology. His major works includes: *Faith Among Faiths: Christianity & the Other Religions* and *Buddhists and Christians: Through Comparative Theology to Solidarity*. In 2002, he received U.S. Frederick J.Streng Book Award.

Fu Youde (1956–) is director of Center For Judaic and Inter-Religious Studies of Shandong University, Chairman of the Department of Religious Studies, Distinguished professor of the Tanshan Scholars. He is also a member of the standing committee of Foreign Philosophy Society of China, of Society of Religious Studies in China; Chairman of Philosophy Society of Shandong Province; editor in chief of *Jewish Studies*. He has numerous writings and won a number of awards.

Fukuyama, Francis (1952–) is a Japanese-American scholar, political scientist and political economist. Fukuyama is a Senior Fellow at the Center on Democracy, Development and the Rule of Law at Stanford University. His writings are *The End* *of History and the Last Man, Trust: Social Virtues and Creation of Prosperity, Our Posthuman Future: Consequences of the Biotechnology Revolution*, and *The Great Disruption: Human Nature and the Reconstruction of Social Order.* In *The End of History and the Last Man*, he argued that the final history would be the history of liberal democracies. In the phase of liberal democracies, human gain the recognization of equality, so the history end. Concerning the problems in the Islamic world, he does not think that is the conflict of culture, but essentially is political radicalism, has nothing to do with culture.

Gandhi, Mahatma (1869–1948) was the preeminent leader of the Indian movement for freedom and the Indian National Congress. He was the father of modern India, the greatest political leader of India and also the founder of Gandhism (modern political theory of national bourgeoisie). His spirit and thought led India to independence, which broke away from British colonial rule. His philosophical thought of "non-violence" (ahimsa) affected nationalists worldwide and international movements which strove for peaceful change. 1927–2001

Gernet, Jacques (1921–) is an eminent French sinologist and historian of the second half of the 20th century. He specializes in the study of Chinese social and cultural history. He publishes numerous works. His best-known works are *The Chinese Civilization* (1972) and *China and Christianity* (1982), which was highly spoken of by international sinological circles. On 8 June 1979 Gernet was elected a member of the Académie des Inscriptions et Belles-Lettres.

Ghose, Aurobindo (1872–1950) was an Indian nationalist, philosopher, leader of the Indian movement for freedom. His philosophy of spiritual evolution played an important role in modern Indian history of thought. Aurobindo wrote more than 100 books. There were *The Life Divine, The Human Cycle, The Future Poetry* and so on. In India he was called a sage or spiritual master. His name together with Mahatma Gandhi, Rabindranath Tagore was called as "Three Sages".

Hanh, Thich Nhat (1926–) is a Vietnamese Zen Buddhist monk, author, poet and peace activist. During the Vietnam War, he was the president of Vietnamese Buddhist Peace Delegation, he told the American people the suffering of the silent Vietnamese poor people in the war as well as their desires for peace. In 1967, Dr. King nominated Thich Nhat Hanh for the Nobel Peace Prize. Nhat Hanh has published more than 100 books, including more than 40 in English. Nhat Hanh is active in the peace movement, promoting non‑violent solutions to conflict.

Heim, S. Mark is Samuel Abbot Professor of Christian Theology at the Andover Newton Theological School. Mark Heim is deeply involved in issues of religious pluralism, Christian ecumenism and the relation of theology and science. He is one of the contemporary leading scholars of religious pluralism. He is also the author of *Salvations: Truth and Difference in Religion, The Depth of the Riches: A Trinitarian Theology of Religious Ends* and so on.

Hick, John Harwood (1922–2012) was a contemporary English philosopher of religion and theologian. In theology, he made contributions in the areas of theodicy, eschatology, and Christology, and in the philosophy of religion he contributed to the areas of epistemology of religion and religious pluralism. In 1991, he was awarded the prestigious Grawemeyer Award for Religion.

Hong Yi (Li Shutong, 1880–1942) was a Chinese Buddhist monk, excellent artist, educator and thinker. He was an excellent representative of combining Chinese traditional culture and Buddhist culture. He was not only the most outstanding monk in the history of modern Chinese Buddhism, but also a well‑known person with a great international reputation. He made creative progress on painting, music, drama, calligraphy, seal cutting and poetry.

Hsing Yun (Li Guoshen, 1927–) is a Chinese Buddhist monk, the founder of the Fo Guang Shan Buddhist order and the chairman of the Buddha's Light International Association. Master Hsing Yun makes outstanding contributions to education, culture, charity and preaching career, makes positive efforts to promote cross‑strait relations, and has a huge influence on the political, cultural and other fields' communication. Humanistic Buddhism founded by him has a great influence on over 80 countries, more than 5 million people have accepted the ideal of Humanistic Buddhism. Hsing Yun writes many works, and they have been translated in many languages and published in Europe, America, East Asia, Africa and other regions.

Hu Shi (1891–1962) was a Chinese philosopher, essayist and diplomat. He was one of the leaders of China's New Culture Movement because of his advocation of literature reform. He served as president of Peking University. He had a wide range of interests such as literature, history, philosophy, textual criticism, pedagogy and redology. He also had in-depth studies in these fields. In 1939, he was nominated for a Nobel Prize in literature. Hu Shi was influenced strongly by Dewey and Huxley, devoted his life to prompting Liberalism. He was the forerunner of the Chinese Liberalism. His research methods were "bold assumption and careful verification" and "every word must has its evidence". "Work earnestly, behave seriously" was his way to live. He preached these throughout all his life.

Huntington, Samuel Phillips (1927–2008) was a controversial Conservative political scientist from the United States, Harvard professor. Huntington was famous for his view of "the clash of civilizations", which was put forward in *The Clash of Civilizations and the Remaking of World Order*. Huntington posited that in the post-Cold War world, competition and conflict between the world's major civilizations would occur because of cultural and religious rather than ideological differences.

Jaspers, Karl Theodor (1883–1969) was a German existentialist philosopher, theologist and psychiatrist. In his *Vom Ursprung und Ziel der Geschichte (The Origin and Goal of History)*, he proposed the theory of an Axial Age. Jaspers posed that the period from 800 to 200 BC, especially from 600 to 300 BC, was the Axial Period of human civilizations. During this period, the major breakthroughs of human civilizations' spirit was made. Great spiritual mentor appeared in every civilizations in the Axial Period—such as *Socrates, Plato, Aristotle in Ancient Greek*; *Jewish Prophets in Israel*; *Sakyamuni in Ancient India*; *Confucius, Lao Tzu in China*.

Ji Xianlin (1911–2009) was a Chinese linguist, indologist, literary translator, educator and social activist. He was proficient in 12 languages. He served as committee of Chinese Academy of Social Sciences, head of institute of South Asian Studies, Chinese Academy of Social Sciences, and a vice chancellor of Peking University. He knew Sanskrit, Pali, Tocharian and other languages. He was one of the only few scholars who studied Tocharian in the world.

Jin Kemu (1912–2000) was a famous Chinese writer, translator and scholar. He served as professor of Hunan University, Wuhan University and Peking University. He has translated some ancient India literature and philosophy works into Chinese. His representative works were *The History of Sanskrit Literature, Essays on Indian Culture, Essays on Comparative Culture*, etc.

Pope John XXIII (1881–1963) was an Italian pope from 1958 to 1963. His

227

original name was Angelo Giuseppe Roncalli. He was elected at the age of 77. He served as pope less than 5 years, but he created profound new changes in Catholic Church. During his reign, it was called the beginning of a new era in the history of Catholic Church.

Kang Youwei (1858 – 1927) was a Chinese scholar, political thinker and reformer of the late Qing Dynasty and early Chinese Republic. His ideas inspired a reformation movement, which was called "Hundred Days' Reform". He believed in Confucian doctrine and was committed to transforming Confucianism into a state religion which was adapted to a modern society. He served as president of Confucian Association. His main works included *A Study of the "New Text" Forgeries, A Study of the Reforms of Confucius, Reformation of Meiji Emperor, Reformation of Peter the Great*, and *Da Tongshu*.

King, Martin Luther, Jr. (1929 – 1968) was a famous American leader in the African-American Civil Rights Movement. He delivered his "I Have a Dream" speech in the Lincoln Memorial on August 28, 1963. King became the recipient of the Nobel Peace Prize in 1964. King was assassinated on April 4, 1968, when he came to Memphis to lead the workers' strike, and he was only 39 years old then. Since 1986, American government regarded the third Monday of January each year as a federal holiday to honor Martin Luther King, Jr.

Kapur, Jagdish Chandra (1917 – 2010) was an Indian philosopher and public figure. He was a co-founder and co-chairman of the World Public Forum, Dialogue of Civilizations. He served as President of Kapoor Surya Foundation, Editor-in-chief of *World Affairs*. Among his publications are: *India, An Uncommitted Society, The Human Condition Today: Some New Perspectives* and *Our Future: Consumerism Or Humanism*. He was one of the recipients of the Padma Bhushan in 2010.

Knitter, Paul F. (1939–) is an American theologian and social activist. He is a leading proponent of religious pluralism, committing himself to theoretical study and social practice of fields such as social justice, interfaith dialogue and global ecological concern. His main works are *Towards a Protestant Theology of Religions, No Other Name?, One Earth Many Religions: Multifaith Dialogue and Global Responsibility* and *Jesus and the Other Names: Christian Mission and Global Responsibility*. In addition, he is the editor of a collection of Faith Meets Faith, which is published by Orbis Books.

This collection has published nearly 50 books, it has a broad impact on the fields such as religious dialogue, global theology and social justice.

Krishnamurti, Jiddu (1895 – 1986) was an Indian Buddhist scholar. He was recognize as the greatest spiritual master in the twentieth century. He visited and lectured in more than 70 countries throughout his life. His speeches had been compiled into over 80 books and translated into more than 50 languages. In today's world, including the United States , Europe, India and Australia have Krishnamurti Foundation and schools which are committed to promoting Krishnamurti's mercy and the idea of relief in the present.

Chin Kung (Hsu Yeh-hong, 1927–) is a Chinese Buddhist master. He not only knows well the theory of various schools of Buddhism, but also reads cursorily and widely Confucianism, Taoism and Islam and other religious doctrines. Among many classics, he focuses mostly on Pure Land Buddhism and also attains the most brilliant results. Master Chin Kung is well known for using modern technology to spread the Buddha's teachings.

Küng, Hans (1928–) is a Swiss Catholic theologian, served as professor of ecumenical theology at the University of Tübingen. Since 1995 he has been President of the Foundation for a Global Ethic. Küng advocates Christian thought of a new paradigm, committing himself to promoting the paradigm shift of theology in the so-called post-modern situation. He wrote the *Towards a Global Ethic: An Initial Declaration*, and this Declaration was signed at the 1993 Parliament of the World's Religions for his advocacy.

Lai Pan Chiu (1963–) is a professor of CUHK's Department of Cultural and Religious Studies. His academic interests include modern Christian thought, inter-religious dialogue, Christianity and Chinese culture, environmental ethics, and religion & natural science. After publishing several monographs on Christian theology and a few edited volumes concerning Buddhist-Christian and Christian-Confucian Dialogue, he published recently a book on Mahayana Christian Theology (2011, received the 33rd Christopher Tang Christian Literature Award), another on theology and culture (2011), and a third on religion and science (co-author, 2012).

Li Zehou (1930–) is a Chinese philosopher, esthetician and scholar of Chinese intellectual history. He had served as researcher at the CASS, visiting professor of

University of Tuebingen, Germany, University of Wisconsin, University of Michigan, Colorado College, America, and visiting researcher at the Academia Sinica, Taipei. In 1988 he was elected Paris International Academy of Philosophy. In 1998, he earned a honorary doctorate of humanities degree in Colorado College, America. Sinologist Yu Ying-shih evaluated him that : "By his books, a whole generation of young Chinese intellectuals broke free from the Communist ideology."

Liang Qichao (1873–1929) was a Chinese scholar, journalist, philosopher, and reformist during the late Qing Dynasty and early Chinese Republic. In 1894, he advocated political reform and edited *Shiwu Bao* in Shanghai. Liang published his political ideals in newspapers to inspire the country to innovative ideas. Liang and "Six Gentlemen" jointly participated in the Hundred Days' Reform. He went to Japan after the reform failed. He came back to China after the founding of the Republic of China and involved in the fight against Yuan Shikai's attempt to revive the Chinese monarchy. In his old age Liang was away from the politics, devoted himself to writing and lecturing. He also studied Buddhism deeply. His writing included *The Learning of Mohism, Introduction to the Learning of the Qing Dynasty, Collected Works from the Ice-Drinker's Studio* and *Chinese Academic History of the Recent 300 Years.*

Liang Shuming (1893–1988) was a famous Chinese thinker, philosopher and educator. He was the leader in the Rural Reconstruction Movement. He studied mainly the problem of life and social problem. He was also one of the early representatives of modern New Confucianism. He was called "the last Confucian of China". His main works included *Eastern and Western Cultures and Their Philosophies, The Substance of Chinese Culture, Theory in Rural Reconstruction* and *Introduction to Indian Philosophy*. Now there compiles eight volumes of *Complete Works of Liang Shuming*.

Lindbeck, George (1923–) is an American Lutheran theologian. Lindbeck was born in 1923 in Luoyang, China, now served as Luther professor at Yale University. He is best known as an ecumenicist and as one of the fathers of postliberal theology. He attended the Second Vatican Council as a official observer of Lutheran World Federation. His best-known work is *The Nature of Doctrine: Religion and Theology in a Postliberal Age*, published in 1984.

Liu Xiaofeng (1956–) is a professor of School of Liberal Arts, Renmin University of China. He also serves as researcher of CUHK's Chinese Culture

Research Institute, adjunct professor of Peking University's Institute of Comparative Culture. In 1993, he completed his PhD in Christian theology at the University of Basel in Switzerland. Since 1980s, professor Liu committed himself to the rediscovery of modernity, Chinese and Western civilization. He successively introduces Christian thought, social theory, political theology, classical political philosophy, classicism and other academic resources into China. He promotes the depth of understanding of the Western intellectual tradition in Chinese academic circles.

Ma Jian (1906–1978) was a Chinese Muslim scholar and translator. He was an Arabic linguist and knew Chinese and Arabic Language and Culture. He also was familiar with Persian and English. After 1954, he successively served as professor of Yunnan University's Department of Oriental Languages and Peking University's Department of Oriental Languages. Ma Jian was one of the founders of China Islamic Association. His main achievements were translating Quran and the General History of Arab.

Macquarrie, John (1919–2007) was a Scottish theologian and philosopher, emeritus professor of Oxford University. Among his numerous works were *An Existentialist Theology: A Comparison of Heidegger and Bultmann, Twentieth-Century Religious Thought, Studies in Christian existentialism, Thinking about God, Christian Unity and Christian Diversity, Christian Hope, In Search of Humanity: A Theological and Philosophical Approach, In search of Deity: An Essay in Dialectical Theism, Jesus Christ in Modern Thought* and *Mary for All Christians*. After retirement Macquarie had maintained an active writing and lecturing activities .

Mandela, Nelson Rolihlahla (1918–2013) is a South African anti-apartheid revolutionary and politician who served as President of South Africa from 1994 to 1999. He is the first black South African to hold the office, he is honored as "the father of the nation". On May 11, 1994, Mandela and cabinet members of the first Government of National Unity were sworn in, which indicated that more than three centuries of apartheid and white racist rule had finally come to an end. Mandela had served a prison sentence in jail for 27 years. In his 40-year political career, Mandela won over one hundred awards, the most notable of which is the 1993 Nobel Peace Prize.

Gutiérrez Merino, Gustavo (1928–) is a Peruvian theologian and Dominican priest. He is regarded as the founder of Liberian Theology, he has a thorough insight and critique of Latin America's society, history, and theology. His works includes *A Theology of Liberation: History, Politics, and Salvation* (1973), *We Drink from Our Own Wells: The Spiritual Journey of a People* (1983) and *On Job: God-Talk and the Suffering of the Innocent* (1987).

Mou Zongsan (1909–1995) was a Chinese modern scholar, philosopher and historian of philosophy, an important representative of New Confucianism. His major works included *Substance of Mind and Substance of Human Nature, Idealism of Morality, Philosophy of History, Physical Nature and Speculative Reason, Buddha-Nature and Prajna, Treatise on Summum Bonum* and other 22 books. In addition, there was 3 translations: *Kant's Moral Philosophy*, *Kant's Critique of Pure Reason* and *Kant's Critique of Judgment*. His philosophical achievements stood for the new level of Chinese traditional philosophy in the modern development and had a worldwide influence. Cambridge Dictionary of Philosophy praised him as "the most original and influential philosopher of contemporary New Confucian in his generation".

Nan Huai-Chin (1918–2012) was a Chinese scholar, poet and positive peddler of Chinese traditional culture. After he went to Taiwan in the spring of 1949, he served as professor of Culture University, Fu Jen Catholic University and National Chengchi University. His works mostly based on the record of his lectures. The content of his books usually took the Confucianism, Buddhism, Taoism and other ideas for comparison, having a unique style. His representative works included *Selections from the Analects of Confucius, Modern Translation of The Shurangama Sutra's Principles, How to Cultivate the Buddha Dharma*, etc.

Watchman Nee (Ni Tuosheng, 1903–1972) was born in Fuzhou. He was a church leader and Christian teacher who worked in China during the first half of the 20th century. He was also the founder of the local churches. During his 30 years of ministry, Nee published many books expounding the Bible, including *The Normal Christian Life* and *The Normal Christian Church Life*. His theology has a wide influence in today's Mainland China and Chinese Christian circles.

Nehru, Jawaharlal (1889–1964) was the leader of the Indian Independence Movement, the first Prime Minister of India, and one of the founders of Non-Alignment movement. His birthday, 14 November, is celebrated in India as Children's

Day to commemorate his care for children. On June 1954, Nehru and Chinese Premier Zhou Enlai jointly put forward the famous Five Principles of Peaceful Coexistence. In 1955, he initiated and participated in the first Asian-African Conference, which took place in Bandung, Indonesia.

Neville, Robert Cummings (1939—) is an American philosopher and theologian, who has a broad international impact. He is the most important representative of Boston Confucianism which is rising in recent years. Now he serves as professor of the Boston University School of Theology: in philosophy, religion, and theology. He is also Chairman of the Executive Committee of International Society for Chinese Philosophy. Neville also places great emphasis on Chinese philosophy, especially on Confucian philosophy, and he has been actively promoting the development of international Confucianism. For a long time, his fields of research are comparative philosophy and philosophy of religion. He has published numerous books, and two of them have been translated into Chinese.

Otto, Rudolf (1869–1937) was an German theologian and scholar of comparative religion. He had worked as a professor at the universities of Göttingen, Breslau and Marburg. His research areas included Western philosophy, systematic theology, New Testament and Old Testament religious history and Indology. He devoted himself to researching religious essence and truth, religious feelings and experiences, philosophical epistemology, sacred concepts, mysticism and other issues. His representative work was *The Holy—On the Irrational in the Idea of the Divine and its Relation to the Rational*. and he also wrote many other important books, such as *Naturalism and Religion, Mysticism east and west: A comparative analysis of the nature of mysticism*, and *Christianity and the Indian Religion of Grace*. His study of the religious category "holy" had a far-reaching impact, it created the conditions for the development of phenomenology of religion.

Panikkar, Raimundo (1918–2010) was a Spanish Roman Catholic priest, pioneer of inter-religious dialogue, scholar of comparative religion. He tried to establish a link in the intrinsic philosophical structure of different religious and philosophical traditions. He not only made an effort to distinguish the internal order of a tradition and mystery foundation, but also conducted this under the illumination of the self-understanding of this tradition's philosophy. After this critical screening, he clarified the structural similarity of different traditions, so that they can dialogue with each other. As a result, the fact became that tripartite dialogue: Christianity and Hinduism or Buddhism, as well as contemporary pluralistic society - political - religious ideology.

Pope Paul VI (1897–1978) was an Italian pope from 1963 to 1978, born Giovanni Battista Enrico Antonio Maria Montini. He led and convened the second period of Vatican II, September 29–December 4, 1963. During his 25-year reign, he actively participated in international affairs and played a unique role.

Radhakrishnan, Sarvepalli (1888–1975) was an Indian philosopher and statesman. He served as professor of philosophy at the Universities of Mysore and Calcutta, and Spalding Professor of Eastern Religion and Ethics at Oxford University. After India's independence, he served as the first Vice President of India, in 1962, he was elected the second President of India. One of India's most influential scholars of comparative religion and philosophy, Radhakrishnan built a bridge between the East and the West by showing how the philosophical systems of each tradition are comprehensible within the terms of the other. His representative works included: *Indian Philosophy, The Hindu View of Life, Idealist View of Life* and *Eastern Religions and Western Thought*.

Rahner, Karl (1904–1984) was a German Jesuit and theologian. He was considered one of the most influential Roman Catholic theologians of the 20th century. Rahner played a huge role in the Second Vatican Council as a official theological consultant specified by the Roman Catholic Church, he not only inspired generations of theologians, but also affected the development of the entire Catholic thought since then. In response to the challenges of secularization and modernization to the Catholic Church, Rahner advocated and actively engaged in dialogues inside and outside Christian. His writings almost covered all fields of theology and related ideas, including voluminous *Schriften zur Theologie* (16 volumes).

Ren Jiyu (1916–2009) was a famous Chinese philosopher, scholar in religious studies, historian and honorary curator of the National Library of China. He graduated from Department of Philosophy of Peking University. He served as professor of Peking University, president of History of Chinese Philosophy Society and chairman of China Atheism Society. He devoted himself to studying history of Chinese Buddhism and history of Chinese philosophy with historical materialism. He lectured and paid a academic visit abroad many times.

Schipper, Kristofer (1934–) is a Dutch sinologist. He is regarded as one of the three most greatest European sinologists. He came to China to undertake cultural studies in 1979. He helped build Research Center for World Civilization of Fuzhou University in 2003. He became well known in international sinological circles because of his study of Chinese Taoism. He also made contributions to research areas such as history of thought and culture in ancient China, and anthropology of Religion. His published works are *The Daoist Body*, *Daoist Canon* and so on.

Sheng-yen (1930–2009) was a Chinese Buddhist master, educator. He was also the 57th generational descendant in the Linji school, the 52nd generational descendant in the Caodong school and the founder of the Dharma Drum Mountain in Taiwan. In 1985, he founded the Institute of Chung-Hwa Buddhist Studies in Taipei and the International Cultural and Educational Foundation of Dharma Drum Mountain in 1989. He published nearly 100 works in Asia, America and Europe, which were written in Chinese, Japanese and English. Among his works, the largest circulation was *Orthodox Chinese Buddhism*, it had published more than three million copies; the most translations was *Faith in Mind*, it was translated by 10 languages; the largest number of series books were *A Journey of Learning and Insight* and *Attaining the Way: A Guide to the Practice of Chan Buddhism*. All there books were welcomed by readers.

Smart, Ninian (1927–2001) was Emeritus Professor of Comparative Religion and of Religious Studies at the Universities of California and Lancaster. He was recognized as one of the world's foremost scholars in religious studies and was President of the American Academy of Religion for the year 2000. He authored many acclaimed books, including *The Religious Experience*, *Dimensions of the Sacred* and *The World's Religions*.

Smith, Wilfred Cantwell (1916–2000) was a Canadian professor of comparative religion who from 1964–1973 was director of Harvard's Center for the Study of World Religions. In his 1962 work *The Meaning and End of Religion* he notably and controversially questioned the validity of the concept of religion. Smith wrote abundant works in his life, among them were *Islam in Modern History* (1957), *Questions of Religious Truth* (1967), *Belief and History* (1977), *Faith and Belief* (1987), *Towards a World Theology* (1989) and *What Is Scripture?: A Comparative Approach* (1993).

Soderblom, Nathan (1866–1931) was a famous Swedish theologist and historian of religion. He devoted his life to the career of religion, actively promoted unity of the Christian Church in various countries, and unswervingly strove for world peace. As a result, he received the 1930 Nobel Peace Prize. Soderblom was the first religious person to win the Nobel Peace Prize. His activities had great influence on twentieth-century worldwide Christian movement.

Spengler, Oswald (1880–1936) was a German historian and philosopher of history, the founder of historical morphology. His philosophy of history was called "cultural morphology". It was a revolt against the linear evolutionary pattern, which focused on western history in the previous historical studies. It stressed that every civilization has its own independent status and value. In his book *The Decline of the West* (*Der Untergang des Abendlandes*), he proposed that civilization was a organic process containing rise and fall, decay and death. We had seen the decline of the ancient civilizations, and the revelation of the decline of the west had appeared.

Stuart, John Leighton (1876–1962) was an American Presbyterian missionary, diplomat and educator. He was born in Hangzhou, China, on June, 1876, of Presbyterian missionary parents from the United States. He began to preach in China after 1904. He participated in the founding of Hangchow Presbyterian College (which later became the Hangchow University). In January 1919, Stuart became the first president of Yenching University. In 1946, Stuart was appointed the U.S. Ambassador to China and he left China in August 1949.

Suzuki, D. T. (1870–1966) was a Japanese Buddhist scholar, Zen thinker, and world cultural celebrity who was famous for introducing Zen to the West. His major works were *Studies in Zen Buddhism, Essays in Zen Buddhism, A History of Chinese Ancient Philosophy, Christian and Buddhist, Studies in Huayan School*, etc. All his works were contained in *Collected Works of Suzuki Daisetz*.

Swidler, Leonard (1929–) is Professor of Catholic Thought and Interreligious Dialogue at Temple University, he has studied and promoted interreligious dialogue and intercultural dialogue for a long time. In 1991, he issued an appeal and called for the drafting of the Universal Declaration of a Global Ethic, he maintained that the declaration should integrate various studies and thinking results of global ethic and related issues. Then we can distribute it to various seminars of all religious and ethical groups and make appropriate modifications, so as to be accepted by all religious and ethical groups.

Tagore, Rabindranath (1861–1941) was an Indian poet, philosopher and nationalist. In 1913 he became the first Asian to win the Nobel Prize for Literature. His poetry enjoyed an epic status in India, and masterpieces of them were *Gitanjali* and *Stray Birds*. His works reflected the Indian people's strong desire to change their fate under the oppression of imperialism and feudal caste system, described their unyielding struggle. His works were full of distinctive spirit of patriotism and democracy

Taixu (1890–1947) was a famous modern Chinese eminent monk, activist and thinker who advocated the reform and renewal of Chinese Buddhism. He served as president of the World Buddhist Court, of Academy of Chinese Buddhism; director of Commission for the Preservation of Chinese Buddhism. Taixu was a great person for Buddhism who made a historic turnaround for Chinese Buddhism and even world Buddhism. In 1928, Taixu went to European and American countries and preached Buddhism. On the recommendation of French scholars, Taixu prepared to establish the World Buddhist Court in Paris, which pioneered the spreading Buddhism through European and American countries by Chinese monks.

Tan Sitong (1865–1898) was a Chinese modern revolutionary pioneer and one of the well-known "six gentlemen of the Hundred Days' Reform". The heroic scene of his brave death was the important spiritual resources of the Chinese revolution. His masterpiece *Ren Xue* strongly criticized the feudal monarchy. His poems conveyed sincere feelings, heroic inclination, and grand realm. There was *Complete Works of Tan Sitong* left the world.

Tang Junyi (1909–1978) was a Chinese modern scholar, philosopher and historian of philosophy, who was one of the representatives of New Confucianism. He had taught in University of West China, Central University and University of Nanking. He also served as provost in Jiangnan University. In 1958, Tang Junyi, Xu Fuguan, Mou Zongsan and Zhang Junmai jointly drew up and published a document entitled *A Declaration of Chinese Culture to the Scholars of the World*, which was a programmatic article of New Confucianism.

Tang Yongtong (1893–1964) was a Chinese philosopher, educator, and master of sinology. He graduated from Tsinghua School and then studied in the United

States. After returning to China, he successively served as professor of National Southeast University, Nankai University, Peking University, and Southwest Associated University. In 1951, he served as vice president of Peking University. He was one of the handful masters of sinology who combined Chinese and Western culture, connected Confucianism and Buddhist, and was erudite and informed. His academic writings were *The History of Buddhism During Han, Wei, Jin and Southern-Northern Dynasties, A Brief History of Indian Philosophy, Papers on the Metaphysics During Wei and Jin Dynasties*, etc.

Mother Teresa of Calcutta (1910–1997) was an India world famous Catholic charity worker, who mainly serviced for the poor in Calcutta, India. She became the recipient of the 1979 Nobel Peace Prize because of her lifelong contribution to removing poverty. She was beatified by Pope John Paul II on October 2003, giving her the title "Blessed Teresa of Calcutta".

Tillich, Paul (1886–1965) was a German-American Christian existentialist philosopher and theologian. Tillich is widely regarded as one of the most influential theologians of the 20th century. He is best known for his major three-volume work *Systematic Theology* (1951–1963). His theological and philosophical views was influential for Protestant theologians in the the United States and Federal Republic of Germany after World War II.

K. H. Ting (Ding Guangxun, 1915–2012) was one of representatives of the Chinese protestant Three-Self Patriotic Movement and Modernist Theology. He was an Anglican Bishop in the 1940s and 1950s. He successively served as chairperson and chairperson emeritus of the Three-Self Patriotic Movement (TSPM) which is supported by the PRC government, president and president emeritus of the China Christian Council, vice-chairman of the Chinese People's Political Consultative Conference (1989–2008), and a member of the standing committee of the National People's Congress.

Toynbee, Arnold Joseph (1889–1975) was a famous British historian. *A Study of History* and *Mankind and Mother Earth* were two of his most important masterpieces. *A Study of History,* his twelve-volume great work, told of the rise and fall of the world's major nations, which was praised as the most great achievement of the modern scholars. In his treatment of history, Toynbee rejected the concept of modern nationalism and maintained that civilizations were the units of history. He divided the world history into 21 civilizations, and explained that civilizations rise and fall depending on the challenges it faced and its responses to them.

Tu Weiming (1940–) is an ethicist and a New Confucian. Tu was Harvard-Yenching professor of Chinese history and philosophy and of Confucian studies in the Department of East Asian Languages and Civilizations at Harvard University. He was director of the Harvard-Yenching Institute and director of the Institute of Culture and Communication at the East-West Center in Hawaii. He is research professor and senior fellow of Asia Center at Harvard University. He is a fellow of the American Academy of Arts and Sciences. Tu Weiming conducts research on Confucian culture placed in the context of the world trend. He directly focuses on how to integrate Chinese culture into china's modernization. He outlines the basic framework of the theory of the contemporary Neo-Confucianism, which has a considerable impact on the East Asia and the Western world.Tu was appointed by Kofi Annan as a member of the United Nations' "Group of Eminent Persons" to facilitate the "Dialogue among Civilizations" in 2001. He gave a presentation on inter-civilizational dialogue to the Executive Board of UNESCO in 2004.

Tutu, Desmond (1931–) is a famous black South African bishop, and he was the first black South African Archbishop of Anglican Church. Tutu is a staunch fighter of South Africa leading black people against racial oppression. He consistently opposed the racial discrimination and apartheid in South Africa and fought bravely for the liberation of black people. He received the Nobel Peace Prize in 1984. To praise his promotion of culture of human rights both domestically and internationally, the UNESCO gave Tutu the Bilbao Prize in 2012.

Wang Zhicheng (1966–) is a professor of Zhejiang University. He is one of the main advocators of religious dialogue in China. His representative works are *Interpretation and Salvation: On Religious Pluralism* and *Religion, Interpretation and Peace: A Constructive Research on John Hick's Religious Pluralism*.

Weber, Max (1864–1920) was a German sociologist, philosopher, and political economist. He systematically elaborated the influences of the differences between Eastern and Western religious ethics on the social modernity and the development of modern capitalism. Weber and Durkheim had been called the founder of sociology of religion. Weber's book *The Protestant Ethic and the Spirit of Capitalism* was the earliest study of sociology of religion. In this book, Weber held that the influences of religion was the major cause for different developments between eastern culture and western culture and he emphasized that the Protestant ethic played an important role in capitalism, bureaucracy and the development of legal authority. His other masterpieces were *The Religion of China: Confucianism and Taoism, The Religion of India: The Sociology of Hinduism and Buddhism*, and *Ancient Judaism*.

Xiong Shili (1885–1968) was a famous Chinese philosopher and the founder of New Confucianism. He wrote *A New Treatise on Consciousness-only, Origins of Confucianism, Essay on Substance and Function, Illuminating the Mind, A Comprehensive Explanation of Buddhist Terms* and *On Change*. His doctrine had a far-reaching influence and its own style in the philosophical circles. The researchers of his theory were also throughout the country and abroad. *Encyclopedia Britannica* stated that "Xiong Shili and Feng Youlan were the outstanding figures of contemporary philosophy in China".

Xu Fuguan (1904–1982) was one of the representatives of New Confucianism. He published numerous treatises on topics such as Confucianism and Chinese Traditions; Confucianism and Cultural Issues; The Personality, History and Destiny of Chinese Intellectuals. He made important contribution to studying and spreading Chinese traditional thought and culture, so that he became a famous modern Confucian at home and abroad. He wrote more than 10 books.

Xu Jialu (1937–) Chair of Nishan Forum, Vice Chair of the National People's Congress Committee, an established humanity scholar, with an expertise in Chinese classic literature. In recent years, he has been engaged in promoting cultural dialogues among world civilization.

Yan Fu (1854–1921) was a very influential Chinese Enlightenment thinker, translator and educator in the late Qing Dynasty. He was one of the "advanced Chinese" who looked to the West for truth in the Chinese modern history. Yan Fu systematically introduced western sociology, political science, political economy, philosophy and natural science to China. His translation is the China's most important enlightenment translations in the 20th century. His chief work was *Evolution and Ethics*.

Yang, C. K. (1911–1999) was a Chinese-American sociologist. His ancestral home was Nanhai, Guangdong. In 1939, he earned a doctorate in sociology in University of Michigan, United States. In 1951, he served as a researcher at Center for International Studies, MIT. In 1953, he served as associate professor, professor at Department of Sociology, University of Pittsburgh. In the 1970s he founded the Department of Sociology of the Chinese University of Hong Kong. He wrote *Chinese Communist Society: The Family and the Village* and *Religion in Chinese Society: A study of Contemporary Social Function of Religion and Some of Their Historical Factor.*

Yu Ying-shih (1930–) is a Chinese world-renowned scholar of contemporary history. He is regarded as one of the representatives of "the third generation of Neo-Confucianism". He served as professor of University of Michigan, Harvard University and Yale University, head of New Asia College in Hong Kong and also the pro Vice-Chancellor of University. He is an Emeritus Professor of East Asian Studies and History at Princeton University, Academician of "Academia Sinica" in Taiwan. Yu Ying-shih's scholarly research began with science of history. His modern interpretation of Confucianism and Chinese Confucian culture formed his own style. He publishes dozens of books in Chinese or English, including *Trade and Expansion in Han China, Intellectuals and Chinese Culture, Science of History and Tradition, Chinese Culture and Modern Changes,* and *Modern Confucianist Theory.* On November 15, 2006, Yu Ying-shih was named the third recipient of the John W. Kluge Prize for lifetime achievement in the study of humanity.

Yakunin, Vladimir (1948–) is president of the state-run Russian Railways company. He has been a visiting professor at the Stockholm School of Economics. Since 2010 he is the Head of State Policy Department of the Moscow State University Faculty of Political Science. Yakunin is also the founding president of the "World Public Forum-Dialogue of Civilizations"

Zhao Dunhua (1949–) is Professor at Peking University and renowned scholar in philosophy and religious studies. He has published several books, such as *The Christian Philosophy in the Medieval Ages*, *The Historical Philosophy of the Bible*, and so on. He has been engaged in establishing the Biblical scholarship in Chinese academia.

Zhuo Xinping (1955–) is a world-renowned expert of religious studies, famous scholar and leader in the field of Christian Studies. He currently serves as Director and Researcher of CASS's Institute of World Religions, President of Chinese Academy of Religion. He earns a doctorate of philosophy at the University of Munich in Germany. His representative works are *World Religion and Religious Studies, Religious Understanding, On Christianity*, etc. In 2006, he was elected a member of the European Academy of Sciences and Arts.

Compilers: Xu Huan, Li Jianyu, Xie Yipin